INDUSTRIAL CONFLICT IN BRITAIN

Industrial Conflict in Britain

Edited by

E. W. EVANS
Senior Lecturer in Economics at the University of Hull

and

S. W. CREIGH
Lecturer in Economics at the University of Hull

FRANK CASS

First published 1977 in Great Britain by
FRANK CASS AND COMPANY LIMITED
Gainsborough House, Gainsborough Road,
London E11 1RS, England

and in the United States of America by
FRANK CASS AND COMPANY LIMITED
c/o Biblio Distribution Center,
81 Adams Drive, Totowa, New Jersey 07512

ISBN 0 7146 3023 3

Printed in Great Britain by offset lithography by
Billing & Sons Ltd, Guildford, London and Worcester

CONTENTS

Acknowledgements   vii

Introduction   1

WORK STOPPAGES: THE BRITISH EXPERIENCE

1   **H. A. Clegg**   :   Strikes   19

2   **P. Galambos and**   :   Work Stoppages in the United
    E. W. Evans   Kingdom 1951–1964: A
         Quantitative Study   31

3   **J. F. B. Goodman**   :   Strikes in the United Kingdom:
         Recent Statistics and Trends   59

4   **T. G. Whittingham**   :   Strikes and the Economy   77
    and B. Towers

5   **M. Silver**   :   Recent British Strike Trends:
         A Factual Analysis   89

THE CAUSES OF STRIKES

6   **G. C. Cameron**   :   Post-War Strikes in the North-
         East Shipbuilding and Ship-
         Repairing Industry 1946–1961   133

7   **W. McCarthy**   :   The Reasons Given for Striking
         An Analysis of Official
         Statistics 1945–1957   159

8   **J. H. Pencavel**   :   An Investigation into Industrial
         Strike Activity in Britain   175

9   **G. V. Rimlinger**   :   International Differences in the
         Strike Propensity of Coal
         Miners: Experience in Four
         Countries   195

INTERNATIONAL COMPARISONS

10   **K. Forchheimer**   :   Some International Aspects of
         the Strike Movement   219

11   **C. Kerr and**   :   The Inter-industry Propensity to
    A. Siegel   Strike–An International
         Comparison   233

         Technical Supplement   283

12   **A. M. Ross and**   :   Influences on Relative Strike
    P. T. Hartman   Activity   255

13   **W. E. J. McCarthy**   :   The Nature of Britain's Strike
         Problem   267

    Bibliography   289

ACKNOWLEDGEMENTS

(1) From *The Political Quarterly*, Vol. 27, 1956, Reproduced by permission.

(2) From the *Bulletin of Economic Research*, Vol. 25, No. 1, 1973, Reproduced by permission.

(3) From the *International Labour Review*, Vol. 95, No. 5. May, 1967, pp. 465-481, published by the International Labour Office, Geneva, Switzerland.

(4) From *The National Westminster Bank Review*, November, 1971 by kind permission.

(5) From *The British Journal of Industrial Relations*, Vol. XI, No. 1, 1973.

(6) From *The British Journal of Industrial Relations*, Vol. II, No. 1, 1964.

(7) From *The Bulletin of the Oxford University Institute of Economics and Statistics*, Vol. 21, 1959.

(8) From *Economica*, Vol. 37, 1970.

(9) Reprinted with permission from the *Industrial and Labor Relations Review*, Vol. 12, No. 3, April, 1959. Copyright © 1959 by Cornell University. All rights reserved.

(10) From *The Bulletin of the Oxford University Institute of Economics and Statistics*, Vol. 10, 1948.

(11) From *Industrial Conflict* (chap. 14 "The inter-industry propensity to strike: an international comparison" by C. Kerr and A. Siegel) Edited by A. Kornhauser, R. Dubin and A. M. Ross. c. 1954. McGraw-Hill Book Company Inc. Reproduced by permission.

(12) From A. M. Ross and P. T. Hartman, *Changing Patterns of Industrial Conflict* (John Wiley 1960) by kind permission of Professor Hartman.

(13) From *The British Journal of Industrial Relations*, Vol. VIII, 1970.

INTRODUCTION

This volume is an attempt to bring together in convenient form some of the most important studies of work stoppages in post-war Britain. Limitations of space and difficulties in obtaining permission to reprint have, of course, influenced the process of selection, a process which, in itself, must be to some extent arbitrary. But it is probably fair to say that the articles presented here include most of the factual evidence, and theoretical analysis of industrial conflicts which have appeared in recent years. For reason of convenience the selections have been grouped under three headings, namely British Experience, the Causes of Strikes and International Comparisons. This, again, must be regarded as a partly arbitrary classification, since many of the articles could have been attributed to at least two of the groups. The moral seems to be that the collection should be treated as a whole, in order to obtain a general view of the subject. For the convenience of those wishing to pursue specific matters further a short bibliography has been added which should make the appropriate sources obvious.

As will be clear from reading the selections, there is still room for substantial disagreement about most aspects of strikes. The data available are by no means satisfactory in all respects, and even if this problem could be solved, there would still be grounds for different interpretations of the facts. Whether the method of study chosen is statistical or econometric, analysis of official returns or detailed inquiries at the level of the firm, it is certain that work stoppages are a complex phenomenon capable of treatment in terms of economics, sociology, psychology and other disciplines. The continuing (and growing) interest in disputes may be due in part to their fascinating complexity. But at a more fundamental level it no doubt arises from a general belief that they are in some sense damaging to the economy and, as a corollary, from a desire to find out why they have become more frequent and how they can be averted.

STRIKES AND THE ECONOMY

Since a strike is intended to bring economic pressure to bear upon the company affected, in order to induce it to accede to the workers' demands, it is to be expected that adverse economic consequences will arise for the company due to the stoppage of work. However, little investigation has actually been carried out into this matter, at least in the modern context in Britain. The general themes of certain American studies may, however, be useful in considering the matters involved.[1] Essentially the tangible costs to the firm of a work-stoppage may be analysed under two headings.

Firstly there is the effect of the loss of production and revenue whilst fixed costs continue to be incurred as the dispute unfolds. Secondly there are the special expenses incurred directly as a result of the stoppage, including such items as additional warehousing, publicity and security costs. Equally, or perhaps more important, however, are the intangible costs, about which only an educated guess can be made. These costs are basically reflections of the impact of the stoppage upon the consumer, the supplier and public relations, and upon the long-term industrial relations in the establishments concerned.

From the labour side the costs of the stoppage hinge upon the income lost during the dispute, and, if the stoppage is officially endorsed, the drain upon the trade union's resources in terms of dispute benefits. In the British context loss of wages by strikers may be offset not only by trade union dispute benefits, but also by supplementary allowances paid to their dependants and, in cases of exceptional need, to the strikers themselves under the Social Security Act. Income tax refunds may also help to reduce the gap between the earnings a worker receives when in normal employment, and the sum received during a stoppage.

One of the few disputes for which calculations have been made of the impact upon the parties involved, is the official stoppage in the printing industry during the summer of 1959. This stoppage arose following the 'breakdown in negotiations concerning claims for increased wages, a forty-hour week, and other terms and conditions of employment'[2]. It was settled after the employers conceded a further $2\frac{1}{2}$ per cent pay rise. This new rate of pay would have had to be maintained for 260 weeks in order to recoup lost wages, and the cost of the concession to the employers, if not passed on, was to reduce profit margins by a mere $1\frac{1}{4}$ per cent of total turnover. Such a situation has been likened to one in which both workers and employers 'scored equally in a long and punishing game but each side scored through its own goal'[3].

Since the dispute discussed above is far from unique in its outcome, it is clear that even so far as official strikes, where rational argument and calculation are likely to be most important, are concerned, there are two distinct aspects to the situation. On the one hand there is the economic motivation and costs of the stoppage, and on the other the peak of frustration which is reached in relations between the parties before the decision to strike is taken.

In recent years, however, public attention has been increasingly focused upon the costs of work-stoppages to the economy as a whole, rather than to the parties directly involved. The most commonly used yardstick of the general effects of stoppages, viz. the number of working days lost (a rather emotive term), is itself inadequate for the task. The most important statistical weakness of this measure is that it fails to take account of the workers indirectly affected by stoppages outside the establishments directly affected.[4] Quite apart from this problem, the use of the aggregate total of working days lost to indicate the economic disruption caused has been likened to 'estimating air-raid damage by reference to the bomb-tonnage dropped, irrespective of target or type of bomb'[5]. The general economic situation must thus be borne in mind, when any assessment of the effects of work stoppages is made.

As several authors have pointed out, even on the basis of such a dubious criterion the economic impact of work stoppages is hardly impressive relative to the losses due to sickness, accidents and unemployment.[6] A common retort to such arguments is that losses incurred during work stoppages are not strictly comparable with those due to say, sickness, since the impact of the former is more highly concentrated. A little elementary economic analysis may at this point be used to attempt to discover the likely impact of such concentrated losses on the economy. The indictment that work stoppages are damaging to the national economy seems to turn upon three main charges. Firstly there is the impact of stoppages upon the level and timing of the economy's output, secondly their impact upon inflation and finally their psychological effects.

Taking the output effects first, it is clear that provided, in common with most employers of modern times, the management of the firm concerned halts production operations until the dispute has ended, the output of the establishment will fall to zero. The impact of this temporary closure upon the economy will, in general, according to the analysis of Chamberlain, depend upon three factors.[7] The first is the ability of consumers of the strikebound establishment's products and the suppliers of its raw materials to switch their orders and supplies to competitive firms or establishments. The economic impact of a stoppage is thus negatively related to the degree to which other firms' products and orders may be substituted for those of the plants on strike. Secondly, the level of stocks, which the strike-bound establishment's suppliers and customers are respectively able to build-up and run-down during the stoppage, will be another essential factor with which economic impact will be negatively correlated. Such stock effects seem likely to be especially crucial when an entire industry is affected by a stoppage.

Consumers and producers will feel the impact of the stoppage only after both the substitution and the stock effects have proved insufficient to offset the disruptive influences of the strike. Even in this case the impact of the dispute depends upon a third factor, the necessity of the product concerned. The 'cultural' necessity of the product to consumers is related to the dispensability and deferability of consumption; similarly the 'market' necessity to suppliers and 'production' necessity to industrial customers are related to the dispensability of the strike-affected product and the recoverability of affected production. In connection with this effect it is noteworthy that in Britain's most strike-prone manufacturing industry, namely motor vehicles, an intensive study has revealed that in periods of low orders what is tantamount to a conspiracy to strike occurs. At such times it seems that 'the strike becomes almost a form of "work-spreading" . . . (since) it is more interesting and sociable than other forms of idleness, and helps to keep workers from drifting away to other jobs'[8]. Working days 'lost' at such times are, in fact, likely to be lost even in the absence of stoppages, due to increased lay-offs later in the year.

Evidence from a plant in the engineering industry suggests that when orders for the strike-affected plant's output do exist, 'lost' output may well be substantially made up. This occurs through overtime working and because of productivity increases once the men return to work, following the release of frustration during the dispute.[9] The same study argued that the deterioration in performance which preceded and accompanied the stoppage was far more serious than the stoppage itself in affecting the level of output.[10]

From the simple arguments above it seems likely that the major impact of stoppages is calculated in terms of the loss of time in the productive process, rather than in terms of a loss of output which is never recovered. Whilst it must of course be recognised that in the case of highly 'perishable', non-deferable commodities such as newspapers, the practical effects of these two impacts are identical, such cases are the exception rather than the rule.

On the basis of the analysis carried out so far, these time-lags seem likely to be the main source of the 'ripple effects' said to constitute the main disruptive factor arising from stoppages. Internally such effects disrupt the flow of goods and services between domestic firms, the effects being presumably most severe in the case of stoppages in basic or highly inter-linked industries. Furthermore, it is also argued that such effects have external influences, especially since the main manufacturing industries involved are regarded as 'image makers' abroad.[11] While such arguments are at first sight highly plausible, the nature of the British work stoppage pattern somewhat undermines their validity. During 1972, the year with the worst strike record of the post-war period, disputes of not more than three days' duration accounted for some 48·5 per cent of all stoppages.[12] Accordingly it seems likely that the bulk of time-lags induced must be correspondingly brief in duration, and their importance must be reduced in proportion.

It is clear that in order to have a dramatically adverse effect on the national economy, a work stoppage must have a number of special characteristics. Hildebrand, working on the basis of U.S. experience, has set forth four conditions which must all be met before a 'national emergency' dispute can develop. These conditions are that the dispute's impacts must be national, and that the product affected must be 'essential' in the sense of being either vital to the external and internal safety of the people, indispensable to the immediate health and safety of final consumers, or essential to the sustained flow of real and money income to much of the population. Furthermore, the dispute must involve all or a substantial part of the industry, and also the emergency must be actual, or imminent, and not merely a remote prospect. [13]

Bernstein, using slightly different criteria for analyzing emergency disputes, has been able to identify only three potential industries in the U.S. economy in which such disputes could occur: bituminous coal, railroads, and basic steel. [14] Whilst no space is available here to carry out an analysis on the same basis as Bernstein's, it seems clear that in Britain a greater number of industries are potentially areas in which a stoppage of exceptional duration could produce emergency conditions. This is because of the greater prevalence of industry-wide bargaining in British industry, the greater range of industries producing for the national market, and Britain's much greater dependence upon international trade.

On this basis the port and sea transport industries must be added to the list of vulnerable sectors. Furthermore, with the passage of the 1971 Industrial Relations Act, which repealed the provisions of the 1875 Conspiracy and Protection of Property Act and the 1919 Electricity (Supply) Act, the range of vulnerable industries must be extended to include the public utilities: gas, water and electricity. [15] Most of the industries mentioned as potentially key sectors have been under public ownership for all, or part, of the post-war period. The two industries to which this does not apply, namely port and sea transport, have both experienced considerable Government regulation in their industrial relations systems. In the port industry this intervention has taken the form of both port ownership and decasualisation through the National Dock Labour Board Scheme, but in the sea transport sector intervention has been limited to special legal provisions, which restrict the freedom of seamen to take strike action. [16]

In these circumstances a decision by the union or unofficial movement concerned to take strike action will be the last resort. The employers involved will have been subject to pressure from the Government during the negotiations, and should negotiations break down a trial of strength between the strikers and the Government is likely to develop. A stoppage of this type is thus hardly likely to be a brief one, and the corresponding 'ripple effects' are likely to be especially powerful and far reaching. Under such circumstances the Government usually takes special measures under the Emergency Powers Act of 1920, which was amended in 1964, in order to safeguard essential supplies and services.[17] Such measures have been taken during only a handful of disputes in the post war period: the dock strikes of 1948, 1949, 1970 and 1972, the coal disputes of 1972 and 1974, the rail stoppage of 1955, the seamen's strike of 1966 and the electricity supply workers overtime ban and work to rule of 1970.

Under the provisions of the 1971 Industrial Relations Act, the Secretary of State could apply to the Industrial Court for the imposition of a 'cooling-off' period of not more than sixty days. Such an application could be made when a dispute posed a threat to the economy, to national security, or of public disorder, disease or injury. In addition, powers were granted to the Court to order a ballot when the Secretary of State requested one in the belief that the workers involved in the industrial action were not acting in accordance with their wishes. During the period when the ballot was taking place no industrial action could be taken or threatened.[18] The only large scale use of these powers occurred during the railway workers' overtime ban and work to rule of 1972, when both a cooling-off period and a ballot were used, with little success, in attempts to terminate the dispute.

A second charge levelled against work stoppages is that they result in increased inflationary pressures. In the case of stoppages over wage issues[19] it may be argued that, where such action is successful in raising wages more rapidly than productivity, increased labour costs will result at least in the short-run. Where a stoppage over a wage issue is unsuccessful, or where a stoppage arises over a non-wage issue, costs may still rise since overtime and bonus payments may be needed to catch up on production. While some authors have gone so far as to regard wildcat strikes and wage inflation as 'Siamese twins', the available statistical evidence, for Britain at least, suggests a looser relationship.

In the most intensive study of these matters, Knight, considering data for British manufacturing industry over the period 1950 to 1968,[20] argues that the most important source of variation in strike incidence is related to past money wage increases, although changes in output per man hour and profits do appear to have played some part. As far as money wage inflation is concerned, the most important contribution appears to have come from the labour market and price expectation variables. The role of strikes was a minor one, which essentially consisted of linking present wage changes to frustrated expectations of money wage increase in the past. The relatively minor role of strikes in the wage inflationary process is hardly surprising in view of the vast number of workers covered by collective bargaining, compared to the relatively small number of workers involved in stoppages in any given year. Whilst it may be argued that the bulk of unaffected workers attain wage increases by the threat of industrial action, there are considerable sectors of the economy, especially in the large tertiary sector,[21] where the threat of sustained strike action is, on historical precedent at least, a very hollow one indeed.

The evidence so far considered seems to support the conclusion reached several years ago by Knowles that 'the direct effect of strikes in pushing up wages or arresting their fall does not seem to have been very great, and the direct loss to production has usually been very small by any criterion; although a few very big strikes have caused exceptional losses, the losses have usually been made up very quickly'[22].

The final charge brought against work stoppage activity is that it has adverse psychological impacts. Reasoning of this type is to be found in the Donovan Commission's Report, where it is argued that 'some managements lack confidence that the plans they make and the decisions they reach can be implemented rapidly and effectively or, in extreme cases, at all . . . the country can ill afford the crippling effect which such managerial attitudes are liable to have on the pace of innovation and technological advance in industry'[23]. Whilst the Report itself argues that the number of establishments where strikes seem to be 'endemic' is small (e.g. during 1965 and 1966 the Report cited 31 and 27 establishments respectively which experienced more than five unofficial stoppages), it was clearly worried lest such situations should spread. Thus reference was made to the 'growing number of establishments where occasional strikes and other forms of industrial action take place, and here managements tend to be worried lest the situation deteriorate'[24].

Evidence for a dispersion of strike activity, however, is not strong. One of the most recent surveys, in the engineering industry in 1968, revealed that '. . . under 1 per cent of the establishments had over 40 per cent of the stoppages and 5 per cent had 65 per cent of the stoppages. Three exceptionally strike-prone establishments accounted for 41 per cent of all strikes recorded'[25].

Even in the case of establishments where strikes may justifiably be regarded as endemic, the nature of their impact may be far from clear. Paterson's study of a factory in which thirteen strikes and five go-slows occurred between 1947 and 1953 casts doubts upon the validity of conventional arguments about strike impacts. Clack has gone so far as to argue that, in the case of brief 'downers' in a car plant, a useful role is played in helping to clarify issues and propel unions and management towards acceptable agreements. Stoppages may thus act more as lubricants than as abrasives within a plant's industrial relations system.[26] It can therefore be argued that the adverse psychological impacts of stoppages must be fairly highly concentrated on relatively few establishments. This would presumably limit their impact on the national economy, and facilitate their counteraction.

In summary, it is clear that the conventional wisdom that work stoppages have a severe effect upon the British economy is far from confirmed by much of the evidence and analysis set out above. It seems to have been established that really serious disputes, with regard to output and time-lags, are very few in number indeed and confined to a few lengthy stoppages in basic sectors of the economy. Outside these sectors it seems that the economic impact of stoppages is very difficult to analyse in terms of conventional economic theory. Leibenstein's concept of 'x-efficiency'[27], which relies on the empirically established possibility of variable performance for given units of input i.e. the ability of apparently identical plants to differ considerably in productivity and unit costs, may well be of crucial importance in this connection. The degree of 'x-efficiency' attained by a plant is related to competitive pressure and other motivational factors. The relative importance of the latter is shown by the fact that the terms 'motivation' or 'incentive' efficiency were initially considered as the name for this effect, only to be rejected subsequently on grounds of failure to be all-embracing.[28] Should work stoppages, through the psychological effects outlined earlier, have appreciable effects upon the motivation of the workers and managers concerned, appreciable adverse consequences for the 'x-efficiency' of the firms concerned might be expected. Empirical evidence on such a hypothesis is unfortunately not available, so that no comment upon its validity can be made.

On the whole it seems reasonable to argue that on close scrutiny, many of the charges levelled against strikes on economic grounds seem to rest upon rather dubious evidence. In these circumstances it is to non-economic factors, notably the political and ideological implications of work stoppages as signs of the overt conflict of interest between capital and labour, that much of the recent anxiety over industrial disputes should be attributed.

THE RECENT INDUSTRIAL UNREST

The first four years after World War II were relatively peaceful in the industrial field, especially when compared with 1919–23, and strikes were mainly local and brief. In the interests of the national economy the trade unions accepted continuance of wartime controls, and even endorsed voluntary wage restraint until rapid rises in the cost of living due to devaluation and the Korean war forced its abandonment. Fortunately the rise in prices halted with the end of this conflict, and pressure of wage demands abated in 1953 and 1954, although 1951 had seen a rate of growth in weekly manual earnings which was not to be equalled until 1971.[29] The full flowering of the wage system based on national level bargaining, so painfully built up during and between the two wars, was thus associated with a degree of industrial peace quite comparable with that of the previous two decades. As Flanders observed at the time, 'National agreements and the acceptance of arbitration . . . tended to eliminate the strike as a bargaining weapon in union strategy used on a national scale to advance wage claims. Instead, it has increasingly become a form of local protest by a group of workers within the union, either against the actions of the management in a particular establishment or against the decisions or settlements of their own union'[30]. In the circumstances, it was perhaps not surprising that references were made to the withering away of the strike.

With hindsight it now seems clear that the mid-fifties in fact saw the beginning of an upward trend in strike activity. In 1953 more than two million man days were lost through disputes, and although this figure had been exceeded on frequent occasions previously, since 1953 the loss rate has never fallen below this level except in 1963. The number of stoppages, too, passed the two thousand mark in 1955 and since then the total has only once dropped below this figure notably, in 1966. Until the early sixties, of course, coal mining retained a dominant role, accounting for between one-half and three-quarters of all stoppages. But losses in other industries certainly increased in importance. In 1953 a one-day token stoppage occurred in shipbuilding and engineering, while a national railway strike was only narrowly averted. A national strike by footplatemen actually occurred in 1955, to be followed by national stoppages in shipbuilding and engineering in 1957 and 1962, in printing in 1959, and in railway workshops and construction in 1963. By the latter year, as Turner observed, 'The large *official* strike, which virtually disappeared from our industrial scene for twenty years after 1932, has made a new, if still occasional, appearance'[31].

The sharp rise in working days lost was almost entirely due to a series of large official strikes for wage increases, but these perhaps merely reflected the effect of growing rank-and-file militancy upon union leaders. The increase in the total of stoppages outside mining, on the other hand, marked the emergence of small, short and usually unofficial strikes, a problem with which the Donovan Commission became preoccupied in the mid-sixties. Apparently, full employment and market forces had created a 'two-tier' system of bargaining under which nationally determined wage rates had lost much of their influence upon actual earnings, which were determined informally at plant level, giving rise to the phenomenon of wage drift. Unofficial strikes were seen as reflecting the inadequacy of procedural and institutional arrangements at plant level for avoiding disputes.

This is not the place to consider objections to this appraisal of the situation, though they are numerous and often valid. The fundamental point is that localised small stoppages today, as in the pre-1914 era, have no special importance for the community as a whole, nor, as Turner has argued, perhaps even for the parties immediately concerned.[32] It has been questioned above whether the total incidence of stoppages has any measurable effect, but leaving this aside, there is no reason to assume that numerous small strikes are proportionately more serious than large stoppages. Nor does this mean, of course, that all large stoppages are damaging, since short token strikes in construction or engineering may cost 300,000 or 500,000 man-days almost unnoticed, as happened in 1963 and 1968 respectively. Full scale national stoppages in shipbuilding (e.g. in 1957 costing over two million man-days) or in printing (costing four million days in 1959) have scarcely more significance for the community at large. Arguably, strikes become an acute problem only when the public is seriously affected, and this requires more or less protracted national stoppages in public utilities, coal and transportation. It is in the public sector, broadly defined, that big strikes matter. Partial stoppages in the traditionally strike-prone industries, although perhaps undesirable, do not create a strike problem comparable with that of national stoppages in vital industries, some of them traditionally strike-free.

If this view is accepted, the 'two-tier' system, representing the decay of national bargaining, may well be at the root of Britain's current strike problem, although not for the reasons suggested in the Donovan Report. Plant bargaining, while no doubt widespread in engineering and manufacturing, has not superseded the national agreement as the main determinant of earnings in most of the key sectors mentioned.[33] There is virtually no 'two-tier' system in national or local government service, in the nationalised industries, for merchant seamen or in public utilities.[34] Since the National Power Loading Agreement of 1966 effective national bargaining has even been introduced for miners, in the sense that control over earnings has been largely removed from the pits.[35]

On purely *a priori* grounds it is likely that workers in the nationally bargained wage sector will suffer most in times of inflation. Firstly, wage drift (defined to exclude overtime) will be less than in sectors where plant bargaining flourishes. Secondly, in so far as national bargaining occurs on an annual (or longer) basis, rapid inflation may offset the gains of any particular settlement before the next round of discussions. Thirdly, when incomes policy or wage restraint of any type is being imposed, the national wage bargain sectors are likely to bear the brunt of government pressure because their settlements achieve widespread publicity, they are regarded as crucial to the economy and have, in many cases, the Treasury as their ultimate paymaster. As a corollary, of course, if national bargaining is unsuccessful in maintaining real wages or even traditional relativities, it is likely to produce national stoppages, and since national bargaining usually (though not invariably) implies powerful unions, these stoppages are likely to be official. Thus rapid inflation coupled with wage restraint will tend to produce national stoppages (or other industrial action) in the key sectors.

Since half a dozen attempts have been made to restrain incomes since the war and the retail price index has steadily risen, it is perhaps surprising that a wave of national strikes in key sectors has not occurred until so recently. However, a number of obvious explanations exist for this phenomenon. Perhaps most important, the annual rate of rise in the retail price index since 1968 has no parallel in the previous period. Devaluation of sterling in 1967, and its depreciation since June 1972, coupled with a world commodity boom, unusual increases in the price of seasonal foods and the new system of indirect taxation have all contributed to rapid inflation.[36] Also, it is clear that until the late fifties, wage drift did not increase sufficiently to leave national bargaining at a disadvantage. It should also be remembered that until the statutory freeze of 1966, wage restraint had been on a voluntary basis and very largely ineffective, except during 1948–50. Even where attempts were made to curb wage increases in the public sector these were either half-hearted as in 1957, or short-lived, as in 1961. In addition, some portions of the key industries were able to avoid serious problems in the short-term, either by winning the principle of comparability (as industrial civil servants did by the Priestley Report in 1955), or by disregarding the 'guiding lights' (as the Civil Service Arbitration Tribunal did in

1962) or by accepting productivity deals (such as that in electricity supply in 1965) or by actual or threatened strikes (the railwaymen during 1950–60). Indeed, even during the era of the National Board for Prices and Incomes generous awards were given to the higher civil service, London busmen, fire brigades and electricity supply workers, while other groups avoided restraint by using the argument of low pay or high productivity loopholes.[37] Arguably, the wave of unrest really began in the aftermath of devaluation, higher indirect taxation and the effect of S.E.T. on prices, as an Incomes Policy was abandoned. During the period from mid-1970 to November 1972 the government sought to exert 'influence' on the public and private sectors to resist highly inflationary pay claims, no doubt more successfully in the former than in the latter since monetary and fiscal policy was not being used. After November 1972 the standstill and Phase II added further pressure to wage demands in the key sectors, more especially because no exceptions on grounds of low pay or productivity were permitted.

It is immaterial whether the mechanism outlined above began to show its effects in the national official seamen's strike of 1966, the road passenger transport strike of 1965 or the postal strike which affected large towns in 1964. National disputes followed in the postal sector in each year from 1968 to 1972; in the local government manual employees sector and among teachers in 1969 and 1970; in the coal mines in 1972 and 1974; and in the hospital ancillary services in 1972. Apart from stoppages, there have been national overtime bans or similar action in the municipal and company-owned bus sector and on the railways in 1972, by two groups of electricity workers in 1970, and in the mines and again among electricity workers in 1973.

It would be naive to accept any single explanation of industrial unrest, and many important factors are not quantifiable either in principle or in practice. But the hypothesis that key sectors where national bargaining predominates have lost ground over recent years to those better able to exploit the two-tier system is at least supported by some evidence.[38] When average weekly earnings of male manual workers in certain industries are expressed as a percentage of the average for all industries, and compared over the period 1948 to 1972, significant changes appear in the ranking of some groups. Public administration, defined as manual workers in national and local government establishments not classified to specified industries (such as transport, medical or educational services) and excluding police, fire and defence services, ranks second only to agriculture as a low pay sector. Moreover, weekly earnings were 82 per cent of the national average in 1948 but only

75 per cent in 1972, a level only slightly higher than that at the lowest point, namely 1969. Similarly, earnings in coal mining were some 33 per cent above average in 1952–3, but had actually declined to the average level by 1970. In the public utilities (gas, electricity and water) weekly earnings were below average for the whole period, but declined from being over 97 per cent in 1964 to just 90 per cent by 1968, and a dramatic improvement in 1971 does not appear to have been sustained. The conciliation grades of railway workers (i.e. wages staff other than workshop), on the other hand, enjoyed earnings above average for the first time in 1966, and contrived to retain this position at least until 1971. Dock workers, too, appear to have improved their position dramatically between 1966 and 1970, no doubt because of the possibility of local bargaining. It may be significant that, to date, national stoppages on the railway (in 1972) and in the docks (in 1970 and 1972) have not hinged upon higher pay but on other matters.

It should be borne in mind, however, that these statistics are no more than suggestive, since they are only partial in coverage and no doubt mask differences in pay within the broad groupings adopted for analysis, as well as differences in working hours. But it is perhaps important that for all the sectors mentioned (except railways, for which no data were included for 1972, and coal mining) the period 1971–2 saw a deterioration in their relative pay, which does not augur well for industrial peace in the key sectors. It cannot, of course, be said that this declining position holds good for all parts of the public sector, but there is no doubt that teachers, for example, have also fallen behind in terms of relative pay since the early sixties, and that their increased money wages over the later sixties produced no gains in real pay.[39] This latter point is not surprising because even before the recent upsurge in prices, all those groups whose pay was tied to the norm laid down by a formal Incomes Policy would have suffered a fall in real pre-tax pay of 1·6 per cent in 1965–6, 2·5 per cent in 1966–7, and, at least, of 2 per cent in 1968–9.[40] After allowance for tax and social insurance contributions, the *median* wage earner with a wife and two children would have increased his real income by 1 per cent per annum over 1964–8, and perhaps 2·7 per cent in 1968–70.[41] But this comparison only underlines the different achievements of those tied to the norm and those who were able to disregard it.

In brief, the arguments so far analysed are as follows: sectors where meaningful national wage bargaining occurs are at a disadvantage relative to those where a two-tier system is operative; national bargaining is prevalent in key sectors, defined as those where strikes cause hardship to the community – these fall primarily in the broadly defined public sector; the public sector is where wage restraint is likely to be most effective, and, consequently, is where the adverse effects of inflation on real pay are most serious; and given a sufficient degree of unionisation, national stoppages are probable in these key sectors. In a sense, therefore, the unrest of the early seventies was due to a failure either to control inflation or to operate a wages policy on any but the most arbitrary and partial basis. It was also, however, perhaps ultimately due to the difficulties inherent in having two systems of wage determination existing at the same time.

Historically, the wave of strikes around 1890 was associated with the changeover from a wage system based primarily on custom to one involving collective bargaining, whereas the incidence of strikes around the first World War coincided with the movement from localised to national bargaining. It is not certain that recent years have really witnessed an abnormal increase in disputes, since although the number of stoppages exceeded three thousand for the first time ever in 1969 and 1970, the following years failed to maintain this level, and the highest figure for man-days lost, nearly 24 million in 1972, is still below the levels of 1919–21, and of 1912, not to mention 1926. If the contribution made by seven large stoppages are excluded from the figures for 1970–72 the man-days lost in each year remain around the seven million mark. The propensity to strike had no doubt increased over these years, but if the problem had, in fact, reached crisis proportions it was largely because of the re-emergence of the national stoppage in key sectors where workers had been forced to use their power to remedy their increasingly disadvantageous position *vis-à-vis* workers elsewhere. In other words, it was a problem created by the co-existence of two wage systems, one susceptible to government influence and perhaps not sufficiently swift-acting to give protection against inflation, while the other (especially in the absence of fiscal and monetary restraint) is largely uncontrolled and better able to offset rising prices by raising wages.

This problem is serious because, while the economic impact of disputes is, as argued above, highly dubious, large stoppages in key sectors clearly do cause hardship and inconvenience to the community. A further dimension is added, however, by the fact that national stoppages, especially those in key areas which fall within the public sector, tend to become conflicts between unions and the government. Militancy in the British context still means merely that bigger demands are pushed further, and not that they are qualitatively different demands from those made in the past. A general strike for purely political purposes has not been a real possibility in Britain since 1920, but this may not always be the case in future if government-union confrontation becomes endemic.

E. W. Evans
S. W. Creigh

NOTES

1 e.g. Alfino, A. P., 'Figuring Strike Costs', *Management Record*, Vol. 21 (1959), pp. 235–237.

Dorbandt, M.P., 'The Impact of a Strike upon Customer and Supplier Relationships', *Management Record*, Vol. 21 (1959), pp. 194–197. Knowles covers similar ground in relation to an earlier period in his *Strikes, A Study in Industrial Conflict*, (1954), p. 262.

2 Ministry of Labour Gazette, Vol. LXVIII (1960), p. 184.

3 Cyriax, G. and Oakeshott, R. *The Bargainers*, (1960).

4 The Department of Employment Gazette, usually in a footnote, does calculate the total of such repercussions in the motor industry coming to its notice, e.g. Ministry of Labour Gazette, Vol. LXVIII (1960), p. 185.

5 Knowles, K. J. G. C., 'Strikes and their Changing Economic Context', *Bulletin of the Oxford University Institute of Statistics*, Vol. 9, (1947), p. 287.

6 Whittingham, T. G. and Towers, B., 'Editorial Comment' *Industrial Relations Journal*, Vol. 2. (1971), calculate the total loss of output as a proportion of G.N.P. during 1971 to be only 0·2 per cent.

7 Chamberlain, N. W. and Schilling, J. M., *The Impact of Strikes*, Harper (1954), p. 13.

8 Turner, H. A., Clack, G. and Roberts, G., *Labour Relations in the Motor Industry*, (1967), pp. 118–119.

9 Paterson, T. T., *Glasgow Limited*, (1960), pp. 203–205.

10 Paterson, T. T., op. cit., p. 212.

11 Whittingham, T. G. and Towers, B., 'Strikes and the Economy'. *National Westminster Bank Quarterly Review*, November 1971, pp. 41–42.

12 'Work stoppages due to Industrial Disputes in 1972', Department of Employment Gazette, Vol. LXXXI, No. 6. (1973), p. 555, 1972 was the most strike-prone of all the post-war years, some 23·9 million working days being lost.

13 Hildebrand, G. H., 'An Economic Definition of the National Emergency Dispute', Chapter I in Bernstein, I., Enarson, H. L. and Fleming, R. W. (eds.) *Emergency Disputes and Public Policy*, Harper (1966), p. 6.

14 Bernstein, I. 'The Economic Impact of Strikes in Key Industries'. Chapter II in Bernstein, I., Enarson, H. L. and Fleming, R. W. (eds.), op. cit., p. 28.

15 Harvey, R. J., *Industrial Relations*. (1971) II. 134. p. 297. Under the former acts it was a criminal offence for a worker to break his contract of service having reasonable cause to believe that the consequence of his action would be a substantial deprivation of the supply.

16 Wedderburn, K. W., *The Worker and the Law*, (Penguin: 1971), p. 389–390.

17 A 'State of Emergency' may be proclaimed under these Acts when it appears that there have occurred or are about to occur events of such a nature as to be calculated, by interfering with the supply and distribution of food, water, fuel and light or with the means of locomotion, to deprive the community or any substantial portion of the community of the essentials of life.

18 Harvey, R. J. op. cit., Chapter 17, pp. 113 to 118.

19 During 1972, for example, of the 2,497 stoppages some 1,477 were over wage issues viz. 59·2 per cent.

20 Knight, K. G., 'Strikes and Wage Inflation in British Manufacturing Industry, 1950–68', *Bulletin of the Oxford Institute of Economics and Statistics,* Vol. 34., (1972), pp. 281–294.

21 In 1972, for instance, the largest single Industrial Order, on the basis of the 1968 S.I.C., was the Professional and Scientific Services group, with 12·9 per cent of total employment. Distribution, with 11·6 per cent of total came second. The 'tertiary' sector as a whole accounted for 52·3 per cent of employment, and if the strike-prone transport group is excluded it is still responsible for 45·3 per cent.

22 Knowles, K. G. J. C., *Strikes, a Study in Industrial Conflict,* (1954), p. 262.

23 Royal Commission on Trade Unions and Employers' Associations 1965–68 (Chairman Lord Donovan) Cmnd. 3623. H.M.S.O. (1968) p. 112.

24 Ibid., p. 112.

25 Marsh, A. I., Evans, E. O. and Garcia, P., *Workplace Industrial Relations in Engineering,* (1971), p. 24.

26 Clack, G. 'How Unofficial Strikes Help Industry', *Business* (July 1965, pp. 42–47).

27 Leibenstein, H., 'Allocative Efficiency vs. "X-Efficiency".' *American Economic Review,* Vol. LVI (1966), pp. 392–415.

28 Ibid., p. 392.

29 Pelling, H., *A History of British Trade Unionism,* (Penguin: 1971), p. 236.

30 Flanders, A., *Trade Unions,* (1952), pp. 106–7.

31 Turner, H. A., *The Trend of Strikes,* (1963), p. 15.

32 Turner, H. A., *Is Britain Really Strike Prone?* (1969), chap. 6.

33 Roberts, B. C. and Gennard, J., 'Trends in Plant and Company Bargaining', in Robertson, D. J. and Hunter, L. C. (eds), *Labour Market Issues of the 1970s,* (1970), p. 47.

34 Johnston, T. L., 'Public Sector and White Collar Bargaining', in Robertson, D. J. and Hunter, L. C. (eds), op. cit., p. 52.

35 Hughes, J. and Moore, R. (eds), *A Special Case: Social Justice for the Miners,* (Penguin: 1972), p. 106.

36 'The Use of Prices and Incomes Policies in Britain: the search for a new instrument', *Midland Bank Review,* August 1973.

37 Fels, A., *The British Prices and Incomes Board,* (1972), p. 47.

38 See 'Trends in Earnings', Department of Employment Gazette, May, 1973, pp. 442–449.

39 Thomas, R. B., 'Post-war Movements in Teachers' Salaries', *Industrial Relations,* Vol. 4, No. 3, Autumn 1973, p. 13.

40 Fels, A., op. cit., p. 31.

41 Ibid., p. 29.

Work Stoppages: The British Experience

1

STRIKES

H. A. Clegg

Between January and September 1955, 553,400 British workers were involved in 1,778 strikes during which an aggregate of 3,199,000 working days were lost. Since 1932 only two complete years, 1937 (London Coronation Bus Strike) and 1944 (Porter Award Coal Strike), have higher totals of working days lost, and only slightly higher at that. Only three years have higher figures for workers involved, 1943, 1944 and 1953, and the last can be explained away by a one-day strike in the engineering industry. Five years, 1943, 1944, 1945, 1946 and 1954, have had larger numbers of strikes.

These statistics show that the final score for 1955 may be the highest since 1932; and, even if it is not, they appear to support the widely-held view that losses through strikes have become so high that a remedy must be found.

Selective comparisons of this kind can, however, be misleading. If we go further back, or to other countries, the figures for 1955 appear less alarming. Supposing that the rate of working days lost in the first nine months of 1955 is maintained until the end of December, a little over four million working days will have been lost. Since 1932 the average has been just under two million, and in every year since the war the total has stood just under or just over the two million mark. The average since 1901, however, is over ten million working days lost a year, despite the absence of any year after 1926 which has come near that mark. Even if 1926 is excluded, as exceptional by any standard, the average is well over seven million. Two periods maintain the height of the average, the years just before and just after the first world war. From 1908 to 1914 the average was over thirteen million; from 1919 to 1925 it was nearly twenty-eight million.

The *International Labour Review* for July, 1955, gives interesting tables of international comparisons.[1] The figures show days lost

per thousand persons employed in mining, manufacturing, construction and transport. The averages for 1947 to 1954[2] shows
Britain above Switzerland, the Netherlands, the Scandinavian
countries and West Germany. But with a score of 151 we remain in
a quite different class from the United States (1,520), France (1,244)
and Italy (1,023). Our performance is also modest in comparison
with Australia (941), Japan (786) and Canada (736). Even if our
1955 figure is double the average of previous years it will not bring
us into competition with records like these.

Comparisons with the first thirty years of the century, and with
other countries, should quieten alarmists, but it would be unwise
to conclude from them that the British strikes of 1955 give no cause
for concern. So far figures for working days lost have been used.
They are by no means a perfect guide to the damage done by strikes,
but since numbers involved can be swollen by one-day strikes, and
since a large number of small short strikes cause far less loss than a
major national dispute, they reveal more than the other measures
available. Nevertheless it is worth remarking that whilst the total
days lost each year since 1932 have been far below the average for
previous years, the number of disputes has risen to new heights.
Strikes have grown in number; but they involve fewer workers than
before, and are briefer.[3]

This trend is in part explained by the change from official strikes
to unofficial strikes, due to the changed philosophy of trade union
leadership, and to the Conditions of Employment and National
Arbitration Order which made strikes illegal from 1940 to 1951. In
earlier years in which losses from strikes were heavy, the great bulk
of them were due to a few official disputes which tied up a whole
industry. The coal strike of 1912, the railway strike of 1911, and the
cotton spinners' strike of 1908 account for the bulk of the days lost
lost between 1908 and 1914. From 1919 to 1925 nearly 150 million
out of 194 million working days were lost in seventeen official
national disputes (out of a total of over 6 thousand disputes), 72
million of them in the coal lock-out of 1921. In 1926, 160 million out
of 162 million working days were lost in the General Strike and the
coal lock-out; the remaining 321 disputes shared the odd 2 million
working days. Of the 30 million days lost from 1927 to 1933, over 18
million are accounted for by five national textile strikes. From 1933
to 1954 there was only one official national dispute, and that the
one-day engineering stoppage in December 1953.

The danger signal of 1955, then, is not the number of strikes, the
number of strikers, or the days lost. It is the railway dispute, which
was the first serious official national stoppage for so many years.
If it is unique, we have little to worry about. If it is the first in a

series of national disputes, alarm may be vindicated and the search for remedies justified.

Before examining proposed cures, it is worth inquiring after causes. If we fear an outbreak of national disputes, we would do well to ask what caused the national disputes of 1908–14, 1919–26 and 1929–32. A simple economic explanation can be offered for the heavy losses of 1919–23. During those years the cost of living was first rising and then falling faster than ever before or since (except during the 1914–18 war when strikes were illegal). It was almost impossible for the system of collective bargaining to cope with the consequent alterations in wages. A crop of strikes for increases was followed by an even heavier crop of lock-outs for decreases, or strikes against decreases. No self-respecting union could peacefully accept the series of reductions of 1921–22, and sooner or later almost every major industry, coal, engineering, shipbuilding, cotton, wool, and printing, had had its dispute.

Thereafter the price level flattened. Indeed in 1924 it rose and railway enginemen and dockers struck for an increase. The subsequent slow decline in prices up to 1934 called for no large reductions in wages in most industries; but the prices of the staple exporting industries fell faster than the average. Coal was the first to suffer in 1925–26. Hence the General Strike and the coal lock-out. From 1929 to 1932 cotton and wool had their turn.

The difficulty with this explanation of large upward or downward movements in prices is that it does not fit the years 1908–14. The usual economic explanation of the high rate of working days lost in this period is that prices were rising, but only slowly, from 1900 to the outbreak of war, and wages were failing to keep pace, so that it was the one considerable period of years since the Napoleonic wars in which real wages in Britain have declined. If this was the reason for industrial unrest, the pre-war and post-war periods cannot have a common explanation. Non-economic causes have also been suggested. The Taff Vale Judgement of 1901 placed legal hazards in the path of would-be strikers, and the law was not revised until the Trade Disputes Act of 1906. It has been supposed that discontent, bottled up during these years, flooded out once the cork was removed. Revolutionary syndicalist notions took hold of some sections of the trade union movement at that time, and these have also received their share of blame.

If a change in the law is the explanation, a parallel can be found in the period immediately after the 1914–18 war when the prohibition of strikes and lock-outs under the Munitions Acts was removed. But it is not easy to believe that the coal strike of 1912 was caused by the Act of 1906, nor that the General Strike of 1926 was the result of the repeal of clauses in the Munitions Act in 1918. Moreover, there is no parallel for the 1929–32 textile strikes.

Revolutionary notions were still current in the trade union movement after the war. They had reached their greatest strength in the shop stewards' movement of the war years, which declined rapidly after the armistice. Before industrial unrest can be ascribed to revolutionary ideas, however, several difficulties must be surmounted. At no time were revolutionaries more than a minority of active trade unionists, and more than a very small minority of trade union leaders. The incidence of strikes was not closely related to the spread of revolutionary doctrines. The conservative cotton workers, for example, were responsible for four major national disputes between 1908 and 1926. The 'red' engineers had only one national stoppage, and that a lock-out, in the same period. This explanation also fails to account for the textile strikes of the years of depression.

Unless we fall back on some such vague notion as mounting social anger, or growing class conflict–which immediately pose the question: Why did they increase then?–there is no single cause for the high strike losses in the three periods under review. Besides this, none of the explanations offered fit the circumstances of 1955. Prices have been rising, but not nearly so fast as in 1919 and 1920, nor so fast as at other times since 1945. In contrast to 1910–14, wages have, on the average, kept pace with retail prices. Only the most shadowy ghosts of syndicalist doctrines can be found in the trade union movement. It is true that the prohibition of strikes and lock-outs was lifted in 1951, when the Conditions of Employment and National Arbitration Order was replaced by the Industrial Disputes Order, but if that is the cause of current unrest, why should it have waited until 1955 to take effect?

Since examination of previous periods of industrial unrest does not provide the clue to unrest in 1955, it may serve our purpose to inquire into the causes of industrial peace since 1932, and ask whether these have now ceased to operate.

After 1932 the price-falls of the twenties, affecting first all industries and then the exporting industries, ceased, and were soon replaced by a gentle general increase. This provided the opportunity for trade union leaders to practice the new strategy which they had been developing since the disaster of 1926. This strategy had two objectives, to avoid the major conflicts which, in the economic conditions of the twenties, had been doomed to failure, and to win for the unions, individually and collectively, the position of respected and responsible institutions within industry, within society and within government.

The war changed the economic conditions, but gave the unions the status which they had sought; and the war effort was supported by the unions with a much more common consent than in 1914–18. After the war economic conditions continued to promise success to strikers, but the new status of the unions was repected by the Labour Government, which could also call on the affections of the unions both as a partner in the Labour Movement, and for its extensive reforms. Trade unionists began to develop a philosophy of confidence: we have now a recognized stake in the economy, individual shares can only increase if total output is raised by common effort; why strike against outselves?

The Conservative Government has maintained, and manifestly maintained, the position of the unions and the main measures of the 'welfare state'. By comparison, however, with the coalition government of the war, and the Labour Government, it has stressed individual incentives more and common effort less. Tax changes have favoured the rich and the middle income groups. Profits have continued to rise, dividends have been increased, and bonus issues have caught the headlines. When controls are removed and luxury expenditure increases, the argument that only an increasing national income provides increased individual shares becomes tarnished, if not plain silly. The economic incentive to strike is still present, and social restraints, far more important than legal restraints, are losing their force.

This account perhaps carries some conviction, but it is a blunt explanation for an increase in working days lost from two to four million, or for the first major national dispute since 1932. In addition, although conditions affecting trade-union action have somewhat changed since 1951, they still look far more like those of 1951 than of any period before the last war.

There remains the possibility of explaining the unrest of 1955 in terms of the events of 1955 itself; but it is a venture with little chance of success. The causes of particular strikes are notoriously complex. The contribution of industrial sociologists to the study of strikes has not been to explain them by translation of causes into their vocabulary of 'tensions', 'statuses' and 'motivations', but to show that the causes are even more complex than previous students have thought. By far the best British contribution to industrial sociology is a study of Manchester dock workers.[4] One of its virtues is that, although it devotes attention to an account of a dock strike, it clearly and honestly fails to 'explain' it.

Several of the major disputes of 1955–the railway, dock, and newspaper strikes–were in part disputes between unions. It will not do, however, to say that the cause of the 1955 strikes was inter-union conflict. For the extraordinary structure of the British trade-union movement has provided enough strains in each of the past fifty years to set off as many major disputes. In most years it has not done so, and the greatest disputes have not been of inter-union origin.

The railway strike can as well be 'explained' in terms of the vacillation and delays of the British Transport Commission and the government, or the apparently contradictory awards of arbitration tribunals, as in terms of the jealousies of the Associated Society of Locomotive Engineers and Firemen and the National Union of Railwaymen, but this 'explanation' would neglect the hundreds, or perhaps thousands, of difficult negotiations which have not ended in strikes.

A more attractive argument is that the main strikes of 1955 have been of groups of workers whose earnings have not kept pace with general increases in recent years. Railwaymen have notoriously fallen behind. Highly-paid newspaper workers have lost some of their advantage. Dockers are still above the average, but by much less than in their peak year, 1944, when they stood 40 per cent above the national average for men. The North-Eastern Division of the Coal Board has been more obdurate than its neighbours in resisting price-list revision, and the earnings of Yorkshire coal-miners rose less between 1947 and 1954 than those of any other coal-field. It is easy to accept that this had something to do with it. But why 1955 rather than another year? And why just these occupations and not the others–including most public services–which have also fallen behind?

We cannot then, arrive at a confident knowledge of causes, and cures must be examined without its aid.

Most proposals for reducing losses through disputes can be classified under two headings: proposals for legal restrictions on the freedom to strike, and proposals to alter the machinery for avoiding disputes.

The former include full prohibition of strikes and lock-outs and provisions that strikes should be prohibited unless certain requirements are met. It has been proposed, for instance, that unofficial strikes should be banned, and that strikes should be legal only if preceded by a publicly supervised ballot.

One of the main difficulties which such proposals have to meet is enforcement. Laws are not likely to serve as deterrents unless they can be enforced. If the penalty is a fine exacted from the union, unofficial strikes are not covered, and the result may be to transform all strikes into unofficial strikes. If strike-leaders are to be punished, there is the same danger, and also the likelihood of creating popular martyrs. If penalties are prescribed for all strikers, there are the enormous administrative problems of punishing tens or hundreds of thousands of transgressors, together with the probability that public opinion in a democracy will not permit the application of the law.

Experience of the prohibition of disputes in Britain is not completely conclusive. Certainly the law was rarely enforced, and strikes were not prevented in the two periods of illegality, 1915–18 and 1940–51. Indeed, in the second period their number greatly increased. During the first world war, however, the number of working days lost was far lower than in the preceding or following years, and during the second world war the total could hardly be lower than before or after, since it was already close to its minimum before the war, and remained there afterwards.

It is important to remember that prohibition was only enacted with trade union consent, and was withdrawn as soon as the trade unions demanded; so that the fall in working days lost may have been due to trade union restraint, partly bolstered up by inoperative penalties.

Other countries provide more conclusive evidence. Australian states, for instance, have experimented with most forms of prohibition in peace as well as during war, and with or without trade union consent. South Australia has tried a straightforward prohibition. Queensland has tried the authorization of only those strikes approved by majority in secret ballot. The provisions seem to have had little effect, as can be judged from the *cri de coeur* of the Queensland premier in 1928: 'You can see no difficulty in imposing penalties on hundreds and hundreds of men. You think I need only wave my hand to make these men load sugar.'[5]

France has found a more successful legal deterrent. Since the renegade syndicalist Briand discovered the method in 1912, French governments have from time to time broken strikes by 'mobilizing' or 'requisitioning' workers under national service legislation. The legislation currently used is the National Service Law of 1938. It is important to note, however, that requisitioning has succeeded when it has appeared that leaders are trying to force unwilling trade-union members to strike, sometimes for political ends as in the 'general strike' of 1938. Then workers have failed to strike, thankful of the excuse. On several occasions since the war, however, the majority of workers have refused to comply with orders, despite the penalties, and then the government has failed to prosecute.[6]

Prohibition of strikes may serve as a protection for leaders who do not wish to call official strikes desired by their members, and for members who do not want to comply with orders of their leaders to come out on official strike. They cannot prevent unofficial strikes, nor official strikes which have the support of union membership. How many British strikes of the last ten, twenty, or indeed fifty years, would fail to come into one or other of these categories?

There is also the even more telling argument that prohibition of strikes is morally wrong, at least if successful. The right to strike is one of the most important principles of a free society. Even in the years of peak strike losses before and after the first world war Parliament upheld the right to strike. The Emergency Powers Act of 1919 gave governments emergency powers to maintain essential services, but not to force strikers to work. Even after 1926 the Conservative Government did no more than enact a vague and probably unworkable measure prohibiting strikes which were both 'political' and 'sympathetic', but not straightforward industrial disputes. Has there been some radical change in the nature of disputes, or in our beliefs, that four million working days lost in a year should drive us to destroy a liberty that was then upheld under far greater provocation?

Proposals to change the machinery for avoiding disputes do not suffer from this defect. Here the first difficulty is that our provisions are already so varied and elaborate, that it is not easy to believe that further additions will make much difference.

Two suggestions have come from the 'rade unions: one, accepted by this year's Trades Union Congress, that the General Council of that body should have power to intervene – but only as a conciliator – in the early stages of disputes; the second, which was rejected, that the government should be asked to establish an Arbitration Appeal Tribunal, to which the decisions of our many existing tribunals could be appealed.

There is some foreign experience to guide us. Many national trade union centres have far more power in disputes than the T.U.C. General Council had, or now has. This is true, for instance, of the Scandinavian countries. Their strike record over recent years has been very good, but they had the same provisions when their strike record was very bad. The French had a National Arbitration Court as part of their system of compulsory arbitration from 1936 to 1939, but its task was to administer a very different system of industrial relations from ours, and no one could ascribe to it unqualified success, in preventing disputes or in other respects.

No one could predict that these or similar changes would have no effect on disputes in Britain. The recent railway stoppage, for example, might perhaps have been avoided if there had been an Appeal Tribunal to which the apparently contradictory decisions of the Railway Staff National Tribunal could have been referred. The changes are, however, small refinements. We have already many arbitration bodies; how many disputes amenable to arbitration which are not settled by them would be resolved by an appellate tribunal? We have already a wealth of professional and amateur conciliatiors; how many disputes in which they fail would the T.U.C. General Council avert? How many of the great disputes in British history would have been resolved by the earlier intervention of the General Council?

Furthermore, new machinery for avoiding disputes seems to be more a symptom than a cause of strikes. The government conciliation service was first built up to a significant service in the Labour Department of the Board of Trade in the very years before the first world war when strike losses were reaching then unequalled heights. No one would, of course, ascribe the losses to the service, and it may have prevented even worse, but it did not stop the figures racing up. The Industrial Courts Act, 1919, added two most important elements to the British system for dealing with disputes—the Court itself, and provision for Courts of Inquiry—and was followed by the greatest strike wave Britain has ever known. Again it would be silly to ascribe the strikes to the Act, but it would be hardly less foolish to interpret the industrial peace of 1927–28 or post-1932 as a long-term effect of the Act. Machinery can and does avoid and contain particular disputes; it cannot deal with the causes.

In recent years the first week or so of a strike of higher-paid workers has been financed from pay-as-you-earn income-tax rebates. The families of strikers—but not the strikers—are eligible for national assistance. It has been suggested that legislation should be introduced to debar strikers from one or both of these sources of income. The ethics of the matter are clear. If the right to strike is to be upheld, it should not be nibbled away by curtailing the rights of strikers as citizens. If the right to strike should be limited, it should be limited directly. Even as a device of expediency the proposal has little to recommend it. If the British workers could run up 86 million working days lost in 1921 or 162 million in 1926 without income-tax rebates or a National Assistance Board, does anyone suppose that the withdrawal of these advantages now would prevent them improving on a figure of 4 million a year if they chose to do so?

To sum up the argument so far: although the recent railway dispute is an unwelcome return of the type of dispute which was responsible for the great bulk of working days lost before 1932, the causes of the three periods of heavy strike losses in the twentieth century, so far as we can isolate them, do not appear to be operating to-day. Compared with the past, working days lost in 1955, though double the average of recent years, are still insignificant. There is little or nothing to be said in favour of altering the law relating to disputes. Changes in the procedures for avoiding disputes might be of some use, but could not prevent a serious outbreak.

There are some grounds for concern, but there seems to be so little justification for panic, and most proposals for cures appear so irrelevant, immoral, or stupid (or have more than one of these qualities) that one is driven to ask: what is the explanation of the fuss over strikes in recent months?

One defence of the alarmists is that industrial disputes cause more serious losses at times of full employment than in times of unemployment. This is obviously true. At the beginning of the 1921 and 1926 coal lock-outs home stocks of coal were high. It was possible to buy coal abroad from producers who were only too happy to find markets. If there was a coal dispute now the country would enter it with low stocks and have to compete in sellers' markets for coal abroad and sellers' markets for coal shipments. What is not clear is the exact weight to be attached to this consideration. Does it make 4 million days lost in 1955 equal to 86 million in 1921, or 27 million in 1920, or 8 million in 1929?

We have little British experience to help us. Frequent dock strikes have shown us that many goods are delayed, some spoilt, and some business transferred to other ports, but that there is no significant long-term effect on the country's rate of economic progress. The national railway strike was a more serious affair than partial dock strikes. It scarcely interfered with production. It delayed deliveries. It also came as a godsend to manufacturers who needed an excuse to offer their customers for delays caused by the expanded order-books of the current super-boom. No one can separate out the blame properly attributable to the strike. The indices of prosperity for the year are running as high as the government or anyone else dared hope.

The high post-war rate of strikes in the United States and France have not had major consequences for their countries' prosperity. Neither country is so dependent as Britain on foreign trade, but France is very far from self-sufficiency. Amongst her most serious strikes have been a 'generalized strike', and national coal and railway strikes. In the 1948 coal strike over a month's output was lost. There were no stocks and dollars had to be diverted to pay for coal imports. The French economy has, however, continued to progress, and if the rate of progress has not been entirely satisfactory, several reasons in the structure of French business and the behaviour of French business men take precedence over industrial disputes.

Strikes are more serious under full employment, but are they so serious that the loss of 4 million, or even 8 million working days, is to be accounted a national disaster?

A more subtle argument is presented by those who say that it is the *threat* of strikes under full employment which forces wage concessions from employers and thereby causes wage inflation. Inflation is indeed the economic malady of our age, and increases in labour costs beyond the rate of progress in productivity must cause rising prices. It takes two parties, however, to make a collective agreement. It is in the nature of trade unions that they should seek increases. It is not in the nature of employers to grant them. They grant them now because industry is so profitable that they can afford to do so. Public services and less profitable industries follow suit in order to preserve what labour force they have. Not only do employers grant increases in collective bargaining; they also give them away. Everyone can quote instances, without going far afield, of employers paying over the rate in order to attract, or merely to hold labour. Full employment gives rise to wage inflation, but it is at least as sensible to blame the profitability of industry, or the avarice of employers, as the use of threats of strike by trade unions. He who can find a means of maintaining full employment without inflation in a free society will deserve all the praises we can give; but candidates offering strike prohibition are not in the running.

There is still no satisfactory explanation for the alarm of recent months. Sociologists tell us that the industrial dispute is of great symbolic significance. In most ages but our own, in many countries to-day, violence plays a large part in social affairs. In western democracies violence is almost totally suppressed, but the strike is a licensed revolt against society, in which may be expressed all the worker's spiritual grievances against the world, his boss, and his fate, as well as his current demands. The middle classes have no such licence. Men are usually over warm in their moral denunciation of the enjoyment by others of licences they would secretly like to share, if they could. Perhaps the spiritual significance of strikes outweighs their material importance for the critic of strikes, as well as for the striker.

Our theory of personal incomes is not logically consistent. The successful actor or author, the man who cashed in on the synthetic detergent market after the war, are objects of praise, and begrudged nothing of that part of their incomes, or expenses, that the Inland Revenue permits them to retain. The man or woman who seeks to increase his or her income by a wage demand backed by a strike is to be condemned. Does this make sense? Perhaps our condemnation of the striker is all the stronger for our consciousness that our case against him lacks full conviction.

We are all democrats. We venerate political opposition, and sanctify the electoral procedures on which it rests. We also venerate industrial democracy—the voluntary settlement of wages and conditions of employment. This, too, rests on opposition (although currently we are given to stressing the importance of co-operation in industry at the expense of opposition) and is ultimately guaranteed by the freedom to strike or to lock out. The exercise of these rights, however, we condemn. With such muddled political thinking, can anyone wonder that our attitude to strikes is remarkable rather for its vehemence than for its close reasoning?

Each of these explanations may seem improbable and far-fetched, but at least they direct attention to the right place. An individual may justifiably fear the loss of a month's or a year's income; fortunately we have social and private insurance to allay such fears. If he is so obsessed with increasing his income as to fear a day's illness or other causes of marginal variation, we might advise a holiday or a visit to a psychiatrist; we should not sympathise with the fears, nor try to ensure that there was no danger of their realization. The analogy between the fears of such an individual and a nation's anxiety over relatively insignificant strike losses is not perfect. A loss of half of one per cent of the national income may be a loss of 10 per cent in a major industry, which must cause national concern. It is, however, a close enough analogy to allow us to conclude that, although a series of major disputes would be highly unpleasant, and must, if possible, be avoided, the explanation of fright over 4 million working days lost in a year, or a single official national dispute, cannot be provided by the student of strikes, but only by the social psychologist.

NOTES

1 *Industrial Disputes*, 1937–1954, pp. 78–91.
2 A table of averages, based on the International Labour Review figures, is given in 'Strike Trends in Britain and Other Countries', *The Times*, 12th September 1955.
3 For a full demonstration and explanation of this proposition, see K. G. J. C. Knowles, *Strikes*, 1952.
4 Department of Social Science, University of Liverpool, *The Dock Worker*, 1954.
5 Quoted in Mark Perlman, *Judges in Industry*, Melbourne, 1954.
6 See Val. R. Lorwin, *The French Labor Movement*, Harvard, 1954, pp. 244–9.

2

WORK STOPPAGES IN THE UNITED KINGDOM

1965–70: A QUANTITATIVE STUDY

P. Galambos and E. W. Evans

INTRODUCTION

This study brings up to date a previously published survey of the period 1951–64.[1] The continued interest in, and increased incidence of, work stoppages seems to justify the exercise. It remains true that the man-days lost per thousand workers in the economy due to stoppages of work is considerably lower than before the First World War, and that several other nations suffer more severely than the United Kingdom in this respect. More time is also lost through unemployment, absenteeism and short-time working than as a result of disputes. These losses, however, do not affect output, exports and the public's well-being to anything like the same extent as strikes. Perhaps most important of all, they also differ in their effects from strikes in that they do not add impetus to wage-drift and inflationary pressure in the way that work stoppages so often do. Our intention is to provide a factual and quantitative examination of the work stoppages which occurred during the period. Detailed explanation of the data is beyond the scope of this work since it would require an intimate knowledge of the special characteristics of each of the industries studied.

All the data used in this survey are derived from the *Ministry of Labour Gazette* up to May 1968, the *Employment and Productivity Gazette* from June 1968 to December 1970 and the *Department of Employment Gazette* for the subsequent period. The major source has, of course, been the annual survey article 'Stoppages of Work Due to Industrial Disputes', which appears in the May issue of the *Gazette* in each year with the exception of 1966, when it appeared one month later. Use has also been made of the statistics on 'Estimated Numbers of Employees' for June in each year, published in the *Gazette* for March of the following year (except during 1967, when publication occurred in February). The unemployed have been

excluded for the data by reference to the series 'Numbers Unemployed: Industrial Analysis' in June of each year, published in
the July issue of the *Gazette*. Where necessary changes in the
Standard Industrial Classification after 1968 have been taken into
account to maintain comparability.

THE INCIDENCE OF STOPPAGES 1965–70

The available data make it possible to consider the incidence of
work stoppages over time in three ways, namely in terms of the
number of man-days lost, the number of workers involved in
disputes and the actual number of stoppages occurring each year.
It may be doubted, however, whether any one of these measures is
an accurate expression of the impact of work stoppages, even disregarding any limitations imposed by the statistics themselves. The
most often quoted indicator, man-days lost, is virtually meaningless
without reference to the number of employees in employment, and
it should also be remembered that a 'man-day' may not be a standard
unit of measurement if the normal working day varies between
industries. More important, since the impact of a five-day stoppage
by 1,000 men may well differ from that of a twenty-five day strike of
200 men, man-days lost can be misleading. Consideration of the
number of stoppages taking place, and of the number of workers
involved or taking part is obviously desirable in order to qualify
the crude evidence on lost man-days. On the other hand, the number
of stoppages occurring is also imperfect as a measure of the impact
of disputes. Between 1958 and 1959, for example, the number of
stoppages fell some 20 per cent while the total of man-days lost rose
by over 50 per cent. Moreover, the impact of the number of strikes
will clearly vary between industries, depending upon how essential
it is to achieve continuous operation, how costly it may be to stop
and restart processes and the extent to which capital costs are
relatively heavier than labour costs. Finally, it must also be recognised that the number of workers involved in stoppages is also
subject to limitations as an indicator of strike incidence. During
1964–5, for example, the number of workers directly involved in
disputes fell, although the total of man-days lost rose very substantially. In addition, for an economy characterised by interdependence, the overall impact of a stoppage involving a given
number of workers will vary according to the extent to which other
firms are affected. Information on this matter is virtually non-
existent, but it is known that within the motor vehicle industry in
1969 some 860,000 working days were lost through stoppages at
establishments not involved in the dispute, in addition to the
1,636,000 officially recorded.[2]

It seems safe to say that the true economic impact of work stoppages, even in purely monetary terms or in terms of output forfeited, is not measurable. But if any statements are to be made, or conclusions to be drawn, regarding changes in the industrial relations climate over time it is clearly essential that all three measures be utilised and account taken of variations in the size of the labour force. Other possible indicators of course exist, such as the amount of strike pay disbursed by unions or the level of social security benefits paid to strikers' dependants. But, as is true of these examples, data are either not available over time or, if available, not disaggregated on an industry basis. We have therefore confined our index to the three generally accepted elements. The fact that these are qualitatively dissimilar has, of course, no importance for an index which is a pure number.

It has been suggested that the three components should be weighted since their importance will vary according to the structure of the industry in question but, while recognising the difficulties involved,[3] we have constructed an index using the unweighted arithmetic mean, as is explained below. On *a priori* grounds it is likely, for example, that where shut-down and start-up costs are high the number of strikes may be more significant to management than the man-days lost. But even if some way existed of devising weights to reflect these differences (which does not appear to be the case), the exercise would be pointless unless 'importance' or 'significance' were defined. The importance or significance of stoppages may be thought of as loss of profits, loss of wages, loss of output, loss of exports or even hardship to the community. No doubt the three elements, when studied in terms of any or all of these measures of importance may vary in their impact between firms or industries contemporaneously or over time. But no weighting system would be logical unless related to a specific effect (e.g. on profits) which the index was meant to reflect. Our index is not intended to measure hardship, loss of output, damage to the economy or any other of the possible consequences of stoppages. It is only meant to show changes in the level of strike activity, defined as the arithmetic mean of the three elements selected. Since no implications are drawn as to the results of such variations no weighting system is required in logical terms. This is perhaps fortunate since it has not proved possible to deduce from theory general criteria by which a given mathematical construction could be justified. Moreover, any system of weights derived on an empirical basis, even if this were feasible, would inevitably be subject to variation over time due to technological change as well as between industries.

THE COMPARATIVE INCIDENCE OF STOPPAGES BETWEEN INDUSTRIES

The purpose of the index is to provide a comprehensive numerical expression of the incidence of stoppages in sixteen industrial groups within each year from 1965 to 1970 on a basis that permits comparisons to be made. It must be emphasised that the indexes presented are only comparable between groups within the same year, and not over time. If, for example, the index for a particular industry group is greater in one year than in another it does not necessarily follow that the incidence of stoppages was greater in the former than in the latter. This will be clearly seen when the construction of the indexes is explained in the following paragraph. The comparison of the incidence of stoppages in the several groups over time will be considered in the following section.

In any particular year, t, let S_{it} stand for the numbers of strikes, W_{it} for the number of working days lost and Y_{it} for the number of workers involved in stoppages within group i ($i = 1, \ldots, 16$), and let S_{Tt}, W_{Tt}, Y_{Tt} be the corresponding totals for all groups in that year. Let X_{it}, X_{Tt} denote the average employment in group i and in all groups respectively in that year. The index is constructed from the following three components:

(1) The relative strike frequency $s_{it} = \dfrac{S_{it}}{S_{Tt}}$; that is, the ratio of strikes occurring in group i to strikes in all groups.

(2) The ratio of the 'worker-days' lost in an industry to the total 'worker-days' lost relative to the possible maximum number of working days available in a given year, this being taken as broadly proportional to employment. Thus, with the notation defined above, this component of the index is

$$w_{it} = \frac{W_{it}/W_{Tt}}{X_{it}/X_{Tt}}$$

(3) The effect of numbers of workers involved upon the strike index, which is obtained analogously to w_{it} and is given by

$$y_{it} = \frac{Y_{it}/Y_{Tt}}{X_{it}/X_{Tt}}$$

Indexes have not been calculated for Agriculture, Forestry and Fishing; Insurance, Banking and Finance; Professional and Scientific Services; Miscellaneous Services; Public Administration and Defence; Bricks, Pottery, Glass and Cement; and Paper, Printing and Publishing.

The main reason for these exclusions is a desire to maintain comparability with our previous study. The sectors excluded are in general those in which stoppages have been few or non-existent for most years since 1951, such as agriculture and the services; or where total employment is very small, such as Bricks, etc.; or those for which disaggregated statistics for other matters, notably the causes of stoppages, are not available, such as Paper and Printing. It will be noted that Mining has also been excluded in the first instance, although the data have been analysed in a separate table. This somewhat ambivalent treatment simply reflects the peculiar nature and characteristics of coal-mining which, as H. A. Turner has shown, is clearly a special case.[4]

Table 1 shows the magnitude of the indexes for the remaining sixteen groups from 1965 to 1970, the index for group i in year t being denoted by I_{it}.

TABLE 1

The Index I_{it} of the Comparative Incidence of Stoppages Between 16 Groups

	$t =$	1965	1966	1967	1968	1969	1970
1.	Food, drink and tobacco	0·340	0·069	0·275	0·127	0·295	0·512
2.	Chemicals and allied industries	0·142	0·165	0·331	0·147	0·203	0·434
3.	Metal manufacture	1·097	0·799	1·163	1·469	1·408	1·125
4.	Engineering and electrical goods	0·825	0·802	0·835	1·538	0·880	0·934
5.	Shipbuilding and marine engineering	2·429	0·733	2·109	2·522	1·773	1·879
6.	Motor vehicles, cycles	6·204	4·136	4·703	3·631	4·728	2·939
7.	Aircraft	1·379	1·307	0·897	2·141	1·400	1·497
8.	Locomotives, carriages	0·282	0·167	0·335	0·670	0·535	2·271
9.	Metal goods, n.e.s.	0·474	0·282	0·371	0·830	0·268	0·478
10.	Textiles	0·164	0·071	0·141	0·091	0·297	0·317
11.	Clothing and footwear	0·063	0·011	0·069	0·038	0·108	0·426
12.	Other manufacturing industries	0·676	0·501	0·621	0·485	0·511	1·009
13.	Construction	0·309	0·447	0·436	0·266	0·301	0·257
14.	Transport and communications	0·941	2·201	1·422	0·614	1·386	1·260
15.	Distributive trades	0·044	0·017	0·014	0·012	0·015	0·028
16.	Public utilities (gas, electricity, water)	0·130	0·071	0·080	0·036	0·130	0·059

Strike incidence, as measured by the index, has been very high in Motor Vehicles and in Shipbuilding as compared with other groups. These two industries almost invariably hold first and second place respectively in the rank ordering, the exceptions being that Shipbuilding was relatively trouble free in 1966 and took third place in 1970. At the other extreme, Distribution, Clothing and Public

Utilities consistently show very low index values. Chemicals, Textiles and Food, Drink and Tobacco also show moderately low values. Metal manufacture, Engineering, Aircraft and Transport, on the other hand, yield index values clustered towards the upper end of the range.

These facts emerge more clearly from Table 2, which summarises the data in simpler form. Ranks ranging from 1 to 16 were assigned to the I_{it} in descending order of magnitude within each year; the table shows how often, if at all, a particular rank was attained by the index for any of the 16 groups during the years from 1965 to 1970.

It will be observed that the ranks assigned to the index for Motor Vehicles, Shipbuilding, Aircraft, Metal Manufacture, Engineering and Transport are invariably low. Conversely, those assigned to Distributive Trades, Public Utilities, Clothing, Textiles, Chemicals and Food, Drink and Tobacco are consistently high. The remaining groups do not lend themselves so easily to generalisation, but it is arguable that Other Manufacturing should be included with the 'strike prone' sectors.

It is interesting to compare these results with those obtained for the period 1951 to 1964. That Motor Vehicles has displaced Ship-building as the most 'strike prone' industry may be due to the dis-aggregation of Aircraft from the former group. With this change in mind, however, the broad division of industries in terms of their vulnerability to stoppages discovered in the previous study holds. Not only are some groups of industries more subject to stoppages than others, but there seems to be little tendency for the composition of this group to change. Mining, however, is apparently an exception to this generalisation.

THE COMPARATIVE INCIDENCE OF STOPPAGES OVER TIME

The I_{it} index only provides a basis for comparison between the sixteen groups within a given year. Even when the index for group i in year t is greater than in year t_1 it does not necessarily mean that the absolute incidence of stoppages in the group was greater in year t than in year t_1. The comparison of strike incidence in each group, and in all groups combined, over time is clearly of interest, and for this purpose a temporal index, denoted by J_{it}, for group i in year t has been constructed. The first year of the period under consideration, namely 1965, has been adopted as the base year.

The construction of the J_{it} index is analogous to that of I_{it} and requires little explanation. As before, let S_{it}, W_{it}, Y_{it}, X_{it} stand for the number of strikes, working days lost, workers involved and average employment respectively in group i and year t. The index is

TABLE 2

Distribution of Ranks Assigned to the Index I_{it} over the Six Years 1965–70

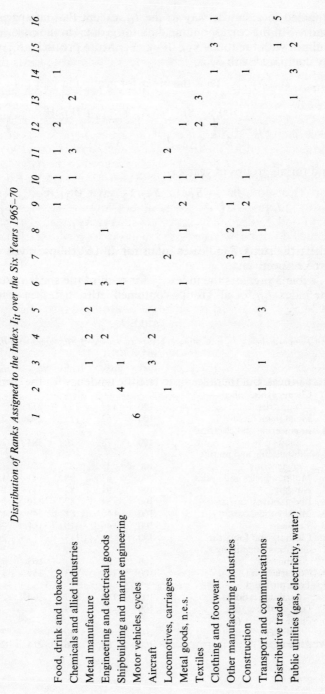

	1	2	3	4	5	6	7	8	9	10	11	12	13	14	15	16
Food, drink and tobacco									1	1	1	2	1			
Chemicals and allied industries										1	3		2			
Metal manufacture			1	2	2	1										
Engineering and electrical goods			1	2		3										
Shipbuilding and marine engineering		4				1		1								
Motor vehicles, cycles	6															
Aircraft			3	2	1											
Locomotives, carriages						1	2				2	1				
Metal goods, n.e.s.		1						1	2			2				
Textiles												1	3	2		
Clothing and footwear														1	3	2
Other manufacturing industries							3	2	1							
Construction							1	1	2	1				1		
Transport and communications			1		3			1		1						
Distributive trades															1	5
Public utilities (gas, electricity, water)													1	3	2	

obtained in a similar way to the I_{it}, except that comparisons are made with the corresponding data for group i in the base year 1965 and not with the totals S_{Tt}, W_{Tt}, X_{Tt} More precisely, S_{it}, W_{it}, X_{it} are compared with S_{i1965},

Y_{i1965}, and X_{i1965}. Thus the index for group i in year t is

$$J_{it} = \frac{100}{3}\left(\frac{S_{it}}{S_{i1965}} + \frac{Y_{it}/Y_{i1965} + W_{it}/W_{i1965}}{X_{it}/X_{i1965}}\right)$$

and for all groups in year t is

$$J_{ot} = \frac{100}{3}\left(\frac{S_{Tt}}{S_{T1965}} + \frac{Y_{Tt}/Y_{T1965} + W_{Tt}/W_{T1965}}{X_{Tt}/X_{T1965}}\right)$$

where the suffix T indicates totals for all 16 groups in year t and in 1965 respectively.

Table 3 presents the index J_{it} for each of the sixteen groups and the index J_{ot} for all groups combined. Although firm conclusions

TABLE 3

The Temporal Index J_{it} to Compare Yearly Incidence of Stoppages with that in 1965
(J_i 1965 = 100)

	$t =$	1965	1966	1967	1968	1969	1970
1.	Food, drink and tobacco	100	35	126	128	253	504
2.	Chemical and allied industries	100	125	259	277	332	858
3.	Metal manufacture	100	62	113	290	235	265
4.	Engineering and electrical goods	100	78	110	383	220	301
5.	Shipbuilding and marine engineering	100	38	87	179	129	172
6.	Motor vehicles and cycles	100	67	98	147	163	150
7.	Aircraft	100	91	82	341	271	368
8.	Locomotives, carriages	100	34	82	420	276	1379
9.	Metal goods, n.e.s.	100	50	81	340	123	265
10.	Textiles	100	46	110	161	284	478
11.	Clothing and footwear	100	34	113	113	266	1561
12.	Other manufacturing industries	100	62	101	165	175	350
13.	Construction	100	111	133	159	175	193
14.	Transport and communications	100	182	159	164	296	349
15.	Distributive trades	100	37	39	56	81	180
16.	Public Utilities (gas, electricity, water)	100	41	80	73	210	124
17.	All groups	100	80	106	214	200	255

cannot be drawn from a series of only six observations, the variation of the index J_{ot} may give some indication of the presence of some systematic movement in the incidence of stoppages and of an improvement or deterioration in the industrial climate. Although in 1966 its value falls below 100, in the four subsequent years the index exceeds 100 and reaches very high values in 1968, 1969, and 1970. It can therefore be said that, with the exception of 1966, the incidence of stoppages has become more severe during the period under consideration, for the total of industries being studied.

It should be remembered, of course, that these are not the total of all industries in the economy, and that comparison of the index with the statistics published in the *Gazette* is consequently not legitimate. These statistics show that from 1965 to 1966 the number of stoppages, man-days lost and workers involved in disputes all declined, which confirms the result indicated by the index. Similarly, a comparison of all three measures for 1966–7 shows a deterioration, which is also consistent with the index. More significantly, however, the official data for 1965 and 1967 reveal that the totals for all three measures of stoppages were lower in the latter than in the former year, whereas the index stands six points higher. The answers to this apparent inconsistency are threefold. Firstly, although for the total of all industries the number of stoppages fell by some 10 per cent, the number of workers involved by about 18 per cent and the number of lost man-days by 5 per cent, this apparent improvement ignores the fact that total employees in employment also fell by some 318,000. Secondly, for the industries covered by the index, the reduction in employment was 460,000 while the number of stoppages and man-days lost (though not of workers involved) actually increased. Thirdly, Coal Mining, which is not included in the index, was much more trouble-free in 1967 than in 1965, the fall in its total of stoppages and days lost being greater than that recorded for all industries in aggregate. Unfortunately, this cross-check on the effectiveness of the index cannot be repeated in subsequent years because, although the total of stoppages and days lost for all industries rose consistently, the number of workers involved actually declined over 1968–9. It may nevertheless be argued that the index not only takes into account all three measures of industrial action but also reflects a factor not incorporated in the official figures, namely the size of the employed work-force, and, by excluding Coal Mining, avoids its distorting effect upon these figures.

Turning next to the industry indexes, it will be seen that for all groups except Chemicals, Construction and Transport the index for 1966 was below that of the base year. It is perhaps worth noting that for these three exceptions a steady deterioration is observable for the whole period, reaching the peak level in 1970, although in 1966 the index for Transport was above the levels of 1967 and 1968. The remaining industries can be classified under four headings. Firstly, after an initial improvement from 1965 to 1966 a steady deterioration occurred in Food, Drink and Tobacco; Textiles; Clothing and Other Manufacturing, to reach a peak in 1970. The Distributive Trades should perhaps also be included with this group since the same general pattern emerges although only in 1970 did the index rise above the base year level. Secondly, a group of industries can be identified for which the index falls below the base year in 1966, rises above it in 1967 and reaches a peak in 1968 with some evidence of an improvement in the industrial climate during 1969–70. This group includes Metal Manufacture and Engineering. Thirdly, for some industries both 1966 and 1967 yielded index values below that of 1965, but were followed by high values in 1968 which were not surpassed in the remaining two years, namely, Shipbuilding and Metal Goods. Finally, there are three industries for which the 1966 and 1967 indexes are below those for 1965 but for which the peak values are recorded either in 1969 (Vehicles) or 1970 (Aircraft and Locomotives). Public Utilities also follow this pattern, although the index values only exceed the base values in 1969 and 1970, the former being the peak year.

In our previous study rank inversion counts were used to determine whether or not an observable trend existed for the period 1951–64. This method does not appear to be appropriate for the small set of observations involved in the study of 1965–70. On the other hand, the data seem to indicate a general deterioration in the industrial climate over the six years even on the basis of simple inspection. For the sixteen groups over the period 1966–70 eighty index values are presented in Table 3, and of these fifty-seven exceed the base year level. Put in other terms, for 1966 only three of the groups have an index value higher than that for 1965; for 1967 the number rises to nine; for 1968 to 14; for 1969 to 15; and for 1970 to 16.

It is not possible to link the data set out in Table 3 to our series for 1951–64. Apart from the effects of excluding Mining and Quarrying from the later study, problems of reclassification under the S.I.C. also arise. The most serious is that relating to the Vehicles, Aircraft and Cycles sector which was not disaggregated in the earlier period. To permit some longer term comparisons, however, the data for 1964 to 1970 inclusive have been recalculated, with Vehicles, Aircraft and Cycles aggregated, and related to 1954 = 100. Mining and Quarrying has, of course, been excluded. The results, set out in Table 3 (A), broadly confirm those obtained when the period 1965–70 was considered in isolation.

TABLE 3(A)

The Temporal Index J_{it} to Compare Yearly Incidence of Stoppages with that in 1954
$(J_{it_{1954}} = 100)$

	1954	1964	1965	1966	1967	1968	1969	1970
Food, drink and tobacco	100	908	3077	1077	3877	3939	7785	9999
Chemicals and allied industries	100	141	234	293	606	648	777	1862
Metal manufacture	100	455	374	232	423	1085	879	998
Engineering and electrical goods	100	638	685	534	753	2624	1507	2020
Shipbuilding and marine engineering	100	133	169	64	147	303	218	235
Motor vehicles, cycles and aircraft	100	567	890	614	837	1513	1531	1367
Locomotives, carriages	100	1115	856	291	702	3595	23631	4654
Metal goods, n.e.s.	100	478	711	356	576	3417	875	1503
Textiles	100	663	942	433	1036	1517	2675	4661
Clothing and footwear	100	147	103	35	116	116	274	1453
Other manufacturing industries	100	237	259	161	262	427	453	777
Construction	100	132	151	168	201	240	264	229
Transport and communications	100	134	99	180	157	162	293	317
Distributive trades	100	337	324	120	126	181	262	609
Public utilities (gas, electricity, water)	100	416	472	194	378	345	991	554
Total	100	214	236	189	250	505	472	556

It will be noted that the temporal indexes for three groups, namely, Shipbuilding, Construction, and Transport, are lower than those for the aggregate of all industries in every year. Conversely, indexes higher than those for the aggregate of all groups occur in every year for seven sectors, namely, Food, Drink and Tobacco; Metal Manufacture; Engineering; Vehicles and Aircraft; Locomotives; Metal Goods; and Textiles. For the remaining groups this criterion yields doubtful results, and indeed gives no result for Other Manufacturing. It is clear, however, that the indexes for Chemicals and Public Utilities are above those for the aggregate in all but two years. For Clothing, on the other hand, they lie below the aggregate values in all years with one exception.

It is interesting to compare these results with those obtained from the I_{it} index, in order to see how far 'strike prone' industries were also those whose performance as measured by J_{it} deteriorated over 1965–70. There are, as has been mentioned, a number of groups whose relative position, in terms of either or both indexes, is ambiguous. But it is obvious that the Vehicles, Aircraft, Metal Manufacture and Engineering groups, already isolated as 'strike prone', continue to deteriorate during this period. The Clothing sector, on the other hand, was not 'strike prone' nor did its good record in this respect worsen except in 1970, and the same is broadly true of

Distribution, Shipbuilding and Transport, although associated with high values of I_{it}, did not show a marked worsening. It is, however, noticeable that two industries not classed as 'strike prone' did in fact, experience a rapid rise in their J_{it} index values relative to the aggregate of all sectors, namely, Food, Drink and Tobacco; and Textiles. Although it should be some time before the ranking of strike prone industries changes, the evidence suggests that such a change may eventually occur as traditionally strike-free industries become affected by unrest.

Two final observations must be made regarding Table 3 (A). Firstly, it is noteworthy that, with the exception of Construction and Public Utilities, the highest index values for the seven years 1964–70 invariably occur in 1968 or 1970. The coincidence of the peaks for so many industries strongly suggests a generalised outburst of discontent. Secondly, it will be noticed that those industries for which index values reached a maximum in 1968 were all within, and only within, Metals and Engineering in a broad sense. The one day engineering stoppage of 15 May 1968, involving 1,500,000 workers, is probably the common factor which explains this phenomenon.

THE DISTRIBUTION OF STOPPAGES BETWEEN INDUSTRIES

Table 4 sets out the proportion of stoppages occurring in each of seventeen groups, Mining and Quarrying being included. The most striking fact that emerges from Table 4 is the sharp decline in the share of Mining in the total of strikes. In the period 1951–64 this industry accounted for 78·4 per cent of all strikes at a maximum and 42·6 per cent at a minimum, when no other single industry ever contributed more than 11·3 per cent. The pre-eminence of Mining as a 'strike maker' was clearly being challenged in the early sixties. But the phenomenal decline shown in Table 4 could hardly have been expected. It should be mentioned that in each year during 1965–70 the proportionate share in total stoppages is in fact higher than in any year between 1951 and 1964 for Food, Drink and Tobacco; Engineering; Metal Manufacture; Metal Goods and Transport. Similarly, the shares over 1966–70 (though not in 1965) are all higher than any of those achieved in 1951–64 for Chemicals and Vehicles, while the same is true of the 1967–70 proportions in Textiles. No obvious deterioration is revealed by such comparisons for Shipbuilding, Construction, Locomotives, Clothing, Distributive Trades, Other Manufacturing, or Public Utilities. No comparison has been made for Aircraft since this group was amalgamated with Vehicles in the 1951–64 series, a point which must also be borne in mind when comparing the results for Vehicles in the two periods.

TABLE 4

Proportional Shares of the 17 Groups in the Total Number of Stoppages (Per Cent)

	1965	1966	1967	1968	1969	1970
Mining and quarrying	33·4	30·1	19·8	10·2	6·7	4·6
Food, drink and tobacco	1·3	1·3	3·1	2·8	4·0	4·1
Chemicals and allied industries	0·7	1·6	1·7	2·1	1·8	2·7
Metal manufacture	5·7	4·9	6·8	6·5	7·7	9·1
Engineering and electrical goods	13·3	14·2	16·8	18·1	22·1	23·7
Shipbuilding and marine engineering	5·8	4·5	4·8	6·0	3·1	3·4
Motor vehicles, cycles	7·4	9·2	11·1	10·4	9·6	9·4
Aircraft	1·7	2·2	2·0	3·0	3·1	2·0
Locomotives, carriages	0·9	0·2	0·4	0·8	0·3	1·1
Metal goods, n.e.s.	3·8	2·8	3·3	4·5	4·0	5·0
Textiles	1·3	1·1	2·0	2·4	2·5	2·7
Clothing and footwear	0·6	0·5	0·9	0·7	0·8	0·8
Other manufacturing industries	1·9	1·8	2·4	2·8	3·0	2·5
Construction	11·7	14·3	12·7	12·4	9·9	9·4
Transport and communications	8·0	9·6	10·3	15·3	18·8	16·6
Distributive trades	1·8	1·3	1·3	1·4	1·5	2·3
Public utilities (gas, electricity, water)	0·7	0·4	0·6	0·6	1·1	0·6

Table 4 (A) sets out the same data, but with Mining excluded. It seems clear that the proportion of total stoppages occurring in Transport, Engineering and Food, Drink and Tobacco increased, and the same is probably true of Textiles. Finally, it is interesting to note that Engineering, Vehicles and Construction alone accounted for between 45 and 54 per cent of all stoppages in the period and, with the inclusion of Transport, for between 61 and 68 per cent.

TABLE 4(A)

Proportional Shares of the 16 Groups in the Total Number of Stoppages (Per Cent)

	1965	1966	1967	1968	1969	1970
Food, drink and tobacco	2·0	1·8	3·9	3·1	4·3	4·3
Chemicals and allied industries	1·0	2·3	2·1	2·3	1·9	2·8
Metal manufacture	8·6	7·0	8·5	7·3	8·2	9·6
Engineering and electrical goods	19·9	20·3	20·9	20·1	23·7	24·9
Shipbuilding and marine engineering	8·7	6·5	5·9	6·7	3·3	3·6
Motor vehicles, cycles	11·1	13·1	13·8	11·6	10·3	9·9
Aircraft	2·5	3·2	2·5	3·3	3·3	2·1
Locomotive, carriages, etc.	1·3	0·2	0·6	0·9	0·4	1·2
Metal goods n.e.s.	5·7	4·0	4·1	5·0	4·3	5·2
Textiles	2·0	1·6	2·5	2·7	2·7	2·8
Clothing and footwear	1·0	0·7	1·2	0·8	0·9	0·8
Other manufacturing industries	2·8	2·6	3·0	3·1	3·2	2·7
Construction	17·6	20·5	15·8	13·8	10·6	9·9
Transport and communication	12·1	13·8	12·8	17·0	20·1	17·2
Distributive trades	2·6	1·8	1·6	1·6	1·6	2·4
Public utilities (gas, electricity and water)	1·1	0·6	0·8	0·7	1·2	0·6

INDIRECT INVOLVEMENT

Although not immediately concerned in the matter at issue, considerable numbers of workers in fact become idle as a result of stoppages. It should be emphasised that the data available only relate to workers indirectly involved at the establishment where the dispute occurred, and do not take account of men who cease work elsewhere in the economy as a result of the stoppage. The proportion of indirectly to directly involved workers in stoppages between 1965 and 1970 is given in Table 5. The percentage for 1967 is, in fact, the second highest recorded for the whole period 1951–70, the highest (27·0 per cent) having occurred in 1952. Those for 1965 and 1966 were only exceeded on two occasions in the period, namely, 1952 and 1963. On the other hand, in only three years years between 1951 and 1964 was the proportion of indirectly involved workers lower than that for 1968. There seems to be no clear conclusion to be drawn from the figures.

Statistics of indirect involvement by industrial groups are only

TABLE 5

Indirect Involvement in Stoppages
Number of Workers Involved

	Total (thousands)	Indirectly involved (thousands)	Proportion of indirectly involved in total involved (per cent)
1965	868	195	22·5
1966	530	116	21·9
1967	732	180	24·6
1968	2256	182	8·1
1969	1656	230	13·9
1970	1793	333	18·6

available for the period after 1959. There have been summarised for the years 1965–70 and the results appear in Table 6. It will be noted that indirect involvement is consistently high in Vehicles and low in Transport and, especially, Construction.

TABLE 6

Percentage Share of the Number Indirectly Involved in the Total Number of Workers Involved in Stoppages

	Mining and Quarrying	Metal and Engineering	Shipbuilding and Marine Engineering	Vehicles	Textiles and Clothing	Construction	Transport and Communication	All Other Industries
1965	35·8	18·6	19·8	40·5	4·1	0·1	0·1	9·1
1966	10·9	14·2	20·2	52·9	19·4	2·2	9·1	16·5
1967	20·2	20·4	5·7	48·1	14·0	1·9	7·7	13·7
1968	32·0	2·1	7·9	28·9	15·6	1·9	15·1	8·1
1969	4·0	20·0	18·7	31·3	3·9	1·6	5·6	7·1
1970	0·7	24·4	21·6	39·8	28·1	2·8	6·6	12·3

DURATION OF STOPPAGES

Table 7 summarises the data concerning the duration of stoppages, in terms of working days, for the period 1965 to 1970. It is clear that stoppages lasting not more than one day constitute decreasing proportions of the total, as was also observed in the years 1951–64. Their proportionate share for each year from 1965 to 1970 was lower than for any years between 1951 and 1964. This may be due to the declining number of stoppages in Mining, since many stoppages in this industry are of very brief duration. It was also noticed in the survey of 1951–64 that stoppages lasting three days or less accounted for 73 per cent of the total at a minimum (in 1961) and 83 per cent at a maximum (in 1958); moreover, such stoppages contributed 75 per cent or more to the total in all but two of the

TABLE 7

Proportion of Stoppages by Duration in Working Days of the Total Number of Stoppages (Per Cent)

Duration in working days	1965	1966	1967	1968	1969	1970
—1	34·3	33·3	29·1	28·6	29·9	24·6
1·1—2	21·6	21·9	23·7	20·5	19·7	16·9
2·1—3	12·9	12·8	12·8	11·9	12·7	13·4
3·1—4	7·7	8·3	7·8	8·0	7·7	7·8
4·1—5	5·6	6·2	6·2	6·0	6·3	7·3
5·1—6	3·0	3·4	3·1	4·3	3·4	4·8
6·1—12	7·6	8·1	9·2	11·1	11·1	12·2
12·1—18	2·8	2·6	2·9	4·0	2·4	5·4
18·1—24	1·2	1·0	1·8	2·0	1·9	2·3
24·1—36	1·7	0·8	1·8	1·7	1·8	3·1
36·1—60	1·2	1·0	1·0	1·1	1·2	1·5
60·1—	0·4	0·6	0·6	0·8	0·9	0·7

fourteen years. During 1965–70, however, stoppages of less than three days never exceeded 69 per cent of the total despite the one day engineering strike. It seems, therefore, that the length of stoppages, on average, is increasing. This effect is noticeable in each of the duration ranges above that for 3·1–4 days, and especially in the 6·1–12 days range, which remains the most important of all the three to sixty days ranges. If the 6·1–12 days range is excluded, it nevertheless remains true that each successively greater duration range accounts for a decreasing proportion of the total of stoppages.

As an alternative it is also possible to analyse the duration of stoppages in terms of the number of working days lost per worker involved. This has been done in Table 8. It should perhaps be mentioned that the number of working days lost per worker involved does not represent the average duration of stoppages for a given group in a particular year. In many cases numbers of workers only become involved in the dispute some time after it has begun. This means, of course, that the number of working days lost per worker involved tends to be smaller than the average duration of the stoppage. It was noticed in our study of the 1951–64 data that, with one exception, Shipbuilding, the number of days lost per worker involved was smaller in the groups where relative incidence of stoppage, as measured by the I_{it} index, was larger. This no longer seems to hold true for the years 1965–70. No firm conclusion can be based on so short a period, but it seems likely that stoppages are becoming longer even in the traditionally 'strike prone' industries.

TABLE 8

Number of Working Days Lost Per Worker Involved

	1965	1966	1967	1968	1969	1970
Mining and quarrying	3·5	2·4	2·6	1·9	7·1	9·3
Food, drink and tobacco	1·9	2·4	2·6	2·8	4·1	8·5
Chemicals and allied industries	1·6	2·5	3·5	3·7	3·2	5·1
Metal manufacture	5·5	4·7	4·1	2·2	6·6	7·6
Engineering and electrical goods	3·0	3·1	3·2	1·3	4·0	5·8
Shipbuilding and marine engineering	5·6	3·7	6·2	6·9	3·8	10·2
Motor vehicles, cycles	3·8	2·6	3·3	2·2	5·9	4·1
Aircraft	1·1	1·9	1·4	1·1	3·4	6·2
Locomotives, carriages, etc.	2·5	1·8	2·5	1·3	6·0	6·2
Metal goods n.e.s.	2·9	3·1	4·7	1·5	4·3	8·1
Textiles	7·7	3·6	3·5	2·7	6·6	5·5
Clothing and footwear	1·7	1·4	1·9	2·0	1·9	6·4
Other manufacturing industries	3·4	2·8	2·2	3·4	3·1	6·5
Construction	4·9	4·1	5·4	5·0	6·3	4·8
Transport and communication	2·3	9·3	7·3	3·8	2·0	3·8
Distributive trades	2·3	5·0	5·0	2·4	4·6	3·8
Public utilities (gas, electricity, and water)	3·8	0·9	2·4	2·3	1·7	7·0

BEGINNING AND ENDING OF STOPPAGES

From data relating to principal stoppages, that is, those which cause the loss of 5,000 or more working days, published in the *Gazette*, it is possible to discover whether stoppages are more, or less, likely to begin or end on certain days of the week rather than on others. The data have been analysed from 1965 to 1970 and the proportions, by the days of the week, are shown in Table 9. Monday remains the most usual day for the commencement of stoppages, as was noted in the period 1960–4, with Tuesday and Wednesday occupying the next ranks. It seems that Thursday and Friday have

TABLE 9

Percentage Share by Days of the Week of the Number of Principal Stoppages Beginning and Ending 1965–9

	Stoppages beginning						Stoppages ending					
	1965	1966	1967	1968	1969	1970	1965	1966	1967	1968	1969	1970
Mon.	30·4	36·5	27·2	28·4	29·8	26·6	9·0	13·4	13·0	18·1	17·6	16·5
Tues.	19·1	17·3	18·5	12·9	19·3	18·7	9·0	7·7	15·2	11·2	10·5	10·1
Wed.	11·2	19·2	19·5	17·2	19·3	18·7	15·7	19·2	15·2	14·7	14·0	14·6
Thurs.	15·7	13·5	16·3	21·6	15·8	18·0	10·1	11·6	9·8	5·1	8·8	8·6
Fri.	18·0	11·6	15·2	13·8	14·0	14·2	48·3	40·4	35·9	42·3	42·1	46·8
Sat.	5·6	—	1·1	3·5	1·2	3·0	4·5	7·7	9·8	5·1	4·7	2·3
Sun.	—	1·9	2·2	2·6	0·6	0·8	3·4	—	1·1	3·5	2·3	1·1

increased their share in the total since the previous period, however, while Saturday has become less popular. One obvious change when the two periods are compared is the sudden increase in the proportion of stoppages commencing on Sunday. In general, the very marked 'day effect' noted for the years up to 1964 seems to have diminished, with the commencement of stoppages being more evenly spread over the week. Friday, on the other hand, remains the most usual day for the termination of stoppages, with Sunday and Saturday the least usual.

SEASONAL VARIATION IN THE OCCURRENCE OF STOPPAGES

Table 10 shows the number of stoppages beginning in each month from January 1965 to December 1970, and the average number in each of the twelve calendar months over the six years. The overall average of stoppages beginning per month equals 211·6 and the estimated standard deviation of the average number of strikes beginning in each calendar month is about 34. When the deviations

TABLE 10

Number of strikes beginning in:

	Jan	Feb	Mar	Apr	May	June	July	Aug	Sept	Oct	Nov	Dec
1965	197	242	263	206	265	187	137	163	201	183	197	113
1966	207	186	266	172	206	153	99	138	104	178	155	73
1967	174	200	156	179	187	181	142	178	278	130	205	106
1968	167	167	183	191	238	175	214	193	230	240	263	117
1969	205	231	271	240	274	233	240	256	264	377	314	211
1970	279	341	371	382	298	317	195	245	326	256	203	110
Average number of strikes beginning in month	205	228	252	228	245	208	171	196	234	227	223	122

of the twelve monthly averages over the six years are compared with the standard deviation, then monthly averages of not less than $211·6 + 2 \times 34 = 279·6$ may be regarded as significantly high, and averages not exceeding $211·6 - 2 \times 34 = 143·6$ as significantly low. On this basis no clearly defined peak emerges, although the March average represents the nearest approach. A clear trough emerges for December, and, much less clearly, for July. These results are interesting when compared with those for the period 1951–64. In the earlier period, a very marked peak occurred in October and the May average very nearly approached the significantly high level. The figures for December and July were clearly abnormally low and constituted obvious troughs. It seems certain that in the later period (1965–70) the December seasonal trough continued, although July ceased to yield the unusually low average noted in the past. No unequivocal seasonal peak emerged for these years but the nearest approximation was the March average, with May replacing October in second place. This pattern suggests that workers are still reluctant to lose income through stoppages immediately prior to Christmas, and, to a lesser extent, before the summer holiday. The peak has clearly remained in March, which might yield advantages to strikers in terms of tax rebate.

THE FREQUENCY OF STOPPAGES

Table 11 shows the frequency of stoppages in various industries in each year from 1966 to 1970, expressed as a percentage of the frequency in 1965. In our previous study an inversion test was applied to isolate any consistent trend in the frequency of stoppages. This procedure is not appropriate for the period 1965–70 in view of the small number of observations, but some general comments can be made.

TABLE 11

Number of Strikes Beginning in Year as a Per Cent of the Corresponding Number in 1965 (to the Nearest Per Cent)

	1965	1966	1967	1968	1969	1970
Mining and quarrying	100	75	54	31	26	22
Food, drink and tobacco	100	77	210	210	380	493
Chemicals and allied industries	100	200	227	307	340	647
Metal manufacture	100	71	108	114	172	255
Engineering and electrical goods	100	89	114	137	215	286
Shipbuilding and marine engineering	100	65	74	104	69	94
Motor vehicles, cycles	100	103	135	141	167	205
Aircraft	100	111	108	181	238	197
Locomotives and carriages	100	16	47	95	53	221
Metal goods n.e.s.	100	61	78	118	136	208
Textiles	100	70	137	180	240	320
Clothing and footwear	100	64	136	107	171	193
Other manufacturing industries	100	81	114	148	205	217
Construction	100	102	98	106	109	129
Transport and communications	100	99	116	191	302	326
Distributive trades	100	59	67	82	107	213
Public utilities	100	50	81	88	194	125

The frequency of stoppages clearly diminished in Mining, and equally obviously increased in Chemicals and Motor Vehicles. An upward trend is also discernible for Metal Manufacture, Engineering, Aircraft, Construction and Transport. The same is true, with less certainty, of Food, Drink and Tobacco, Textiles, Other Manufacturing and Clothing despite a temporary improvement during 1966. It can be argued that no obvious upward trend emerges in the Shipbuilding, Distributive Trades, or Public Utilities groups, and the existence of such a trend in the Metal Goods and Locomotives sectors is also doubtful.

The analysis of the causes of disputes is difficult for a number of reasons. The published statistics ignore stoppages involving fewer than ten workers or lasting for less than one day unless the aggregate loss of working days exceeds one hundred. Nor do they cover any loss of time caused by lack of materials or similar reasons at establishments indirectly affected. Moreover, the published data deal only with the principal causes of industrial disputes. This means that where several distinct issues are involved, as often happens, the published data may be misleading. This is especially likely since the choice of principal cause is, in many instances, a subjective matter.

Analyses by cause of the number of strikes beginning in each year and of the workers directly involved are available for the aggregate of all industries and services for the whole period under consideration. Statistics concerning the causes of stoppages in terms of the number of working days lost have also been published since 1957. The incidence of stoppages arising from the several causes varies considerably between the industrial groups, so that the aggregated data conceal important differences. Ideally, therefore, the causes of stoppages should be studies for each industry individually. In this section of the study the statistics relating to principal causes of stoppages in eight major industrial groupings, and in all industries and services, are analysed.

The index of the relative incidence of stoppages by cause within each of the eight groups and for each year from 1965 to 1970 has been constructed in the following way: for group i ($i = 1, 1, \ldots, 8$), let S_{ijt}, Y_{ijt} and W_{ijt} be the percentage shares in the number of stoppages beginning, the number of workers directly involved and the number of working days lost respectively, arising from cause j ($j = 1, 2, \ldots, 9$) in year t; the index of relative incidence for group i, due to cause j in year t is

$$C_{ijt} = \tfrac{1}{3} (S_{ijt} + Y_{ijt} + W_{ijt})$$

The index makes it possible to rank the incidence of stoppages by cause for each group and each year by means of a single quantity. The magnitude of C_{ijt} for each group, and also for the total of all industries and services is presented in Table 12 for each year from 1965 to 1970.

It will be noted that the index C_{ijt} is similar to the Index I_{it}, used above. In this instance, however, the inclusion of the level of employment as a scaling factor was unnecessary, since comparisons between causes are made within the same group and the same year. It is also clear that the magnitude of the index can never exceed 100.

It can be seen from Table 12 that the major causes of stoppages in All Industries and Services, in descending order of importance, are: 'wage disputes', 'other working arrangements, rules and discipline', and 'disputes concerning the employment of discharge of workers'. In the six years from 1965 to 1970 the index of incidence for these causes taken together is always between 82 and 91 approximately. It is worth noting that no change has occurred in the ranking of the indexes relating to these causes over the period since 1959. The indexes for 'hours of labour', 'other disputes mainly concerning personnel questions', and 'demarcation disputes' are consistently small. The same is true of 'trade union status' and sympathetic action', except in 1969.

If it is accepted that wages and hours of labour are the issues with which collective bargaining is mainly concerned, it would appear that deficiencies in, or failures of, the normal bargaining process accounted for between 52 and 73 per cent of the incidence of stoppages as measured by the causal index. Similarly, if demarcation disputes, trade union status and sympathetic action can be taken as matters mainly affected by trade union organisation, then the defects in this quarter are revealed by the causal index between 6 and 15 per cent. Finally, if the remaining issues are essentially those lying within the prerogative of management, then the causal index relating to managerial practices is between 20 and 38 in the six years.

Turning to the seven individual groups of industries, we see that Table 12 reveals some similarities between them. In all groups and for all years, with one exception, wage disputes appear to be the most important cause of stoppages. Only for the Textiles and Clothing sector in 1966 do wage disputes fall to second place after 'employment and discharge'. With the exception of the All Other Industries and Services group in 1965 and 1966, for all groups in all years 'claims for increase' are far more important as a cause of pay disputes than 'other wage disputes'. For Mining and Quarrying the data have been presented separately in Table 13. It will be noticed that except for 1970 in this industry 'other wage disputes' account for the vast majority of pay disputes with 'claims for increases' being consistently small, though pay is far less important than 'other working arrangements.'

More appreciable differences exist between the groups analysed in Table 12 with regard to the importance of non-wage disputes in the total. In Construction 'employment and discharge' disputes

TABLE 12

Index Cijt of the Relative Incidence of Stoppages by Cause Within the Nine Groupings 1965–9

	Metals and Engineering						Shipbuilding and Marine Engineering						Vehicles						Textiles and Clothing					
	1965	1966	1967	1968	1969	1970	1965	1966	1967	1968	1969	1970	1965	1966	1967	1968	1969	1970	1965	1966	1967	1968	1969	1970
1. Claims for increases	42·5	35·6	36·8	75·0	59·4	69·4	61·1	41·3	42·3	54·2	48·4	72·9	45·2	40·7	51·6	63·2	56·2	57·2	62·6	24·3	23·2	45·8	68·8	78·3
2. Other wage disputes	7·8	20·0	11·0	4·0	3·5	3·0	2·7	4·8	6·7	5·9	11·5	6·0	8·6	14·7	11·0	10·8	7·9	8·1	5·5	12·7	17·8	4·6	7·3	3·4
All wage disputes	50·3	55·6	48·7	79·0	62·9	72·4	63·8	46·1	49·0	60·1	59·9	78·9	53·8	55·4	62·6	74·0	64·1	65·3	68·1	37·0	41·0	50·4	76·1	81·7
3. Hours of labour	3·1	1·1	0·8	0·3	0·2	0·1	—	—	1·2	—	8·3	—	19·9	1·8	2·5	1·0	1·5	0·6	2·9	—	12·4	2·1	0·3	1·0
4. Demarcation disputes	3·9	1·2	3·0	0·9	1·7	0·6	7·7	17·5	5·6	24·5	4·8	2·9	1·7	1·0	2·4	2·9	2·0	2·1	—	—	0·5	—	1·3	0·7
5. Disputes concerning the employment or discharge of workers	20·2	21·6	20·5	9·0	9·3	10·2	9·0	7·4	8·5	7·7	8·9	8·8	10·7	18·8	9·3	6·2	9·4	10·3	12·7	43·5	27·0	16·9	6·6	5·5
6. Other disputes mainly concerning personnel questions	1·9	1·2	1·9	1·7	1·4	0·9	1·3	7·4	1·8	1·8	3·2	1·7	2·0	4·0	2·6	1·6	2·5	2·9	—	—	1·5	—	1·4	1·1
7. Other working arrangements, rules and discipline	15·4	12·4	16·3	5·1	11·5	10·2	8·5	21·2	10·2	2·9	2·9	2·8	10·3	15·8	16·4	11·9	12·5	14·5	13·7	19·5	16·5	27·7	7·9	2·2
8. Trade Union status	4·7	6·4	6·7	3·5	8·5	4·9	9·7	—	—	0·6	9·0	2·9	1·4	3·2	3·1	1·6	3·1	3·6	2·6	—	1·1	7·9	6·1	2·8
9. Sympathetic action	0·5	0·5	2·1	0·5	4·5	0·7	—	0·4	23·7	2·4	3·0	2·0	0·2	—	1·1	0·8	4·9	0·7	—	—	—	—	0·3	5·0

TABLE 12

Index C_{ijt} of the Relative Incidence of Stoppages by Cause Within the Nine Groupings 1965–9

	Construction						Transport and Communication						All Other Industries and Services						All Industries and Services					
	1965	1966	1967	1968	1969	1970	1965	1966	1967	1968	1969	1970	1965	1966	1967	1968	1969	1970	1965	1966	1967	1968	1969	1970
1. Claims for increases	27·7	22·8	20·6	34·5	35·5	30·1	50·4	44·8	42·8	59·6	62·8	61·2	22·8	15·7	26·0	45·0	41·3	71·2	38·1	36·2	37·5	63·7	50·7	66·5
2. Other wage disputes	11·7	16·9	17·5	14·6	6·0	8·0	17·9	9·0	9·4	8·5	5·9	8·9	28·7	32·5	20·1	13·0	5·4	7·4	16·0	17·7	13·2	7·9	5·6	6·3
All wage disputes	39·4	39·7	38·1	49·1	41·5	38·1	68·3	53·8	52·5	68·1	68·7	70·1	51·5	48·2	46·1	58·0	46·7	78·6	54·1	53·9	50·7	71·6	56·3	72·8
3. Hours of labour	1·0	1·0	1·5	—	1·1	0·7	4·2	1·0	0·9	1·9	0·5	0·6	1·1	1·5	1·6	1·2	0·4	0·3	6·8	1·1	1·3	0·6	0·8	0·3
4. Demarcation disputes	6·3	3·2	5·6	5·9	6·8	1·9	1·4	7·6	5·9	2·2	2·4	6·8	1·0	2·5	2·5	1·8	0·4	1·0	2·3	3·4	3·7	3·5	1·8	2·4
5. Disputes concerning the employment or discharge of workers	37·7	34·7	31·3	21·7	23·6	31·2	5·2	4·7	4·3	2·8	2·5	4·6	5·0	10·0	11·0	8·5	5·5	6·0	11·8	14·6	13·3	8·0	7·5	8·4
6. Other disputes mainly concerning personnel questions	2·9	5·2	0·9	1·8	2·1	1·5	1·4	2·6	2·2	1·1	1·7	0·6	1·3	3·1	2·7	3·8	0·6	0·6	1·6	2·5	2·0	1·7	1·5	1·0
7. Other working arrangements, rules and discipline	8·6	11·2	18·0	13·5	13·0	15·1	17·5	23·6	31·1	21·6	10·3	13·1	37·4	29·3	30·1	20·0	39·5	9·4	20·1	19·5	22·5	10·9	18·6	10·2
8. Trade union status	2·8	4·1	1·8	3·8	8·3	6·6	1·3	4·4	1·1	1·0	3·4	2·2	2·3	3·5	4·2	5·9	4·2	2·6	2·9	3·9	3·6	2·8	8·5	3·4
9. Sympathetic action	1·3	0·9	2·8	4·2	3·6	4·9	0·7	2·3	2·3	1·3	10·5	2·0	0·4	1·9	1·8	0·8	2·7	1·5	0·4	1·1	2·9	0·9	5·0	1·5

rank second only to wage disputes in each year, and also in Metals and Engineering with the exception of 1969. This cause also achieves second place for the Vehicles group in two years. In the other sectors except Shipbuilding 'other working arrangements' are usually the second most significant cause of disputes. It is worth noting that in groups where the causal index for 'employment and discharge' ranks second, that for 'other working arrangements' generally takes third place, and conversely. The exceptions are Mining and Quarrying (Table 13), where 'personnel questions' ranks third after 'other working arrangements' and 'wage disputes', and Shipbuilding, where 'demarcation disputes' take second or third place in some years. It is interesting to note that, compared with the period 1959–64, 'sympathetic action' in Mining has decreased in importance as a cause of stoppages. Once the two dominant causes through which stoppages arise have been considered, it is difficult to discern a clear pattern in the ranking of the indexes for those that remain. It will be seen from Table 12, however, that the incidence of stoppages arising from 'hours of labour' attains in no group a rank higher than the fourth. 'Sympathetic action' ranks fifth or lower in all cases with the exception of Shipbuilding and Mining in 1967. Indeed, this cause only contributed to stoppages in Textiles and Clothing on two occasions, namely, 1969 and 1970. The index by cause for 'demarcation disputes' also ranks fourth or lower in all groups except Shipbuilding and Transport, where it achieves higher ranks in three years. 'Trade union status' invariably occupies the fourth or a lower rank except in Shipbuilding for two years and All Industries in one year. 'Disputes mainly concerning personnel questions' consistently fails to rise above the fourth rank outside Mining.

CONCLUSION

(1) In terms of the I_{it} index the incidence of stoppages is clearly low in Distribution, Clothing and Public Utilities, and high in Vehicles and Shipbuilding. Chemicals, Textiles and Food, Drink and Tobacco show moderately low index values, while Metal Manufacture, Engineering, Aircraft and Transport, on the other hand, yield index values clustered towards the upper end of the range.

(2) There has been an upward trend in the incidence of stoppages over the period 1965–70 for the aggregate of all industries, with the peak value of the index being attained in 1970 and the trough in 1966. When compared with the index values for all industries certain sectors show a slower rate of deterioration

TABLE 13

Mining and Quarrying

	1965	1966	1967	1968	1969	1970
1	1·5	3·3	3·1	2·1	0·9	61·9
2	40·0	46·3	36·7	41·6	11·6	11·1
3	41·5	49·6	39·8	43·7	12·5	73·0
	—	—	2·6	0·1	—	—
4	0·4	0·2	0·5	—	—	—
5	1·0	3·2	1·7	2·4	1·1	0·9
6	1·2	4·3	4·9	4·7	0·8	0·9
7	55·5	42·0	47·0	46·9	85·3	25·0
8	—	—	—	—	0·3	—
9	0·4	0·7	3·5	2·2	—	0·2

All Other

	1965	1966	1967	1968	1969	1970
1	52·2	30·3	42·1	55·7	67·3	72·6
2	11·8	16·2	8·7	5·8	3·4	6·9
3	64·0	46·5	50·8	61·5	70·7	79·5
	3·0	3·8	1·1	1·5	0·6	0·3
4	2·0	4·6	3·0	2·3	0·4	1·3
5	12·4	20·7	18·1	10·8	7·8	7·2
6	1·9	1·7	1·5	3·7	0·5	0·6
7	10·0	11·6	16·3	12·2	8·5	6·0
8	6·3	7·7	7·3	7·4	6·6	3·2
9	0·4	3·4	0·9	0·6	4·9	1·9

during 1964–70, namely, Shipbuilding, Clothing, Construction and Transport. Conversely, a more rapid deterioration has occurred in the Food, Drink and Tobacco, Metal Manufacture, Engineering, Vehicles and Aircraft, Locomotives, Metal Goods and Textiles groups. The same is also probably true, though less clearly so, of the Public Utilities and Chemicals sectors. It is tempting to conclude, in the light of the data, that much of the recent wave of unrest is attributable to the metal working and engineering sector broadly defined.

(3) With regard to the number of stoppages occurring and the proportionate shares of various sectors in the total, the outstanding result is the sharp decline in the importance of mining. The noticeably increased share of the engineering and metal sectors is also worthy of comment, as is the evidence for a deterioration in the strike record of Food, Drink and Tobacco; Transport; Vehicles and Chemicals.

(4) Stoppages lasting not more than one day constituted a decreasing proportion of the total during 1965–70, as was also observed for the period 1951–64. The share of stoppages lasting less than three days also fell. In general, it is clear that the average duration of stoppages is increasing.

(5) A survey of the data relating to principal stoppages (i.e. those which cause the loss of 5,000 working days or more) confirms the existence of the 'day effect' noted for the period 1960–4. Monday remained the most usual day for the commencement of stoppages, and Friday the most common day for their termination. The 'day effect', however, was less clear in the 1965–70 data than previously, partly due to the noticeable increase in the proportion of stoppages that commenced on Sundays and partly because of the tendency for Thursday and Friday to increase their share.

(6) The seasonal variation in the commencement of stoppages noted for the period 1951–64 has lost some of its strength. No unequivocal peak month emerged from the study of 1965–70, although March has some claim to that distinction. December was obviously a quiescent month, as, indeed, it was for the earlier period. In general, however, the marked peaks in March and October noted for the earlier period do not persist in the later data.

(7) The frequency of stoppages has clearly declined in Mining and Locomotives and equally clearly increased in Chemicals and Vehicles. An upward trend can also be postulated for Metal Manufacture, Engineering, Aircraft, Construction, and Transport.

(8) The analysis of disputes by cause shows that 'wage disputes', 'other working arrangements', and 'employment and discharge' remain the dominant causes in that order. The indexes for 'hours', 'personnel questions' and 'demarcation' remain consistently small, as do those for 'trade union status' and 'sympathetic action' except in 1969. Differences exist between the various industry groups, but 'claims for increase' are almost always far more important than 'other wage disputes.'

(9) As a broad generalisation, it appears reasonable to conclude that during 1965–70 the industrial climate deteriorated in Britain, with the metals and engineering sector acting as pacemaker, and with claims for wage increases dominating the range of issues over which disputes occurred.

NOTES

1 P. Galambos and E. W. Evans, 'Work Stoppages in the United Kingdom, 1951–64: a quantitative study', *Bulletin of the Oxford University Institute of Economics and Statistics*, Vol. 28, no. I, 1966.

2 *Employment and Productivity Gazette* (May 1970), p. 398.

3 P. Galambos and E. W. Evans, 'Work Stoppages in the United Kingdom, 1951–64: A Reply', *Bulletin of the Oxford University Institute of Economics and Statistics*, Vol. 28, no. 4, 1966.

4 H. A. Turner, *Is Britain Really Strike Prone?* (Cambridge University Press, 1969).

3

STRIKES IN THE UNITED KINGDOM: RECENT STATISTICS AND TRENDS

J. F. B. Goodman

The use of the strike as a sanction is traditionally the ultimate weapon of trade unionists against employers, and its exercise has frequently been the subject of analysis by students of industrial relations.[1] The purpose of this paper is to review recent changes in the level, distribution and 'causes' of strike activity in the United Kingdom, which may help to inform participants in the current debate over the nature of the 'strike problem'.

Strikes are complex phenomena which can be analysed from a variety of points of view, academic disciplines and ethical or utilitarian standards.[2] Indeed an examination of published statistics throws little or no light on the circumstances surrounding particular disputes, and the factors which channelled the expression of conflict into this particular form. Some strikes may be relatively spontaneous outbursts against a particular action or decision by management, being as much demonstrative as combative. In other instances strikes are timed as part of a strategy to improve terms and conditions of employment and take place when they are most likely to be successful in gaining these ends.[3] In yet other cases participants have no eye for tactics, but they or their leaders see only what they regard as a grievance requiring urgent attention and feel a sense of injustice. In a few workplaces distrust reaches the point where strike action becomes the first rather than the last resort. Thus different strikes can be accurately described in different ways; some have a strategic or planned element, others come closer to spontaneity; some are demonstrations, others are lengthy struggles; in some stoppages the initial demands made by workers have a certain novelty vis-à-vis existing practice and customs, in others workers are defending advances or rights which they feel are being challenged by management. Certainly the vast majority of strikes, in the United Kingdom at least, are both unofficial and unconstitutional[4] and nave their origin and leadership in the workplace rather than in the local or (still less likely) national union offices. This change in the pattern and nature of strike activity is indicative of the shift in the nature and location of contentious industrial relations activity which has occurred in the past two decades.[5]

A strike is not, of course, the only collective sanction available to workplace or union leaders, or indeed to the rank-and-file union members. Resistance to management policies and practices, opposition to specific changes, or support for desired improvements can be expressed by other means, of which the overtime ban and the go-slow are perhaps the best known. However, other, often less open, methods are at hand, e.g. the withdrawal of informal co-operation or goodwill in day-to-day operations on the shop floor; insistence on the rigid observance of conventions or rules which have been left unobserved when relationships were good; an unco-ordinated increase in the reluctance of individuals to work overtime; the obstruction or delay of new management policies which need the consent of workplace representatives before they can be effectively implemented; refusal to participate in established joint management-employee committees; following up or exaggerating complaints which would normally not be pursued, in order to waste management's time. The list, certainly a descriptive list, of alternatives is extensive. Thus the absence of strikes does not mean the absence of overt conflict; nor, still less, does it automatically mean that industrial relations are good. Unfortunately the extent to which these alternative or supplementary techniques are used is extremely difficult to gauge, and no attempt can be made in this paper to quantify their presence, or indeed other unorganised symptoms of unrest or dissatisfaction. Their variety and range do, however, serve to remind us that the problems in industrial relations are of greater consequence and complexity than the mere prevention of strikes.

STATISTICAL SOURCES AND THEIR LIMITATIONS

In the United Kingdom the source of statistics of strike activity due to industrial disputes is the Ministry of Labour.[6] The Ministry obtains its information from its Industrial Relations Officers, Employment Exchange Managers, certain nationalised industries and statutory authorities, the press and, for larger stoppages, the workers' and employers' organisations concerned. Over the years there have been a number of changes in classification and presentation, which have generally improved the information available. However, there remain a number of limitations, and it is important to bear these in mind in any examination of trends.

(1) The Ministry does not distinguish between strikes and lockouts, both being grouped under the heading of 'stoppages of work'. It would, of course, be very difficult to do this accurately and, even where the distinction appears clear, provocation by the other side may make it unreal. However, the number of clear-cut lockouts in the United Kingdom is negligible.

(2) The statistics exclude stoppages involving fewer than ten workers and those which lasted less than one day, except where the aggregate number of working days lost exceed 100.

(3) The statistics include time lost by workers who were thrown out of work at establishments where a stoppage took place, but who were not parties to the dispute. These are classified as 'indirectly involved'. They do *not* include any loss of time caused at other establishments, e.g. through shortage of materials. The number of days lost through such external repercussions will vary considerably, depending primarily on the technology and structure of the industries concerned and on the length of the stoppage.

(4) The statistics do not include instances of other forms of industrial action, e.g. overtime bans, work-to-rule, go-slow. It seems that these sanctions are being used more frequently, especially overtime bans in industries where overtime has become customary and is relied on for normal production. The Ministry's figures do not enable this subjective impression to be quantified.

(5) The categorisation of industrial stoppages by single cause is necessarily arbitrary. Where several causes are involved, the classification is based on what appears to be the principal cause, i.e. the main reason given by those involved at the time. The accurate isolation of the principal cause is made additionally difficult by the probability of subsequent rationalisations, and by the displacement of grievances from topics of doubted legitimacy to more accepted issues, e.g. wages. The wide range of problems and the differing degrees of emphasis they may be given in a particular stoppage suggest that some strikes will be forced, rather than fitted, into the Ministry's categories.

(6) The Ministry has admitted that 'there are undoubtedly many strikes which, though not too small to be included in the Ministry's figures, in practice escape inclusion'[7]. This is especially true of the private sector, where there are numerous employers. Further, it can be added that very brief 'lightning' strikes, e.g. those taking place within one shift, will largely go unrecorded. The conclusion is that the figures underestimate

the number of strikes, as well as excluding other overt and organised expressions of conflict.

Since the measures of 'numbers involved' and 'days lost' are susceptible to large fluctuations (e.g. in the case of a one-day token stoppage throughout an entire industry), the number of strikes will be used as the primary basis of analysis. This is further justified since, on this criterion, the United Kingdom's international record is poor, whereas on 'days lost' only six countries have a better record.[8] Moreover, an examination of strike frequency has more diagnostic value than has a study of magnitude or duration, particularly as the 'typical' stoppage in this country is both small and short.

NUMBER OF STRIKES

The number of stoppages in the United Kingdom might be expected to rise, other things being equal, with the increase in the number of persons in employment. Alternatively, it might be expected that this tendency would be offset by the increasing proportion of the labour force employed in occupations or sectors where the use of the strike weapon is neither customary nor considered legitimate. The number of strikes tends to rise in times of prosperity (i.e. low and falling unemployment and rising prices). This, *inter alia*, would suggest increased strike activity in the post-war period. A comparison of the post-war and inter-war periods certainly validates the correlation (see table I), which can also be demonstrated by reference to shorter time periods; for example the level of unemployment rose to relatively high levels in 1959 and 1963, and in the same years the number of stoppages fell.[9] But, on the whole, post-war employment conditions have been favourable to the unions. They and their members have been in a stronger position to pursue grievances, to extend their influence and to secure acceptance of new principles in their relationship to employers. In so far as these pressures are resisted an increase in strike activity can be anticipated.

The number of strikes reached a record level in 1957; but, although this number has not been exceeded, the figures for subsequent years have consolidated at a level higher than that for earlier years. The average number of strikes per year in the decade 1956–65 was almost 40 per cent higher than for the decade 1946–55.[10] Strikes have thus become much more frequent within these two decades of consistently low unemployment levels and of increasing prosperity.

Whilst this general view illustrates the upward trend in the number of strikes, as an analytical tool it is relatively blunt. Indeed, the fact that the number of strikes has not passed the 1957 figure is in one

TABLE I

Stoppages of Work Beginning in Each Year, 1914–65

Year	No. of stoppages in year	No. of workers involved*	Aggregate working days lost (in thousands)	Year	No. of stoppages in year	No. of workers involved*	Aggregate working days lost (in thousands)
1914	972	447	9,360	1940	922	299	940
1915	672	448	2,970	1941	1,251	360	1,080
1916	532	276	2,370	1942	1,303	456	1,530
1917	730	872	5,870	1943	1,785	557	1,830
1918	1,165	1,116	5,890	1944	2,194	821	3,700
1919	1,352	2,591	36,030	1945	2,293	531	2,850
1920	1,607	1,932	28,860	1946	2,205	526	2,180
1921	763	1,801	82,270	1947	1,721	620	2,400
1922	576	552	19,650	1948	1,759	424	1,940
1923	628	405	10,950	1949	1,426	433	1,820
1924	710	613	8,360	1950	1,339	302	1,380
1925	603	441	8,910	1951	1,719	379	1,710
1926	323	2,734	161,300	1952	1,714	415	1,800
1927	308	108	870	1953	1,746	1,370	2,170
1928	302	124	1,390	1954	1,989	448	2,480
1929	431	533	8,290	1955	2,419	659	3,790
1930	422	307	4,450	1956	2,648	507	2,050
1931	420	490	7,010	1957	2,859	1,356	8,400
1932	389	379	6,430	1958	2,629	523	3,470
1933	357	136	1,020	1959	2,093	645	5,280
1934	471	134	1,060	1960	2,832	814	3,050
1935	553	271	1,950	1961	2,686	771	3,040
1936	818	316	2,010	1962	2,449	4,420	5,780
1937	1,129	597	3,140	1963	2,068	590	2,000
1938	875	274	1,330	1964	2,524	873	2,030
1939	940	337	1,350	1965	2,354	868	2,932

*Directly and indirectly.

sense misleading. For each post-war year until 1962 the coal industry was responsible for over half of the stoppages, accounting for over 70 per cent of the total number of stoppages from 1952 to 1958 (see table II). The number of stoppages in the coal industry reached a record level in 1957, and this to a large extent accounted for the over-all record number in that year. Since 1957 the number and proportionate share of strikes in the coal industry have fallen consistently, reaching their lowest post-war level in 1965, when the industry contributed only 31 per cent of all strikes. Between these years the numbers employed in the coal industry declined by about 30 per cent, but the number of strikes fell by 67 per cent. However, this dramatic reduction in strike activity in the coal industry has been offset by the increased frequency of strikes elsewhere. The incidence of strikes in other industries and services has more than doubled since the late 1950s and has reached new record levels in each year of the 1960s except 1963–a year of relatively high unemployment.

Thus the coal industry's long domination of the statistics is rapidly disappearing.[11] Not all industries and services have shared equally in this over-all increase outside the coal industry. Comparing the period 1953–55 with 1963–65, the number of stoppages outside the coal industry rose by 60 per cent. As shown in table III, different industries show different rates of increase in the number of strikes between these two periods. For example the number in non-electrical engineering nearly quadrupled; in electrical machinery, apparatus and goods it rose by seven times; in motor vehicles and cycles it trebled; in construction it more than doubled. Amongst the industries in which the rate of increase did not reach the national average are ports and inland water transport, where the number rose by just over half, and shipbuilding and marine engineering, where it rose by only one-third. Between these two periods the number of strikes in the coal industry fell by almost 40 per cent and more than halved after 1956–58.

TABLE II

Strikes in the Coal Industry, and Elsewhere, 1945–65
(Stoppages in progress during the year)

Coal industry

Year	Number	Percentage of total	Percentage of days lost	No. of strikes outside the coal industry
1945	1,306	56·9	22·6	987
1946	1,329	60·2	19·5	876
1947	1,053	61·1	37·4	668
1948	1,116	63·4	23·8	643
1949	874	61·2	38·7	552
1950	860	64·2	31·1	479
1951	1,058	61·5	20·4	661
1952	1,221	71·2	36·7	493
1953	1,307	74·8	18·0	439
1954	1,464	73·6	18·8	525
1955	1,783	73·7	29·3	636
1956	2,076	78·3	24·4	572
1957	2,224	77·7	6·1	635
1958	1,963	74·6	12·9	666
1959	1,307	62·4	6·8	786
1960	1,666	58·8	16·2	1,166
1961	1,458	54·2	24·2	1,228
1962	1,205	49·2	26·7	1,244
1963	987	47·7	16·3	1,081
1964	1,058	41·9	13·2	1,466
1965	740	31·4	14·0	1,614

This dramatic rise in the number of strikes outside the coal industry is all the more notable as data collection from the private sector is less comprehensive than from the nationalised coal industry. Thus the upward trend is probably even stronger than the figures indicate.

TABLE III

Strikes in Selected Industries Outside the Coal Industry[12]
1953–55 and 1963–65

	1953–55		1963–65	
Industry	Total	Average	Total	Average
Electrical machinery, apparatus and goods	38	13	268	89
Non-electrical engineering	140	47	522	174
Motor vehicles and cycles	145*	48	459	153
Construction	251	84	651	217
Shipbuilding and marine engineering	209	70	286	95
Ports and inland water transport	159	53	263	88
National figures (excl. coal industry)**	1,600	533	4,161	1,387

*This figure includes aircraft.
**Showing an over-all increase of 160 per cent over the period.

DISTRIBUTION OF STRIKES

Stoppages of work through strikes are, as we have seen, much more frequent in some industries than in others. Over the post-war period from 1946 to 1965 the coal industry accounted for 62 per cent of all strikes, though the proportion fell to 45 per cent in the period 1961–65. For the same periods it accounted for 22 and 19 per cent of the aggregate days lost respectively.

If the criterion of 'days lost per thousand employees' is applied a consistent concentration emerges. Using this criterion, the motor vehicles, ports and transport, and shipbuilding groups are to be found among the five most affected industries every year since 1960. Coal mining has been similarly located each year except 1962. No other industry group has appeared among the five most affected industries per thousand employees more than once in the past six years, except iron and steel, which is present twice. However, even in the industries most afflicted by strike action the loss of working days remains relatively small. For example in the three industries which lost the largest number of working days per thousand employees in 1965 the amount of time lost was less than one-third of 1 per cent of working days in shipbuilding and coalmining, and slightly more than two-thirds of 1 per cent in motor vehicles.

If the number of strikes is taken as a guide, a consistency is found amongst industry groups[13] similar to that apparent on the 'days lost per thousand employees' criterion. Of the 49 industries and services in the Ministry of Labour's Standard Industrial Classification, excluding the coal industry as a special case, five groups account for a large proportion of all strikes. For each of the eight years from 1958 to 1965, i.e. after the dramatic and continued increase in strikes outside the coal industry began, the construction industry headed the table. For the last five years non-electrical engineering was second, and motor vehicles and cycles third. Both were among the top five for each of these eight years. Other groups which appeared there are shipbuilding (six times), ports and inland water transport (seven times) and iron and steel (twice). The five industries most frequently experiencing strikes (excluding coal) contributed over half the total number of strikes in each of these eight years. However, this proportion showed a downward trend, within the rising aggregate number, i.e. from 69 per cent in 1958 to 52 per cent in 1965. This demonstrates that strike activity is becoming more broadly based and, whilst the concentration does remain, it is becoming less marked.

If the coal industry is included in the figures for the five industry groups most frequently experiencing strikes, then the decrease in the proportion was even larger, i.e. from 90 per cent of all strikes in 1958 to 63 per cent in 1965.

Inter-industry disparities are not the only ones revealed by an analysis of strike statistics. There are also regional variations. For example over the period 1960–64 Yorkshire accounted for 46 per cent of all days lost in the coal industry, but the proportion of mining employees in that area was only 20 per cent. In the same five-year period Scotland had 23 per cent of the employees in shipbuilding but accounted for 38 per cent of the days lost. The north-west region had 11 per cent of all employees in construction in the period 1960–64 but had 43 per cent of all days lost in the industry.[14]

Strike activity also appears to follow a seasonal pattern, with a high incidence in the early months of the year leading to an annual peak in March or April, falling to lower levels in July and August, rising to a secondary peak in September and October and falling dramatically in December.

SIZE OF STRIKES

Table I shows that for a period of almost 30 years after the General Strike of 1926[15] the number of workers involved in stoppages of work reached over 500,000 in only seven years. The number has not been lower than this since 1955. This reflects the increase in the number of strikes and particularly illustrates the increase in the numbers 'indirectly involved', which reached post-war record levels in 1963, 1964 and 1965. This figure has risen each year since 1958, except in 1960 and 1961, and illustrates the increasing interdependence of processes in modern technology. It is of particular importance in the motor industry.[16] Even these figures are an underestimation of the numbers affected indirectly, for they exclude workers laid off at establishments other than those at which the stoppage has taken place. In many ways the figures for those 'indirectly involved' are a cause for concern, and may be of more meaningful long-term significance than those for workers 'directly involved'. The latter are periodically inflated by large-scale stoppages, which may be of a token nature; for example, of 4,296,000 workers directly involved in stoppages in 1962, 3,785,000 were involved in token stoppages in engineering and shipbuilding (two days), and on the railways. The median figure for the numbers directly involved over the past ten years is 673,000; for 'indirectly involved' it is 123,000.

However, the most apparent feature of the size of strikes is their small scale. In 1965 stoppages involving (directly and indirectly) less than 50 workers constituted 38 per cent of all strikes. Those involving less than 250 workers formed 75 per cent of all strikes. It is also found that, while most strikes involve relatively few workers, the greater proportion of workers involved are concerned in larger strikes; for example in 1965, 1,758 strikes (75 per cent of the total), involving less than 250 workers, accounted for only 14 per cent of all the workers involved in stoppages; but 34 per cent of all the workers involved were concerned in the 23 stoppages (1 per cent of the total) affecting over 5,000 workers.

The typical strike is a relatively small one. This pattern of small-scale strikes became increasingly characteristic in the war and post-war years. Recently, however, the trend has begun to change. Strikes involving less than 250 workers still constitute three-quarters of all strikes, but in the late 1950s the proportion was always over 80 per cent, and it reached 84 per cent in 1956 and 1957. The subsequent fall may be the result of fewer strikes in the coal industry and more in the motor industry with its large manufacturing plants. Strikes of this size normally account for around 15 per cent of the aggregate days lost.

LENGTH OF STRIKES

Long stoppages have not been a characteristic feature of strike activity in the United Kingdom since the General Strike. In the early part of this century the unions were much readier to confront

the employers with large, long and official strikes[17] which fully
extended the resources of both. Fortunately, prolonged struggles
of this kind are now rare, though the 1966 seamen's strike[18] illustrated
that they have not been abandoned. Usually, individual companies
or single factory managements have not been prepared to face long
strikes. However, it remains noticeable that even in the post-war
period strikes have been less numerous but more lengthy in periods
of recession.[19] Similarly, strikes over matters of 'principle', e.g.
closed shop, victimisation, 'management prerogatives', etc., tend
to be longer than wage disputes.

Over the past ten years between 70 and 80 per cent of all stoppages
have lasted not more than three days. Strikes of this length account
for about 20 per cent of the days lost, though this figure varies
widely with the occasional incidence of large but short strikes; for
example in 1962 they accounted for 73 per cent of all days lost.
However, the proportion of short strikes has been declining over
recent years; it fell from over 80 per cent in 1957 and 1958 to 68
per cent in 1965. This too may be the direct result of the lower
incidence of strikes in the coal industry since 1957. The same trend
is apparent in very short strikes; for example the proportion of
strikes lasting one day or less was higher than 40 per cent in all post-
war years until 1960 (with the exception of 1955), but it has not
subsequently been above this level and fell to 34 per cent in 1965. At
the other end of the scale the number of strikes lasting longer than
24 days has risen continuously since 1958 (again with one exception),
and there have been more than 50 in each year since 1960. These long
strikes normally contribute around 15 per cent of the days lost, but
it is difficult to speak of normality here, as the proportion rose to 75
per cent in 1959 but was as low as 6 per cent in 1962.

ANALYSIS BY THE NUMBER OF WORKING DAYS LOST

Again the pattern is one of a majority of strikes with limited direct
repercussions: 63 per cent of all strikes recorded between 1960 and
1965 involved the loss of less than 250 working days. However, an
examination of individual years shows that the proportion of stoppages in this category fell from 72 per cent in 1958 to 58 per cent
in 1965. This movement may be associated with the decline in importance of strikes in the coal industry. The trend corresponds with
the falling proportion of short strikes and of very small strikes
mentioned in the two preceding sections.

The aggregate number of days lost is shown in table I, which
brings out the disproportionate influence of national strikes,
illustrated, for example, by the following figures:

1955: of the 3,790,000 working days lost (the highest figure since 1932), the railway strike accounted for 865,000;

1957: of the 8,400,000 working days lost, national strikes in engineering and ship-building accounted for 6,150,000;

1959: of the 5,280,000 working days lost, the six-week strike in the printing industry accounted for 3,500,000;

1962: of the 5,780,000 working days lost, two national one-day token strikes in engineering and shipbuilding and one on the railways accounted for 3,785,000.

These occasional large strikes account for the periodic increase in working days lost to levels in excess of 3 million. However, the comparative freedom of large sections of employment from strike activity has been noted earlier, as has the low amount of time lost per employee even in the most strike-prone industries. The amount of time lost through strikes in 1964 was equivalent to about one-tenth of a working day per person in the employed population. In that year working days lost through sickness and injury, i.e. certified incapacity, amounted to 306,490,000, compared with 2,030,000 lost through stoppages. Obviously the nature of these two is vastly different; for example absence due to certified incapacity can be calculated and allowed for by firms, whereas strikes cannot. However, these figures put the situation into some perspective.

REASONS GIVEN FOR STRIKING

The Ministry of Labour publishes annually a breakdown of strikes analysed by the cause of each stoppage, or rather by principal cause. 'Where several causes are involved (e.g. a claim for an advance in wages accompanied by a claim for some other change in working conditions) then the classification is based on what appears to be the principal cause'[20].

This necessarily involves some arbitrary placement. Secondly, it may record not the causes of disputes but rationalisations of causes; and as such it is a classification by reason given, which is not invariably the same as *the* cause. The results of this tabulation for stoppages *outside the coal industry* for the period 1959–65 are given in table IV.

CLAIMS FOR WAGE INCREASES

The number of disputes in this category in industry as a whole has increased very markedly in recent years, from an average of around 110 in 1953–55 to 642 in 1965. An increase in the proportion of disputes in this category also took place in each year after 1953, when it accounted for 5·5 per cent of all disputes, until 1965 when

TABLE IV

Number of Stoppages of Work Outside the Coal Industry Analysed by Cause, 1959 to 1965
(Stoppages beginning in each year)

Cause	1959 No.	1959 Per-centage	1960 No.	1960 Per-centage	1961 No.	1961 Per-centage	1962 No.	1962 Per-centage	1963 No.	1963 Per-centage	1964 No.	1964 Per-centage	1965 No.	1965 Per-centage
Claims for wage increases	216	28	420	36	399	33	343	28	362	34	531	36	642	40
Other wage disputes	129	16	172	15	181	15	175	14	136	13	159	11	182	11
All wage disputes	345	44	592	51	580	48	518	42	498	46	690	47	824	51
Hours of labour	6	1	37	3	22	2	8	1	17	2	23	2	44	3
Demarcation disputes	31	4	48	4	50	4	58	5	58	5	58	4	60	4
Disputes concerning the employment or discharge of workers (including redundancy questions)	174	22	186	16	242	20	276	22	215	20	249	17	301	19
Other disputes mainly concerning personnel questions	44	6	51	4	46	4	102	8	32	3	47	3	41	3
Other working arrangements, rules and discipline	123	16	161	14	183	15	164	13	167	16	279	19	260	16
Trade union status	42	5	63	5	69	6	100	8	73	7	97	7	69	4
Sympathetic action	17	2	25	2	25	2	24	2	15	1	16	1	12	1
All causes	782	100	1,163	100	1,220	100	1,242	100	1,075	100	1,461	100	1,611	100

its share was 27·5 per cent–except for temporary falls in both the numbers and percentage in 1958 and 1962. Finally, the number of strikes caused by wage claims more than doubled between 1959 and 1965, when it accounted for 46 per cent of working days lost.

As already noted, the coal industry has had a dominant influence on strike statistics generally. However, claims for wage increases are not an important cause of strikes in the coal industry, and in any case even the small number attributable to this cause has been decreasing, thus acting as a slight brake on the aggregate rate of increase. If stoppages in the coal industry are excluded altogether, claims for wage increases accounted for 40 per cent of all strikes and 53 per cent of working days lost in 1965. The actual number of wage-claim strikes has trebled outside the coal industry since 1959, though this upward movement has not been consistent and stoppages due to this cause appear to be sensitive to the state of trade.[21] To the extent that this is true of industries other than coal we may expect the aggregate number of strikes to vary even more markedly with the level of economic activity, since wage-claim strikes are becoming proportionately more important.

OTHER WAGE DISPUTES

This also is an important category, and includes disputes over systems of payment, calculation of earnings, claims for the application of conditions and other allowances, etc. In industry as a whole, however, its importance has declined both absolutely and relatively, having fallen from 1,035 disputes (accounting for 42 per cent of all disputes) in 1955 to 532 (22 per cent) in 1965. Its percentage share fell in each year within this period except 1958.

However, the coal industry has regularly accounted for over 75 per cent of all stoppages in this category. Consequently the reduction in the number of strikes in the coal industry, and of those stemming from this cause, in each year since 1960 has considerably affected this category's share of all strikes.

If the coal industry is excluded, 'other wage disputes' accounted for an average of about 13 per cent of all strikes between 1959 and 1965, with some discontinuous tendency to fall–from 16 per cent in 1959 to 11 per cent in 1965. The proportion of stoppages due to this cause is higher than the national average in both construction and transport (which is dominated by the docks).

Thus, outside the coal industry, i.e. in the sector where the frequency of strikes is rising, there is a tendency for 'claims for wage increases' to become relatively more important and 'other wage disputes' to become relatively less important. The increase in the former category is larger than the decrease in the latter, and so we find that 'all wage disputes' accounted for 51 per cent of all strikes outside the coal industry in 1965 compared with 44 per cent in 1959. Over-all–including the coal industry–the figures are 50 per cent and 46 per cent respectively.

HOURS OF WORK

This category is relatively unimportant. It has never accounted for more than 4 per cent of stoppages over the past 20 years, and has been the cause of less than 1 per cent of all stoppages in three out of the past five years.

DEMARCATION DISPUTES

Stoppages in this category have been separately classified only since 1959. They have averaged about 60 each year, accounting for between 2 and 3 per cent of all strikes. Demarcation does not, therefore, appear to be an important cause of strikes, but it has a high incidence in certain industries. The most notable of these is shipbuilding and marine engineering, in which demarcation disputes have constituted between 9 and 15 per cent of all stoppages in each year since 1959. This industry regularly experiences around 15 per cent of all demarcation dispute stoppages.

FRICTIONAL CAUSES

This classification was made by Knowles[22] to include disputes arising from 'employment of particular classes or persons' (which has now been amended to 'disputes concerning the employment or discharge of workers (including redundancy questions)'), and 'other working arrangements, rules and discipline'. To this frictional category we can add 'other disputes mainly concerning personnel questions', for which figures have been given since 1959. These three categories include disputes of a widely varying nature, for example the whole range of disciplinary issues, disputes over supervision, changes in working conditions or systems which do not involve changes in pay or hours. Knowles found that stoppages in his frictional category rose from 22 to 39 per cent of the total between the two periods 1911–25 and 1927–47. From 1945 to 1957 frictional strikes rose to 48 per cent of the total. However, this upward tendency has been reversed since then, and over the period 1959–65 only 44 per cent of all stoppages were placed in this category. There has been some change in the classification of strikes over this period, chiefly in 1959, and so the figures may not be strictly comparable. For example demarcation disputes were previously included in 'employment of particular classes or persons'. If demarcation disputes are added to the frictional category, then the 1959–65 figure would rise (to 46 per cent), but insufficiently to affect the slightly downward proportionate trend. Further, a residual category ('Other') was included by the Ministry of Labour until 1953, after which the small number of disputes normally placed in this section were spread amongst the remaining categories. From 1959 this category re-emerged as 'other disputes mainly concerning personnel questions' which has been included in the frictional category.

Thus there is little doubt that the proportion of stoppages due to frictional problems has been declining over the recent period, after rising for about 50 years. However, the changes in classification make it difficult to quantify this trend exactly.

Again the coal industry affects the figures. Since 1959 an analysis of strikes by cause within major industry groups has been available. The coal industry dominates disputes over 'other working arrangements, rules and discipline', though the number of coal industry strikes in this category has fallen continuously, from 745 in 1960 to 366 in 1965. Similarly coal's share of all disputes in this single category fell from 82 per cent in 1959 to 58 per cent in 1965. If the coal industry is excluded, the proportion of frictional disputes has averaged only 38 per cent of all stoppages since 1959, with little trend. Stoppages over wages issues have averaged 47 per cent for the same period, with an upward trend. However, the aggregate number of stoppages due to frictional issues has risen with less fluctuation than the number due to wage claims, from 341 to 602 between 1959 and 1965, with a fall in only one year (1963). 'Claims for wage increases' have shown much greater fluctuations numerically. The number of strikes outside the coal industry has risen by 160 per cent since 1959; 'claims for wage increases' have accounted for over half of that increase, and frictional issues for less than one-third.

An examination of broad industry groups reveals even wider disparities. For example in 1965, in the metals and engineering group, wage disputes accounted for 53 per cent of all disputes, with frictional issues causing only 35 per cent; but in construction, frictional disputes usually outnumbered all wage disputes.

TRADE UNION STATUS AND SYMPATHETIC ACTION

These two categories together account for an average of around 4 per cent of all stoppages. The former category includes stoppages over union recognition, closed shop, etc., whilst the latter is self-explanatory.

CONCLUSIONS

(1) It is apparent that in recent years there have been several important changes in the nature and distribution of strikes, with the decline in the relative importance of the coal industry exerting a profound influence on most of the indices. Thus the traditional concentration of strike activity in five or six industry groups is less marked, even if the strike-prone coal industry is excluded from the statistics – and even more so if it is included. Strike activity has become more diffuse, and the reduced frequency of strikes in the coal industry has been generally offset by increases elsewhere.

(2) Secondly, there has been a fairly constant upward movement in the proportion of stoppages due to 'claims for wage increases' and a dramatic reduction in 'other wage disputes'. The latter is largely due to falls in the coal industry, although the proportion of stoppages due to this cause has also shown a downward tendency outside the coal industry. Wage-claim stoppages have their own dynamic, numbers having trebled between 1959 and 1965 outside the coal industry, but there have been large fluctuations in the number of stoppages classified in this category, and this now exerts considerable influence on the aggregate number of stoppages. The number of such stoppages appears to be responsive to the 'economic climate' and other variables.

(3) Thirdly, the proportion of aggregate stoppages over frictional issues has been relatively stable or falling, in contrast with its upward tendency throughout most of the century so far. If stoppages in the coal industry are excluded – and the reduction in the number of these has influenced the above trend – then it emerges that the number of disputes over frictional issues has been closer to one-third than to one-half of total stoppages in five out of the past seven years, whilst wages topics have always been over 40 per cent and twice over 50 per cent of all stoppages in the same period. If it is assumed that the Ministry has been consistent in its categorisation of stoppages, there has been a change of emphasis in strike causation.

Previously employee pressure and employer resistance on questions of status, management prerogatives, discipline, styles of treatment, etc., were thought to be of increasing relative importance as a direct cause of stoppages, but it appears that wages topics have assumed the ascendency, particularly in those sectors where the frequency of strikes is increasing.

In many ways employer unwillingness to accept joint regulation of a broader range of workplace topics was thought to stem from the less calculable results of concessions on these topics, whereas the effects of increased wage costs did not suffer from such vagueness and could usually be offset by being passed on to the consumer. However, given the continued devolution of wages and earnings bargaining to the shop floor or local establishment in many industries and the fairly widespread extension of the range of monetary topics included in that bargaining, it is not surprising that the pattern of strike activity – and its level – is reflecting this change of emphasis. Government pressure on wages and earnings negotiations at both national and factory levels, through the imposition of a pay freeze and the enactment of legislation to impose penalties on workers who strike in support of the early payment of their claims, should serve to check the rate of increase in the number of strikes for which this reason is given. So, too, should the downturn in the economy induced by the government economic measures of July 1966. The effect of the first two changes, however, may be to transfer 'causes', either in reality or by subterfuge, into other categories of the Ministry's classification, or into other forms of pressure or resistance. Unfortunately the extent of this latter movement will not be quantifiable.

NOTES

1 See, for example, K. G. J. C. Knowles: *Strikes* (Oxford University Press, 1952); W. E. J. McCarthy: 'The reasons given for striking', in *Bulletin of the Oxford Institute of Statistics*, Feb. 1959; and H. A. Turner: *The trend of strikes* (Leeds University Press, 1963).

2 See J. E. T. Eldridge and G. C. Cameron: 'Unofficial strikes: some objection. considered', in *British Journal of Sociology* (London), Vol. 15, 1964.

3 See G. C. Cameron: 'Post-war strikes in the north-east shipbuilding and ship repairing industry, 1946–61', in *British Journal of Industrial Relations* (London), Mar. 1964.

4 The Minister of Labour said in the House of Commons on 21 February 1966 that between 90 and 95 per cent of all strikes in this country were unofficial, and that this figure was true of the past six years, i.e. 1960–65. The Ministry has estimated that in the 1960–64 period unofficial strikes – defined as strikes not called or recognised by a trade union – accounted for nearly 60 per cent of days lost, though if 'unusual' national strikes in 1962 are excluded the proportion rises to over 75 per cent. The Ministry has also observed that the vast majority of unofficial strikes are 'unconstitutional' in the sense that they occur before the procedure for dispute settlement has been exhausted. (Ministry of Labour: *Written evidence to the Royal Commission on Trade Unions and Employers' Associations* (London, H.M. Stationary Office, 1965), First Memorandum, para. 127.)

5 For an outline of some of the factors influencing this change of emphasis see J. F. B. Goodman and T. G. Whittingham: *Shop stewards in British industry*, Chapter VIII.

6 Unless otherwise stated all the statistics in this paper have been obtained directly

from the *Ministry of Labour Gazette,* or are derived from these. The presentation of statistics in the *Gazette* has been much improved since 1959.

7 *Written evidence to the Royal Commission on Trade Unions and Employers' Associations,* op. cit., p. 38.

8 *See Ministry of Labour Gazette,* Oct. 1966.

9 Unemployment was particularly high in the early months of 1963, and the number of stoppages in the first six months of that year totalled only 75 per cent of the totals for the similar period of both the immediately preceding and subsequent years.

10 This may in part be due to improved reporting, but there is no tangible evidence to support this. Indeed the impression is gained that there has been an increase in very short strikes, i.e. begun and settled within a shift, and these may very easily not be reported.

11 This trend appears to be continuing. According to the figures so far available for 1966, i.e. for the first nine months, the coal industry accounts for only 27 per cent.

12 Owing to changes in the Standard Industrial Classification the industries are not strictly comparable between these two periods, but such definitional variations have not greatly affected the figures in the industries mentioned.

13 This criterion does not, however, take account of differences in the size and structure of the industries, numbers employed, and type of labour.

14 *Written evidence to the Royal Commission on Trade Unions and Employers' Associations,* op. cit., First Memorandum, para. 133.

15 The so-called General Strike lasted from 4 to 12 May 1926. It was called by the Trades Union Congress (T.U.C.) in support of the Miners' Federation's resistance to wage cuts and lengthening of the work week proposed by the employers in the coal industry. This proposal had first been put forward in 1925, but its implementation was delayed by the establishment by the Government of a Royal Commission to investigate the future of the industry. In the meantime the Government paid a temporary subsidy to maintain miners' conditions at existing levels. The Commission's report was rejected by the Miners' Federation, and the T.U.C., which had latterly been negotiating on its behalf, was given powers to undertake the conduct of the dispute. On 4 May 1 million miners were already on strike, and a further $1\frac{1}{2}$ million workers were called out from the transport, iron and steel, heavy chemicals, power, printing, and building industries. After a week workers in engineering and shipbuilding were called out. The strike ended with the acceptance by the T.U.C. negotiating committee of proposals broadly in line with the Royal Commission's report, although the Miners' Federation rejected these and continued their strike until the end of November.

16 In 1959 the Ministry of Labour made some changes in its Standard Industrial Classification, and this makes strict comparisons difficult. However, the groupings have been corrected to allow for this as far as possible.

17 For example, between 1919 and 1925, 17 official national strikes caused the loss of 150 million working days.

18 This stoppage lasted from 16 May to 1 July 1966 and was in support of a claim for, *inter alia,* the immediate introduction of a 40-hour week during service at sea. The number of workers involved rose, as vessels docked in the United Kingdom, to about 30,000, and the loss of working days has been estimated at around 850,000.

19 See, for example, H. A. Turner and J. Bescoby: 'Strikes, redundancy and the demand cycle in the motor car industry', in *Bulletin of the Oxford Institute of Statistics,* second quarter, 1961.

20 *Ministry of Labour Gazette.*

21 See Turner and Bescoby, op. cit.

22 K. G. J. C. Knowles, op. cit., pp. 234–236.

4

STRIKES AND THE ECONOMY

T. G. Whittingham and B. Towers

The Government's Industrial Relations Act was conceived, born and reared in a period of continuous economic crisis. Thus it is hardly surprising that in the Commons debate on the bill on 15 December 1970, the Prime Minister should have stated that the legislation was 'necessary . . . for our industrial health and for an expanding economy'. He went on to argue that it was vital for dealing with the pressures underlying the collective bargaining system which were inflation and the consequences of industrial disputes and disruptions. Hence among the major objectives of the Industrial Relations Act is the curbing of the incidence of strikes. Thus in the introductory section of the Act (General Principles) it is stated that:

'The provisions of this Act shall have effect for the purpose of promoting good industrial relations in accordance with . . . the principle of developing and maintaining orderly procedures in industry for the peaceful and expeditious settlement of disputes by negotiation, conciliation or arbitration, with due regard to the general interests of the community . . .'

Earlier the Solicitor General, Sir Geoffrey Howe, pointed out that the act had much to do with curbing strike activity. Referring to the British strike pattern he said:

'All the time the picture has been going from bad to worse. By the time the Donovan Commission was appointed in 1965, the number of strikes in industries, apart from coal-mining, had risen from six hundred a year during the 1950s to exactly twice as many in the 1960s.'

The figure had risen to 1,700 in the year before the Donovan Commission reported that 'the prevalence of unofficial strikes and their tendency (outside coal-mining) to increase have such serious economic implications that measures to deal with them are urgently necessary'. By 1969 the figure had risen to 2,930—and that figure has

TABLE I

Stoppages, workers involved and working days lost, beginning in each year 1931–70

Year	Number of stoppages	Number of workers involved (thousands)	Aggregate working days lost (thousands)
1931	420	490	7,010
1932	389	379	6,430
1933	357	136	1,020
1934	474	134	1,060
1935	553	271	1,950
1936	818	316	2,010
1937	1,129	597	3,140
1938	875	274	1,330
1939	940	337	1,350
1940	922	299	940
1941	1,251	360	1,080
1942	1,303	456	1,530
1943	1,785	557	1,830
1944	2,194	821	3,700
1945	2,293	531	2,850
1946	2,205	526	2,180
1947	1,721	620	1,400
1948	1,759	424	1,940
1949	1,426	533	1,820
1950	1,339	302	1,380
1951	1,719	379	1,710
1952	1,714	415	1,800
1953	1,746	1,370	2,170
1954	1,989	448	2,480
1955	2,419	659	3,790
1956	2,648	507	2,050
1957	2,859	1,356	8,400
1958	2,629	523	3,470
1959	2,093	645	5,280
1960	2,832	814	3,050
1961	2,686	771	3,040
1962	2,449	4,420	5,780
1963	2,068	590	2,000
1964	2,524	873	2,030
1965	2,354	868	2,932
1966	1,937	530	2,395
1967	2,116	732	2,783
1968	2,378	2,256	4,672
1969	3,116	1,656	6,789
1970	3,906	1,793	10,854

Source: Department of Employment, DEP, and Ministry of Labour Gazette.

Note: These figures do not distinguish between strikes and lockouts or between official, unofficial, constitutional and unconstitutional stoppages. They also exclude stoppages involving less than ten workers and those which last for less than one day unless the aggregate number of working days lost exceeds one hundred. Time lost at establishments other than those at which the stoppages occurred is also excluded. Other forms of industrial action, e.g. overtime bans, go slows, etc., are also omitted. Finally, it should be noted that not all stoppages are notified to the Department of Employment.

been exceeded in the first nine months of this year. Donovan described the problem as serious and urgent. The gravity and urgency of the problem has certainly not diminished. More significantly, perhaps, Donovan observed that, 'the problem is peculiar to this country'. Sir Geoffrey also said that students of industrial relations had commented that Britain suffered from unofficial strikes to a greater extent than any other western democracy and that in no other did the law play such a passive part.

Given such clear indications of the thinking of the Government about strikes it is highly pertinent to examine the strike pattern in the United Kingdom. Hence, in this article, we analyse trends in strike activity on a national and comparative basis, examine some of the more important economic effects of strikes, assess the nature and importance of what is often referred to as the British strike problem and, finally, offer some conclusions on this contentious and difficult subject.

TRENDS IN STRIKE ACTIVITY

It is perhaps useful initially to take a long-term view of the trend of strikes in this country. This is done in Table I. From this Table it is clear that there has been, since 1967, a dramatic upsurge in the number of stoppages and especially in the aggregate of working days lost. This upturn is in contrast to the relative stability evident from 1933 onwards. Furthermore, this upsurge has continued in 1971. In the first quarter of 1971 some twelve million days were lost in aggregate. However, the postal workers' strike, the Ford workers' strike and strikes against the Industrial Relations Bill accounted for over 80 per cent of this total. Again, if different indicators are used it can be argued that we have now returned to what was normal three years ago.

INCREASING DURATION OF STRIKES

Returning to Table I we can see that the recent increase in the number of stoppages has been substantially less pronounced than the increase in aggregate working days lost. The average annual number of stoppages for the years 1945–67 was 2,153. The 1968 figure showed a 10.5 per cent increase and there were increases of 44.7 per cent and 81.4 per cent for 1969 and 1970 respectively, all calculated on the 1945–67 annual average. As regards aggregate working days lost, the annual average for 1945–67 was 2,901,000 and there were increases for 1968, 1969 and 1970 of 61.0, 134.0, and 274.1 per cent respectively on this figure. Hence although there has been a marked increase in the 'propensity to strike' this has been overshadowed by the growing economic impact of strikes as measured by the growth in aggregate working days lost. This can largely be explained by the fact that strikes are, on average, tending to increase in duration, as can be seen from Table II.

TABLE II

Analysis of stoppages by duration

Stoppages beginning in year	1960 %	1965 %	1968 %	1969 %	1970 %
Not more than 1 day	39.2	34.3	28.6	29.9	24.6
Over 1 and not more than 2 days	24.9	21.6	20.5	19.7	16.9
Over 2 and not more than 3 days	12.6	12.9	11.9	12.7	13.4
Over 3 and not more than 4 days	6.7	7.7	8.0	7.7	7.8
Over 4 and not more than 5 days	4.4	5.6	6.0	6.3	7.3
Over 5 and not more than 6 days	2.2	3.0	4.3	3.4	4.8
Over 6 and not more than 12 days	5.6	7.6	11.1	11.1	12.2
Over 12 and not more than 18 days	1.4	2.8	4.0	3.4	5.4
Over 18 and not more than 24 days	1.0	1.2	2.0	1.9	2.3
Over 24 and not more than 36 days	1.1	1.7	1.7	1.8	3.1
Over 36 and not more than 60 days	0.4	1.2	1.1	1.2	1.5
Over 60 days	0.5	0.4	0.8	0.9	9.7
	100.0	100.0	100.0	100.0	100.0

Source: Ministry of Labour, *DEP* and *DE Gazettes* (various issues).

This observation concerning the tendency for strikes to increase in duration needs some qualification. In the first place, although there is a trend towards greater length, the 'typical' British strike lasts less than three days, as can be seen from Table III.

Secondly, the trend towards longer strikes has not, apparently, continued into 1971, as Table IV makes clear.

Thus there is support for the return-to-normal thesis; but here one

TABLE III
Stoppages of less than three days duration as percentages of all stoppages beginning in each selected year

1960	1965	1968	1969	1970
76.7	68.8	61.0	62.3	54.9

Source: Table 2.

TABLE IV
Stoppages of less than three days duration as percentages of all stoppages ending in each month, January to April 1971

January	February	March	April
45.0	48.8	52.2	55.8

Source: DE Gazette, February, March, April, May 1971.

should be cautious because of the obvious pitfalls in comparing a four-month trend with one encompassing a decade. What is widely accepted is that the vast majority of these strikes must be unofficial because of their short duration relative to the time necessary to convene the body responsible for declaring them official. Even here there would appear to have been a smaller proportion of unofficial stoppages in 1970 and the first three months of 1971 as compared with the sixties. However, this conclusion must remain tentative since it is based upon the proportion of strikes that last six days or less; and in most unions it takes at least six days for the national officials to learn of the strike, convene the appropriate body to consider making it official, and then transmit the decision to the strikers.

UNCONSTITUTIONAL STRIKES

Equally, it is now widely accepted that many short-duration strikes are also unconstitutional. Some evidence for this is found in the Government Social Survey's study of 'workplace industrial relations', for which 1,161 shop stewards and 121 personnel officers were questioned about the duration of the last strike experienced. According to the stewards, 84 per cent of strikes lasted less than six days, and according to the personnel officers, 88 per cent. On the question of whether procedure had been exhausted within the firm or nationally before the strike (that is was it constitutional or not?) the stewards said that in 58 per cent of the strikes it was and in 34 per cent it was not. The personnel officers, interestingly, stated that in 19 per cent of the strikes procedure was exhausted, while in 79 per cent it was not.[2]

It is useful at this stage to summarise the statistical findings so far. The two more important aspects would seem to be:

(a) Over the last three years, the aggregate of days lost by strikes has increased much more rapidly than the number of strikes.

(b) The typical British strike is still brief, unofficial and unconstitutional.

In addition, there are two less important and more challengeable aspects:

(c) It is possible to detect some slackening off in the proportion of unofficial strikes in the total.

(d) The upsurge in strikes may have passed its peak and we may be returning to the pre-1968 situation.

THE ECONOMIC IMPACT OF STRIKES

Any discussion of strikes will be influenced, consciously or unconsciously, by the economic background. Much of the widespread concern over strikes in the United Kingdom reflects the persistence and apparent intractability of some of our economic problems, especially the relatively low rates of growth and productivity and the difficulty of securing a healthy balance of payments. It is perhaps no exaggeration to say that much of this concern would probably evaporate should the major economic problems be solved. However, in present circumstances there appears to be considerable public concern over the issue of strikes. A recent National Opinion Poll, based upon a systematic probability sample of 1,867 electors in one hundred representative constituencies and carried out between 8 and 14 June 1971, found that strikes were given a third ranking in a question concerning the prime issues facing Britain today.[3]

What is the economic impact of strikes? Here it is convenient to analyse at two levels – that of the national economy and major industries and that of the single firm.

At the national level, in terms of working days lost as a proportion of total working days, the effect of strikes, even over the last three years and particularly over the first five months of 1971, appears insignificant. In crude terms, the total loss of output in 1970, as a proportion of gross national product, amounted to 0.20 per cent, and that year, as can be seen from Table I, was exceptional in terms of aggregate working days lost. Inevitably, these calculations are imprecise and they ignore possible 'ripple effects'. These may be external or internal. Externally, our strikes record may affect foreign attitudes towards Britain both as a supplier of goods and services and as a recipient of investment. Internally, a strike in one firm or sector may affect others. The fact that these effects are

International comparison of days lost through industrial disputes, 1957–69
(Days lost per 1,000 persons employed)[1] Annual Averages

	1957–61	1962–66	1957–66	Rank based on average for ten years 1957–66	1960–64	1965–69	1960–69	Rank based on average for ten years 1960–69
Australia[2]	306	356	331	10	350	456	403	12
Belgium	636	180	408	13	164	156	160	6
Canada	596	764	680	15	460	1,556	1,008	16
Denmark[3]	700	110	405	12	708	110	409	13
Finland	248	338	293	8	340	206	273	10
France	288	322	305	9	352	243(a)	303(b)	11
Federal Republic of Germany[4]	26	34	30	3	34	10	22	3
India	760	498	629	14	498	976	737	14
Ireland	342	1,188	765	16	686	1,350	1,018	17
Italy	676	1,386	1,031	18	1,220	1,574	1,397	18
Japan	470	250	360	11	302	198	250	8
Netherlands	61	16	38	4	62	12	37	4
New Zealand	50	170	110	5	154	242	198	7
Norway	140	98	119	6	212	4	108	5
Sweden[5]	10	26	18	2	6	28	17	2
Switzerland	—	10	5	1	10	—	1	1
United Kingdom[6]	352	230	291	7	242	294	268	9
United States[7]	1,166	792	979	17	722	1,232	977	15

1 Industries covered are mining, manufacturing, construction and transport.
2 Including electricity and gas.
3 Manufacturing only.
4 Excluding West Berlin (and the Saar up to 1958).
6 All industries included.
Owing to changes in industrial classification figures from 1959 onwards not strictly comparable with previous years.
7 Beginning 1960: including Alaska and Hawaii. Figures cover also electricity, gas and sanitary services.
(a) Average for 1965–67 and 1969 only.
(b) Average for 1959–67 and 1969 only.

Sources: Ministry of Labour Gazette, November 1967 and DE Gazette, February 1971.

difficult to quantify should not be taken to mean that they are not important. Perhaps the more important of these two types of effect is the external, given Britain's position as a trading nation. Table V shows our record as compared with those of other countries.

It is perhaps stating the obvious to say that international statistical data must in general be treated with caution. For example, there are differences in national official definitions of strikes. Given these problems, too much significance should not be attached to relatively small differences in the figures. However, the ten-year averages in Table V show that the United Kingdom has moved from seventh to ninth place in terms of working days lost per thousand workers employed. This may indicate a downward trend, especially in the light of the figures for 1970 and 1971.[4]

Of course, differences in aggregate days lost between countries are a function of many variables. Among the more important of such variables would appear to be the industrial structure, the propensity to strike, the impact of the culture, the government and its agencies and other relevant non-governmental agencies.

NEED FOR GOVERNMENT INTERVENTION

Despite this complexity there appears to be a kind of political consensus in Britain regarding the need for a degree of governmental intervention, in that both parties have at least attempted to use legislation as an instrument of change in the industrial relations system. Probably the major reason for such a consensus is that the centre of British strike activity is to be found in the 'key' industries serving export markets and those home markets in which there is a high propensity to import. Mechanical and electrical engineering and motor-vehicle manufacture consistently rank high in terms of number of stoppages, number of workers involved, total working days lost and days lost per thousand workers employed. These industries are, of course, key exporters. For example, in 1969, mechanical and electrical machinery and transport equipment accounted for 48 per cent of exports of manufactures and 41 per cent of all exports. In the same year the import figures were approximately 32 per cent and 16 per cent respectively. These figures underline the significance of strikes in these industries.

Such industries may also be regarded as 'image makers' in the eyes of foreign customers (that is the reliability or otherwise of firms within them as suppliers of goods, providers of services and so forth, is an oft-quoted factor underlying the decision of foreign customers to buy from British manufacturers or their competitors). Hence, strike patterns in these industries are important in the psychology of decision-making in markets for British exports.

Mr. Robert Carr commented recently on the foreign impression of the British at work in the following terms:

'I know that in recent years there has grown up a too widely held impression that the most typical picture of the British at work is of the British on strike. I once saw in a European journal a series of cartoons depicting different national characteristics. The British one bore the caption "757 varieties of strikes".'

Mr. Carr went on to point out that the actual facts do not support this image.[5] Perhaps we can take the argument further and suggest that action may often be more a function of belief than fact.

STRIKE PROBLEM SECTORAL

It would probably be reasonable to conclude from this part of the analysis that in economic terms, if there is a British strike problem, it is sectoral rather than national. A final statistic bearing on this point is that the three key industries mentioned above contained 13 per cent of employees in employment in September 1970.[6]

When we move to the level of the organisation, there is evidence, according to Professor Turner, suggesting an even heavier concentration of strikes.[7] He points out that in 1965, some 31 establishments experienced five or more officially-recorded strikes, and in 1966 the number was 27, several of them appearing in both lists. The statistics supplied by the motor manufacturers to the Donovan Commission imply that some 60 per cent of the time lost from disputes 'within the companies' occurred in a single firm. An unpublished study of disputes in a major shipbuilding region shows that the company which experienced most strikes over the post-war period ranked sixth in shares of local output. In the metal-working trades he deduces from the Department of Employment and Productivity's summaries of 'principal stoppages' supported by press reports that nearly half the strikes occur in one hundred firms.

DANGER OF STRIKE NEUROSIS

The danger here would appear to be that managers may develop a strike fixation which can easily grow into a more serious state of strike neurosis. This problem may often be compounded by an attitude on the shop floor which converts the use of the strike weapon from an exceptional to a normal action. This attitude may be reinforced by the knowledge that striking brings economic rewards to the strikers. The point is frequently made that striking in pursuit of inflationary wage settlements is self-defeating. However, this view fails to take into account the fact that a wage increase is certainly not immediately eroded by prices, and also that for small groups of workers gains may be made at the expense of others. Of course, in macroeconomic terms all inflationary wage increases are ultimately self-defeating, but such a global argument often fails to influence particular groups, especially when it runs counter to their own experience.

It is useful at this stage to summarise the points made in this section.

(a) At the level of the national economy and major industries, in terms of aggregate working days lost as a proportion of total working days, strikes are statistically insignificant. This is true even over the last three years and the first five months of 1971. However, this statement ignores the possible 'ripple' effects. Internally these are the effects of a strike in one firm or sector upon others. Although they are difficult to quantify they are important in assessing the overall effects of strikes.

(b) Perhaps more important than the internal are the external ripple effects–given Britain's position as a trading nation.

(c) In this context it is a serious matter for the United Kingdom that the centre of the strike pattern is in industries which have great importance both in export markets and in those home markets where there is a high propensity to import. Such 'key' industries are also important as 'image makers' in the eyes of foreign customers.

CONCLUSIONS

Such problems as Britain has in the matter of strikes are largely associated with particular organisations. Many of these organisations are to be found within industries which would seem to be particularly strike prone. Given this situation, any attempt to deal with the problem ought surely to reflect its nature: that is, its solution should be sought on a piecemeal, selective basis. Perhaps this suggests a role for the Commission on Industrial Relations. It could be given a strategic role in the analysis of strike-prone sectors, companies and establishments within the economy. Its specific task might be to seek out such organisations, conduct an analysis of their problems and make recommendations. Perhaps such recommendations would need legal backing. But whatever course is followed, it needs to be recognised that we are dealing with a very complex problem. Alvin W. Gouldner has reminded us of this when he notes that, 'a "strike" is a social phenomenon of enormous complexity which, in its totality, is never susceptible to complete description, let alone complete explanation'.[8]

NOTES

1 In a speech to the Industrial Law Society in London on 21 November 1970.
2 SS 402 HMSO, London, March 1968, pp. 141–2.
3 Reported in the *Daily Mail*, 21 June 1971.
4 See Table 1 for the 1970 figures. For the first five months of 1971, 10,397,000 days were lost (excluding days lost from strikes against the Industrial Relations Bill). *Source: Department of Employment Gazette*, June 1971.
5 Speech to the Third Annual Forum of the Institute of Collective Bargaining and Group Relations, New York, Tuesday, 25 May 1971.
6 *DE Gazette*, May 1971
7 H. A. Turner, *Is Britain Really Strike-Prone?* CUP, Cambridge, 1969.
8 *Wildcat Strike*, Routledge and Kegan Paul, London, 1955, p. 65.

5

RECENT BRITISH STRIKE TRENDS: A FACTUAL ANALYSIS

Michael Silver

The statistics of industrial conflict present the would-be scientist with a difficult dilemma. Incomplete and sometimes arbitrary in design, they must be regarded as lacking in reliability and being of very dubious validity for many purposes.[1] On the other hand, they are all we have; the only tangible thermometer of organized and overt industrial conflict and, as such, central to government policy-making. Regardless of whether or not they are perceived as the great unsolved social problem of the age, strikes are a dramatic and fascinating aspect of industrial relations and trends in strikes are a focal point of almost any analysis of industrial relations systems at work. The only sensible way out of this dilemma is to be realistic. If strike statistics are inescapable and necessary tools of analysis, then let them be used as resourcefully and systematically as possible. Whenever they are capable of honest refinement, let them be so treated. Where they can be supplemented by alternative sources of information, let them be so embellished.

Recent analysis of Britain's strike statistics have demonstrably failed to measure up to these criteria and have suffered from a number of other weaknesses. In the first place, the treatment of the statistics has been insufficiently careful and comprehensive to uncover important trends and to avoid making substantial errors in the interpretation of the figures. Secondly, discussion of the characteristic features of British industrial conflict has been weighted too heavily towards the aspects of unofficiality and unconstitutionality. Thirdly, there has to date been an absence of research work into the strike statistics of very recent years and the way in which, if at all, they differ from those of the past.

This paper will attempt to make a first step towards remedying these deficiencies. Rather than setting out to support a particular argument, an effort will be made to furnish the statistical raw materials from which more general conclusions can later be drawn. It may of course be argued that by not going into the meaning of the figures one is inviting their misuse. For example, one of the following sections attempts to establish the comparative trends of authorized and unauthorized industrial disputes. It is only proper to admit that such information of itself can provide little concrete understanding of the changing role of the workplace in industrial conflict. It can still be argued, however, that there is considerable justification at the present time for undertaking the more pedestrian task of returning to the sources of quantitative information on strikes and presenting them in a form in which they can usefully be applied to some of the key issues in the discussion of strike trends. The present paper will attempt only to perform the task of getting the facts straight, rather than interpreting them, and this will be done with special reference to the published strike statistics of the last thirteen years. First, however, we must attempt to assess the meaning and significance of these statistics.

THE NATURE OF THE STRIKE STATISTICS[2]

As the Department of Employment points out in every issue of its statistical *Gazette*, British statistics on stoppages of work due to *industrial* disputes are inclusive of both strikes and lockouts and limit their coverage to stoppages where at least ten workers are involved and the dispute lasted at least a day–unless in either case more than 100 working days were 'lost' as a result of the stoppage. The implications of this statistical definition of the strike should be carefully considered. To begin with, the combining of figures for strikes and lockouts has only a negligible effect on the overall statistics. We know, for example, that the residual category used by the Ministry of Labour in analysing strikes in the mid-1960s for the Donovan Commission was made up of lockouts, strikes by non-unionists and unclassifiable disputes. This group *in toto* only accounted for about 25 strikes a year and under 4 per cent of the annual number of days lost.

The exclusion of so-called 'political' disputes from the statistics is a rather more contentious matter, since although such stoppages may lack even latent industrial causes, they certainly have industrial *consequences*. There are also certain 'political' strikes which are so basic to building up a picture of a particular year's strike activity that they cannot be ignored. The one-day strikes against the Industrial Relations Bill in 1971 are a case in point–in all there were more than twice as many workers involved in these three stoppages as in the whole year's industrial disputes.

Finally, only those strikes which come to the notice of local officers of the Department of Employment find their way into the statistics. Hyman has suggested that this system of collecting strike data leaves too much to the discretion of employers, some of whom may be

> more efficient or scrupulous than others. Situations may tempt companies to be liberal or restrictive in their recording: a firm wanting to give an impression of harmonious industrial relations may turn a blind eye to certain disputes; employers keen to provide evidence for legal restrictions on the right to strike may record numerous minor incidents which would otherwise go unrecorded.[3]

In short, strike statistics are incomplete, and therefore represent a 'sample' of the entire 'population' of strikes which actually occur. It is difficult to know exactly how representative this sample is, nor do we know how complete it is in its coverage. In the current context of strikes in Britain these deficiencies constitute quite serious limitations, since attention has tended to focus upon the relative significance of strikes which are small in size and brief in duration and these are the very ones which are most likely to escape the Department of Employment's net. Turner cites figures of about 30 per cent and 80 per cent respectively as the proportions of strikes noted 'internally' which did not find their way into the official statistics in the coal mining and motor industries respectively in certain years in the 1960s.[4] It may be added, however, that the use of uniform standards for determining the eligibility of a stoppage for inclusion in the government statistics also has advantages, going some way to meet Hyman's charge of employer manipulation of strike records.

A more serious challenge to the usefulness of strike statistics is raised by the fact that strikes are by no means homogenous phenomena. At the heart of any statistical aggregation of data there is an assumption that each datum is equivalent to every other datum in the same category; that is why they can legitimately be added together. In the case of strikes, not even the use of apparently standardized units of measurement for assessing strike activity, such as the number of workers involved or the number of days lost can overcome this problem. The social and economic significance of neither of these indices can be predicted from their magnitude alone – any given number of days lost, for example, could be the product of a one-day stoppage which gave a whole industry the chance to off-load stocks, or the result of a protracted dispute which bankrupted a single company.

Are we, then, to be reduced to a historical case-by-case approach to industrial conflict in order to give meaning to strike statistics?

Fortunately not, because it can be demonstrated that strike statistics, especially after secondary computations have been made, evince a degree of patterning and regularity which is suggestive not only of unitary characteristics which embrace the diverse components of the aggregate statistics, but also of the operation of some kind of 'invisible hand' evenly guiding *trends* in strike activity at many levels and in many places. Basically these assertions rest on two types of evidence.

(1) As will be demonstrated later, the strike behaviour of different industries exhibits highly comparable trends, in both the frequency and incidence of strikes.[5] Particularistic factors are obviously responsible for differences between industries in their levels of industrial conflict, but relative changes in those levels appear to be reasonably uniform across nearly all industries, suggesting that they are subject to common influences. Knowles has explained this 'correspondence' as being 'due not only to the fact that economic and political changes tend to affect all industries together, but also . . . (that there is) . . . a certain "momentum" which develops when workers come out on strike in a major industry. Strikes tend to be contagious, especially if established wage differentials are altered'.[6]

(2) Multivariate analysis of strikes and macro-economic indicators has provided convincing mathematical evidence of the existence of generalized influences operating on the national frequency of strikes and being largely responsible for trends in their number from year to year. For example, Pencavel's study of the frequency of strikes outside coal mining in the U.K. between 1950 and 1967 found that 87 per cent of the variance in strike activity over this period was attributable to four variables: the time of year, the unemployment rate, the level of real wages, and the ratio of profits to wages.[7] Similar analysis of data for several individual industries confirmed that changes in macro-economic variables are strongly associated with trends in the frequency of strikes.

It seems reasonable to conclude that, while the meaning of given levels of industrial conflict is subject to important qualifications, strike trends constitute a valid and relevant subject for study, and it is to this task that we now turn.

BRITAIN AMONG THE NATIONS

Considerations of the strike situation of the U.K. invariably begin, as the Donovan Commission did, with speculation about Britain's strike proneness in comparison with other countries. The word 'speculation' is used advisedly–the complications inherent in making inter-country comparisons of strike behaviour, which were brought home so forcefully by the debate between Turner[8] and McCarthy,[9] appear to rule out reliable use of the international statistics for this purpose. Nevertheless, it does seem to be generally accepted that the number of working days lost per thousand workers constitutes a useful comparative measure, firstly because it automatically adjusts for differences between countries in the sizes of their labour forces, secondly because it constitutes a rough index of the economic cost of strikes, and thirdly because it is unlikely to be severely affected by international differences in the scope of strike statistics, since these differences mainly bear on the smallest and shortest strikes (which usually contribute relatively little to the total number of days lost).

If one accepts the assumption–inherent in the analysis of the strike statistics of a single nation–that the scope of the statistics and the method of collecting them have not undergone significant changes over time, it seems reasonable to expect that any alteration in the position of a given country in an international 'league table' of days lost per thousand workers would be indicative of a genuine change in the incidence of strikes in that country compared with all the others.

In 1971 Whittingham and Towers attempted just such an analysis of the figures for days lost through industrial disputes per thousand persons employed which the Department of Employment now publishes each year for eighteen countries.[10] They then assigned ranks (from lowest to highest) to each country's average for two ten-year periods, 1957–66 and 1960–9. Their conclusion was that 'the United Kingdom, using ten-year averages, has moved from seventh to ninth in terms of working days lost per thousand workers employed. This may indicate a downward trend (i.e. a rise in Britain's relative strike-proneness)'.[11]

Unfortunately, the use of ten-year 'moving averages' to analyse a period of only thirteen years, and the fact that only two such averages were compared, rendered the technique less effective than it should have been. Britain's strike record is such that the particular ten-year averages calculated by Whittingham and Towers were bound to conceal the actual changes in the position of the U.K. which did occur from 1957–69. The two ten-year periods they used were 1957–66 and 1960–9. Thus the years 1960–6 are common to both periods, and the years 'unique' to each one are 1957–9 in the first, and 1967–9 in the second period. Yet both of the 'unique' periods had abnormally high numbers of days lost in comparison with the years between them. To compound the difficulties, a full third of the countries for which information is available have gaps in their figures for various years, in fact in some cases only one or two figures are available for the whole series. By coincidence, with a few minor exceptions, all six of the countries concerned are consistently less strike prone than Britain. Since Whittingham and Towers ranked their data in ascending order their calculations were bound to be distorted by irregular omissions of data.

If the countries with gaps in their information are excluded from consideration and the remaining twelve ranked in *descending* order, it can be shown that with the exception of one year (1962), the figures fall into three discrete periods: 1957–60, in which Britain's modal rank was seven; 1961–7, in which it fell to nine; and 1968–70, when it rose once more to seventh. In view of the high degree of internal consistency in each of these periods, it seems fair to conclude that in the last few years Britain's strike-proneness in international terms has suffered a fairly significant increase; one which will doubtless be seen to have continued when the record figures for 1971 and 1972 are incorporated in the analysis.

THE COAL INDUSTRY AND THE TREND OF STRIKES IN THE U.K.

Any discussion of the national pattern of strike activity in the U.K. must begin by examining the position of the coal mining industry. In terms of numbers employed, the industry has for long had a conspicuously high level of strike incidence. But at least until very recently the significance of coal mining for strikes analysis has been a product of the enormous *number* of coal strikes, rather than their contribution to the time each year that Britain's workers spend on strike. In the post-war era the frequency of coal strikes reached an all-time peak in 1957, at which time the industry was responsible for over three-quarters of the total number of strikes. The number of coal strikes had in fact been steadily rising throughout the 1950s, while at the same time the frequency of strikes in the rest of the economy had been remarkably stable, and thus it was the coal mining sector alone which was behind the apparent upward trend in Britain's strike-proneness in this period.

In the 1960s, however, almost the opposite 'distortion' occurred, as the number of coal strikes fell rapidly and steadily downwards (until in the last few years they have represented only around 5 per cent of all strikes), while the number of stoppages outside of coal mining was rising quite considerably. Once again the overall figures for strike frequency, if looked at in isolation, paint a very misleading picture of the underlying forces at work. The changing contribution of the coal industry to the national frequency of strikes since 1959 very clearly demonstrates the tremendous increase in strikes outside mining over almost the whole of the period (they had increased nearly five-fold by 1970) compared with the relative stability of the nation-wide frequency of strikes (which, in 1970, was barely double its 1959 level).[12] The importance of excluding coal strikes from the analysis of national trends can also be demonstrated by comparing a centred index of the national frequency of strikes (Column 1 of the Statistical Appendix) with the comparable figure for non-mining strikes (Column 8). It can be shown in this way that in three of the thirteen years under consideration (1961, 1962 and 1965) the inclusion of coal strikes in the total has the effect of actually *reversing* the trend of strikes elsewhere.

The 'withering away' of the coal strike since about 1959 has, then, created a situation in which trends in national strike frequency cannot possibly be comprehended unless a differentiation is made between strikes in coal mining and those in all other industries.[13] The position of the coal industry as a 'special case' is underlined by the fact that at precisely the same time as the relative significance of coal strikes was being subjected to such a radical alteration, virtually all other inter-industry variations in strike behaviour were remarkably stable.[14]

In addition to the statistical evidence of the uniqueness of strike trends in the coal industry, empirical studies of industrial relations in coal mining lend support to the hypothesis that the forces making for a decline in coal strikes have been largely confined to this industry alone.[15] A fragmented bargaining structure and fluctuating earnings due to frequent changes in working conditions at the coal face were at one time the key features of industrial relations in the coal industry. These factors have been very largely eliminated by the introduction of mechanization into mining together with increasing centralization of the system of collective bargaining, most notably as a consequence of the National Power-loading Agreement of 1966. Coupled with a decline in the size of the industry's labour-force, these changes appear to have been at the root of the fall in the frequency of coal strikes over the last decade. Interestingly, however, research on the coal sector has shown that this fall has certainly not meant an end to industrial conflict in the wider sense. At the same time as the level of overt conflict has been declining, there appears to have been a compensating increase in absenteeism, accidents, and voluntary wastage.[16]

The pattern as well as the level of industrial conflict has been undergoing important changes. Stoppages have become fewer but also larger in scale and longer in duration (this is the case even without taking into account the national coal strike of 1972). Further, by compounding coal statistics with those for the rest of the economy not only is the overall frequency of strikes distorted, but so also is the number of stoppages of a particular *character*– the brief, small-scale, localized strike which is directed at an adjustment of piece-rates. Thus the inclusion of coal industry data in nation-wide statistics on the size, length and causes of strikes would also create spurious trends or conceal genuine ones. Wherever possible, therefore, the coal mining figures have been excluded from the statistics calculated for this paper.

THE INDUSTRIAL DISTRIBUTION OF STRIKES

The enormity of the decline in coal strikes is underscored by the very large increases in the frequency of strikes in other industries which have occurred in recent years. Thus in the brief period 1963–70 (1970 was the year in which U.K. strike activity reached its highest level ever) only two of the fifteen industry groups considered in this study less than doubled their strike frequencies (they are Coal, of course, and Shipbuilding); and in a full half of all the industries under consideration there was a four- to six-fold rise.

It is important, however, that the exact degree to which there has been inter-industry uniformity in the rise in strike frequency should be ascertained. H. A. Turner, for example, took the view that the strike activity formerly concentrated among coal miners had been 'dispersed' elsewhere, mainly into the metal-working sector of the economy, and he described this 'counterbalancing increase in strike-proneness' as having occurred on a 'comparatively narrow front'.[17] On the one hand it is perfectly true that the metal-working industries, when considered together, do indeed constitute much the same proportion of *total* strike activity today as coal mining did a decade ago. Thus in 1971 the combination of strike totals in the Engineering, Vehicles, Metal, and Shipbuilding industries produces a figure of 43 per cent of all strikes in that year, compared with, for example, a figure of 45 per cent for coal mining strikes in 1962. But if coal strikes are excluded from consideration, it turns out that these same metal-working industries accounted for 46 per cent of all non-mining strikes in 1971, as against 42 per cent in 1968, 44 per cent in 1965, 40 per cent in 1962, and 43 per cent in 1959. Clearly, the relative position of these industries has hardly altered throughout the period of the decline in coal strikes. The present-day prominence of the metal-working sector in the total strike picture is not a result of any alteration in the relative strike-proneness of the various industries outside of coal, but is a simple and direct consequence of the drop in mining disputes.

The constancy of inter-industry strike propensities outside mining is most clearly borne out by the application of statistical tests to the data for the fourteen non-mining industries found in the statistical Appendix (Columns 26–40). The Kendall Coefficient of Concordance, w, can be used to measure the degree of stability over time in the relative ranking of the various industries on some scale of strike-proneness. Applying it to the frequency of strikes from 1959–71 yields a value for w of 0·92 indicating a degree of association significant at better than the 1 per cent level. Thus, while the metal-working and 'Un-named' industries are now the most predominantly strike-prone industries, most of the others have been expanding their shares of the strike cake as well–and at roughly the same rate.

Examination of the degree of correlation between strike trends in single industries and those in the nation as a whole (outside of coal mining) furnishes additional evidence of the even industrial spread of the increase in strikes. If values of r_S (the Spearman Rank Correlation Coefficient) are computed for 1959–71, it is found that all industries except Ship-building are positively correlated at 0·5 or better with the overall trend, and indeed, that nearly half of them have a value for r_S of over 0·9. It is true, as Turner claimed, that most of the metal-working industries are among what might be termed the 'trend-setters', but they are not alone in exhibiting a close association with total strike activity. Thus the five highest values of r_S are attributable to the Un-named Industries (0·99), Metal Manufacture (0·99), Mechanical & Instrument Engineering (0·98) Overland Transport (0·96), and Electrical Engineering (0·95). Interestingly, those industries which are most removed from the overall trend are on the whole the least strike-prone, although Construction ($r_S = 0·57$) and Shipbuilding ($r_S. = -0·50$) are important exceptions.

While there have been no major shifts in relative strike-proneness between the non-mining industries, the overall rise in strike frequency has meant that, as Hyman has pointed out, 'disputes are becoming common in industries which previously were relatively immune'.[18] This is doubtless the case, but both Hyman and Goodman[19] before him have tried to go one step further by suggesting that strike activity has been becoming broader-based in the sense that the industrial strike leaders have been 'losing' part of their strike-proneness to other industries.

On the one hand, it is of course true that some of the traditionally strike-free industries–most notably in the public sector–have been resorting to the strike weapon far more frequently than would have been expected if increases or decreases in strike activity were uniformly distributed in every case. This is doubtless one of the reasons why the 'Unnamed' industries of our classification, employing nearly half of the labour force, have risen in strike frequency from third place in the early 1960s to second in the mid-sixties, and now, since 1968, into first place. It can also be shown that some of the less strike-prone industries have been increasing their strike totals no less rapidly than their more prominent associates. If strike frequency in the various industries is indexed, taking 1963 as the base year (and assigning it the value 100), the average of the index numbers since 1963 can be taken as a crude means of comparing the extent of the changes in strike frequency. Three of the four 'highest flyers' according to this measure have been Public Utilities, Food & Drink, and Overland Transport–industries which are certainly not the leaders in either strike frequency or incidence.

Even so, the Hyman-Goodman conclusion is far too sweeping. It cannot be disputed that it is the *evenness* of the spread of increased strike activity which has been the primary feature of its industrial distribution. Furthermore, it would appear that the evidence put forward by the above authors was, by chance, actually the product of the choice of industrial groupings analysed and the years for which data was computed. Hyman claims that the share of the five industries with the most stoppages in the total number of non-mining strikes dropped from 69 per cent in 1959 to 52 per cent in 1965 and 47 per cent in 1970. On the other hand, the industry data used in this paper yield values, for the same years, of 62 per cent, 54 per cent and 49 per cent respectively, which have the effect of somewhat deflating the postulated downward trend. But if three-year moving averages are calculated, to minimize the effect of short-term fluctuations, it becomes clear that very little change in this proportion has in fact taken place over the last thirteen years. The figures thus obtained are totally confined within the narrow range of 53–8 per cent and indicate that there is only a very slight trend towards a reduction in the role of the strike-prone industries. Furthermore, the *composition* of the 'Top Five' has shown considerable stability, with Construction, Vehicles, and Mechanical & Instrument Engineering present in all thirteen years, Metal Manufacture in ten, the Docks in seven, Shipbuilding in five, Electrical Engineering in three, and Overland Transport in one.

So far the evidence for uniform industrial trends in strike-proneness has been derived from changes in strike frequency rather than from the days lost through strikes. A convenient way of arriving at the relative incidence of strikes in the various sectors of the economy is by computing the annual number of working days on strike per thousand employees. This index indicates simply the number of days the 'average' thousand employees spent on strike in a given year. In the data under consideration (Columns 26–40) it has varied from as little as two days per thousand employees (in Distribution) to over 6,500 on the Docks – that is to say, a range of roughly five minutes to six and a half days spent on strike per annum by the average worker. Such direct comparisons are, of course, somewhat superficial. As the Department of Employment points out, figures for the

> days lost per 1,000 employees in employment in the industry group(s) . . . should be used with caution when comparing one group with another. Total numbers of days lost comprise those lost at the establishment concerned by workers indirectly involved as well as those directly involved . . . Moreover, 'employees' include administrative, technical and clerical workers, who are normally less involved in stoppages, and the proportion of these varies considerably between industry groups.[20]

Regional variations in strike liability, which appear to be a significant influence in their own right, also affect industrial strike incidence (and frequency too, of course) because of the uneven geographical distribution of the different industrial groups. On the other hand, the argument used in relation to international comparisons also applies here – namely, that in the short term such problems of comparability should not constitute any serious obstacle to a useful comparison of *trends* (as opposed to absolute levels) of strike incidence. With this is mind, the statistical test (Kendall's w) already performed for strike frequency was applied to the data on strike incidence. The value of w thus obtained was 0·81 – lower than for the concordance of the strike frequencies, but nevertheless significant once again at better than the one per cent level. In addition, since a significant proportion of the days lost through industrial disputes are a result of 'major confrontations' (which are unevenly spread both through time and between industries) it is likely that further analysis of concordance in strike incidence which omitted these bigger stoppages would reveal an even closer association between industries in their strike behaviour.

THE DISTRIBUTION OF STRIKE ACTIVITY AT THE MICRO LEVEL

Up to now we have been emphasizing the relative uniformity in strike trends among different industries. This, it will be remembered, was the evidence on which we based our earlier conclusion that there was some kind of 'invisible hand' at work spreading changes in strike activity evenly over almost the whole of the economy. It would be quite wrong, however, to ignore the very real differences in *levels* of strike activity and incidence in the different sectors of the economy. One of the most important points in Professor Turner's paper was contained in the following statement: 'The problem of industrial unrest in Britain may be, not so much that its incidence is high, as that it is not too well distributed'.[21]

Regrettably, strike statistics are too broad in scope to afford more than a superficial understanding of the circumstances associated with conditions of strike-proneness. We know, of course, that particular firms, towns and industries–some of them central to the health of the economy–suffer an enormously disproportionate share of industrial strife. Unfortunately, however, the use of statistics for the analysis of strike behaviour carries with it a built-in tendency to try and arrive at averages for everything. For example, considering the number of strikes and the number of days lost per thousand trade unionists over the last decade or so, and allowing for occasions when workers go on strike more than once a year or are involved in stoppages indirectly, then a very rough calculation can be made indicating that the average union member goes on strike once (and sometimes more) every twelve years, for a period of about two and a half days at a time. Averages, however, are notorious for their obscurity, and a number of studies have shown this to be particularly so in relation to strike statistics.

The engineering industry is perhaps the most prominently strike-prone sector of the economy, and a fair amount of quantitative information has been collected about its strike patterns. Marsh and McCarthy showed that from 1960–6 unconstitutional stoppages (which amounted to about 96 per cent of all strikes by manual workers) took place in an average of only 9 per cent of the 1,000 federated firms under investigation.[22] A more recent survey by Marsh, Evans and Garcia revealed that of 432 federated establishments, 38 per cent had not suffered even one stoppage (of half an hour or more) throughout 1967 and 1968. It appears in fact that just *three* of the 432 establishments in the sample accounted for *41 per cent* of all the strikes reported, and the authors estimate that 'it would not be surprising to find that upwards of 80 per cent of federated engineering managements would think of themselves as strike-free'.[23]

The Workplace Relations Survey conducted for the Royal Commission in 1966 brought to light a number of factors associated with strike-proneness in a broader spectrum of industries than just the engineering sector.[24] For example, it was found that 'large' plants (those with 500 or more employees) were over twice as strike-prone as smaller ones. Turner also cites examples of this extreme variability in liability to industrial conflict which are drawn from studies further afield than engineering–namely from motor-car manufacture and shipbuilding.[25] And yet he too falls victim to the lure of averages.

One of his major complaints has been against the Donovan Commission's thesis that one of the principal costs of unofficial stoppages can be their dampening effect on managerial initiative. The Report in fact suggested that

it is characteristic of unofficial action that it is unpredictable. For the most part it concerns issues which are not regulated by written collective agreements. . . The upshot is that *some* managements lack confidence that the plans they make and the decisions they reach can be implemented. . . This situation is found in its most acute form in the *small number* of establishments where there is what might be termed an 'endemic' strike situation.[26]

In his article 'The Donovan Report' Turner attacked the Commission's view on the grounds that the average manager is rarely involved in a strike. 'If the threat involved amounts to one small strike in twenty years it can hardly be so bad for the average management's nerves as the Commission supposed'.[27] Apart from the fact that the Commission was explicitly drawing attention to the problem of the *atypical* manager, Turner's use of the statistics appears to have been inaccurate. His 'once in twenty years' conclusion is derived from the finding of the Workplace Relations Survey that 'only one-third of the trade unionists consulted could recall there ever having been a strike at their place of employment–at which their average period of personal service was six years'.[28] However, average length of service was actually ten years–so assuming that those who had not yet experienced a strike never would do so, their 'average' strike liability was once in *thirty* years.

Nonetheless, both this figure and Turner's are overridden by one important qualification, namely that a large number of those respondents who had experienced a stoppage since taking up their current job had been involved in *more than one*. Indeed, the Survey revealed that less than half of the trade unionists who recalled having experienced strike action were reporting on just a single stoppage.

Clearly, it is precisely the skewed distribution of strike activity which was the inspiration for the Donovan thesis, and even a careful discussion of *average* experience would be unable either to prove or disprove this thesis. Turner's attitude towards the problem of skewness is in fact somewhat ambivalent. At one point in *Is Britain Really Strike-Prone?* there is the suggestion that 'Of course, . . . the risk (of a strike) is substantially greater in certain sectors of the economy . . . But even . . . in the motor industry, . . . during the two years 1967 and 1968 together, one can reckon from the D.E.P.'s data that the *average* employee was involved in (only) one strike 'within the company' which was big enough to be recorded in the official statistics'.[29] Five pages later, however, one reads that the motor industry is a prime example of unevenly distributed conflict, since 'it appears that from 1962 through October 1965, some 60 per cent of the loss of working time from disputes "within the companies" was attributable to one firm alone, which seems to have had an incidence of disputation (measured in these terms) four times as high as that of the rest of the car-assembly industry'.[30]

TRENDS IN WORKER INVOLVEMENT AND DAYS LOST

Strike frequency, on which most of our attention has so far been concentrated, is of course only one of the three major strike indices, the other two being strike incidence (working time foregone) and worker involvement. Each of these indices, it must be stressed, is capable of serving only limited purposes, and these purposes may overlap very little. They are not simply alternative ways of measuring the same phenomenon, but are representative of at least partially independent features of industrial conflict.

The degree of association between the different measures of industrial conflict – especially strike activity and worker involvement – is quite high. The interrelationship between the three indices is significant in statistical terms (the Kendall Coefficient of Concordance yields a w of 0.7, $0.02 < p < 0.01$). The relative independence of the trend of working days lost compared with those for strikes and strikers may be explained by the fact that this index is a product of the other two indices and a third factor – the duration of stoppages. In 1959, for instance, the number of days lost was falling while the numbers of strikes and of strikers were both rising; exactly the opposite occurred in 1971, and in both cases this was, of course, due to the independent influence of changes in the length of strikes. Clearly, the pattern of conflict in any one year may consist of an unique combination of statistical variables. It is, therefore, of some importance that trends in each of these variables be looked at independently rather than in conjunction with the others.[31]

Following Knowles, we can take 'the number of strikes, as indicating the prevalence of separate outbreaks of discontent; the number of workers involved, as showing the extent of militancy; . . . (and) . . . the number of working days lost, as revealing, in addition, something of the stubbornness of the parties'.[32]

. There are, however, a number of straightforward secondary indices which are rather more useful for deciphering trends in 'militancy' and 'stubbornness'. Thus if we divide the number of strikers by the number of strikes ('strikers per strike') some impression can be gained of the average size of strikes and hence of the scale of episodes of industrial conflict. The 'stubbornness' of the parties is basically another aspect of militancy, in the sense of willingness to *stay* on strike, and is indicated by the duration of stoppages. It is a mistake, however, to use the average length of strikes as a measure of their duration, since wide variations in the size of strikes make the result of such a computation very difficult to interpret. The best index of duration is therefore the amount of time which the 'average' striker spends on strike, i.e. the 'days lost per striker'. In a later section trends in the size and length of stoppages will be discussed with reference to these secondary indices rather than to the numbers of strikers and days lost. The latter are, however, of interest for other purposes.

Worker Involvement in Strikes

The aggregate number of workers involved in strikes (Columns 2 and 9) is not a very sensitive indicator of trends in the extent of worker participation in industrial conflict, for a number of reasons.

(1) In the first place, only the occurrence and not the *degree* of 'involvement' is indicated by this statistic, and hence in years when the numbers involved appear to rise (as was the case in the peak years of 1962 and 1968), it is necessary to ask whether this was the result of widespread escalation of industrial strife or merely the effect of a change in the *form* of strike activity. In the years referred to above just such an innovation did occur, in the form of 'very occasional industry-wide official stoppages as a means of pressure in national wage-negotiations (in the engineering industry)'.[33]

(2) Although we have loosely referred to the number of workers involved in disputes as the number of 'strikers', the statistics are actually inclusive of employees *in the same establishment* who are 'thrown out of work' because their fellow-workers are on strike. In recent years this number has constituted a quarter of all workers involved in industrial disputes. In the 1960s changes in the estimated number of workers 'indirectly' involved in strikes have tended to lag behind trends in the *total* numbers involved (Columns 2 and 4). Thus the proportion of 'genuine strikers' in the total number of workers involved in strikes have tended to lag behind trends in the at about 75–80 per cent in the middle of the decade, rose again in 1968 but has since been steadily dropping back to pre-1968 levels. The implication would seem to be that lately an increasing number of workers have been laid idle because of

industrial conflict through no wish of their own. However, there are factors such as changes in technology and in the size of enterprises which have major implications for the secondary effects of strikes but which the statistics obviously cannot take into account. Furthermore, given the difficulties faced by the Department of Employment in collecting accurate information on numbers indirectly involved, and the fact that the statistics anyway do not include workers at non-struck establishments who have stopped work involuntarily,[34] not too much confidence can be placed in apparent trends in this index.

(3) There are some workers in the more strike-prone sectors of the economy who go on strike more than once in a year and hence are counted more than once in figures for total worker involvement. In 1967, the last year for which rough estimates were made of the 'net' number of strikers, the proportion which individual strikers constituted of the total figure for workers involved was put at 93 per cent and it appeared to have been rising—presumably an indication that 'multiple strikers' were becoming proportionately less important. (See Column 3).

(4) Finally, the number of workers involved needs to be adjusted for changes in the size of the labour force and changes in the number of workers belonging to trade unions, since both of these parameters clearly set limits to the number of potential strikers. In spite of the contraction in the size of the labour force since about the mid-1960s, trends in strikers per thousand workers have followed those for the total number of strikers fairly closely. The same is broadly true of strikers per thousand unionists (Column 11), although the relative expansion of union membership in recent years has had the effect of making the simultaneous rise in the number of strikers appear slightly less dramatic.

Despite these various reservations which must be borne in mind when assessing the significance of trends in worker involvement it can safely be said, in considering figures outside the coal industry, that the years since 1968 have seen the aggregate number of workers involved in strikes, like the number of strikes, enter a new dimension of magnitude. Considering the period since 1959, 1968 was the first year in which the number of strikes reached and even exceeded the two thousand mark, and the first (apart from 1962) in which the number of strikers was more than a million; so far there has been no return to earlier levels in either case, notwithstanding the reduction in strike activity in 1971.

Working Days Lost

This index (Columns 5 and 12), being compounded of the aggregate number of strikers and the average duration of the strikes in which they took part, produces trends which are not easily explicable without reference to its component factors. It is, however, usually thought of as a useful rough-and-ready guide to trends in the economic cost of strikes–which, of course, helps to explain why public concern about Britain's so-called strike problem has been increasing in recent years. Looking again at all industries outside coal mining, we find that in the period 1959–68, with the exception of the years 1959 and 1962 (in which strike incidence was exceptionally high), the number of working days lost through industrial disputes fluctuated between $1\frac{1}{2}$ and $2\frac{1}{2}$ million a year. Since then it has risen enormously–by four million days in both 1970 and 1971– until in 1971 the total number of days lost was the highest since the General Strike of 1926. This is all the more remarkable when one considers that in 1971 both the number of strikes and the number of strikers fell considerably–and the increase in the number of working days lost was therefore entirely a result of the fact that the duration of strikes (in terms of days lost per striker) doubled in a single year.

TRENDS IN THE SIZE AND DURATION OF STRIKES

It is useful in discussing trends in the size and length of strikes to distinguish between the characteristics of the *average* strike and those of the *modal* (most common) dispute. In average terms (the overall number of strikers per strike) the stoppages of the 1960s have been considerably larger in scale than those in the earlier post-war years. However, as the figures in Column 10 of the Appendix demonstrate, within this phase of apparently bigger strikes, the trend from year to year has not been particularly consistent. The average duration of strikes, i.e. the overall number of days lost per striker (Column 13), has shown trends of a similarly variable nature.

However, this is not the whole of the story. For a number of years now, by far the majority of Britain's strikes have been small in size and brief in duration. But in the period covered by our figures (Columns 6 and 7) the relative significance of these small, short strikes has been declining. Between 1959 and 1971 the proportion of all strikes which were 'small' (involved less than 250 workers) dropped slowly but steadily from 80 per cent to 72 per cent and in the same period the percentage of days lost in 'short' strikes (lasting three days or less) fell from 78 per cent to 51 per cent. However, both of these indices are unfortunately only available for the strike activity of the economy as a whole, and it is probable that the decline of strikes in coal mining – which were almost universally of the brief, small-scale variety – has been responsible for some or all of this apparent change in the character of strikes.

A method has, however, been found to overcome this problem. The annual strike statistics published by the Department of Employment include figures for the distribution of each of the three major strike indices into various categories of size (number of strikers). Although these figures are not broken down into industry groups (and hence are inclusive of coal industry data) information on large-scale coal strikes can be found in the annual list of 'Prominent Stoppages'. This list consists of brief descriptions of strikes which resulted in the loss of 5,000 or more working days. If one is prepared to accept 5,000 strikers as a useful (if arbitrary) cut-off point for distinguishing between larger and smaller stoppages, it is possible to identify, and subtract from the overall data for 'Big' stoppages, those 'prominent' mining strikes which involved this number of workers.[35] The remaining non-mining strikes then constitute the 'Small' stoppages.

It was on this basis that a comparative analysis of 'Big' and 'Small' strikes was carried out for the period 1959–71 (Columns 21–5). On average, only nineteen strikes a year, just a tiny fraction of the total, are of the 'Big' variety; although it is not without interest that in each of the years under study except 1961 and 1968 the *number* of strikes, both 'Big' and 'Small', followed similar *trends*. In any event, these 'Big' stoppages, while insignificant in number, have been responsible for a very large proportion of all working days lost – in fact in the last few years this proportion has ranged from one-third to three-quarters of the total (Column 23). The Donovan Report contains perhaps the most direct evidence of this skewness in the size distribution of strikes in Britain.[36] It was calculated by the Commission that between 1957 and 1966 over two-fifths of all working days lost through strikes were the product of just eight industry-wide disputes. Clearly one would expect the average size of the 'Big' strikes to have been far greater than that of the smaller ones, as indeed it has been. The massive one-day 'token' stoppages in engineering in 1962 and 1968 make those years abnormal ones, but if they are omitted from the calculations then the average 'Big' strike in the years 1959–71 involved roughly 14,000 workers, while the average size of the other strikes was about a mere 300 strikers. What is possibly even more significant is that the typical (i.e. 'Small') strikes have shown amazingly little variation in size from year to year, while it is the 'Big' stoppages which have been exhibiting the distinctive cyclical variations present in the aggregate data for all strikes.[37]

Similar peculiarities can be observed in relation to the *length* of strikes. This has shown quite erratic tendencies from year to year in the case of the 'Big' strikes, which on average are sometimes longer and sometimes shorter than 'Small' ones. The 'Big' strike may take the form of a national one-day stoppage, as in 1968, when the average duration per 'Big' striker was only 1·2 days. But there is another type of 'Big' strike–the protracted struggle–which produces a very different statistical picture, as in 1971, when two disputes–in the Post Office and the motor industry–were largely responsible for an average 'time out' of over eighteen working days per 'Big' striker. Turning to the duration of the 'Small' strikes, however, we find a clear tendency since the mid-1960s for these stoppages to be increasing in duration (see Column 25).

The distinction between 'Big' and 'Small' strikes is also valuable in explaining a puzzling feature of the relationship between the average size and average length of strikes. The data in Columns 10 and 13 of the Appendix, if considered together, indicate that in ten of the thirteen years 1959–71 there was a consistently inverse relationship between the size and duration of stoppages–in other words, the smaller the average strike in any one year the longer it tended to last, and *vice versa*. However, if Columns 24 and 25 are compared it will be seen that while it is possible to detect such a relationship between the size and length of 'Small' strikes, the national trends in this direction are primarily a product of the inclusion of data for the few very big strikes each year.

TRENDS IN THE CHARACTER OF STRIKES

The 'Causes' of Disputes

Although the Department of Employment uses the term 'causes' in its reports on industrial disputes, McCarthy's formulation of the statistics as referring to 'the reasons given for striking' is rather more accurate.[38] The Department classifies stoppages by a single cause– which is taken to be the main reason given by those involved at the time of the dispute. The pitfalls inherent in such a procedure are obvious, but we would agree with McCarthy that there is neverthe- less much to be gained from cautionary use of the available data.

Column 15 presents the grouping of strikes into five classes of reasons given for striking. What is immediately apparent is that by far the lion's share of the rise in strike frequency since the early 1960s is attributable to disputes over wage claims. Doubtless this trend is partly the result of governmental restraint of incomes at the end of the 1960s, but whatever the explanation it is apparent that the sources of discontent behind the recent strike are quite clearly attributable to material aspirations rather than (as is more fashionable to claim) to a greater desire for effective industrial democracy – that is to say, for more control over life at the workplace. Strikes over working conditions and 'employment' issues form a smaller proportion of the total today than they did at the beginning of the period, although there have been considerable increases in absolute terms – the frequency of strikes in both categories has more than doubled. The proportion of stoppages on 'union' matters has remained more or less static throughout at slightly over the 10 per cent level.

What is surprising about these figures is the fact that there has been virtually no increase, even in absolute terms, in the number of stoppages concerned with 'other wage matters'. Disputes over the operation of wage incentive schemes have been widely regarded as a major and increasing source of industrial conflict, yet in relative terms their share of total strike activity has never in the period been more than one-sixth and has recently sunk to as little as 6 per cent. One reason why commentators have emphasised the operation of wage payment systems as a source of industrial strife is that strike-proneness is often synonymous with instability of earnings.[39] Another factor to be taken into account is that until the decline in coal strikes, the relative insignificance of stoppages on 'other wage matters' was obscured by their pre-eminent position in the mining sector. Whereas coal miners have nearly always struck in support of wage disputes of this kind, workers elsewhere have been primarily and increasingly concerned with straightforward wage rises rather than with the mechanics of wage regulation.

This point can be illustrated by comparing the years 1959 and 1971. In 1959, 730 disputes (one-third of the total for that year) were classified under the heading of 'other wage disputes': 601 of these stoppages occurred in Mining and Quarrying. In 1971 the proportion of disputes on 'other wage' matters had fallen to just over one-tenth – and of the 165 stoppages thus classified, Mining and Quarrying accounted for only 31. As the total number of strikes was slightly higher in 1971 than in 1959, it is easy to see how misleading it would be to include minimg disputes in the analysis and how the significance of the 'other wage disputes' outside of this sector has not been very great.

The Trend of Unofficial Strikes

Writing of the character of strike activity in Britain as it was some fifteen years ago, W. E. J. McCarthy described two very different stereotypes of the British strike. The first was the small, localised unofficial strike, normally a response to 'some umpopular proposal for change, or threat to established customs and practice', which tended to be centred on wage payment methods or working arrangements in the plant.[40] Such strikes were invariably brief in length, and normally occurred in breach of procedure. The Donovan Commission later confirmed, for the years 1964–6, that the average unofficial strike was small (involving some 300 workers) and short-lived (the average stoppage lasting a little over $2\frac{1}{2}$ days, and the vast majority–over 80 per cent–being over within a week).[41]

In stark contrast to these unofficial disputes–which the Commission reckoned to have constituted 95 per cent of all strikes from 1964–6–are the very small number of major official strikes which are another prominent feature of British industrial conflict. McCarthy characterised this second stereotype as the more prolonged and widely-based strike which comes about because of failure to reach agreement over the amount or manner of execution of a nationally negotiated wage increase. The Donovan Report added that the average official strike involved four to five times as many workers and lasted nearly three times as long as its unofficial counterpart. Further, as we had occasion to point out earlier, the Report also noted that a mere eight official, industry-wide disputes over pay or hours of work or both were the source of over 40 per cent of the working days lost between 1957 and 1966.

McCarthy's stereotypes were conceptualised on the basis of his analysis of the reasons given for striking. Since that time the Donovan Commission has made available figures for the distribution of unofficial strikes into various types of 'causes', and from these the following table has been derived.

TABLE I

The Reasons Given for Official and Non-Official Strikes
(Average annual figures, 1964–66)

Reason	Official[1]		'Non-Official'[2]		Ratio of Official : Non-Official
Wages	38	(49%)	1,052	(48%)	1:28
Working Conditions	4	(5%)	676	(31%)	1:169
Employment	20	(25%)	326	(15%)	1:16
Union	17	(21%)	138	(6%)	1:8
TOTAL	76	(100%)	2,196	(100%)	1:29

1 Includes stoppages declared official by some but not all of the unions involved.
2 Appears to include other than unofficial strikes.

Source: Royal Commission, op. cit., p. 97. and p. 101.

Unfortunately no differentiation was made between strikes over wage claims and those over the operation of wage payment systems, so the popular assumption that unofficial strikes are mainly concerned with the latter type of wage dispute remains untestable. Apart from the finding that one half of both official and unofficial strikes derive from some kind of grievance over wages, it emerges that, relative to the number of official strikes over working conditions, the number of unofficial disputes in this category is disproportionately large. Relatively speaking again, it seems that employment issues are more often the reasons for official than unofficial strikes, and the same is true of stoppages relating to union matters. But the numbers of official strikes are so small, and the categories of causation so wide in scope (even without the grouping of causes performed here) that the figures must be evaluated with caution. They seem to verify that the circumstances which are said to give rise to official and unofficial strikes are subject to systematic differences.

The first governmental statistics on unofficial strikes were released in 1937, and they indicated that in the year 1936 the ratio of official to unofficial strikes for the whole economy was just over 1:2.[42] Since that time the importance of unauthorised stoppages in the pattern of industrial conflict has increased considerably. For example, the figures released by the Donovan Commission for the period 1964–6 yield a ratio of official to unofficial disputes of nearly 1:30. Although the unofficial strikes of 1936 were, on average, larger than those of 1964–6 (483 strikers per strike, compared with 301), they share with the unauthorised stoppages of recent years the characteristic of being much shorter in duration than other strikes.

Unfortunately, the use of the 1936 data is subject to certain qualifications which appear to have sometimes been overlooked. In the first place, as Knowles has stated, 'the years 1935 to 1937, and especially 1936, were particularly notable for unofficial strikes', so the data cannot be regarded as being representative of any greater period.[43] In addition, the 1936 figures, in contrast to those of more recent years, indicate that there was a very sizeable proportion of stoppages – about a quarter in fact – which were neither official nor unofficial, but which fell into the residual category of lockouts, strikes by non-unionists, or stoppages whose status was unknown.

Only by comparing directly the numbers of official and unofficial strikes is it possible to avoid a misleading interpretation of the data. This can be illustrated by Turner's statement that, 'On the one occasion in the 1930's, for instance, when the then Ministry of Labour attempted an estimate of the proportion of strikes which was *unofficial*, it concluded that only a quarter had received *official* union support'[44] (Emphases added). The implication of this statement–that three-quarters of all stoppages in 1936 were unofficial–is, of course, erroneous.

In September 1972 information was made public by the Department of Employment which, for the first time, allows us to examine the trends of official and unofficial conflict over the whole of the last decade.[45] When these figures are adjusted as far as possible to exclude the coal mining industry, three important conclusions may be drawn.

(1) Since 1960 there have been fairly continuous rises in the frequency of both official and unofficial stoppages.

(2) With some exceptions, the trends of official and unofficial strikes over the last twelve years have exhibited a good deal of comparability.

(3) The relative significance of unofficial disputes has varied from year to year.

Although it is only recently that figures on unofficial strikes have been available for the years since 1967, earlier discussions of the trends of official and unofficial stoppages were remarkably inadequate in failing to recognise any of the above points, or even to reach definite conclusions as to what the trends had been. Commenting on the data for 1960–67, Turner claimed that 'if one allows for . . . fluctuations relating to the general level of economic activity, the numbers of official strikes over the above years seem to suggest a certain increasing trend'.[46] The Donovan Report, on the other hand, argued that 'there is no tendency for official strikes to rise from year to year'.[47] The application of three-year moving averages to the data to smooth out short-term fluctuations confirms that, since the period 1961–3, the trend in the frequency of official strikes has been almost consistently upwards.

Turner also pointed out that the trend in the total number of unofficial stoppages had been 'pretty clearly downwards'.[48] He admitted that this trend was reversed if strikes in the coal industry were excluded, but did not cite the relevant figures (and neither did the Donovan Report, or any other commentary). Table 2 shows that unofficial strikes outside mining were on the increase over almost the whole of the period and that their rate of increase–with the exception of two of the later figures–was very similar to that of official strikes. Furthermore, when the whole series of annual data from 1960–71 (Column 16) is subjected to statistical testing, the parallel between the trends in the frequency of both types of dispute is confirmed. (The correlation coefficient r_s is 0·86.)

The other strike indices have not evidenced such parallels in official and unofficial trends. Table 2 indicates that from the early

TABLE 2

Trends in the Authorisation of Strikes Outside Coal Mining*
(3-year moving averages, 1960–71. Centred trend: 1962–64 = 100)

	Stoppages				Strikers				Days Lost			
	Number		Index		Number		Index		Number		Index	
	Official	Non-official	Official	Non-official	Official	Non-official	Official	Non-official	Official	Non-official	Official	Non-official
1960–62	68	1,145	105	95	134	487	73	108	656	1,583	110	145
1961–63	62	1,123	95	94	156	419	85	93	666	1,206	112	110
1962–64	65	1,199	100	100	183	451	100	100	595	1,093	100	100
1963–65	72	1,315	111	110	112	518	61	115	594	1,275	100	117
1964–66	76	1,412	117	118	102	542	56	120	809	1,343	136	123
1965–67	88	1,485	135	124	60	580	33	129	724	1,745	122	160
1966–68	86	1,668	132	139	50	581	27	129	755	1,922	127	176
1967–69	99	2,171	152	181	128	847	70	188	902	2,944	152	269
1968–70	117	2,828	180	236	215	1,088	117	241	1,877	4,337	315	397
1969–71	140	2,783	215	232	318	1,126	174	250	4,980	4,673	837	428

Source: Department of Employment Gazette, September 1972.
*Excludes data on the one-day Engineering stoppages of 1962 and 1968.
Source: Statistical Appendix of this paper.

to the late 1960s, the number of official strikers was declining while unofficial strikers were at the same time becoming more numerous. Since the late 1960s, however, worker involvement in both types of strike has been rising quite rapidly. As far as strike incidence is concerned, since the mid-1960s there have been almost continuous and very considerable rises in the numbers of both official and unofficial days lost. Before that time, however, there was no apparent connection between the official and unofficial trends.

While it is not the case that there has been a tendency for unofficial strikes to become disproportionately frequent, it is, however, true that the position of unofficial stoppages in the makeup of total strike activity has been subject to significant variation. Until now this point has gone unrecognised, perhaps because of the way in which the Donovan Commission presented its data on unofficial strikes. In reference to the national total of strikes, the Commission announced that 'the overwhelming majority of stoppages–some 95 per cent (were) due to unofficial strikes'.[49] By combining the figures into a period average, variations from year to year were bound to be concealed. The use of a percentage to represent the relationship between the two types of strike, one numerically very much superior to the other, also has the effect of understating changes. Thus when the Labour Government's White Paper, *In Place of Strife*, updated Donovan's figures to include those for 1967, it was possible to calculate that in the year 1967 the proportion of strikes which were unofficial remained at 95 per cent.[50] However, examination of the figures in terms of the ratio of official to unofficial strikes gives a radically different picture, demonstrating that whereas in 1964–6 for every official strike there were 29 unofficial, in 1967 the ratio fell to 1:19. Column 16 of the Appendix indicates that, if attention is shifted to unofficial strikes outside of coal mining, the ratio of official to unofficial stoppages has tended to fluctuate, within a range of between 1:12 (1971) and 1:29 (1969).

There is another way in which it can be shown that the Donovan Commission's widely-quoted figure of 95 per cent is open to question. The 1966 Survey of Workplace Industrial Relations sampled 1,161 shop stewards belonging to six major unions. 40 per cent of them had experienced a strike since taking up their present position as a steward (six years ago, on average). Asked whether, in the case of the last strike experienced, permission had been obtained from the union before the strike took place, some three out of ten stewards replied in the affirmative. In contrast the small sample of personnel officers (who reportedly had the least experience of official stoppages of any of the sub-samples) registered proportionately only half as many official strikes as the stewards.

In answer to another question it was found that–in respect of *all* strikes–11 per cent of the stewards reported that the decision to stop work had been made by the union at national level, while another 7 per cent recalled the decision as having been made at a branch meeting of the union. In other words the origins of the strike had, in at least a formal sense, involved the machinery of the union in some 18 per cent of cases. The judgments of those in the managerial sub-samples corresponded quite closely with those of the stewards on this question.

It therefore appears that an estimate of between 75 and 85 per cent of Britain's strikes as being unofficial is at least as worthy of consideration as Donovan's 95 per cent.[51] Indeed, there are a number of factors which suggest that the proportions in the Survey were actually *inflated* compared with those in the official statistics. Firstly, unlike the Department of Employment statistics, the Survey had no limitations (in terms of size or length) on the strikes eligible for inclusion. The combined experience of all the sub-samples was that in an unknown number of cases their last strike had involved less than ten workers, while 20 per cent of them claimed it had lasted less than a day. In either case, unless such strikes had caused the loss of at least 100 working days they would not have appeared in the official statistics. Secondly, it seems a reasonable assumption that shop stewards, being at the heart of unofficial strike activity, would be more accurate in reporting the occurrence of such stoppages, especially those which are relatively minor in stature, than would the officers of the Department of Employment responsible for collecting the national statistics. Thirdly, the definition of official strikes adopted by the Survey was more restrictive than that of the Department of Employment, since only the latter included strikes given union authorisation after they began.

Not only the trends in the frequency of official and unofficial stoppages but also their other statistical characteristics are of interest. With the exception of two years (1960 and 1971) unofficial strikes have accounted for at least three-quarters of all the workers involved in industrial disputes and, except for 1966 and 1971, for between 60 and 85 per cent of all days lost. As with the frequency of strikes, the importance of these unofficial stoppages for both of these indices has been fluctuating from year to year. The source of these fluctuations can be traced to changes in the size and duration of official and unofficial disputes. The picture here is markedly similar to that which resulted from the comparison of 'Big' and 'Small' strikes: This is of course hardly unexpected, since the dichotomy of 'Big' and 'Small' describes the scale of most official and unofficial strikes respectively.[52] (See also Appendix, cols. 17–20.)

While the average size of official stoppages has varied considerably from year to year, unofficial strikes have undergone little alteration in scale, averaging below 400 strikers per strike. Similarly, while the duration of official stoppages has fluctuated widely, unofficial strikes have shown consistent trends in duration, first dropping in length in the early 1960s and then rising a good deal after 1966. Despite the variable character of official stoppages revealed by these statistics, a tendency for both their size and duration to increase has been evident in the last few years. By 1971 official strike activity accounted for one-third of all strikers and two-thirds of the total number of days lost.[53]

The recent release of unofficial strike data has made possible limited inter-industry comparisons of the propensity for unofficial strikes. Of five industry groups, the median proportion of days lost in unofficial strikes in the period 1961–71 was lowest in the Unnamed Industries (63 per cent) and highest in Construction (93 per cent). The Engineering sector and Transport and Communication both yielded a median value of 75 per cent, while that for Textiles and Clothing was 78 per cent. Thus it appears that there are both similarities and differences between industries in unofficial strike incidence. The figures for the metal-working industries are of particular interest. It will be recalled that we were earlier able to demonstrate that the share of this sector in total (non-mining) strike activity has not, as some commentators claimed, been increasing faster than those of other industries. However, the Engineering industries have also been singled out as having quite atypical patterns of industrial relations in general, and unofficial strike activity in particular.

In his scathing critique of the Donovan Report, H. A. Turner claimed that one of the Commission's major errors was to have been 'persuaded to accept as the typical situation of British industrial relations that of the mass production operative in a large engineering establishment'. The available evidence appears to support the view that, as far as unofficial strikes are concerned, while their relative significance is not particularly greater in Engineering than elsewhere, the *trend* of unofficial strike incidence in Engineering is peculiar to that sector. On the first of these points, the median percentage of days lost in unofficial strikes during 1961–71 was 69 per cent in the non-metal-working industries, compared with the only slightly higher figure of 75 per cent for the combined data of the Metals, Engineering, Shipbuilding and Vehicles industries. With respect to the *trend* of unofficial strike incidence in the Engineering sector, however, there is virtually no correlation between the Engineering and total (non-mining) trends ($r_S = 0.22$), while that between the non-Engineering sector and the total is very high indeed ($r_S = 0.92$). (These figures are exclusive of the 'token' Engineering stoppages of 1962 and 1968–which means they inflate the correlation between Engineering and the total.)

The peculiarity of the Engineering trends extends, however, only to the *form* of industrial conflict, and not to its *level*. The degree of correlation is very high, in respect of both strike frequency and incidence, between the overall figures for the metal-working industries and those for the non-mining industries as a whole. But going back to the character of strikes, the particularistic nature of Engineering disputes extends beyond the question of authorisation, and also exists in relation to the size and length of strikes. Taking once again the period 1960–71 and disallowing the one-day Engineering stoppages, the average size of strikes in Engineering was 348 strikers per strike, while outside of this sector it was 521. While they were smaller in size, however, the Engineering disputes were much longer in duration–the average days lost per striker was 5.6 in Engineering, compared with only 2.8 in the non-Engineering industries (exclusive of coal mining). Trends in the size and length of strikes were also quite different in Engineering from those in the economy as a whole. If one compares the correlation between Engineering and the total non-mining figures, and that between the non-Engineering industries and the total, the figures, respectively, are $r_S = 0.26$ and $r_S = 0.93$ for the size of strikes, and $r_S = 0.56$ and $r_S = 0.93$ for their duration. Once more the metal-working industries evince patterns of strike behaviour conspicuously different from those in the economy as a whole. In short, Turner's point that the Engineering industries constitute a special case as far as industrial relations is concerned, is fully validated insofar as the character of industrial disputes is concerned.

Unconstitutionality in Industrial Conflict

An integral part of the small-strike stereotype is that such stoppages usually take place in breach of an agreed disputes procedure. In fact the adjectives unofficial and 'unconstitutional' have come to be seen in practice as being almost synonymous. There appear to be only two sources of quantitative information on the extent to which strikes are unconstitutional and these are the Workplace Relations Survey and the statistics collected and published annually by the Engineering Employers' Federation (E.E.F.).

When questioned as to whether the plants in which they worked had a disputes procedure, no less than 89 per cent of the respondents in any of the Survey's sub-samples replied in the affirmative. Only 37 per cent of the shop stewards who fell into this category admitted that the last strike they experienced took place before procedure had been exhausted. Of the constitutional strikes (i.e. the other 63 per cent of strikes experienced) three out of ten had exhausted both the national and plant-level procedures, and the remainder the plant-level only. In contrast, those interviewed on the management side reported unconstitutional strikes in a far higher proportion of cases–62 per cent of foremen, 68 per cent of works managers, and 81 per cent of personnel officers. As a group they judged that 45 per cent of the constitutional strikes had exhausted procedure both nationally and within the firm. These results suggest that there are strong grounds for questioning the widely-held assumption that the '95 per cent' of strikes commonly regarded as unofficial are also unconstitutional.

The E.E.F. evidence on unconstitutional strikes is also of considerable interest, although it can certainly not be treated as typical of the whole of British industry. The 'York' disputes procedure for the engineering industry which existed until the end of 1971 was widely regarded as being exceptionally archaic, cumbersome, and slow to produce results. Trade unionists had always bitterly opposed the strong 'managerial rights' position built into the agreement against their will half a century ago, and it was this feeling of distrust which was partly responsible for the C.S.E.U. unilaterally abandoning the procedure in favour of independently-negotiated domestic agreements. All things considered, therefore, it is hardly surprising to find that there was a very high rate of unconstitutionality in engineering stoppages. Neither is it surprising that, as Turner puts it, 'it has become pretty well recognised that a settlement in formal grievance or conciliation procedure . . . (was) . . . more likely to be achieved–or more likely to be achieved quickly–if an issue's reference to that procedure had been preceded by a suitably demonstrative strike'[54].

The E.E.F. Annual Report for 1971–72 indicates that, on average, during the period 1961–71 there were 56 strikes of 'staff' workers reported each year of which 41 ($\frac{3}{4}$) were unconstitutional. Among manual workers the yearly average was 710 stoppages of which 684 (96 per cent) were in breach of procedure. Analysis of the ratio of constitutional to unconstitutional manual worker stoppages in each year of the series, shows that the relative significance of stoppages in breach of procedure has varied considerably from year to year (from ten times the number of constitutional strikes, in 1964, to fifty-nine times their number, in 1969). Furthermore, at least in Engineering, the relative significance of unconstitutionality in the pattern of strike activity has shown no clear trend towards either an increase or a decrease. This, it will be remembered, was also true of the national data on the unofficiality of strikes.

CONCLUSION

In the introduction to this paper the suggestion was made that the published literature on strike trends in the U.K. is badly in need of revision. One of the most recent and widely-accepted analyses of strikes in Britain is that of H. A. Turner. In *Is Britain Really Strike-Prone?* Turner offers the following description of strike trends in the recent past:

> In the . . . phase from the 1930's to the present day, there was an increase in the frequency of strikes in the Second World War . . . and this trend resumed again in the post-war period up to the late 1950's. But this increase was very largely concentrated in a narrow range of industries and was not, apparently, maintained in the 1960's. And the typical strike became and stayed relatively small and short (p. 18).

A more accurate summary might be that if the strong and continuing downward trend in the number of disputes in the coal mining industry is set aside, the frequency of strikes fell after the war to a notably low level and remained remarkably stable throughout the 1950s, since which time it has risen almost continuously to the highest levels ever recorded. In the last decade the relative contribution of the various sectors of the economy to the overall rise in strike frequency appears to have undergone very little basic change, although the decline of stoppages in the coal industry has tended to highlight the centrality of certain other industries for Britain's strike statistics. The rate of increase in the number of stoppages has been rising in all the industries examined, and to a significantly similar extent. This is certainly the dominant impression which emerges from our analysis, notwithstanding the fact that the frequency of strikes in some of the traditionally strike-free industries has been rising at a faster rate than in certain others which are better known for their strike-proneness.

The average strike in the post-war period has been somewhat smaller in size and considerably briefer in duration than those which came before. On the other hand, the relative significance of small, short stoppages in the whole country's strike pattern has been declining, although (in the 1960s at least) trends in both the average size and average length of strikes have been subject to a good deal of variability. On analysis this variability outside coal mining has proves to be the result primarily of trends which have occurred in the size and length of 'Big' strikes. In contrast, the 'Small' stoppages, which constitute almost the entirety of the total in numerical terms, have exhibited remarkable stability in size but a significant increase in their average duration in the last few years.

Our other principal findings were, in brief that:

(1) The incidence of strikes in the U.K., relative to that of other countries, has risen significantly in recent years.

(2) In stark contrast to the broad industrial base over which *changes* in Britain's overall strike-proneness have been evenly spread, strike-proneness itself appears to be a highly localised phenomenon which is exceptionally uneven in its distribution throughout the economy.

(3) In recent years not only the frequency of strikes (outside of coal mining) but also the number of workers involved in strikes and, most of all, the amount of working time foregone, have shown strong upward tendencies.

(4) The rise in strike activity has been caused above all by discontent over wage rates.

(5) Unofficial stoppages, while constituting the vast majority of the total number of strikes, have increasing in frequency to an extent similar to that of official stoppages.

(6) The degree both of authorisation and of observance of procedure are aspects of strike behaviour which have been subject to variability over time.

(7) The statistical importance of unofficial and unconstitutional strikes is less than is conventionally assumed.

Emergent Trends

If the statistics on industrial conflict analysed in this paper are examined for major variations during the period since 1959, it becomes clear that, not only are many of the current orthodoxies about Britain's strike problem replete with statistical inaccuracies, but they may also be seriously out of date. In some respects the period in the mid-sixties which provided the statistical raw material for these various diagnoses has proved to be unrepresentative of the pattern of industrial conflict both before and since. The Donovan Commission based its assessment of the strike situation on figures prepared by the Ministry of Labour and its secretariat for the years 1964–66. When the Labour Government made its recommendations for reform it incorporated data from 1967. Professor Turner's is one of the most recent statistical analyses and it ends with figures for 1968, and in some cases earlier. For the sake of analysis we shall divide the years since 1960 into three four-year periods: the 'early

TABLE 3

Selected Strike Indices* (Average Annual Figures) in Three Recent Periods
(Figures for coal mining excluded, unless otherwise indicated)

	The Early Sixties 1960–63	The Donovan Era 1964–67	The Current Period 1968–71
NUMBER OF STRIKES			
All Industries	2,509	2,233	2,907
Outside Coal	1,180	1,547	2,732
NUMBER OF STRIKERS (000s)	576	655	1,264
NUMBER OF DAYS LOST (000s)	2,031	2,279	8,019
SIZE OF STRIKES			
Strikers Per Strike	488	424	463
Size of 'Big' Strikes	16,840	11,180	14,580
Size of 'Small' Strikes	292	310	310
Size of Official Strikes	1,909	1,018	1,996
Size of Unofficial Strikes	407	390	388
DURATION OF STRIKES			
Days Lost per Striker	3.6	3.5	6.3
Duration of 'Big' Strikes	3.2	4.1	9.5
Duration of 'Small' Strikes	4.0	3.3	4.8
Duration of Official Strikes	5.2	8.3	15.3
Duration of Unofficial Strikes	3.1	2.8	4.1
REASONS GIVEN FOR STRIKING			
Wage Claims	33%	36%	49%
'Other Wage'	14%	13%	8%
Working Conditions	16%	21%	16%
Employment	24%	21%	17%
Union	13%	10%	10%
AUTHORISATION OF STRIKES			
Official: Unofficial Strikes	1:18	1:17	1:20
Proportion of Strikers (Unofficial	79%	87%	80%
Proportion of Days Lost (Unofficial)	69%	69%	51%

*The effects of the one-day Engineering stoppages of 1962 and 1968 have been excluded from the calculations for 'Big' strikes and those on the authorisation of strikes. Apart from this, definitions of each statistical index are as given in the Appendix.

sixties', 1960–63; the 'Donovan era', 1964–67; and the 'current period', 1968–71. The periods selected, while varying in their degree of internal consistency, are sufficiently suggestive of important basic changes in the pattern of industrial conflict to be worthy of comparison.

Compared with the early-sixties, the Donovan era was lower in overall strike frequency, though non-mining stoppages rose by nearly a third. (From now on, unless otherwise stated all comments refer to non-mining strikes.) Strike incidence was virtually unchanged from the previous years, still not quite reaching 100 days lost per 1,000 workers. Unofficial strikes were no more numerous in relation to official ones than they had been before–though the decline in coal strikes meant that, for the economy as a whole, the unofficial strike proportion was lower than before. However, examination of the characteristics of unofficial and 'Small' stoppages in the Donovan era (when the combination of these two characteristics reached the peak of its renown as a stereotype) shows that the period was especially and unusually prone to such stoppages. In the first place, an especially high proportion of both its strikers and its days lost was attributable to 'Small' and unofficial stoppages. Further, on average the period's 'Big' strikes and its official ones were very much smaller in size, and its 'Small' and unofficial stoppages were significantly briefer in duration than in the other periods.

In the last few years a remarkably different pattern of industrial conflict appears to have emerged. Both strike frequency and the number of strikers are nearly double their 'Donovan' average, and the number of days lost has risen enormously–by $3\frac{1}{2}$ times in fact. The 'causes' of strikes have also altered–nearly half now relate to wage claims, compared with about a third earlier on. The industrial composition of strike activity has also undergone a change, as it is only in the current period that the coal mining industry has finally been deposed as strike leader by the 'un-named' industries. The position of the latter has also been strengthened by the newfound militancy of public employees.

While the significance of unofficial strikes has increased in the current period, both in terms of their frequency and their duration, the length, and most significantly the scale of authorised disputes has risen a good deal. Implied in this is perhaps the most significant change of all, namely the emergence–or in a sense re-emergence–of the major confrontation as a central focus of industrial conflict. The most dramatic manifestation of this trend was the coal strike in 1972, which alone caused the loss of more working days than all of the 8,931 stoppages which took place during the four years of the Donovan era.

The average dispute of the current period is 75 per cent longer and slightly larger than its earlier counterpart; but the major increases are in the enormous impact which 'Big' strikes have now achieved. These large-scale stoppages were responsible during 1968–71 for over half of the total days lost, compared with a quarter in the

Donovan era and slightly more before then. On the other hand, $\frac{2}{3}$ of the nation's strikers and nearly 99 per cent of its strikes continue to fall into the category of 'Small' stoppages. The difference today is that the 'Big' disputes have become far more conspicuous – bigger, longer, and therefore more severe in their impact. What is more, this is a trend which shows signs of continuing.[55]

Strike trends, however, are clearly unpredictable in their changes of direction. The alterations in the pattern of industrial conflict which have occurred since Donovan could never have been foreseen by statisticians. But the situation now is that the niggly unofficial strikes which seemed to be bringing Britain to the verge of economic destruction only five years ago are lessening in significance because of the massive and lengthy confrontations in coal and cars, and by dockers, dustmen and train drivers, that have become part of the industrial scene of the 1970s.

NOTES

1 By reliability is meant consistency of measurement, and by validity that units of measurement are a valid representation of the phenomenon they are intended to describe.
2 This subject has been extensively discussed elsewhere, e.g. by K. G. J. C. Knowles, *Strikes: A Study in Industrial Conflict*, Blackwell, Oxford, 1952, pp. 299–306.
3 R. Hyman, *Strikes*, Fontana/Collins, London, 1972, p. 26.
4 H. A. Turner, *Is Britain Really Strike-Prone?: A Review of the Incidence, Character and Costs of Industrial Conflict*, Occasional Paper No. 20, Cambridge University Press, 1969, p. 8.
5 Following Turner, the word 'incidence' is used here to refer to the impact of strikes in terms of lost working time. The terms 'strike frequency' and 'strike activity' have been adopted to refer to the number of strikes.
6 Knowles, *op. cit.*, p. 51.
7 J. H. Pencavel, 'An Investigation into Industrial Strike Activity in Britain', *Economica*, Vol. 50, No. 147, 1970, pp. 239–55.
8 Turner, *op. cit.*
9 W. E. J. McCarthy, 'The Nature of Britain's Strike Problem', *British Journal of Industrial Relations*, Vol. VIII, No. 2, 1970, pp. 224–36.
10 T. G. Whittingham and B. Towers, 'The Strike Record of the United Kingdom: An Analysis', *Industrial Relations Journal*, Vol. 2, No. 3, 1971, pp. 2–8.
11 Whittingham and Towers, *ibid.*, p. 6.
12 It may be added that due to exceptionally thorough strike reportage by the coal industry since nationalisation, the increase in non-mining stoppages is undoubtedly understated by the official statistics.
13 The pivotal position of the year 1959 in inaugurating the decline in coal strikes favoured the choice of that year as the starting point for the statistical analysis in this paper. This choice was also influenced by the fact that 1959 marked the close of the post-war era of very low strike frequency.

14 Inter-industry strike differentials are examined in detail later in this paper (pp. 73–76).
15 For a summary of the special features of industrial relations in the coal industry, see H. A. Clegg, *The System of Industrial Relations in Great Britain*, Blackwell, Oxford, 1971, pp. 325–7.
16 L. J. Handy, 'Absenteeism and Attendance in the British Coal-Mining Industry', *British Journal of Industrial Relations*, Vol. VI, No. 1, 1968, pp. 27–50.
17 Turner, *op. cit.*, pp. 24–5.
18 Hyman, *op. cit.*, pp. 30–1.
19 J. F. B. Goodman, 'Strikes in the United Kingdom', *International Labour Review*, Vol. 95, No. 5, 1967, pp. 465–81.
20 See, for example the *Department of Employment Gazette*, May 1972, p. 438.
21 Turner, *op. cit.*, p. 42.
22 A. I. Marsh and W. E. J. McCarthy, *Disputes Procedures in British Industry*, Research Paper No. 2, Part 2, Royal Commission on Trade Unions and Employers' Associations, 1966, p. 25.
23 A. I. Marsh, E. O. Evans and P. Garcia, *Workplace Industrial Relations in Engineering*, Federation Research Paper 4, Engineering Employers' Federation, London, 1971, pp. 24–5.
24 Government Social Survey, *Workplace Industrial Relations*, H.M.S.O., London, 1968. A summary of the findings relevant to industrial disputes may be found in W. E. J. McCarthy and S. R. Parker, *Shop Stewards and Workshop Relations*, Research Paper No. 10, Royal Commission on Trade Unions and Employers Associations, 1968, pp. 45–8.
25 Turner, *op. cit.*, p. 46.
26 *Royal Commission on Trade Unions and Employers' Associations 1965–8: Report*, Cmnd 3623, H.M.S.O., London, 1968, paras. 414–5 (Emphases added).
27 H. A. Turner, 'The Donovan Report: A Critical Analysis', *Economic Journal*, Vol. 79, No. 313, 1969, p. 3.
28 *Ibid.*, p. 3.
29 Turner, *Is Britain Really Strike Prone?*, p. 41 (Emphasis added).
30 *Ibid.*, p. 46.
31 For this reason it was felt wise to reject the approach of those statisticians who have attempted to analyse strike trends by amalgamating the data of all three primary strike indices. (See P. Galambos and E. W. Evans, 'Work-Stoppages in the United Kingdom, 1951–64: A Quantitative Study', *Bulletin of the Oxford University Institute of Statistics*, Vol. 28, No. 1, 1966, pp. 33–57).
32 Knowles, *op. cit.*, p. 145.
33 Turner, *op. cit.*, pp. 19–20.
34 Estimates of worker involvement at non-struck establishments are compiled for the motor industry, where there is of course an exceptional degree of interdependence between establishments. The ratio of 'struck' to 'non-struck' worker involvement has ranged from 1:2 to over 30:1 in the last decade; but it is normally the case that there are between two and five times as many workers involved at the struck establishment as at the non-struck one(s).
35 All stoppages involving 5,000 or more workers are included among the 'Prominent Stoppages' *except* of course for any of this size which lasted less than a day and therefore caused the loss of less than 5,000 working days.
36 Royal Commission, *op. cit.*, para. 366.
37 It should be noted, however, that a comparison of trends in the size of 'Small' strikes with those of all non-mining stoppages shows that, with the exception of three of the years under study, the direction of change has in both cases been the same. Nevertheless, the extent of the fluctuations in the size of 'Small' strikes has been very minor indeed, whereas changes in the average size of all non-mining

strikes have been quite marked. Our analysis makes it clear that the source of this variation in the overall size of strikes can be traced almost entirely to the size of the very small number of large-scale stoppages which occur annually.

38 W. E. J. McCarthy, 'The Reasons Given for Striking', *Bulletin of the Oxford University Institute of Statistics*, Vol. 21, No. 1, 1959, pp. 17–29.

39 Clegg, *op. cit.*, p. 326.

40 McCarthy, *op. cit.*, 1959, p. 21.

41 Royal Commission, *op. cit.*, para. 368.

42 The information concerned was originally presented by the then Minister of Labour in the House of Commons on July 1st, 1937 (Hansard, Vol. 35, Col. 2167).

43 Knowles, *op. cit.*, p. 33.

44 Turner, *op. cit.*, p. 21. It should be pointed out that it was Knowles (*op. cit.*, footnote, p. 33) who first made the statement that a quarter of all strikes in 1936 were official. However, Knowles did present the complete set of figures, including those in the residual category.

45 *Department of Employment Gazette*, September 1972, pp. 810 and 864–5. Note that throughout the following discussion the term 'unofficial strikes' will refer to *non-official* stoppages (outside of coal mining) as defined in the notes to Columns 16–20 of the Appendix.

46 Turner, *op. cit.*, p. 24.

47 Royal Commission, *op. cit.*, para. 71.

48 Turner, *op. cit.*, pp. 23–4.

49 Royal Commission, *op. cit.*, para. 368.

50 *In Place of Strife: A Policy for Industrial Relations*, Cmnd 3888, H.M.S.O., London, 1969, p. 39.

51 Part of the gap between these two estimates may be due to shop stewards and other interviewees in the Workplace Relations Survey having classified as official those stoppages which received *post facto* authorisation in the form of retroactive dispute benefit.

52 Note, however, that the parallels in the characteristics of the polar aspects of size and authorisation cannot be taken as implying that the two are synonymous (i.e. that all 'Big' strikes are official and all 'Small' ones unofficial). While there is a strong tendency in this direction, there are cases of both '*Big*' *unofficial* strikes and '*Small*' *official* ones.

53 Department of Employment statistics for the first six months of 1972 indicate that the enormous rise in the proportion of days lost from official strikes during 1971 may have since declined to earlier levels.

54 Turner, *op. cit.*, p. 23.

55 At the time of writing, figures on non-mining strikes are available for the first eight months of 1972. The average size of strikes sustained yet another increase, and their average duration, while much below the comparable figure for 1971, was still considerably higher than in earlier years. The frequency of strikes was almost indentical to that in the first eight months of 1971, the number of strikers rose, and the number of days lost dropped, but again was still above that for the years prior to 1971. Finally, wage claims retained their position as the cause of every second strike.

Selected U.K. Strike Statistics, 1959–71

All Industries

	(1) Number of Strikes		(2) Number of Workers Involved (000s)		(3) Number of Individuals Involved		(4) Workers Indirectly Involved		(5) Number of Days Lost (000s)		(6) Size of Strikes		(7) Duration of Strikes	
	No.	Index	No.	Index	% of Total	Index (For No. of Workers)	% of Total	Index (For No. of Workers)	No.	Index	% Strikes with under 250 Strikers	% Days Lost by 10,000 or more Strikers	% Strikes 3 days or less	% Strikes over 6 days and not over 18 days
1959	2,093	101	645	109	78	105	19	91	5,257	304	80	68	78	7
1960	2,832	137	814	138	78	132	14	86	3,001	173	78	24	77	7
1961	2,686	130	771	131	82	132	13	73	2,998	173	80	29	74	8
1962	2,449	118	4,420	749	55	505	3	91	5,757	333	78	69	73	9
1963	2,068	100	590	100	81	100	23	100	1,731	100	77	33	75	7
1964	2,524	122	872	148	82	150	20	127	2,011	116	76	10	75	8
1965	2,354	114	868	147	87	156	22	144	2,906	168	74	27	69	10
1966	1,937	94	530	90	91	101	22	86	2,372	137	77	36	68	11
1967	2,116	102	731	124	93	141	25	133	2,765	160	74	15	66	12
1968	2,378	115	2,255	382	—	—	8	135	4,672	270	72	32	61	15
1969	3,116	151	1,654	280	—	—	14	169	6,799	393	67	29	62	15
1970	3,906	189	1,793	304	—	—	19	247	10,854	627	70	34	55	18
1971	2,228	106	1,171	198	—	—	26	228	13,497	780	72	67	51	19

Notes   for column: (1) Only strikes beginning in each year are included. Excludes 'political' strikes. Excludes strikes involving less than 10 workers and strikes lasting less than 1 day (unless more than 100 working days are lost). A small number of lockouts and strikes by non-unionists (about 25 annually) are included as stoppages.

(2) Workers involved directly and indirectly in stoppages beginning in each year.

(3) As for Column (2), but only counting once cases where an individual was involved in more than one strike in the year.

(4) Excludes workers indirectly involved at non-struck establishments.

(5) Number of working days lost within each year from stoppages beginning in the year.

(6) and (7) Based on stoppages beginning in each year, but allowing for days lost from those which continued into the following year.

*The index numbers in this Appendix are 'centred trends', with the base year (1963) assigned the value 100.

†The following Government publications were drawn upon for information: *Department of Employment Gazette* (formerly *Employment and Productivity Gazette* (1969–70) and *Ministry of Labour Gazette* (prior to 1969); *British Labour Statistics: A Historical Abstract; Annual Abstract of Statistics; Monthly Digest of Statistics.*

All Industries Except Coal Mining

	(8)		(9) 'Strikers': Workers Involved (000s)		(10) Strikers per Strike		(11) Strikers per 1,000 Unionists			(12) Number of Days Lost (000s)		(13) Days Lost per Striker		(14) Days Lost per 1,000 Workers			(15) Reasons Given for Striking (% of Total)				
	Number of Strikes																Wage Claims	Wage Issues	Other Working Conditions	Employ-ment	Union
	No.	Index	No.	Index	No.	Index	No. (a)	No. (b)	Index (b)	No.	Index	No.	Index	No. (a)	No. (b)	Index (b)					
1959	786	73	454	104	578	143	67	51	109	4,894	348	10.8	338	239	230	365	28	16	16	28	12
1960	1,166	108	577	132	495	122	83	64	136	2,507	178	4.3	134	133	115	183	36	15	17	20	12
1961	1,228	114	522	119	425	105	78	57	121	2,261	161	4.3	134	131	102	162	33	15	17	23	12
1962	1,244	115	4,265	938	3,718	918	447	464	987	5,449	388	1.3	41	259	243	386	28	14	14	30	14
1963	1,081	100	438	100	405	100	59	47	100	1,405	100	3.2	100	75	63	100	34	13	17	23	13
1964	1,466	136	700	160	477	118	87	74	157	1,709	122	2.4	75	86	75	119	36	11	21	20	12
1965	1,614	149	750	171	465	115	85	78	166	2,494	178	3.3	103	123	108	171	40	11	19	21	9
1966	1,384	128	480	110	347	86	52	50	106	2,254	160	5.1	159	100	97	154	31	16	21	23	9
1967	1,722	159	690	158	401	99	73	73	155	2,660	189	3.9	122	119	117	186	37	12	21	20	10
1968	2,157	200	2,225	508	1,032	255	225	233	496	4,618	329	2.1	66	202	203	322	43	10	19	18	10
1969	2,930	271	1,509	345	515	127	160	153	326	5,760	410	3.8	119	295	254	403	53	6	16	14	11
1970	3,746	347	1,675	382	447	110	163	158	336	9,764	695	5.8	181	474	434	689	57	7	14	13	9
1971	2,093	194	1,148	262	549	136	—	—	—	13,434	956	11.7	366	600	607	963	42	11	14	24	9

Notes for Column: (8) and (9) As for Columns (1) and (2) respectively, except that the figures for Workers Involved which were deducted for coal mining relate to stoppages in progress rather than the stoppages beginning in each year.

(10) = (9) ÷ (8).

(11) (a) Includes strikes and members of unions in the coal mining industry.

(b) Excludes strikes and members of unions in coal mining (the latter had to be estimated from 1969–70).

(12) As for Column (5), except that the days lost in coal mining (deducted from the total) are for stoppages in progress.

(13) = (12) ÷ (9).

(14) (a) Refers to all U.K. days lost (Column 5) and all employees in employment at each mid-year.

(b) Excludes days lost and employees in employment in coal mining (the latter was estimated for 1970).

(15) Figures are based on stoppages beginning in the year, and exclude strikes in Mining and Quarrying.

'Working Conditions' includes the D.E.'s categories of 'Hours of work' and 'Other working arrangements, rules and discipline'.

'Employment' includes 'Disputes concerning employment or discharge of workers (including redundancy questions)' and 'Other disputes mainly concerning personnel questions'.

Authorisation of Strikes Outside Coal Mining

	(16) Number of Strikes			(17) Workers Involved			(18) Days Lost			(19) Strikers per Strike (000s)		(20) Days Lost per Striker	
	Official	Non-Official	Official:Non-Official	Official (000s)	Non-Official (000s)	Proportion Non-Official %	Official (000s)	Non-Official (000s)	Proportion Non-Official %	Official	Non-Official	Official	Non-Official
1960	68	1,098	1:16	14	563	98	497	2,010	80	0.21	0.51	35.5	3.6
1961	60	1,168	1:19	80	442	85	861	1,400	62	1.33	0.38	10.8	3.2
1962	76	1,168	1:15	309	456	60	609	1,340	69	4.07	0.39	2.0	2.9
1963	49	1,032	1:21	80	358	82	527	878	62	1.63	0.35	6.6	2.5
1964	70	1,396	1:20	161	539	77	648	1,061	62	2.30	0.39	4.0	2.0
1965	97	1,517	1:16	94	656	87	607	1,887	76	0.97	0.43	6.5	2.9
1966	60	1,324	1:22	50	430	90	1,172	1,082	48	0.83	0.32	23.4	2.5
1967	108	1,614	1:15	36	654	95	394	2,266	85	0.33	0.41	10.9	3.5
1968	90	2,067	1:23	65	660	91	699	2,419	78	0.72	0.32	10.8	3.7
1969	98	2,832	1:29	283	1,226	81	1,613	4,147	72	2.89	0.43	5.7	3.4
1970	162	3,584	1:22	296	1,379	82	3,320	6,444	66	1.83	0.39	11.2	4.7
1971	161	1,932	1:12	376	772	67	10,007	3,427	26	2.34	0.40	26.6	4.4

Notes for Columns (16)–(20) : (a) Official strikes include those declared official by some but not all of the relevant unions.

(b) The figures for official stoppages are inclusive of coal mining where, as far as is known, official strike activity was virtually negligible (Hyman, *op. cit.*, p. 29). The Department of Employment did however report one figure for coal – 24,000 days lost in 1964 – which was excluded from the data above.

(c) The figures for non-official stoppages were derived by subtracting those for official stoppages from those for all stoppages outside coal mining. Non-official stoppages therefore include lockouts, strikes by non-unionists and unclassified stoppages, as well as unofficial strikes.

(d) The effects of the one-day Engineering stoppages of 1962 and 1968 have been excluded from the data.

Comparison by Size of Strikes: All Industries except Coal Mining

	(21) Number of Strikes			(22) Strikers (% of Total)		(23) Days Lost (% of Total)		(24) Strikers per Strike (000s)		(25) Days Lost per Striker	
	'Big' No.	'Big' (%)	'Small' No.	'Big'	'Small'	'Big'	'Small'	'Big'	'Small'	'Big'	'Small'
1959	11	(1.4)	775	44	56	75	25	18.16	0.33	18.6	4.9
1960	15	(1.3)	1,151	36	64	38	62	13.85	0.32	4.7	4.3
1961	13	(1.1)	1,215	35	65	27	73	14.30	0.28	3.3	5.0
1962	20	(1.6)	1,224	92	8	76	24	196.12	0.28	1.1	3.8
1963	10	(0.9)	1,071	29	71	44	56	12.65	0.29	5.9	3.0
1964	16	(1.1)	1,450	33	67	18	82	14.42	0.32	1.4	3.0
1965	22	(1.4)	1,592	34	66	32	68	11.58	0.31	3.2	3.5
1966	9	(0.7)	1,375	18	82	45	55	9.60	0.29	11.9	3.2
1967	17	(1.0)	1,705	21	79	30	70	8.44	0.32	5.6	3.4
1968	15	(0.7)	2,142	73	27	40	60	107.84	0.28	1.2	4.6
1969	31	(1.1)	2,899	34	66	35	65	16.77	0.34	4.0	3.9
1970	42	(1.1)	3,704	32	68	40	60	12.82	0.31	7.3	5.2
1971	31	(1.5)	2,062	47	53	74	26	17.57	0.29	18.3	5.9

Notes for Columns (21)–(25): 'Big' strikes are those involving 5,000 or more workers. Unless otherwise stated, figures refer to stoppages beginning in each year, but including days lost from those which continued into the following year. Figures deducted for Coal are based on strikes which began in the year for 'Number of Strikes', and on stoppages in progress for 'Strikers' and 'Days Lost'. Data on those strikes in Coal which involved 5,000 or more workers but lasted less than one day were not deducted from the totals for 'Big' strikes.

Strikes, and Days Lost per 1,000 Workers, by Industry

	(26)		(27)		(28)		(29)		(30)		(31)		(32)		(33)	
	Vehicles		Shipbuilding and Marine Engineering		Electrical Engineering		Mechanical and Instrument Engineering		Metal Manufacturing		Docks		Construction		Food and Drink	
	Strikes	Days	Strikes	Days	Strikes	Days	Strikes	Days	Strikes	Days	Strikes	Days	Strikes	Days	Strikes	Days
1959	100	385	85	1,116	31	35	78	57	44	122	55	280	171	97	14	14
1960	129	560	74	1,388	64	128	126	230	68	79	107	2,699	215	75	13	153
1961	102	473	91	1,473	36	118	140	121	78	469	66	1,039	286	188	24	16
1962	116	846	78	1,857	53	844	159	1,183	88	634	66	993	316	143	24	8
1963	129	360	66	460	81	150	130	72	68	179	80	317	168	225	24	12
1964	165	489	91	706	84	147	199	155	120	564	102	908	222	76	21	27
1965	165	991	129	756	103	145	193	200	128	335	81	750	261	79	30	67
1966	170	400	84	145	83	145	179	121	91	176	81	971	265	84	19	11
1967	223	612	96	736	115	228	223	179	138	323	97	4,391	256	126	62	66
1968	233	1,107	134	1,803	136	458	269	615	146	722	193	820	276	150	62	68
1969	276	1,958	89	968	204	649	431	298	336	1,171	368	3,447	285	186	112	170
1970	336	1,312	121	2,060	287	765	559	677	326	1,017	259	6,585	337	177	148	531
1971	241	3,781	83	2,787	135	784	353	460	146	609	151	1,606	234	197	74	178

Strikes, and Days Lost per 1,000 Workers, by Industry

	(34) Chemicals etc.		(35) Overland Transport		(36) Textiles Clothing and Footwear		(37) Public Utilities		(38) Distribution		(39) Coal Mining		(40) Un-named*	
	Strikes	Days	Strikes	Days	Strikes	Days	Strikes	Days	Strikes	Days	Strikes	Days	Strikes	Days
1959	9	141	32	54	29	39	4	13	11	2	1,307	473	123	403
1960	26	98	56	95	44	19	16	56	20	2	1,666	703	208	37
1961	28	45	62	52	48	17	6	8	42	5	1,458	1,103	219	39
1962	17	23	63	294	49	26	7	8	31	10	1,205	475	227	87
1963	21	37	49	22	48	18	5	5	26	8	987	522	186	18
1964	16	10	69	72	62	25	17	29	39	9	1,058	507	259	41
1965	15	23	79	205	48	40	16	34	39	7	740	729	327	29
1966	30	25	85	64	32	10	8	5	23	3	553	228	234	107
1967	34	87	100	255	67	24	13	21	26	2	394	212	272	19
1968	46	84	128	490	73	34	14	17	32	3	221	121	415	73
1969	51	114	151	214	101	112	31	45	42	7	186	2,553	453	96
1970	97	389	285	662	118	315	20	54	83	15	160	2,868	770	333
1971	50	141	83	58	97	61	8	13	54	13	135	171	384	692

Notes for Columns (26)–(40): (a) Figures for the 'Number of Strikes' relate to those beginning in each year, while those for 'Days Lost' are derived from stoppages in progress (except for Textiles & Clothing, where the figures refer to strikes beginning in the year).

(b) It is difficult to be precise about the number of workers in each industry. In the main, calculations of the days lost per thousand workers are based on the number of employees in employment at mid-year. However, in the cases of Electrical Engineering (except for 1970 and 1971), Mechanical & Instrument Engineering (except for 1970 and 1971), Overland Transport, and Coal Mining, figures for all employees (including those unemployed) have been utilised. In a few cases, estimates had to be made of very recent figures.

*On average during the whole period 1959–71 these industries accounted for 44% of the labour force, 15% of all strikes, and 31% of all days lost.

The Causes of Strikes

6

POST-WAR STRIKES IN THE NORTH-EAST SHIPBUILDING AND SHIP-REPAIRING INDUSTRY 1946–1961[1]

G. C. Cameron

I

INTRODUCTION

Over the past few years the British shipbuilding and ship-repairing industry has become known for its troublesome strikes. Statistical support for this notion can be found in Ministry of Labour figures which show that in the decade from 1949 to 1958 only coal-mining had a higher yearly average number of stoppages, and no other industry lost as many days per thousand employees as did shipbuilding and ship-repairing. After the war the loss of working days in shipbuilding tended to fall, but 1954 saw the start of an upward trend which continued throughout the rest of the decade. Part of this rise was due to three nation-wide strikes; one in 1954 and another in 1957 involved all shipbuilding workers, and one in 1960 only apprentices. Despite the importance of these highly organized encounters between unions and employers, the typical strike has been the small local stoppage of limited duration and effect. These local stoppages were nearly always conducted without the approval or the initial leadership of the permanent local or national trade union officials. On the North-East coast, for example, at least 90 per cent of all such disputes during 1946–1961 were started in this way, and could thus be regarded as unofficial.[2]

All kinds of reasons have been given for the outbreak of these local strikes. Drawing a sharp contrast between the length and severity of some disputes, and the apparent triviality of their cause, many commentators have concluded that a few agitators are the source of all the trouble. Other writers have pointed out that even in this strike-prone industry, each worker loses only a very few days per annum though strikes, and far less in any case than he is likely to lose through illness. It is the purpose of this article to show that local strikes can be seen as a response to the methods employed in ship construction. These methods necessitate the employment of the separate trades in turn, creating job insecurity and variability of earnings as well as favourable opportunities for labour claims. It will also attempt to show that job insecurity must be seen not only in terms of yard layout and opportunities for alternative local employment, but also in the light of employers' and unions' efforts, or lack of efforts, to reduce the insecurity. To this end a brief but detailed analysis of strikes in the North-East section of the industry will be attempted, and will be followed by a general analysis of the causes of these strikes with special reference to strikes over wages and demarcation.

II

THE NORTH-EAST AND STRIKES

The North-East has long been associated with the building and repairing of ships. For example, as early as 1840, 64,000 tons of shipping was launched on the Wear.[3] At present the industry is centred on the three main rivers of the region, the Tyne having 56 per cent of the total employment in the industry, the Wear 22 per cent and Tees 13 per cent, with small single-firm centres at West Hartlepool,[4] Blyth and Berwick. In the area as a whole, something over 60 per cent of the industry's employees work in shipbuilding with the remainder in ship-repairing. Seven out of every ten of the ship-repairing workers are employed on Tyneside.[5] In terms of output there is great variety from firm to firm. Some companies concentrate entirely on building or repairing but others combine the two functions, and in a few cases marine-engine works are part of the organization as well. In recent years these output divisions have become blurred by amalgamations and commercial tie-ups.[6] These links have been brought about largely because of the tremendous increase in competition from foreign builders and repairers, which has also induced many firms to modernize their yards and docks in ways which will allow varied sizes and types of vessel to be built. On the labour side, the industry contains an extremely high proportion of skilled craftsmen. For example, of the 27,000 work-people employed in North-East shipbuilding in August 1956, almost 60 per cent were recognized either as fully skilled craftsmen or as training to be skilled craftsmen. The ship-repairing figure for the same date was approximately 54 per cent.[7] As one would expect in this old and highly skilled industry, almost all of the labour force belong to one or other of the many unions, of which the Boilermakers and the Shipwrights are the strongest numerically.

In comparison to other shipbuilding areas the North-East has, over the last hundred years or so, enjoyed a reputation for good labour relations, and the loss of working days per employee due to strikes has been significantly smaller. In this area, collective bargaining and conciliation as a means of solving outstanding disputes has long been accepted. For example, the first local conciliation board in British shipbuilding was formed on the Wear in 1850. In 1894, moreover, the shipbuilders of the Tyne, Wear and Tees came to an agreement with the Boilermakers Society whereby both sides were to give one month's notice of any claim for a change in wage rates. There were no similar agreements on conciliation and wage bargaining in other areas until the national agreement of 1909. Currently, there is strong evidence to show that the loss of working days per employee through strikes is significantly lower in the North-East than in some other shipbuilding centres.

TABLE 1

Area	No. of strikes	Works involved	Working days lost	
			Total	per employee
North-East Coast	237	38,911	148,856	3·4
Scotland	680	184,502	1,128,494	24·8
Rest of U.K.	328	171,190	2,206,431	16·9

Private sources. The number of disputes includes some post-1958 marine engineering stoppages.

Table 1 shows that in the period 1946 to 1961 the average North-East Coast shipbuilding and repairing worker lost only one-seventh of the time of his counterpart in Scotland, and one-fifth of the loss of working days per employee in the rest of the U.K. Nevertheless, by comparison with other U.K. industries, North-East shipbuilding and repairing was highly strike-prone in post-war years. Further, it is clear from the pattern of days lost in strikes that the North-East sector of the industry followed the over-all U.K. trend. Thus a high loss period from 1946 to 1950 was followed by a low stable period from 1951 to 1955, and a high increasing period from 1956 to 1961 (see Table 2).

TABLE 2

Loss of Working Days in Shipbuilding and Ship-repairing, 1946–1961 North-East and U.K.

Period	Loss of Working Days N.E. (annual average)	Loss of Working Days U.K. (annual average)
1946–1950	11,201	185,342
1951–1955	4,215	170,864
1956–1961	11,936	283,387

III

When the over-all North-East picture is examined some particularly interesting facts on the frequency, length and cause of strikes in the different areas of the region from 1946 to 1961 are discernible.[8]

TABLE 3

Area	Number of Strikes	Number of Strikes per 1,000 employees	Loss of Working Days per 1,000 employees
Wear	86	8·2	4,000
Tees	22	3·6	4,100
Tyne	73	2·8	1,900
Hartlepools, Berwick and Blyth	51	12·0	7,200

These calculations are based on Ministry of Labour regional aggregates, and upon newspaper reports. They do not include any disputes in marine engineering works (which were to some extent included in national totals after 1958) and exclude disputes which lasted for less than a day or involved fewer than ten workers except where the total loss of working days exceeded 100.

Table 3 shows quite clearly how much more frequent strikes were in the Hartlepools, Berwick and Blyth area and on Wearside than they were on Teeside and Tyneside. There were also considerable differences in the lengths of stoppages in the four areas. Table 4 indicates that whereas more than one-quarter of all North-East disputes were over in one day or less, and 60 per cent finished within three days, Wearside had an exceptionally high percentage of short strikes (35 per cent concluded in one day or less) but on Tyneside over a third of all strikes lasted longer than five days.

TABLE 4

Length of Stoppage in Working Days	Wear %	Tyne %	Tees %	Other %	Total N.E. %
0 – 1	35	19	27	27	27
1 + to 3	33	28	31	33	31
3 + to 5	17	14	14	14	16
5 + to 10	7	14	18	14	12
10 + to 15	3	9	5	2	5
15 +	5	16	5	14	9
	100	100	100	100	100

Taking all the basic statistics together, it is clear that although Wearside disputes are frequent, they are, on the whole, extremely short. Tyneside disputes, on the other hand, are infrequent, but often of considerable length. The strikes on Teeside were also infrequent and often only a little shorter than on Wearside. Finally, the remaining region – which covers the 'isolated' North-East yards and berths – shows a normal incidence of short strikes, but a particularly high percentage of long disputes.[9]

Differences of frequency and length are of a far greater order than the differences in cause of strikes in the four areas. Even allowing for the immense difficulties in classifying the real cause of a strike,[10] it is clear from Table 5 that in every area wage disagreements were a major source of strife. In three of the four areas, demarcation disputes were also very prominent. On Tyneside, however, only two demarcation disputes were recorded in the sixteen years from 1946 to 1961.

TABLE 5

Cause	Tyne	%	Wear	%	Tees	%	Other	%	All	%
Wages	1,680	86	1,530	38	2,190	54	2,650	37	1,800	57
Demarcation	50	3	1,750	43	1,690	41	3,450	48	940	30
Dismissal and Redundancy	80	4	410	10	90	2	560	8	220	7
Working Arrangements, Rules and Discipline	60	3	250	6	100	3	440	6	140	4
Trade Union Status and Sympathy	80	4	110	3	—	—	70	1	80	2
Total	1,950	100	4,050	100	4,070	100	7,170	100	3,180	100

Two other basic points are worthy of note. First, a large proportion of all the strikes broke out in a few companies. For example, on Wearside two firms employing approximately 25 per cent of the total area labour force accounted for 55 per cent of all Wearside demarcation strikes, and 40 per cent of all Tyneside wage strikes broke out in one company employing less than 15 per cent of the Tyneside labour force. Secondly, on the labour side, the most frequent strikers were the skilled craft workers of the black squads (see Table 6).

TABLE 6

Trade	% of All Strikes	% of Total Loss of Working Days	Trades % of Total Employment
Black squads *	56	70	24
Finishing **	25	24	34
All other ***	19	6	42

* Platers, drillers, welders, riveters, holders-on, caulkers and burners.
** Joiners, shipwrights, riggers, blacksmiths, coppersmiths, plumbers, sheet-metal workers, electricians, painters, mechanics, fitters and turners.
*** Labourers, apprentices and semi-skilled workers.

IV

CAUSES OF STRIKES

The statistics given in Section III raise several questions on the causes of strikes. Why were there considerable variations in the number of strikes and loss of working days in the four areas of the North-East? Secondly, why were wage strikes important in all areas, and how did Tyneside largely avoid the demarcation strikes which affected all the other areas? Again, how did certain companies largely avoid strikes, and why were some trades prone to pursue their grievances by striking? Finally, and more tentatively, do the variations in length of strike suggest that the strike weapon is used differently according to the cause of the strike and the area of incidence?

Insecurity

Insecurity of employment appears to be a major cause of strikes in the shipbuilding industry. This insecurity has arisen from three sources in post-war years. In the first place, shipbuilding is an assembly industry in which the skills of the many trades are used in turn, so when the work of any particular trade is finished on one vessel, there is the possibility that other vessels in the yard will not be at a stage of building which requires the skill of the particular trade which is seeking new work.[11] Moreover, if payoffs are necessary, they can well affect a large percentage of the total numbers of the trade in the yard since each vessel involves a high proportion of total yard output, and consequently of yard employment. Table 7 shows how unemployment in Northern shipbuilding not only varied greatly over the years 1953 to 1961, but tended to be considerably higher than unemployment for the region as a whole.

The figures given do not, however, show the considerable variation in demand for shipbuilding labour which can occur during any given year. Thus even in years such as 1955 and 1957 when the average level of unemployment was low – approximately 1·3 per cent in both cases – some months in each of these years had unemployment averages of three or four times this amount; and although the figures given for May 1959 and May 1960 show a high level of unemployment, they were by no means the highest points reached in either of these years.

Besides the non-continuity of employment which production techniques induce, insecurity has also arisen from the considerable reduction in the labour force which has taken place in post-war years and especially since 1957. This has been caused by a fall-off in orders for both the building and repairing of vessels, and also because

TABLE 7

Year	Tyne incl. Blyth		Wear		Tees incl. West Hartlepool		Total N.E. Shipbuilding		Total all Employment Northern Region
	1*	2**	1*	2**	1*	2**	1*	2**	1*
1953	3·8	3·7	5·9	4·9	1·2	1·2	3·6	3·5	2·3
1954	4·3	4·2	4·3	3·9	1·5	1·5	3·8	3·6	2·3
1955	1·9	1·9	2·3	2·2	1·3	1·3	1·9	1·9	1·7
1956	1·1	1·1	3·1	2·0	1·0	1·0	1·5	1·3	1·4
1957	2·5	2·5	3·4	3·1	1·4	1·4	2·5	2·5	1·7
1958	2·7	2·7	6·0	5·0	2·2	2·2	3·1	3·0	2·2
1959	5·5	5·5	8·2	7·4	4·5	4·5	5·9	5·7	3·3
1960	7·7	7·6	16·2	15·9	5·4	5·0	9·2	9·1	2·8
1961	5·0	4·9	5·8	5·8	3·2	3·2	4·9	4·9	2·3

* Total Unemployed   ** Wholly Unemployed i.e. minus Temporarily Stopped

Source: Ministry of Labour.

(a) Ministry of Labour unemployment figures do not allow an analysis to be made for the four areas of the North-East previously outlined.

(b) The wholly unemployed total excludes men 'temporarily stopped'.

(c) In shipbuilding North-East is the same as the North Region.

(d) The comparison between Northern shipbuilding unemployment and total Northern unemployment is not strictly valid since the former refers to wage earners and the latter to all employees. If comparable figures for regional wage earners were available then these would probably show a higher percentage unemployed than the figure given here.

recent modernization in the yards and docks has led to the introduction of labour-saving equipment.

TABLE 8

1956	41,203
1957	41,831
1958	39,915
1959	38,060
1960	34,241
1961	34,044

Table 8 shows how in the space of five years the run-down in the labour force was of the order of 20 per cent. For some skills the reduction in employment opportunities was even more severe, for not only were they affected by a decline in over-all demand for skill, but also by technical changes which tended to require the use of other skills. Thus some of the riveting trades declined by more than 50 per cent over the period.

Variability of earnings must also be seen in relation to job insecurity. This is partly caused by the system of remuneration by which most trades are paid–piece-work and lieu rates–for these can

bring fluctuating prices as each new job is 'rated'. Of greater importance, however, is the fact that the earnings opportunities for any
trade are related to the changing stages of vessel assembly. Thus
even if a trade is not paid off at the conclusion of its work on one
vessel, it may have its overtime opportunities reduced or completely
removed, or be under-employed.

Insecurity of employment and variability of earnings may thus
be caused by three distinct factors which influence the demand for
shipbuilding labour. First, the production process itself may cause
a trade to be utilized in one week, and surplus in the next. Secondly,
the long-term demand for all shipbuilding skills has been downward, due to the fall-off in orders for vessels and the replacement of
labour by capital equipment. Finally, the need for some skills has
been considerably reduced as a result of the introduction of changed
methods of ship construction and repair.

There are two aspects of the relationship between job insecurity,
earnings variability and strikes.[12] First, we must make clear the
reasons for the actual 'timing' of disputes as distinct from their
underlying causes, and secondly, we must treat the timing and causes
of wage disputes separately from all other disputes.

Insecurity and Wage Strikes

Although there is no statistical way of proving that insecurity is
the root cause of many wage strikes,[13] evidence from personal
interviews and the findings of writers such as D. J. Robertson and
J. R. Parkinson[14] suggest that most workers in the industry expect
variable earnings and possible unemployment, and they therefore
feel that they must earn as much as they can whilst the going is good.
This leads to wage claims at a point when the men of a particular
trade or trades calculate that the management has a great need for
their skill, and when the general level of local employment does not
allow tradesmen to be brought into the yard at short notice. On these
occasions the men's expectancy is that management will accede to
the wage claim, and if the employer proves either tardy or obstinate
in dealing with this claim, then the men are likely to come out on
strike. Thus whilst insecurity provides the basic cause of such disputes, their timing is largely dictated by the state of the market for
labour. For example, between 1950 and 1961 there were eighty-one
recorded wage disputes. The outbreak of a large number of these disputes could be directly related to the level of wholly unemployed in
three separate North-East districts: Tyne (including Blyth), Wear,
and Tees (including West Hartlepool). This relationship was
established by enumerating the highest and lowest annual points of

local wholly unemployed and relating to these points the number of local wholly unemployed at the outbreak of each strike. Fifty-six of the eighty-one disputes started when the level of unemployment was either at the lowest annual point or not greatly in excess of that point. Eleven disputes had an uncertain connection with the level of unemployment, as they occurred when the number of unemployed lay between 30 per cent and 50 per cent above the lowest annual point of local unemployment. Fourteen disputes appeared to have no connection with the level of unemployment. The basic point here is that fluctuations in the demand for ships, and the technique of ship production itself create periods when particular types of labour are in excess of demand as well as providing occasions when particular skills are in short supply. At the root of many wage strikes then, is the strikers' desire to cover for these 'lean periods' by making the most of the 'fat years'.

Insecurity and Other Strikes

Craftsmen may discern another source of job insecurity in management proposals to change the methods of ship construction or repair. All the men in the yard or dock may join together to oppose these changes on the grounds that they will reduce the total demand for labour, or specific craftsmen may fight the proposals because they see their own particular work allocation in jeopardy. The first type of conflict, which is classified as an attack on working arrangements, was particularly likely when local aggregative demand for shipbuilding or repairing labour was falling, and any management proposal which was seen as intensifying this position was promptly met by strike action. Several disputes of this kind occurred on Wearside in 1958, when a particular company was drastically re-organizing its yard layout during a period of rising unemployment. The kind of change which affects the job allocation of particular trades has a more complex relationship to strike action.[15] In general, the trades which were numerically strong, and whose membership was increasing or was more or less constant, were prone to fighting lengthy demarcation strike battles with employers who appeared to be trying to reduce the trades' job allocation. These attempts to change policy by strike action were particularly likely when unemployment was high for the given year. Finally, it is clear that some demarcation disputes broke out not because management introduced new methods, but because craftsmen felt insecure during periods when unemployment was on a rising trend. In these circumstances, claims for particular job-allocations were backed by strike

action at unemployment 'low points', in order to establish precedents
for the expected period of high unemployment.

Other Work Opportunities

The general level of employment of the labour force as a whole or
of particular parts of it does not, however, explain the varying
incidence of strikes by area, company and trade. One explanation
for differing strike activity by company, is the degree of job security
which the particular organization of the yard allows. For example,
the company which operates several building berths and ship-
repairing dry docks may be able to plan the continuous use of its
labour force knowing that tradesmen can be switched from declining
work on one vessel to other work within the company organization.
Internal transfers of this kind are never simply arranged, since most
workers prefer to remain attached either to shipbuilding or ship-
repairing. Furthermore, transfers often involve a degree of geographical labour mobility, and the employers may feel that the
added cost of paying for workers' travelling expenses makes it
more economical to employ local labour. Nevertheless, where
transfers are practicable they can create a greater degree of job
continuity than is possible in smaller single-site, single-function
organizations.

Looked at from a broader perspective, job security can be
furthered by the approximate balance of employment opportunities
between local shipbuilding and ship-repairing. On Tyneside, these
two sections of the industry each employed approximately half of
the industry's labour force. There is evidence, at least in some
months, that when shipbuilding or ship-repairing was laying-off
men, the other section of the industry could take up the slack.

TABLE 9

1951 = 100

	1951	1952	1953	1954	1955	1956	1957	1958	1959	1960	1961
Shipbuilding	100	99	106	107	97	111	118	111	111	105	109
Repairing	100	120	124	104	115	119	128	120	100	98	89
Total	100	108	113	105	105	113	122	114	105	102	106

Source: Shipbuilding Employers' Federation Figures.

Thus in the two years 1952 and 1955, when Tyneside shipbuilding
employed fewer operatives than it did in 1951, ship-repairing
compensated for the shipbuilding decline. Similarly the sharp
decline in ship-repairing employment in 1961 was offset by a rise in
employment in shipbuilding. Clearly the same is not true of 1958,
1959, and 1960 when there was a continuous fall in the total numbers

employed, but the over-all chances of alternative employment can be contrasted to those available on Wearside, where only a very few workers were employed in ship-repairing and transfers from shipbuilding were consequently even more limited than on Tyneside. The effects of these 'organizational' differences are also partially reflected in the rates of local unemployment, which show that Tyneside and Teeside were able to maintain a higher degree of employment than was the case on Wearside as Table 7 indicated.

Job security must also be related to the opportunities for employment outside the shipyards and dry docks. Scattered evidence suggests that in this respect Tyneside and Teeside were areas with reasonable opportunities for other work during the 50's, but that Wearside and the remaining districts were not so favourably placed. In these two latter areas the lack of opportunities was due to the fact that shipbuilding and repairing employed a far higher percentage of the total local working population than was the case on Tyneside and Teeside. Because of this, the prosperity of the local working population was far more closely linked to the fortunes of this one industry, and if lay-offs were current in shipbuilding, other employment was a rather remote possibility.

Obviously, Tyneside-Teeside job security must not be exaggerated, nor can the relative infrequency of strikes in these areas be totally explained in terms of large, diversified company organizations, a balance between local shipbuilding and ship-repairing, or the availability of alternative local employment. Nevertheless, a 'favourable' company organization may have reduced the possibilities of demarcation disputes arising from technical change, in that workers could be moved to other positions within the company whilst the modernization proceeded, or could be found other work if this modernization replaced or reduced their former work. In any event, with reasonably wide alternatives for employment outside the company, any dissatisfaction with a management 'job-reducing' policy could conceivably be answered by labour turnover rather than by strikes.

Managerial Policy

It has been suggested that strikes mainly arise because of the insecurity of employment which production techniques and the long-term decline of the labour force induce. It has also been suggested that strikes are more likely where technical change, the difficulties of internal job transfers and lack of other employment opportunities heighten the effects of insecurity. Yet in themselves these factors do not satisfactorily explain the varied strike activity by area, company and trade. Human factors are of far greater importance. For example, managerial awareness of the connection between job and income insecurity and strikes may well determine whether management policy exacerbates this insecurity or modifies it.

Job Insecurity

Some managers have ameliorated the effects of job insecurity by informing each other in advance of forthcoming redundancies, and by attempting to arrange immediate transfers of labour when the lay-offs actually arose.[16] The statistical correlation between this kind of policy and lack of strikes is hard to establish, but it may be of relevance to note that the increase in Wearside demarcation strikes after 1957 coincided with a drive to reduce the rise in shipbuilding costs, and as part of this policy, advance information on redundancy and firm-to-firm transfers of labour were scaled down.[17]

A closer relationship between management policy and lack of strikes could be seen in those firms which consistently explained to their workers the reasons for technical change and how these changes would affect the labour force. This policy was often backed by a willingness to consult the unions at each stage in the introduction of new equipment and new methods of production. Such explanation and consultation seems to have been of vital importance in preventing strikes, especially where major technical changes were introduced in a very short space of time. For example, one Wearside company was able to alter considerably its methods of plate-cutting by installing a new machine, without any ensuing strike trouble. This was accomplished by reaching an agreement with the union of the men likely to be affected by the machine's introduction, and then by giving these men full-scale information and instruction, in company time, on the operation of the machine. This was all completed prior to the formal introduction of the machine.

Clearly the timing and content of such information and consultation is important, particularly where redundancies or internal job re-allocations are involved. Vague, generalized information, months in advance of the actual changes, not only runs the risk of considerable amendment, but may also provide the kind of uncertainty over job and income security which can lead to 'emotional' strikes against the changes when they are finally introduced. This appears to have happened in one company where information on the radical changes which the management was envisaging was allowed to filter through to the labour force, without precise details being given of how the changes would affect the total size of the labour force or how the individual trades would fare. When the changes were introduced several strikes broke out in protest against the management's handling of the situation. In this case it was clear that the management decided to push through the changes speedily, whatever the strike consequences,[18] and at this stage information to the labour force was clearly regarded as superfluous.

Finally, some managers have tried to eradicate or minimize possible demarcation problems by giving the pre-building design plans of each vessel to the unions concerned, and asking them to agree on the allocation of work amongst the various trades. This appears to have been particularly successful on Teeside in recent years, in that each trade knew exactly what tasks lay in its province before work on the vessel commenced. This scheme may well have reduced the danger of demarcation disputes in Teeside yards.[19]

Wage Problems

In the shipbuilding industry there are several wage problems[20] which have a distinct connection with strikes. We have already suggested that tradesmen may seek to iron out fluctuations in their earnings by making wage claims at a point when management greatly requires their particular skill. Strikes often followed a management rejection or delayed decision on such claims. A good example of this type of dispute is the pre-launching strike of the shipwrights. Amongst the duties of this craft is the preparation and control of the launching of each vessel, and this time-period provides a highly suitable occasion for a wage claim which can, if necessary, be backed by a short strike. In most cases managements simply conceded the shipwrights' claim, although on one occasion on Wearside a management's refusal to conform to this 'normal practice' led to a lengthy strike and the cancelling of the official launching of the vessel.

Some of these strikes were caused not so much by management obstinacy, as by a failure to deal with the wage claim as soon as it arose. These delays may have arisen because the production manager was in control of the rate negotiations. Whatever the merits of having a manager who can make wage decisions on the basis of clear knowledge of what each craftsman does, it would seem obvious that no production manager, however willing, can spend much time on wage-rate bargaining. By the time meetings between the shop stewards and the manager, and then the manager and the local union official have been arranged, the men's impatience with inaction may lead to a strike.

Management is also faced with the problem of fixing new rates, since more than 80 per cent of the labour force have company-bargained incentive payments over and above the basic time rates laid down by national agreements.[21] By and large, most black squad workers (i.e. the steelworking trades) are paid by piece-work or lieu rates, whilst finishing tradesmen work under contract or nominal forms of payment-by-result.[22] The difficulties of these several systems are somewhat different in character, in that piece-work or lieu rates may require too frequent bargaining with a consequent increase in potential dispute, whereas payment-by-result schemes run the risk of causing conflict because of the complexities of relating wage payments to effort.

Piece-work bargaining is complicated by several factors. Because of the wide range of vessel types which each yard or dock undertakes, there may be a continual need for the rating of new work, or 'jobs' as they are called. Rating may also be increased by the introduction of new methods of building or repair, and this faces management with the considerable problem of finding time to conduct rate bargaining and to achieve a 'fair rate for the job' at a point where technical difficulties may be uppermost in their minds. Given the frequency and complexity of rate bargaining, it becomes apparent that the chances of conflict between union officials and the management must be high. Furthermore, this frequent bargaining over new rates provides the trades involved with an excellent opportunity for backing their demands by strike action.

Even allowing for the difficulties which management face in settling new rates, they cannot be completely absolved from responsibility for causing wage strikes of this kind. It has been suggested that the production manager's control of rate bargaining may be a contributory cause of wage strikes, but what may be of more fundamental importance is the failure of managers to recognise that new jobs will require new rates, and to make the necessary arrangements for rate bargaining. For example, the failure of a Tyneside manager to appoint a deputy to conduct rate bargaining led to a strike when this manager had to be absent from the yard and a new rate had to be settled.

The problems of paying finishing tradesmen do not appear as acute as those involved in the payment of the black squads. Most finishing workers are employed on a contract which covers the whole of a particular trade's work on the vessel, and this is broken down into the number of man-hours needed to complete this task. Bonus payments are then added to the standard time rates on the basis of any hours 'saved' by output in excess of the contracted norm. This method of payment caused few disputes in North-East yards, and those that did occur seemed to result either from the difficulty of relating week-by-week effort to a bonus which in essence was supposed to cover a period of months, or from trades-men claiming that their bonus was not as large as that in operation in other companies.

This question of inter-trade and inter-company wage differentials was clearly a continual source of post-war strikes in North-East yards. In this industry – because of close-proximity working (i.e. in and around the berth) and high labour mobility between yards – newly-established rates quickly became known to all the other trades. For example, the success of the growing trades in improving their rates was widely recognised by the declining trades and led to attempts by this group to emulate the success of others. When managements rebuffed these attempts, short 'emotional' strikes resulted. It is difficult to see how management could have avoided these strikes (even if it had wanted to), but management handling of differential rates may not have had such a neutral role in the creation of strike causes. During periods of low unemployment there is evidence to show that in order to attract labour, some managements were willing to pay rates different from those generally prevailing in the locality. Tradesmen working in other yards then claimed comparability increases and threatened strike action if these were not granted. In one case on Tyneside where this happened, the management refused to pay the higher rate; the men came out on strike and then promptly left their employment to join a firm willing to pay the higher rate. On this occasion the failure of the companies to agree on a common local rate, and the willingness of the second management to break traditional practice by employing men involved in a current dispute, created a situation which was fully exploited by the strikers.

The Trades and Strike Incidence

The policies of some companies on job security and wages clearly limited the outbreak of strikes in these firms, but previous figures showed that certain tradesmen were generally more apt to strike than other craftsmen. This was partly due to the greater insecurity which these 'striking trades' experienced. There is a great deal of evidence which shows that the black squads, as a whole, find it much more difficult than the finishing trades to obtain work outside the yards.[23] In some cases this is because the black squad skill is specific to the shipyards (e.g. shipwrights' work), or because the outside demand for the skill has declined even more rapidly than the shipbuilding demand (e.g. riveting). Difficulties of skill transfer may also arise because the shipbuilding craftsmen have concentrated on a different type of work, or failed to learn new techniques of work (e.g. welding). The steelworking trades' greater strike militancy could therefore be explained in terms of a greater dependence for their income on this one industry, and a resulting inability to solve unsettled grievances by voluntary change of employment. An added explanation of the frequent strikes of trades such as riveters is that they are in decline; another possible cause of the proneness of the steelworkers to strike is that they are paid by piece rates which entail a greater chance of conflict, as well as giving more scope for using the frequent rate bargaining as an occasion for striking. These explanations do not, however, give a totally satisfactory evaluation of the strike habits of the different trades. For this, a brief account of union attitudes to strikes and a more detailed study of disputes in terms of length and type of issue selected for strike action are both required.

Trade Union Attitudes to Strikes

Of all the unions with members in the shipbuilding industry only the leaders of the major union, the United Society of Boilermakers, have openly discussed the role of strikes in the union strategy. The attitude of the Boilermakers' General Secretary, Mr Ted Hill, is quite clear-cut as a recent statement shows:

> ... If a strike is on a question of wages we have got to support it. Sometimes it has got to be unofficial but if it is for the purpose for which unions were formed, I can always find a way to justify it.[24]

This view seems to imply three things. First, the official union leaders accept that the unofficial strike is one way of 'backing up' wage claims. Secondly, it accepts that the shop stewards in the yard must have a very wide degree of discretion in calling any strike, and promises that executive support for all wage strikes will be forthcoming, as will support for anything which furthers the 'purpose' of the unions. Finally, there is an almost implicit assumption that strike conflict is inevitable.

Mr Hill's views accord well with recent statements by other rank and file members of his union. For example, one shop steward delegate to the 1960 Trades Union Congress, in rejecting that part of the General Council's *Report on Unofficial Disputes* which called for the disciplining by individual unions of unofficial strikers who constantly flouted the instructions of the union executive, said:

> ... Bro. George Brinham proved yesterday that the class struggle is as acute to-day as it has ever been. Therefore we shall depend more on the

militancy of the rank and file if we are to win our point of view in the struggle for socialism and for the principles of the trade union Movement. I am a shop steward and I have probably committed every crime that the authors of this Report condemn, but no one has ever accused me of disloyalty to the trade union Movement or to the class to which I belong. . . . Our job is to protect the most valuable asset the trade union Movement has, and that is the energetic, militant men and women who accept the responsibilities as shop stewards at workshop level. They are continually faced by a threat of victimisation. They are misrepresented by a hostile Press. Do not let us add any further threats for the work that they are doing. . . .[25]

Further evidence for this rank and file militancy and willingness to bend all efforts to the class struggle is given by the statement of a North-East member of the Boilermakers who said: '. . . you can't lose wages when you are on strike for you are not working for them. . . .'

All these views bring out the militancy of the union and show how the strike, whether official or unofficial, is regarded as one weapon in the continual battle for improving the workers' lot.

Strike Frequency, Length of Strike, and Strike Issues

The reasons for the comparative infrequency of strikes by other unions cannot be understood without further detailed research, but frequency of strikes is not the only guide to a union's attitude to the unofficial strike weapon. Thus although an analysis of the trades involved in wage strikes from 1946 to 1961 shows that the black squads were, for their size, the most active strikers, at least two of the larger finishing trades (the electricians and the joiners) were also involved in several lengthy disputes. It is also noticeable that such frequent strikers as the riveters and holders-on were mostly involved in very short stoppages which tended to disappear altogether as the numbers in the trade dwindled. On the other hand the considerable growth in the number of welders (the trade which has largely super-seded riveting) was not matched by a similar increase in the number of welders' wage strikes. Nevertheless, from 1952 to 1961 the welders failed to strike only in one year and in most cases these strikes were long and tough e.g. on Tyneside several lasted more than fifteen days). The implication of this is that the bargaining power of the crafts was closely linked to their numerical importance. Where a craft was numerically strong, and the demand for its services was increasing or was reasonably constant, managements were much more likely to accede to wage demands without the craft having to resort to strike action. When strikes did break out they tended to be lengthy battles, with neither side willing to concede defeat, for management aimed at showing the 'strong trades' that they must not expect an increased rate whenever they asked for it, and in their turn the 'strong trades' were determined to show management how difficult it would be to operate the yards without their services. The infrequent but long disputes of such trades as the welders, platers, joiners and electricians were thus deliberate trials of strength.

The success of the powerful trades had the effect of persuading the declining trades to attempt to achieve comparable treatment, and this led to the frequent, but short, protest strikes of such trades as the riveters. Although these took the form of an attack on management policy, they were also symptomatic of a weakening bargaining power and a failure to emulate the policy-changing powers of the stronger trades. This success of the strong also led the smaller, but more or less constantly-demanded trades such as the burners and caulkers, to form wage strike alliances with their more powerful colleagues in the hope that this would bring them success.

It could also be argued that the more powerful trades were inclined to engage in strikes on various key issues, whereas the declining trades confined their strike activities to a narrower range of issues. For example, the platers fought on both the wage and the demarcation fronts, whilst the riveters were not highly prone to striking over demarcation–preferring to seek work from yard to yard and to concentrate their efforts on raising or guaranteeing their wages. It seems probable that the stronger trades sought job security and high earnings whilst the declining trades realised that job security was unattainable and did not strike for it.

Demarcation Disputes

Many of the problems discussed in the earlier part of this article are seen to be present when shipbuilding's most charcteristic dispute– that of demarcation, or which craftsman does which work–is closely analysed. Numerically these disputes are nothing like as important as strikes over wages, but except for two 'blank' years there was at least one demarcation strike in every year from 1946 to 1961. Moreover, nearly 40 per cent of the demarçation disputes lasted longer than five days as compared with only a quarter of all other strikes. Many of these disputes involved a very large number of workers.[26] As with disputes over wages, the black squads were the most frequent strikers, taking part in twenty-eight out of the thirty-four North-East demarcation stoppages, with the platers, shipwrights and, to a lesser extent, welders well to the fore. Alliances of trades were far less frequent than in wage disputes, and this itself suggests that the individual trades felt that this was the kind of battle which they alone could fight successfully.

TABLE 10

Length of Stoppage

Working Days	Demarcation Disputes	All Other
	%	%
0−1	21	28
1−3	26	32
3−5	15	16
5−10	23	10
10−15	6	5
15+	9	9

To categorize demarcation disputes by cause is extremely difficult, but with the help of the Ministry of Labour Classifications and newspaper reports it has been possible to separate demarcation into five main types. Of course, several of these causes may be apparent in any strike, and categorization thereafter depends not only upon an estimate of the most important cause, but also on an element of guesswork based on other relevant factors.

Table 11 requires explanation. The most important causes of the incidence and frequency of demarcation disputes appear to be not only the level of local unemployment but also its over-all annual trend. For example, it is significant that there were no category A disputes in years when the trend of unemployment was steadily upward. It is also the case that most of these dilution disputes[27] broke out when local unemployment was very low. It may be that managements were forced into attempts to employ dilutee labour because of the shortage of skilled craftsmen. This of course brought an immediate craft response–particularly from the bigger trades such as the welders and the platers. It is noticeable that these disputes were short, and this suggests that in conditions of skilled-craft shortage the employers were unwilling to antagonize the fully-skilled craftsmen, and consequently withdrew the dilutee labour.

Category C disputes (change of methods and/or materials and allocation of work) show by their length (five out of seven disputes were longer than five days) the immense difficulties involved in demarcation disputes of this kind. Under the Demarcation Agreement of 1912, an employer is entitled to allocate work claimed by different tradesmen, pending a full investigation by a committee of disputing unions and of employers. The unions concerned often regard this temporary decision as precedent-setting, and refuse to act on the allocation, although the 1912 Agreement specifically states that the temporary decision should not prejudice the final

TABLE 11

Demarcation Disputes 1949–1961

Type	Number	Cause	Decisions as to manning	Action	Response
A	4	Shortage of skilled labour (low local unemployment)	Management	Employment of dilutees (apprentices, semi-skilled, unskilled) on skilled work	Strike against dilution of skill
B	1	Long term company policy? No change in work techniques or materials used	Management	Employment of semi-skilled on skilled work	Strike against breaking of written or un-written precedent
C	7	Changes in techniques and/or materials	Management consultation with unions	If no agreement, job temporarily allocated by management	Union which feels it has done badly may strike
D	12	No immediate or current change in techniques/ materials but insecure employment conditions	Trades 'mark out' craft jobs before un-employment brings redundancies	Strike	Management may dispute claims of particular trades; long-drawn-out struggle a strong possibility
E	2	All other			

settlement.[28] What is most noticeable about these disputes is the fact that six out of seven broke out in months when local unemployment was high for the given year. This suggests that a union which finds a management's temporary manning decision unsatisfactory is more likely to fight the decision when unemployment is high. When unemployment is low there is plenty of work for everyone, and even though the decision may be regarded as unsatisfactory, there isn't the urgency to press for an immediate change in the situation. The men will wait, in fact, until the result of the final bargaining over the disputed work is known.

The fourth and major type of demarcation dispute (D) appears to arise when there is no immediately apparent technical or material change, but when future employment appears to be threatened. Here there appears to be a strong connection between strike incidence and the lowest levels of unemployment in the particular year. It appears as if each striking craft had decided to mark out its 'area of employment' in an attempt to establish precedents and to cushion the effects of the ensuing high unemployment. These disputes were most noticeable on Wearside in the highly unstable employment years after 1956.

Clearly the whole question of job security is at the root of demarcation disputes in the industry. This concern for security is not really surprising since in some localities the industry employs up to 30 per cent of the total labour force. Thus, as we have seen, any attempt to de-skill or dilute traditionally fully-skilled jobs is feared by the craftsmen, and is met by a sharp response. The speedy introduction of major technical change can diminish the numerical strength and power of the individual crafts, and create a general atmosphere of job insecurity for all trades; in these circumstances demarcation disputes are always likely. A situation of this kind appears to have existed on Wearside, but on Tyneside the technical changes seem to have been introduced in a much more gradual way.

Besides the fear of losing employment, negotiations over job allocation are bedevilled by the complexities which technical change can introduce. One strike arose because the platers (who were entitled to erect all single plates on the building berth) claimed that two plates, welded together by the welders and sent to the berth equalled a single plate. The shipwrights, however, claimed the work as they said they had the right to erect all prefabricated plates, and these units clearly came into this category. The management made a temporary decision in favour of the shipwrights, whereupon the platers came out on strike. The question at issue here is highly complex. If taken to the extreme the platers' case would mean that all prefabricated plates were theirs by right, as they constituted one plate. On the other hand, with the tremendous increase in prefabricated work, the shipwrights were in a very strong position to wait for an increasing volume of work. It is no small wonder that disputes of this kind often lasted for a considerable time.[29]

SUMMARY

This article has attempted to show that strikes in the shipbuilding and ship-repairing industry can be viewed as a labour-force response to the techniques of ship production and repair, with their pattern of job and earnings insecurity and of favourable opportunities for labour claims. In recent years this insecurity has been increased by the constant run-down in the labour force resulting from the falling demand for British-built vessels and the introduction of labour-saving equipment and methods of production. In some areas and companies insecurity of employment has been further heightened by the kind of yard organisation which does not allow a flexible and continuous use of the yard labour force, or by the lack of alternative job opportunities within the company organisation, in local yards and docks, or in neighbouring industries. Variability of earnings itself is closely linked to the demand for particular skills at progressive stages of the building and repairing process, but earnings are also affected by the uncertainties of frequent price-fixing. Both of these problems are particularly acute in localities where shipbuilding and repairing employ a high proportion of the area's working population.

In view of the uncertain employment conditions and the variability in earnings, many strikes broke out when the workers felt their chances of a successful struggle were favourable. For example, in most wage strikes it is clear that the strikers tried to force management's hand at a time when they knew their particular skill was in short supply within the yard, and when general employment conditions would prevent any of their trade from being brought in from outside. Demarcation stoppages had a less straightforward connection with the level and trend of local employment conditions, but their classification shows that the causes of dispute in the various categories were associated with particular conditions in the demand for shipbuilding labour.

This general analysis provides an explanation of the causes and timing of stoppages. For the actual incidence by area and company, 'human factors' were of greater importance. Some managers tackled job insecurity by arranging transfers of labour from company to company. Many took great pains to explain technical changes in the labour force, and only introduced such changes after consultation with the unions. Some companies sought the co-operation of the unions over job allocation and reached agreement on tasks even before the work on the vessel began. On the other hand some managements seemed to ignore the effects on the labour force of frequent lay-offs, of delay in dealing with wage claims, and of rapid and complex technical change which in some cases considerably altered both the relative strengths of the different crafts and their earning power.

The different unions and trades varied greatly in their use of strikes, and this cannot be completely explained away by their relative insecurity of employment and earnings. Certainly many of the black squads' strikes were extremely short and took the form of an emotional outburst at management delay in handling claims or because management accepted one trade's claim while rejecting a similar effort by another trade or trades. Even allowing for this, it is clear that the Boilermakers Union in particular, adopted a very 'free' attitude to unofficial strikes, and this allowed a considerable degree of latitude to the yard shop stewards in calling such stoppages of work.

Variations in strike activity in the four areas of the North-East can thus be analysed in the light of these preceding factors. For example, the lack of demarcation disputes on Tyneside in comparison to Wearside appears to be due not only to the willingness of the local unions to negotiate rather than strike, but also because yard organisation, employment opportunities and phased technical change all helped to reduce the problem of job insecurity. On the Wear employment seemed to be far less secure, for yards were smaller, ship-repairing employed few workers, and the shipbuilding industry gave work to a larger proportion of the total working force in an area which was prone to a higher level of local unemployment.

Similarly the frequency of wage strikes in all areas was clearly linked with the problems of variable earnings, differential price-fixing and of suitable opportunities for wage claims, but even here the considerable variation in the length of stoppages suggests that the strike weapon may be used differently in the four areas. Thus it could be argued that greater job security on Tyneside lent itself to lengthy strikes, whereas grievances against Wearside job and earnings insecurity found expression in the numerous short strikes.

In conclusion, it is clear that strikes in the shipbuilding industry are not a simple phenomenon to be explained by reference to the work of a few agitators. They can be interpreted as a response to the techniques of ship production and repair, with their pattern of insecurity and the opportunity they provide for labour to make claims; they must also be seen in the light of shipyard layout, local employment opportunities, and the efforts, or lack of efforts, of employers and unions to reduce the job and income insecurity of the labour force.

NOTES

1 This article was started whilst the author was a member of the Durham Colleges Business Research Unit, and he gratefully acknowledges the continual help in its preparation given by the Director of the Unit, Mr A. J. Odber. Other members of the Unit, including Mr J. E. T. Eldridge and Mr G. Roberts, were especially helpful as were Professor D. J. Robertson, Dr L. Hunter and Mr J. B. K. Hunter of Glasgow University.
2 There are considerable analytical difficulties in labelling any dispute as unofficial. The 1960 TUC Annual Report suggested that approximately 50 per cent of the strikes which were initially unofficial were later made official by the rules of the unions concerned.
3 See J. W. Smith and T. S. Holden, *Where Ships are Born – Sunderland 1346–1946*.

4 The firm at West Hartlepool has recently closed as a shipbuilding unit.

5 Shipbuilding Employers' Federation Figures.

6 A good example is the Sunderland Shipbuilding Group which includes J. L. Thompson's, Lang's, Doxford's and Greenwell's.

7 Ministry of Labour figures.

8 The figures of strike incidence in the various areas as shown in tables 1 to 5 make no allowance for the different 'weighting' of ship-repairing as a percentage of total shipbuilding/ship-repairing disputes unemployment, nor has it proved possible to separate ship-repairing from shipbuilding strikes, so there is no statistical way of determining which section of the industry is most strike-prone.

9 The number of long strikes (i.e. those over ten days) per thousand employees was greatest in the Hartlepools, Berwick, Blyth area, followed by Tyneside.

10 See A. Gouldner, *Wildcat Strike* (Routledge & Kegan Paul) for an analysis which shows the diffculty of finding the causes of any strike.

11 'In order to provide steady employment for any one occupational group, it would be necessary to phase the operations of each trade on each ship in such a way as to bring one ship to the required stage as another ship left it, and to join the curves of requirements for each occupation on a number of ships so as to provide a smooth demand for the yard as a whole.'–D. J. Robertson, 'Labour Turnover in Ship-building'–*Scottish Journal of Political Economy*, March 1954.

12 For comparative purposes see J. Bescoby and H. A. Turner, *Manchester School of Economic and Social Studies*, May 1961, and *Bulletin of the Oxford Institute of Statistics*, May, 1961.

13 It could be argued, for example, that more security would bring more wage strikes in this industry, but what evidence there is tends to make this unlikely. For example, the average annual number of wage disputes and loss of working days per employee was lower in the high employment period 1951–1955, than in the high unemployment period 1956–1961.

14 See D. J. Robertson, *Factory Wage Structures and National Agreements* (Cambridge University Press, 1960). p.. 136, and J. R. Parkinson, *The Economics of Shipbuilding* (Cambridge Unibersity Press, 1960), pp.154–181.

15 See later analysis under Trades and Strike Incidence, and under Demarcation Disputes.

16 On at least two of the rivers the Employers' Association had facilities for aiding these transfers of labour. On Wearside the Association itself often arranged the transfer of men, in consultation with the managements concerned, and even directed the transfer of equipment as well, particularly for riveting.

17 This was not, of course, the only cause of demarcation disputes in this period of rapid technical change.

18 This is not to argue that the management's policy was wrong, only that it provoked strikes.

19 There have been no demarcation disputes in Teeside yards since 1959.

20 See J. R. Parkinson, *loc. cit*. pp. 171–181.

21 J. R. Parkinson, *loc. cit*. p. 171.

22 'Productivity in Shipbuilding'–1962 ('The Paton Report').

23 A. J. Odber and J. E. T. Eldridge, 'Shrinkage in Industry', *New Society*, January 17, 1963.

24 Reported in *The Financial Times*, July 20, 1961.

25 TUC Report, 1960, p. 351.

26 See Table 10.

27 It is arguable whether this is in fact a problem of demarcation, but it has been included in order to show managements' difficulty in allocation jobs not only between skills but between recognised skill and 'probationary skill', and between skill and ability to do the job.

28 A complicating feature of this is the fact that the Boilermakers did not sign the 1912 Agreement, although on one North-East river they tend to follow the agreement.
29 The recent amalgamation between the United Society of Boilermakers and the Shipwrights' Association may help to reduce these disputes.

7

THE REASONS GIVEN FOR STRIKING

AN ANALYSIS OF OFFICIAL STATISTICS, 1945–1957

William McCarthy

For over seventy years the government has published estimates of the 'Principal Causes' of strikes. Each year the *Ministry of Labour Gazette* contains a table which lists the number of stoppages, and the number of workers directly involved, as a result of seven different causes. Considering the amount of discussion which has arisen from time to time, concerning the origins of industrial unrest, little systematic analysis of this material has been undertaken. The object of this article is to attempt such an analysis of the period 1945–1957.[1]

One possible reason why the official statistics have been neglected may be the belief that they are essentially suspect. It is sometimes suggested that the whole idea of selecting and isolating the 'principal cause' of a dispute is misconceived. It is possible to argue that any one of a multiplicity of influences has caused a series of strikes. For example, many of the strikes which took place in the years immediately before the first world war have been related to the repeal of the Taff Vale Judgement, or the spread of revolutionary syndicalism; just as the relative increase in strikes since 1953 has been partially explained by reference to the removal of controls, and the increase in luxury expenditure, which has created a situation in which 'social restraints, far more important than legal restraints, are losing their force'[2]. Then again, one can always interpret strikes as being in some way 'fundamentally' caused by still more general considerations–such as the trade cycle, or bad social conditions, just as one can attempt to explain any particular strike in sociological terms, speaking of 'tensions', or 'motivations', or 'indulgency expectations', etc.[3]

Since none of these factors has any place in the system of classification used by the Ministry of Labour it is possible to argue that nothing but confusion can result from attempts to use the official statistics in order to 'explain' strikes. But such an attitude cannot be maintained once one appreciates what the Ministry's sevenfold classification actually represents. In fact the list is wrongly named. It is not an objectively compiled list of the principal causes of industrial unrest. One assigns causes to strikes according to one's personal bias or predilections. A Marxist will draw up one list, and an industrial psychologist another. If the Ministry's classifications were nothing more than a series of personal pigeon holes, selected by some long dead civil servant according to the matrix of his own prejudices, it would be no more acceptable than any other random classification. In fact it is something more precise than this, and something more interesting. It is a classification of strike statistics according to the main or 'principal' reasons most frequently cited by those involved at the time.

This becomes obvious once one considers how the statistics are compiled. The only data available at the time are the speeches and writing of those involved, together with any comment which the conciliation officers and arbitrators may wish to make upon them. It is from these accounts that the officers of the Ministry of Labour must determine their classification. It is from these that they must abstract a more or less commonly agreed reason for the stoppage. Of course there is often more than one reason cited. Then, as the Gazette admits, the strike must be classified according to 'what appears to be' the main or principal reason. Naturally strikes sometimes arise as a result of two or more grievances in circumstances in which it is almost impossible to say which is the most important. This may result in a situation in which the official's choice of the 'principal' reason determines the classification of the strike. In these cases the Ministry officials can only be guided by the form which the argument takes. They may think that underlying the talk about wages there lie wider grievances, they may be convinced that a dispute which is outwardly an argument concerning the right to a particular class of work is actually motivated by the desire to maintain real income. But their selection of categories cannot be influenced by such inferences. They must classify the strike according to the only objective data available, and these are the reasons given for it by those most closely involved.

The sevenfold classifications available to the officials at this point are as follows:
(1) Claims for Increases in Wages.
(2) Other Wage Disputes.
(3) Hours of Labour.
(4) Employment of Particular Classes or Persons.
(5) Other Working Arrangements, Rules and Discipline.
(6) Trade Union Status.
(7) Sympathetic Action.

Each and every dispute must be fitted, or forced, into one of these categories, so that before a final verdict can be delivered upon the utility and significance of the tables which result it is necessary to know what is included in each of them. Unfortunately most of them are not self-explanatory, and the footnotes which seek to elucidate them are far from comprehensive. One footnote informs us that category (4) *'includes e.g. demarcation disputes; for reinstatement of discharged or suspended employee(s); disputes arising from employment of certain officials'*. While another states that category (6) *'includes e.g. refusal of trade union members to work, with non-unionists'*. However, we are not informed of the other kinds of disputes *'included'* in (4) and (6), and we are told nothing about the sorts of strikes classified under (5) or (2). The only category exhaustively defined is (7) i.e. *'in support of workers involved in stoppages at other establishments'*[4].

Fortunately it is possible to obtain further clarification by consulting the long out of print 1913 *Report on Strikes and Lockouts*.[5] This publication contains a fuller list of twenty or more classifications from which the seven published causes of to-day are compiled, together with examples of a large number of disputes and their appropriate classification. With its aid it is possible to ascertain the sorts of disputes which are included in each of the seven categories. Using Tables 1 and 2, which have been compiled from statistics published in the period 1945–1957, and by reference to Graphs 1 and 2 which accompany them, it is possible to go further and discuss the relative importance of each of the categories in the period since the war. Let us take each of these in turn.

(1) CLAIMS FOR INCREASES IN WAGES

This is by far the most straightforward classification and it is virtually self-explanatory. Since 1945 it has accounted for 9.2 per cent of the total number of stoppages and some 42.3 per cent of workers directly involved. Graph 1, however, shows that on two occasions a considerably larger proportion of workers on strike were said by those involved to have withdrawn their labour as a result of disputes over increases in wages. In 1953 84 per cent of all workers directly involved came into this category, while in 1957 the figure was 72.6. Yet in both cases this abnormal increase was largely due to the effects of one particular strike in the engineering industry. The first was a one day token strike which involved over a million workers, the second was the recent national engineering and shipbuilding stoppage which accounted for over 600,000.

These two instances apart the number of workers involved in stoppages as a result of wage increase disputes appears to be relatively constant in each year since the war, while the percentage of the total workers directly involved has usually been in the region of 20 per cent. Moreover, if one measures the effect of wage increase disputes on the total number of stoppages per year there would appear to be even less variation. On average this category has accounted for about 9 per cent of all stoppages, and in no single year has it been given as a principal reason for as much as 13 per cent; only a relatively stable minority of disputes since the war have been justified principally by reference to the demands of workers for increases in wages.

(2) OTHER WAGE DISPUTES

Unfortunately this category is by no means as unambiguous as (1) above. Until a few years ago it was the practice to sub-divide the wages categories into three—strikes for increases, strikes against decreases and other strikes about wages. Presumably because for some years there were virtually no strikes arising out of the attempts of employers to reduce wages, the second category was merged with the third.

'*Other wage disputes*' originally contained merely disputes concerning systems of wage payment. That is to say those which arose principally out of attempts to substitute time for piece-work, or introduce payment by results, etc. Also included were disputes where the principal argument concerned the readjustment of rates, demands for the payment of guaranteed minimums, extra pay for bad work, etc. Present day strikes principally aimed at securing payment for holidays are also classified under this heading.

It is difficult to draw significant conclusions from the figures in this category, even if one assumes that there are still very few wage decrease strikes contained within it. Nevertheless it is worth attempting to make some sense out of the figures, if only because Table 1 shows that they constitute a substantial proportion of the total. Since the war 36 per cent of all disputes come into this category, and even in terms of workers involved they have accounted for some 18.6 per cent. Of additional use here would be an industrial breakdown of this group; as the figures stand one can only infer that it is probably within strike prone industries, such as mining, engineering and shipbuilding, where there is considerable piece work, that this category is most important.

TABLE 1

Principal Causes of Disputes Leading to Stoppages of Work in the Period 1945–1957

Cause	Total No. of Stoppages	% of Total	Workers Directly Involved	% of Total	Average No. of Workers per Stoppage
Wages:					
Claims for Increases ..	2,382	9.2	2,944,100	42.3	1,236
Other Wage Disputes ..	9,299	36.0	1,294,400	18.6	139
All Wage Disputes ..	11,681	45.2	4,238,500	60.9	363
Hours of Labour ..	820	3.2	259,100	3.7	316
Employment of Particular Classes, etc.	3,227	12.5	791,300	11.4	245
Other Working Arrangements	9,172	35.5	1,049,300	15.1	115
Trade Union Status ..	567	2.2	174,200	2.5	307
Sympathetic Action ..	245	0.9	347,900	5.0	1,420
Other*	125	0.5	94,100	1.4	753
All Classes	25,837	100	6,954,400	100	269

*This category was dropped in 1952. It represented miscellaneous disputes not easily classified under other headings and was never very large.

Small stoppages involving fewer than 10 workers and those which lasted less than one day are excluded from the statistics, except any in which the aggregate number of working days lost exceeded 100.

Source: Ministry of Labour Gazette, 1945–1957. Annual article on Stoppages of Work due to Industrial Disputes.

TABLE 2

*Total and Average Number of Working Days Lost as a Result of the Principal Causes of Disputes in 1957**

Cause	Total Working Days Lost	% of Total	Average No. of Working Days Lost per Stoppage
Wages:			
Claims for Increases	7,160,000	85.2	21,896
Other Wage Disputes	327,000	3.9	351
All Wage Disputes	7,484,000	89.1	5,851
Hours of Labour	31,000	0.4	264
Employment of Particular Classes or Persons	341,000	4.1	1,258
Other Working Arrangements, etc. ..	405,000	4.8	425
Trade Union Status	62,000	0.7	984
Sympathetic Action	73,000	0.9	3,173
All Causes	8,399,000	100	2,937

*Earlier figures of this sort are unfortunately not available.

Small stoppages involving fewer than 10 workers and those which lasted less than one day are excluded from these statistics, except any in which the aggregate number of working days lost exceeded 100.

Source: Ministry of Labour Gazette, 1957, Annual article on Stoppages of Work due to Industrial Disputes.

Workers involved, and numbers of stoppages
according to principal causes of disputes, 1945–57

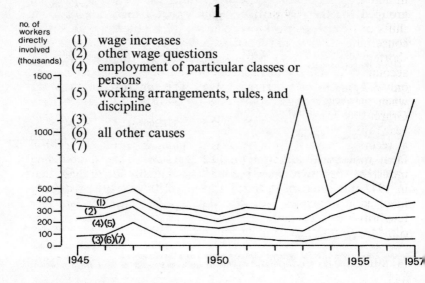

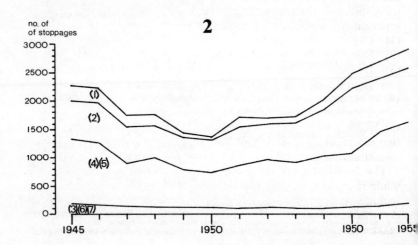

(3) HOURS OF LABOUR

This category is comparatively unimportant. There was a time when separate figures were published showing strikes *for* decreases in hours, as opposed to those *against* increases. These are now all grouped together and strikes against the introduction of night shifts or refusals to work overtime are all counted in with strikes concerning starting and leaving times and the introduction of a shorter working day. Altogether, however, they have never accounted for more than 4 per cent of stoppages, and on an average only 3.7 per cent of workers involved. The only year since the war when the pattern was broken was in 1947, as can be seen from Graph 1. A glance at the Ministry's list of major disputes for that year reveals that there were at that time a number of strikes aimed at securing a reduction of hours in road haulage, together with a fairly widespread strike for the five day week in the shipbuilding industry. These two issues account substantially for the fact that in 1947 this category included 18.5 per cent of workers directly involved in stoppages. Since that date one may conclude that very few British workers have been prepared to strike over reasons concerned with attempts to reduce hours of working.

(4) EMPLOYMENT OF PARTICULAR CLASSES OR PERSONS

This category, together with the one that follows, is both ambiguous and interesting. Both categories are statistical rag-bags. The 1913 Report lists a whole series of widely disparate disputes which have, from time to time, been included within it. It is obvious from this list that the three examples given in contemporary footnotes are incomplete if not misleading. There seem to be no less than six separate types of dispute included. They are:
(1) Demarcation disputes.
(2) Disputes concerning the reinstatement of workmen.
(3) Disputes arising out of the employment of foremen, supervisors, etc., who are objected to for various reasons.
(4) Disputes concerning claims to promotion or re-employment after redundancy.
(5) Refusals to negotiate or recognise more than one trade union.
(6) Disputes as to which of two or more trade unions a worker should join.
The last three are not mentioned in the published footnotes, while it is arguable that the last two might equally well have been included in category (6). As in the case of category (2) the apparently diverse nature of the kinds of strikes included in this group makes it seem difficult at first to draw many conclusions from it.

Yet the accompanying tables show that it is a relatively important one. In terms of workers involved this group has been responsible for 11.4 per cent of the total since 1945, while in terms of stoppages it has resulted in some 12.5 per cent of the total. Its full importance, however, can only be gauged after a consideration of category (4), with which it is closely allied.

(5) OTHER WORKING ARRANGEMENTS, RULES AND DISCIPLINE

The 1913 Report lists a whole series of disputes which are classified under this heading. The list includes strikes for 'the abolition of certain machines', objections to 'new engagement forms', or the 'use of a pneumatic elevator'. Also contained are disputes arising out of the use of certain materials, or the working of gangs, etc. At first glance this category looks like an index of Luddism, but in fact it appears to have been designed to provide a home for two quite distinct types of dispute which it unfortunately classifies together. These are:

(1) Disputes arising out of attempts to change the conditions of employment not covered by categories (2) and (3) above, i.e. alterations in systems of working which do not involve changes in methods of payment or hours.

(2) Disputes arising out of attempts to impose discipline not covered by category (4) i.e. disciplinary issues which do not involve reinstatement, or attempts to secure the removal of foremen, etc.

The need for the first of these is evident once it is realised that there are bound to be disputes in which workers will be trying to resist or advocate some proposal to change their methods of working which does not take the form of an alteration in the system of payment or hours;[6] a pigeon hole must be found for these. Similarly, some issues of discipline give rise to disputes which affect workers generally rather than particular classes of workers and these must be put somewhere too. That this residual role was intended for category (5) is made clear by its old title, which has since been abbreviated but which is given in full in the 1913 report. It runs:

'Working Arrangements, Rules and Discipline–Other than the above'.

Unfortunately this residual appears to be the single most important group affecting post-war stoppages of work. It has account-ed for 35.5 per cent of all strikes. It is less important as a reason given for numbers of workers directly involved, since it only accounts for 15.1 per cent, yet in certain years it has been relatively more important. Moreover, taken with category (4), which it in some ways resembles, it appears to be even more significant – since between them these two groups have accounted for 26.5 per cent of all workers involved and 48 per cent of all stoppages. It is here, surely, that the case for some re-classification of the *Gazette* statistics is most strong. Again what would be desirable would be a much fuller breakdown, if possible industry by industry. In the absence of this is it possible to make any meaningful use of these two groups?

One attempt to do this for the years 1911–1947 was made by K. G. J. C. Knowles.[7] Knowles grouped categories (4) and (5) together as '*frictional*' causes, and compared them with two other groups of categories over various periods since 1911. These he termed '*basic*' causes – i.e. categories (1), (2) and (3), and '*solidarity*' causes – i.e. categories (6) and (7). He found that 'Strikes on basic questions have declined in relative importance, and strikes on frictional issues have correspondingly increased'[9]. He also found that there was a very marked decline in wage increase strikes, expressed as a percentage of all strikes, and a particularly marked increase in strikes about working arrangements rules and discipline. From this he concluded that the character of strikes had perceptibly changed over the period 1911–1947. Strikes had come to be caused less by so-called '*basic*' factors, which directly involved economic questions, such as wages or hours of working, and more by so-called '*frictional*' issues such as amenities, or lack of consultation, etc.

It is clear from our two tables that this trend has continued. Knowles found that the percentage of strikes over 'basic' issues had fallen from 69 per cent in the period 1911–1925 to 54 per cent in the period 1927–47. Taking the post-war period as a whole we can see that it has dropped to 48.5 per cent. Similarly while in the two periods he compared '*frictional*' strikes rose from 22 per cent of the total to 39 per cent, in the years since the war '*frictional*' strikes have risen to 48 per cent. The two groups are now virtually the same size. Even inside the groups the trend continues relatively unchanged. Claims for wage increases have fallen to less than 10 per cent of all stoppages, while other working arrangements now account for over 35 per cent.

In one respect only have the trends noted by Knowles been reversed; the total number of workers directly involved as a result of all '*basic*' issues has actually risen slightly since the figure of 60 per cent for the period 1927–1947. Over the whole of the post-war period it stands at 64.6 per cent. This is still some 10 per cent less than the corresponding figure for 1911–1925, and as we have seen it is largely the result of two isolated engineering disputes.

It would consequently appear that categories (4) and (5) can be used significantly in order to illustrate the changing character of strikes and the increasing relative importance of so-called '*frictional*' issues.

Can any further conclusions be drawn from the continued growth in the importance of these groups? Let us reconsider the sorts of strikes that are included within these two categories; demarcation disputes have in common is resentment at an assault upon establish-behaviour of charge-hands, attempts on the part of unrecognised unions to recruit members, poaching disputes, sudden removals of established privileges, etc. One of the characteristics which *all* these disputes have in common is resentment at an assault upon establish-ed customs and practices which the group is quick to defend – if need be with a strike. Of course this is not to deny that there may often be good economic reasons for such resentment – as in the case of demarcation disputes – but this is not the point. As we have seen these classifications should be primarily regarded in terms of the reasons given for striking. So that what is significant, in the continued rise in the relative importance of categories (4) and (5), is the indication given that more and more British workers are tending to justify their withdrawals of labour in terms of what Burke would have called their 'acquired rights'. Or as they themselves would put it; in terms of 'the custom and practice of the trade'. No doubt Marxists, industrial psychologists, and others will be able to explain this, according to their own general theories of strike determination. What we have to record is that categories (4) and (5) can be regarded as a rough index of the process.

(6) TRADE UNION STATUS

What this category is an index of is not at all clear. A reading of the 1913 Report shows that it is made up of at least three widely different disputes only one of which is mentioned in contemporary footnotes. These are:

(1) Disputes arising out of attempts to eliminate non-unionists.
(2) Disputes concerning attempts to secure trade union recognition, or certain facilities for union activity – *e.g.* the right to send round collectors, etc.
(3) Disputes concerned with alleged victimisation of trade union-ists *as* trade unionists – *e.g.* the removal of shop-stewards, etc.

The category is not a large one, and it has only accounted for 2.2 per cent of all stoppages, and 2.5 per cent of all strikers in the period since 1945. These figures show the declining relative importance of this category, which in the years just before the second world war accounted for just under 10 per cent of strikes and strikers.

In some ways the group is linked to (4) and (5) above, in that many stoppages probably occurred as a result of the defence of various acquired rights–for example the 'right' not to have to work with non-unionists. In other ways the group can be regarded as an indication of attempts to acquire new rights–such as recognition, or a closed shop, the latter being by far the most important since the war. In its present form, however, it is difficult to say which movement it represents on balance, so that little can be done with it.

(7) SYMPATHETIC ACTION

This group seems to be more straightforward than it is. It is defined as 'in support of workers involved in stoppages at other establishments.' The 1913 *Report* lists a number of examples of this; 'refusal to handle goods belonging to certain firms involved in a dispute', 'because of a rumour that a steamer was loading coal for a port where a strike was in progress', etc. This gives the impression that the category includes only 'blackleg' strikes, in fact it embraces any stoppage of work in support of another group's grievances, whether blacklegging is involved or not. Nevertheless the group is not a very large one, involving less than 1 per cent of all stoppages since 1945 and a mere 5.0 per cent of workers. The only year since the war when a substantial number of workers justified their withdrawal of labour by reference to this category was in 1947, when category (7) accounted for some 20 per cent of all strikers. Then, as we have seen, there was an upsurge of strikes in favour of reductions in hours, and some of these received the sympathetic support of the dockers. This somewhat unusual trend helped to swell Knowles' *'solidarity'* category, but in fact since that date they have declined, as a glance at graphs I and II makes clear.

CONCLUSIONS

We have now completed our survey of the Ministry's sevenfold classification of strikes according to their 'Principal Causes' and must attempt to draw some general conclusions from this analysis.

Firstly, it seems fairly clear that significant use can be made of these statistics. As a classification of the reasons given for striking they appear to be basically sound. What they need is further refinement rather than any radical alteration of existing categories. Ideally what would be best would be a return to the pre-1914 practice of classifying strikes according to the twenty odd causes mentioned above, allied to the present method of supplying separate statistics for the 48 industrial groups in the standard industrial classification. If this could be done for total stoppages, workers directly involved and aggregate number of working days lost, it would help in answering a whole series of interesting questions. For example, it would then be possible to tell which industries are most troubled by demarcation disputes; where disciplinary problems are most likely to result in strikes; what groups of workers resist the introduction of time and motion study, or are most concerned with problems of redundancy, etc. At the moment only the larger strikes which are justified by reference to these issues are reported, and while most students of industrial relations could make a number of more or less shrewd guesses concerning the nature and extent of the many other strikes in these categories, a further refinement of Ministerial statistics would provide much more information on which to base such inferences. Indeed it seems possible to argue that information of this sort, by focusing attention on existing centres of unrest, might even help in suggesting ways of avoiding certain stoppages. If such a radical extension of the published figures is out of the question in these days of government economy then one would put in a plea for almost any further refinement even of the most inexpensive sort. If it is at all helpful to suggest priorities then it seems clear that a further refinement of groups (4) and (5) is needed most of all. The published figures for these groups should surely at least allow one to distinguish between demarcation disputes, strikes concerned with various disciplinary issues, and strikes which are really justified by reference to the right to organise and recruit workers into particular unions. At the moment, as we have seen, these three types of strikes are either mixed together in a single composite category, or are distributed amongst one or another of two different categories.

Turning from the possibilities of improving the statistics: what have they revealed to us of the pattern of post-war industrial disputes? In summary we found that many, though not all, of the trends observed by Knowles in the period 1911–1947 continued into the period 1947–1957 – although sometimes a rather different construction was put on these trends. Graphs I and II indicate the relatively constant influence of most categories over the post-war period and Tables 1 and 2 show that large scale official wage disputes aside, the great majority of workers who have struck since the war have not justified their withdrawals of labour by reference to simple wage issues. Nor have they put forward as a reason the need to reduce hours of working, or the closed shop, or a desire to support other workers in dispute.

The reasons which workers have used can be grouped under three broad headings. They are:

(1) Arguments concerning changes in the system of payment.
(2) Arguments concerning changes in other working arrangements.
(3) Arguments concerning alleged assaults on what are termed the
     customs and practice of the trade.

Now it is clear that these three groups, which have accounted, in most years, for some 80 per cent of stoppages and some 70 per cent of workers involved, have much in common. In a sense they are all examples of the continued importance of what we have termed acquired rights. That this is so in the case of (2) and (3) above has already been argued; but even in the case of strikes which arise out of changes in the system of payment there must surely often be a sense in which it is acquired rights which are at stake. After all, in present circumstances, most changes in the system of payment, which involve the introduction of time and motion methods, or the introduction of new ways of fixing rates, or devices for reducing scheduled overtime, etc., are usually initiated by the employer because it is believed that existing methods of payment have led to 'featherbedding' or 'restrictive practices'. But from the workers' point of view these practices may not be regarded in this way. It may seem to them that what is at stake are certain long established rights or privileges, and so their reason for striking takes the form of an appeal to such rights.

Another general conclusion which may be drawn from the above analysis concerns the average size of most strikes in the period 1945–57. These can be found by dividing the number of strikes in any group by the number of workers involved and are set out in Table 1. This table indicates the relatively localised nature of most strikes since the war. Apart from the wage increase strikes, and the relatively few sympathetic strikes, most other groups have an average of under 300. In the important categories (2), (4) and (5) the average is 108 workers involved in each strike. Unfortunately it is not possible to estimate the average number of working days lost in these strikes, because until last year there were no figures available. However, the 1957 table did contain a breakdown of working days lost according to the seven classifications used and in Table 2 these have been used to arrive at the average number of working days lost per strike in each category during 1957. Assuming that 1957, apart from the engineering and shipbuilding wage increase strike is a typical post-war year, these figures demonstrate once again the limited nature of post-war strike activity.[9] Wage increase and sympathetic strikes would appear to be the most drawn out type of dispute, accounting for an average of 21,896 and 3,173 working days respectively. Those two aside most strikes tend to be relatively short, the combined average of groups (2), (4), and (5) being some 678 working days.

In other words the average dispute in these categories is one which involves about 100 workers and lasts about a week. Loosely what emerge from these statistics are two very different stereotypes. Since the war most strikers have approximated to one or another of them. Either they have been taking part in a somewhat prolonged and relatively widely based (usually 'official') strike, justified by reference to the fact that a group of employers had refused to concede a nationally negotiated wage increase–for example the engineering and shipbuilding stoppages of 1953 and 1957, the engine drivers' and fireman's strike of 1955, or the dispute between London Transport and the busmen in 1958. Or, they have been taking part in a strike (usually 'unofficial'), along with a limited local group, and have tended to justify their refusal to work by reference to some unpopular proposal for change, or threat to established customs and practices. In this case a settlement will probably have been effected within a week.

As we have seen in most years since the war the first stereotype–the 'official' wage striker–has appeared but infrequently, whereas the second–the 'unofficial' defender of acquired rights–has put in a more or less constant appearance in markedly similar numbers each year. These facts are at least worth remembering when considering proposals for the avoidance of industrial unrest–particularly those which over-emphasise the role which is played by national leadership.[10]

Which of our two stereotypes will predominate in the next ten years is a matter of conjecture. Just as the 'underlying' or 'fundamental' causes for the emergence of either of them is a task for any economist or sociologist who thinks he can explain these things. All that this article has set out to do is to show that the 'Principal Cause' tables of the Ministry of Labour can be analysed in such a way that they furnish material which enables us to reach meaningful conclusions concerning the reasons men actually give for striking. Presumably any general theory of strike determination will have to take such factors into account.

NOTES

1 The outstanding exception here is, of course, K. G. J. C. Knowles in 'Strikes–A Study in Industrial Conflict', Blackwell, 1952. Some of the arguments set out in that work will be examined in this article. For the moment, however, it need only be mentioned that Mr. Knowles was primarily concerned with the period 1911–1947, and with making broad comparisons within that period. As a result he used no figures later than 1947.

2 Strikes, by H. A. Clegg, The Political Quarterly, January–March, 1956.

3 See '*Wildcat Strike*', by Alvin W. Gouldner, Routledge and Keegan Paul, 1955.
4 *Ministry of Labour Gazette*, May, 1958, p. 170.
5 *Report on Strikes and Lockouts*, 1913, Cd. 7658, pp. 173–8. Ministry officials have assured the writer that the categories outlined in this publication still form the basis of the present classification.
6 So called '*cup of tea*' strikes and similar minor disputes would be included in this group.
7 Knowles, *op. cit.*, pp. 234–6.
8 Knowles, *op. cit.*, p. 235.
9 In fact the 'curve' of total working days lost as a result of all causes, which can be compiled from published figures for each year since the war, follows the 'curve' of the total number of strikes for the same period very closely. This would seem to indicate that generalisations about the whole of the post-war period which are based upon the 1957 breakdown of working days lost by causes may not be wholly inaccurate.
10 See '*The Challenge of Employee Shareholding*', by George Copeman, Batsford, 1958, for the latest example of this perennial error.

8

AN INVESTIGATION INTO INDUSTRIAL STRIKE ACTIVITY IN BRITAIN[1]

John H. Pencavel

In the proliferating diagnoses of Britain's post-war economic performance, its system of industrial relations has come under increasing criticism. Practically every day the news media supply us with examples of the most bizarre of employee–management contretemps, so that the general public must be forgiven if it concludes that these incidents are typical of Britain's system of industrial relations. Above all, attention has been focused on the frequency of industrial disputes, and unfavourable comparisons have been made with the strike record of other countries.

Notwithstanding increasing public concern over industrial conflict and the availability of a large amount of reasonably accurate data, economists have done little to apply to strike activity those techniques of multivariate statistical analysis that characterise so much of current research in economics. This paper embarks on such a statistical analysis by specifying and testing the implications of a model that has been used to account successfully for work stoppages in the United States. As in other branches of economics, these methods complement and do not supplant other methods of enquiry. Thus, the unresolved questions in this study may prove more tractable when examined by alternative analytical tools. However, an investigation into strike activity employing multiple regression techniques should yield some rewards particularly by affording the opportunity to test some standard hypotheses. For instance, one may ask whether there is a statistical foundation for the common belief that industrial conflict has been tending to increase in recent years. Similarly, is there an association between the frequency of strike action and the ideological complexion of the particular party in power? Do different industries display markedly different strike propensities? This paper addresses itself to these and other questions in the belief that the conclusions which follow are not without value.

The plan of this paper is as follows. In the first section, the model is outlined and the question of its applicability to Britain's system of labour–management relations discussed. Section II tests the implications of the model with aggregate data on the number of strikes beginning in each quarter in the period from 1950 to 1967. There follows in Section III an analysis of industrial disputes in four major industries. Finally, Section IV contains a discussion of the limitations of the results and offers some concluding remarks.

I. THE MODEL

According to Arthur Ross's concept of the role of the institution of trade unionism,[2] in addition to the economic welfare of their members, union leaders are concerned with the survival and development of the union as an institution and with their own personal ambition. The reconciliation of these diverse aims occasions union strategies that do not easily lend themselves to explanation in terms of simple maximising behaviour. For instance, it has been difficult to integrate the use of strike action into a consistent maximising model of union conduct. Ashenfelter and Johnson [2] have demonstrated, however, that the invocation of the strike is a tactic consistent with Ross's broader view of the nature of unionism. If the union rank-and-file desires and expects to obtain conditions of employment that management is not willing to concede, the leadership jeopardises its position by accepting the management's terms. On the other hand, in the event of a strike, '. . . the [union] leadership may at least appear as adversaries against management in a crusade which may even raise their political "stock" and will unify the workers. The outbreak of a strike, however, has the effect of lowering the rank-and-file's expectations due to the shock effect of the firm's resistance and the resultant loss of normal income. After some passage of time, the leadership feels that the minimum acceptable wage increase has fallen to a level at which it can safely sign with management, and the strike ends.' [2, p. 37.]

Upon these foundations, Ashenfelter and Johnson construct an optimising model[3] in which the entrepreneur chooses between, on the one hand, accepting the union's wage demands and so avoiding the interruption in production that accompanies a strike and, on the other hand, incurring a strike in the hope that his resilience will moderate union demands and burden him with lower wage costs. The commonsense implication is that the likelihood of a strike depends upon the size of the union's demands and upon management's assessment of the rate at which the worker's resistance will wither under strike conditions. After making simplifying assumptions concerning the parameters of the institutional setting, the authors present the following specification:

(1) $$p(S_t) = \alpha_0 + \alpha_1 \gamma_{0t} + \alpha_2 D_t + \alpha_3 T + \varepsilon_t',$$

where $p(S_t)$ is the probability of a strike in period t, T is a time trend, D is the ratio of profits to total compensation,[4] y_{0t} is the minimum wage increase acceptable to the rank-and-file on the outbreak of the strike, and ε_t' is a stochastic disturbance term. Clearly, when workers are militant and entertain high aspirations, y_0 is high and the likelihood of a strike increases. Hence α_1 is hypothesised to be positive. The sign of α_2 is expected to be negative since management will be more willing to concede to union demands when the firm's opportunity cost in terms of its lost profits during a strike is large. Because strikes over union jurisdictions in the United States have been declining, α_3 is posited to be negative.

Ashenfelter and Johnson proceed to identify y_{0t} negatively with the unemployment rate[5] (U_t), negatively with a moving average of real wage changes[6] ($\sum_{t=0}^{m} \mu_i \Delta R_{t-i}$), and positively with the firm's profits[7] (approximated by D_t). Substituting these variables for y_{0t} in (1) yields the following equation:

$$p(S_t) = \alpha_0 + \alpha_1 U_t + \alpha_2 \sum_{t=0}^{m} \mu_i \Delta R_{t-i} + \alpha_3 D_t + \alpha_4 T + \varepsilon_t.$$

The hypotheses are that α_1 and α_2 are negative whilst α_3 is ambiguous in sign, for, to quote the authors, 'although management is more likely to give in when previous profits are high, the union is also likely to increase its demands' [2, p. 41].

In the industrial relations system of the United States, strikes generally occur over the terms of the collective contract. Since contract expirations have marked seasonal variations, the authors move from an equation accounting for the probability of a strike to an equation accounting for the number of strikes beginning in any quarter by supplementing the previous equation with a set of seasonal dummy variables (N_i):

(2) $$S_t = \beta_0 + \sum_{i=1}^{3} \beta_{1t} N_{it} + \beta_2 U_t + \beta_3 \sum_{i=0}^{m} \mu_i \Delta R_{t-i} + \beta_4 D_t + \beta_5 T + \varepsilon_t$$

where S_t now measures the number of strikes beginning in period t.

In the United Kingdom such collective agreements are not binding by law or by convention and hence labour is not compelled to concentrate strike action in those periods when contracts expire. In this respect the British institutional environment makes the step of substituting S_t for $p(S_t)$ less demanding. Yet a seasonal pattern does exist in British strike activity, and this recommends the inclusion of seasonal dummy variables. In months when the need for current income is high (notably the Christmas and summer holidays), workers will be less prone to withdraw their labour. This would produce a tendency towards greater strike frequency in the post-Christmas and spring months.[8]

Since the British system of industrial relations differs in some important respects from the pattern in the United States, it is pertinent here to discuss the applicability of this model to the institutional environment in Britain. Most strikes in the United Kingdom are described as unofficial – not only are these strikes not recognised by the executive committee, but the senior officials away from the branch organisation are often unaware of the discontent among their members. If the Ashenfelter–Johnson model is to have any meaning in the British context, the leadership's position must be interpreted as being occupied either by the branch official or, more especially, by the shop steward organisations at the place of work.[9] Certainly it seems that the workers view the steward as the effective and relevant union official.[10] Furthermore, from the detailed investigations into shop steward activities emerges a picture of the steward, not as an irritant exhorting the rank-and-file to more and more militant action, but rather as a moderating influence, avoiding conflict where possible and tailoring his strategy according to pressures from the union members and from the man agement.[11] The steward is not a mere broker bringing together management and his rank-and-file; if he recognises that the workers will not be satisfied with management's concessions, rather than allow the initiative to slip into the hands of militants he will safeguard his own position and the solidarity of the union by leading a strike against the firm. Even in industries in which the shop steward does not occupy a pivotal role, there will be equivalent union officers functioning in much the same way. In short, although senior officers in some unions may be divorced from the issues that perturb the rank-and-file, officials lower down in the echelon of authority take on much of that function of trade unionism which relates to the welfare of the member at his place of work, and in this capacity they operate much like the union leadership described by Ashenfelter and Johnson.

II. EVIDENCE FROM AGGREGATE DATA

For much of this century, industrial unrest in the coal mining industry has dominated total strike activity in the United Kingdom.

Miners have been in the forefront of organised labour movements and the characteristics of the industry have lent themselves to vigorous expressions of union militancy. This dominance also held for the first half of the period from 1950 to 1967. However, since 1957 (when coal mining accounted for more than three-quarters of all stoppages) the number of disputes in the coal industry has been declining steadily, yet perceptibly, so that by mid-1967 strikes in coal mining constituted but 20 per cent of the total. Following Turner's example of treating coal mining 'as the special case it is' [18, p. 8], our attention focuses on the number of stoppages in all industries other than mining. This series seems to show a rising trend which would account for the growing public concern over industrial unrest. At first glance, therefore, it does not appear likely that the negative trend in American strike activity over this period will be replicated in the British data.

The results of estimating Equation (2) from quarterly data over the period from the first quarter of 1950 (1950-I) to the second quarter of 1967 (1967-II) are shown in Equation (2a) of Table 1. The dependent variable is the number of disputes beginning in each quarter in all industries excluding coal mining. The seasonal dummies N_1, N_2 and N_3 stand for the first, second and third quarters respectively. The lag coefficients on real wage changes (ΔR) are estimated according to the procedure suggested by Shirley Almon [1].[12] To guard against any simultaneous equation bias, the current change in real wages is not included as a regressor and the lag distribution starts with ΔR_{t-i}. The lag on ΔR_{t-i} is fixed at six quarters.[13]

The results provide remarkable support for the hypotheses advanced above. All independent variables but the third-quarter seasonal dummy are significant, and together they account for 87 per cent of the variance in strike activity over this period.[14] There is a significant tendency for strikes to be higher in the first six months of the year. A rise of one percentage point in the unemployment rate will reduce the number of stoppages by about 40 strikes per quarter.[15] The lag on real wage changes has a shape akin to an exponential decay (see Table 2). Profits as a percentage of total compensation has a small, yet significantly *positive*, effect on the number of stoppages.[16]

There has been a highly significant positive trend in strike activity such that the number of strikes has increased, on average, by 22 strikes per year. A variety of explanations has been offered for this positive trend, explanations that range from the 'agitator theory'[17] to the belief that strikes, along with accidents, labour turnover and absenteeism, are all manifestations of poor industrial morale. The

TABLE 1

Determinants of Aggregate Strike Activity, 1950-I to 1967-II
(Mean of the Dependent Variable = 227.16)

Estimated Coefficients on

Eq.	Constant	N_1	N_2	N_3	U_t	D_t	$\sum_{i=1}^{6} \Delta R_{t-i}$	$\sum_{i=1}^{6} \Delta W_{t-i}$	$\sum_{i=1}^{6} \Delta P_{t-i}$	T	J	L	R^2	DW	SEE
(2a)	−147.88 (88.26)	74.93 (15.01)	38.0 (14.22)	7.01 (14.51)	−41.29 (14.30)	1.87 (0.72)	−42.46 (8.69)			5.50 (0.36)			0.869	1.36	41.9
(2b)	−74.46 (102.94)	70.55 (15.35)	38.45 (14.22)	5.44 (14.55)	−38.73 (15.98)	1.27 (0.85)		−44.20 (11.35)	39.34 (9.06)	5.24 (0.40)			0.873	1.35	41.9
(2c)	−142.25 (97.08)	75.56 (15.40)	37.99 (14.41)	6.71 (14.63)	−50.19 (17.00)	1.97 (0.84)	−52.52 (13.66)			5.71 (0.43)	−10.27 (18.34)	−11.10 (20.54)	0.871	1.41	42.3

Notes: Estimated standard errors of the estimated regression coefficients are in parentheses. *SEE* is the standard error of estimate for the equation, and *DW* the Durbin–Watson statistic, a measure of the first-order serial correlation in the estimated residuals.

Sources: The number of stoppages beginning in each period is taken from issues of the *Monthly Labour Gazette* (or *Employment and Productivity Gazette*, as it is now called). Stoppages involving fewer than ten workers and those lasting less than one day are excluded from the statistics except when the aggregate number of working days lost exceeded 100. The unemployment rate, the index of weekly wage rates (all workers, 31 January 1956=100), and the retail price index (17 January 1956 = 100) are found in the *Monthly Gazette*. Real wage changes (ΔR_t) are defined as $100[((W_{t+2} - W_{t-2})/2W_t - (P_{t+2} - P_{t-2})/2P_t)]$. The variable D_t is defined as gross trading profits as a percentage of wage and salary compensation: the index of gross trading profits (1948 = 100) is contained in Klein *et al.* [9]. and from 1957 the index was extended by using the series of gross trading profits from issues of the *Monthly Digest of Statistics*; similarly Klein *et al.* [9] provided the source for the index of wages and salaries (1948 = 100) until 1953-IV when the series in the *Monthly Digest of Statistics* was used.

Donovan Commission [20] stressed the 'inadequacy of institutions', an explanation given by Turner and his colleagues [19] with respect to disputes in the motor vehicles industry and extended by the Commission to embrace strike activity in all industries. Turner pointed to the role of wage structures in the increasingly strike-prone motor industry: '. . . its combination of a general pay level which seems in relative terms, unusually high, with both marked anomalies in wage-differentials within the car industry *and* a very considerable instability of earnings' [19, p. 331]. This might suggest supplementing the estimated regression equation with regressors measuring movements in the spread of wages across occupations, across firms, or across industries. However, disputes over wage structures are typically the pretext for pursuing wage increases and, as such, lend themselves to interpretation within the confines of the present model.[18] Further, if the Ministry of Labour's (or, now, the Ministry of Employment and Productivity's) classification of strikes according to the principal issue in dispute has any meaning— and some observers believe it does[19]—then the proportion of total strikes categorised as wage disputes other than those for wage increases has fallen from 38 per cent in 1950 to some 23 per cent in 1966. Unquestionably, strikes concerning wage differentials have been and probably will continue to be an important part of total strike activity; but it seems unlikely that the significantly positive trend in the estimates equation is a surrogate for disputes over wage differentials.

TABLE 2

Estimated Lag Coefficients and the Standard Errors for Equations (2a) and (2b)

Lag	(2a) $\Sigma \Delta R_{t-i}$	(2b) $\Sigma \Delta W_{t-i}$	$\Sigma \Delta P_{t-i}$
1	-10.27 (5.21)	-6.52 (6.42)	11.12 (5.43)
2	-9.49 (2.34)	-8.49 (3.11)	9.33 (2.37)
3	-8.34 (1.95)	-9.23 (2.43)	7.51 (2.10)
4	-6.81 (2.70)	-8.78 (3.12)	5.67 (2.96)
5	-4.92 (2.78)	-7.06 (3.19)	3.80 (3.04)
6	-2.64 (1.90)	-4.14 (2.17)	1.91 (2.07)

A more plausible explanation, yet at the same time one more difficult to test explicitly, is that, as memories of depression years faded to be replaced by greater confidence in economic stability, so labour gradually became less reticent about taking up issues that irked it. In the post-war years, management did not have recourse to pools of unutilised labour in the event of their employees striking briefly over some grievance. In some countries (e.g., Sweden and

West Germany), this increase in labour's bargaining power was reflected in the modifications made to the system of industrial relations such that employee grievances could be handled more speedily and more effectively. In others (notably the United States) legal restraints were imposed on labour's use of the strike weapon. But in the United Kingdom the rising expectations of workers tended not to be accompanied by such institutional developments. Though the climate of employer–employee relations was undergoing significant change, the institutional structure had all but ossified. Britain's system of industrial relations has been suffering from the rigidity of an old-established structure inflexible in relation to a change in the relative bargaining power of the participants.

Equation (2b) separates real wage changes into their price and wage change components. The estimated coefficients on the money wage change variable sum to slightly more than those on price changes (see Table 2); so the null hypothesis that the coefficients on wages and price changes sum to zero was tested. Invoking the t distribution in the standard way strongly suggests that wage and price changes act symmetrically with respect to their effect (negatively and positively, respectively) on the frequency of strikes.[20]

The official links between the unions and the Labour Party, and the ideological sympathies which cause many trade union members to support the Labour Party, suggest the hypothesis that workers are 'less reluctant to see a Conservative Government embarrassed by industrial conflicts than a Labour one' [18, p. 10]. In addition, Ashenfelter and Johnson argue that the adoption of an incomes policy will tend to reduce strike activity by lowering y_0.[21] However, if, as is usual, a policy of wage restraint is coupled with attempts to moderate product price increases, the employer will be more intransigent in the wage bargain in the knowledge that his ability to pass on wage increases in the form of higher prices is more limited. For this reason, we form no *a priori* judgement as to whether an incomes policy will increase or reduce the frequency of strikes. These hypotheses were tested by estimating an equation with two dummy variables, one (L) taking the value of unity when the Labour Party was in power and zero otherwise, and the other (J) taking the value of unity when an incomes policy was in effect and zero otherwise.[22] The consequences of adding these dummy variables to the estimated equation are shown in Equation (2c) of Table 1. The estimated coefficients on J and L imply that each has a depressing effect on industrial unrest of about ten strikes per quarter. Both dichotomous variables possess negative signs, yet their estimated coefficients are less than their estimated standard errors. However, since J and L are assigned their unity values for similar periods, and since they are surely related behaviourly, an F test on their joint significance is warranted and this reveals that the estimated coefficients on those dummy variables are indeed significantly different from zero:

$$\hat{F} = 5{\cdot}08 > F_{0{\cdot}05}\,(2{,}59) = 3{\cdot}15.^{23}$$

One possible objection to the interpretation of these results requires consideration. Hines [6] has argued that the change in the percentage of the labour force unionised (ΔT) is a measure of trade union militancy, and has proposed that ΔT itself is a function of the level of union membership, the rate of change of prices and the level of profits. Since two of these variables appear as regressors in the estimated strike equation, the correct specification may be one which includes ΔT, on the argument that, when union membership is increasing, 'unions feel stronger and become more intransigent in the wage bargain'[24]. This hypothesis does not immediately lend itself to test since quarterly data on union membership are absent.[25] Instead, strike equations which included ΔT were estimated using *annual* data from 1950 to 1967; but, with fewer degrees of freedom in these regressions and with high collinearity between the 'independent' variables, it became impossible to draw meaningful inferences from the results. An investigation spanning a period longer than the 18 years covered in this study should be less inconclusive concerning the role of ΔT in a strike equation. Indeed, it would be interesting to consider whether ΔT and S together form a system of labour-market equations.

Finally, the estimated equations were tested for their stability over the given time period. The sample was divided in two, and separate regressions run on the two equal sub-periods. Invoking the F distribution in the standard way, we find the null hypothesis that the estimates from the two linear regressions are drawn from the same structural relation is rejected. For instance, in the case of the equation including the J and L dummy variables, $\hat{F} = 4.5$, which clearly exceeds the critical values of F. A number of explanations for this absence of stability springs to mind;[26] but the most likely draws attention to the problem of aggregation. Theil [17] has shown that, if a macro relation of the form $Y = \alpha + \sum_i \beta_i X_i + u$ is derived from a theory that specified microeconomic behaviour of the form $Y_j = \alpha_j + \sum_i \beta_{ij} X_{ij} + u_j$, where j stands for the n micro decision-makers, then the aggregation bias in estimating the β_i parameters of the macro relationship can be represented as

$$\beta_i - \frac{1}{n}\sum_j \beta_{ij} = n\sum_i \text{cov.} (\beta_{ij}, b_{ij}),$$

where b_{ij} are the slope parameters in the linear equation of X_{ij} on X_i:
$X_{ij} = \alpha_{ij} + \sum_i b_{ij}X_i + \varepsilon_{ij}$. In terms of the analysis here, the β_{ij} may be interpreted as indicators of strike propensities across the j industries; and the next section suggests they are not identical for each j.[27] It is also probable that the b_{ij} differ significantly for various j.[28] If the β_{ij} and b_{ij} vary not only by industry but also over time, there is no guarantee that the aggregation bias in estimating the β_i will remain constant through time. When the problem is viewed thus, the surprising result perhaps is not that the parameters of the strike equation estimated from British data are unstable over time, but that the fit to American data displays a significant stability. In view of the implied importance attached to the microeconomic relations, the investigation proceeds to examine the industry evidence.

III. EVIDENCE FROM INDUSTRY DATA

This section presents the results of testing the implications of the model developed above with data on strikes from four major industries–construction, transport and communications, metal goods, and coal mining.[29] Data limitations compel this industry investigation to span a period shorter than was the case for that of aggregate strike activity. This industry evidence is circumscribed by the absence of a quarterly series of profits by industry for the whole of this period. Since the ratio of profits to wage compensation would almost certainly not be orthogonal with respect to the other independent variables in this disaggregated study, the omission of a profits variable implies a real specification error.[30] In spite of this, the industry evidence should be valuable since decision-makers in the Ashenfelter–Johnson model operate at the firm or industry level and, as has been noted towards the end of the previous section, an analysis at an aggregate level may very well be misleading. If the estimated relationship suggests considerable differences from industry to industry, forecasts made from the aggregative relation will be highly sensitive to, *inter alia*, the industrial composition of the dependent variable.

The explanations offered by Ashenfelter and Johnson in their paper for the negative dependence of y_{0t} (the minimum wage increase acceptable to the rank-and-file) on U_t (the unemployment rate) suggest the use in this industry study of both the unemployment rate for the industry and also the unemployment rate for the whole economy. For when unemployment is low in all industries, the existence of alternative job opportunities encourages workers to press more aggressively for wage increases in their present employment and, in addition, part-time employment is available during strike action; when employment is high in a given industry, the negative employment effects of a wage increase will be less apparent. Therefore, the industry's unemployment rate (U_t^I) is added as an independent variable to the regression equation.[31] The equation fitted to the industry data took the following form:

$$(3) \quad S_t^I = \gamma_0 + \sum_{i=1}^{3} \gamma_{1i} N_i + \gamma_2 U_t + \gamma_3 U_t^I + \gamma_4 \Delta R_{t-j}^I + \gamma_5 T + \gamma_6 J + \gamma_7 L + v_t,$$

where the superscript I refers to the given industry.[32] It was soon discovered that the distributed lag on real wage changes associated with aggregate strike activity was not replicated in the industry analysis. Instead, real wage changes for a *given past quarter* produced results most in accord with *a priori* expectations. Since straightforward experimentation produced a lag of different length in each industry, this suggests that the distributed lag in the aggregate data results not from a uniform response by all workers that decays through time, but rather from aggregating responses the size and length of which differ across industries. If this is the case, the shape of the distributed lag on real wage changes in the aggregate series will be sensitive to the industrial composition of the dependent variable.

Table 3 presents the results from estimating Equation (3) for time-series strike data for the four industries. Each industry reveals a seasonal pattern in its strike frequency similar to the aggregate data, with significantly higher activity in the first quarter of the year. The three industries that formed part of the dependent variable in the regressions of the previous section have significantly positive time trends. The coal mining industry has a strong negative trend. The period of lag on the real wage change variable was chosen according to the coefficient estimates which agreed most with *a priori* expectations. This resulted in a lag of four quarters, zero quarter, one quarter, and one quarter in the four industries, respectively.

The results from fitting the equation to strike activity in the construction industry are given in Equation (3a). Although both U_t and U_t^I, the aggregate and the industry unemployment rate respectively, have the expected signs, their estimated standard errors exceed their estimated coefficients. Since the two variables are highly correlated (the simple correlation between them in 0.83),

TABLE 3

Strike Activity in Four Major Industries

Eq.	Industry and Period	Mean of Dependent Variable	Constant	Estimated Coefficients on									R^2	DW	SEE
				N_1	N_2	N_3	U_t	U_t^l	ΔR_{t-j}^l	T	J	L			
(3a)	Construction 1957-II to 1967-II	56.71	8.01 (18.27)	21.22 (5.53)	3.16 (5.28)	2.54 (5.40)	−6.14 (10.38)	−1.93 (2.35)	−5.65 (3.13) for $j=4$	0.88 (0.27)	15.47 (5.93)	−26.64 (8.27)	0.651	1.68	11.88
(3b)	Metals 1957-II to 1967-II	144.59	−66.77 (50.02)	49.02 (14.28)	38.47 (14.13)	−10.61 (15.18)	−15.04 (24.48)	−20.13 (13.70)	2.26 (10.01) for $j=1$	4.16 (0.73)	−8.20 (15.63)	−9.36 (21.54)	0.775	1.64	31.81
(3c)	Transport 1957-II to 1964-IV	32.77	21.65 (17.07)	7.86 (3.72)	−0.72 (3.57)	−3.90 (4.30)	−23.60 (9.50)	5.73 (17.37)	3.10 (3.10) for $j=0$	0.85 (0.21)	−4.16 (4.05)	1.05 (8.17)	0.736	1.66	6.85
(3d)	Coal Mining 1957-II to 1967-II	313.17	909.77 (108.90)	33.20 (17.34)	48.20 (16.46)	−20.35 (16.78)	−13.15 (29.56)	−13.08 (80.33)	−44.11 (16.58) for $j=1$	−10.10 (2.58)	−37.95 (20.25)	−5.67 (25.29)	0.943	1.48	37.15

Notes: See Notes to Table 1.

Sources: The strike data from the *Ministry of Labour Gazette*. The quarterly indices of weekly rates of wages (31 January 1956=100) were generously provided by the Statistics Division of the Department of Employment and Productivity. I am most grateful to them. Unemployment rates by industry were found in issues of the National Institute's *Economic Review* until 1965-I, and then were calculated from figures on unemployment in the *Ministry of Labour Gazette*. The industry described in the text as metals consists of metal goods, engineering, shipbuilding and motor vehicles.

and F test on their joint significance was performed, and implied that their coefficients were indeed significantly different from zero: $\hat{F} = 3.94 > F_{0.05}(2,31) = 3.3$. A one-tail t test on the coefficient of ΔR_{t-4} suggests it is significantly different from zero at the 5 per cent level. For this industry, the estimated coefficient on the incomes-policy variable is significantly positive, implying that, on balance, the policy served more to stiffen management's resistance in the wage bargain than to reduce unions' wage demands. The estimated coefficient on the Labour Government dummy suggests that strikes are reduced by nearly half their mean level by the existence of a Government ostensibly more sympathetic to the lot of labour.

Equation (3b) for the metal goods industry performs less satis-factorily. Though 78 per cent of the variance in the dependent variable is removed, much of this is apparently the work of the seasonal dummies and the time trend.[33] The dichotomous variables J and L are not significant on a joint F test. On the other hand, the estimated coefficients on U_t and U^I are adjudged significantly different from zero, though the calculated value for F only margin-ally exceeds the critical value: $\hat{F} = 3.45 > F_{0.05}(2,31) = 3.3$. The estimated coefficient on real wage changes in the metals industry possesses a positive rather than the expected negative sign, and is clearly not significant. The same result follows for different lags on this variable. A number of investigators have drawn attention to the large number of strikes over wage differentials in this group of industries and, quite possibly, what this equation lacks is some measure of the wage structure in the industry—ΔR^I_{t-j} is clearly an imperfect substitute here.

The equation accounting for strikes in transport is the least satisfactory of the industry equations. The aggregate unemploy-ment rate, U^I_t, is significantly different from zero by conventional standards, but the estimated coefficients on the industry's unem-ployment rate (U^I_t) and on real wage changes (ΔR^I_t) have signs opposite from what was expected and are clearly not significantly different from zero.[34] The poor performance of the real wage change variable stimulated the search for a more appropriate variable, and regressions were estimated in which it was replaced by a variable measuring the ratio of wages in transport to the general wage level: (W^I_t / W_t). The estimated coefficient on this vari-able was always unquestionably insignificant, and in its lagged form had a positive rather than the expected negative sign.[35]

The fitted Equation (3d) accounts for 94 per cent of the variance in the number of strikes in coal mining beginning in each quarter.[36] The inter-correlation between U_t, U^I_t and T is high, and a joint F test was performed on these three variables. The joint significance of these three variables is unmistakable: ($\hat{F} = 62.2$). The dummy variable for J for incomes policy is not significant on a two-tail t test at the 5 per cent level. (Recall that either a positive or a negative coefficient could obtain for this variable.) Nor is it significant in a joint test with L:$\hat{F} = 2.04 < \hat{F}_{0.05} (2,31) = 3.3$.

Section II concluded on the conjecture that aggregation error was present in the strike equations estimated with aggregate data. A rough indication of the seriousness of this problem is afforded by the industry data examined here. The procedure is first to aggregate (weighting by employment) the industry-specific variables in Equation (3) over the three industries (construction, metals and transport) that constituted some four-fifths of the regressand in Section II. This aggregated regression is then fitted to the 1957-II and 1964-IV periods,[37] and the sums of the squared residuals from the industry equations and from the aggregated equation are compared.[38] The null hypothesis that aggregation errors are absent is rejected for 'high' values of the calculated F. In fact, for this short period, we are unable to reject the null hypothesis: $\hat{F} = 0.985 < F_{0.05} (20,63) = 1.74$. This suggests the working hypothesis that an aggregate strike equation may be employed without excessive aggregation biases over a shorter period than the 17 years or so to which Equation (2) was fitted.[39]

IV. CONCLUSIONS

This paper has applied a model of employee-management relations to the British economy and tested its implications with aggregate and industry data since the 1950s. Though the results are generally encouraging, it is necessary to stress the following cautionary notes.

(1) Theoretical formulations different from that described in the first section of this paper could specify the relationship estimated in Sections II and III. The advantage of the present approach, however, is that it replaces improvised *ad hoc* explanations of strike activity with a behavioural model which, unlike rival bargaining models, does yield refutable implications. Amendments and extensions of the model to take account of particular institutional arrangements should improve its performance.

(2) The high coefficients of determination, especially in some of the industry regressions, tend to conceal rather than reveal explanatory behaviour. The association of strike activity with the level of demand in the labour market seems established, but the significant trend terms are not themselves explanatory variables and call for interpretation. One possibility is that they are proxies for aging institutional structures increasingly unwilling

or unable to accommodate the growing post-war shift in the balance of power between management and labour without the parties having to resort to the strike weapon. Other explanations have been proposed; but many are difficult to quantify in a statistical study of this kind, and the use of other methods of analysis may prove more rewarding. Certainly, in so far as the frequency of strikes is an index of the smooth operation of Britain's system of industrial relations–and surely there are many facets other than strike activity to take into account–there is nothing in the results in this paper to suggest that the mounting criticism of its performance is unwarranted.

Notwithstanding these limitations, the findings reported in this paper suggest that this framework for analysing the frequency of strike activity is not fruitless, and further refinement of the model should enhance our understanding of the relations involved. Further research holds out the promise not merely of a greater insight into the particular workings of the system of industrial relations, but, to the extent that labour–management negotiations exercise an independent influence on labour market variables such as the rate of change of wage rates, there is also the goal of a fuller understanding of their relationships in the economy.

NOTES

1 I am indebted to Orley Ashenfelter, Melvin Reder and Albert Rees for their valuable comments on an earlier draft of this paper.

2 See A. M. Ross [15]. References in square brackets are listed on p. 256, below.

3 For the elegant development of the model, the reader is, of course, referred to Ashenfelter and Johnson's paper [2].

4 This term is a lagged value in the Ashenfelter and Johnson formulation. Since the length of the lag is an empirical question and since the empirical results below report that the effect of D on strike activity is more or less complete within a quarter, this variable appears here in its unlagged form.

5 The costs of strike action to workers tend to be less inhibiting when unemployment is low since alternative job opportunities are available to make up for the loss of normal income that a withdrawal of their labour involves. Moreover, to the extent that the employment effects of a wage increase are smaller or less apparent in prosperous conditions, the union leadership can safely ignore any threat to their political position that would accompany increasing unemployment among the rank-and-file. For earlier evidence on the association of strike activity and the trade cycle see, for the American experience, Rees [13], and for Britain, Knowles [10, pp. 145–9].

6 Ashenfelter and Johnson's neat justification for the effect of lagged real wage changes on y_0 is, in essence, that the larger recent wage changes have been the more they satisfy the constantly rising expectations of workers and hence the less militant labour becomes.

7 High profits raise workers' wage aspirations and simultaneously reduce the union leadership's reluctance to embark on strike action.

8 Knowles [10, p. 159] draws attention to this seasonal pattern from data over the period 1919 to 1939. Hobsbawm [7, p. 131] presents evidence to suggest that, even as far back as the first half of the nineteenth century, there tended to be especial labour unrest in the first six months of the year.

9 In nomenclature, function and structure, there is a great diversity in union organisation at the plant or workshop level. For instance, the printing industry chooses 'chapel fathers' rather than shop stewards, the National Union of Mineworkers generally select their branch officers rather than their stewards for negotiations with the management, and in some motor vehicle firms shop stewards from different unions cooperate to establish a joint shop stewards' committee. When the text here and subsequently makes a reference to shop steward organisations, it should not be inferred that their differences from firm to firm and from industry to industry are not important; but for our purposes the essential point is that each is a response by union officials to represent effectively the wishes of their rank-and-file members.

10 Roberts [14, p. 57] writes: 'For the great majority of members trade unionism begins and ends at the place of work. Most workers probably become members of a union because a steward asks them to join, and to them the steward is the union. It is to the steward that they pay their contributions, it is the steward on whom they rely to keep them informed of changes in the conditions of employment that might affect their workshop, office, or department, and it is to him that they go when in difficulties. The steward, in fact, is often the only contact they have with the union to which they belong.' See also McCarthy and Parker [12, para. 199].

11 Thus in their exhaustive study into industrial relations in the motor industry, Turner, Clack and Roberts note [19, p. 214]: '. . . this series of stoppages, at any rate, hardly makes the shop stewards, and particularly the senior stewards' committee, appear as stimulating and provoking disputes. Rather, they are attempting to control a number of pressures to which they are subject, including those from the management and outside union officials, but especially including pressures from particular groups and sections of workpeople themselves. Which is not to say that leading stewards (or, for that matter, local union officers) may not sometimes indicate that a 'spontaneous' demonstration will help to secure or expedite a settlement. Although, on the whole, the stewards here appear as attempting to minimise trouble; *but when trouble seems inevitable, they attempt to assert their leadership, in order to maintain their authority over the operatives.* This in any case suggests that certain factors act as regulators of the leading stewards' activity and policy. One is a comparative flexibility to membership pressures–at least, in the long run . . . And another major pressure is the stewards' very real–if again, long run–dependence on the management itself. In a sense, the leading stewards are performing a managerial function, of grievance settlement, welfare arrangement and human adjustment, and the steward system's acceptance by managements (and thus, in turn, the facility with which the stewards themselves can satisfy their members' demands and needs) has developed partly because of the increasing effectiveness–and certainly economy–with which this role is fulfilled'. See also *ibid.*, p. 228 and p. 230; and paragraphs 104, 111–13, 201 and 235 of [12].

12 A second degree polynomial is used with the restriction that the estimated coefficients taper off to zero at a finite lag.

13 Since data on earnings are not available on a quarterly basis for most of this period, indices of wage rates were used throughout. If workers respond to movements in earnings rather than wage rates, then the correct specification should be: $S = a + b(\Delta E - \Delta P) + cT + dX + u$, where ΔE is the rate of change of earnings and X a vector of other exogenous variables. Casual inspection suggests that the

movement in earnings can be approximated by the rate of change of money wages plus a positive time trend: $\Delta E = \Delta W + \gamma T$. Substituting this into the previous equation yields the estimated equation $S = a + b(\Delta W - \Delta P) + (b\gamma + c)T + dX + u$. For values of b implied by the equations in Table 1 (say, 50) and for a value of γ of 0.015, an estimate of c is 6.45 instead of the estimated coefficient of 5.7 on T in equation (2c).

14 To guard against the possibility that our statistical inferences are jeopardised by serial correlation of the estimated residuals, the equation was transformed according to the procedure suggested by Cochrane and Orcutt [4]. The results showed that all the independent variables have very similar estimated coefficients and standard errors with the possible exception of D_t whose coefficient tended to fall without a corresponding decline in its estimated standard error. Its coefficient now hovered at the margin of significance.

15 Practically identical results obtain if U_t is replaced by the Dicks-Mireaux–Dow index of excess demand.

16 Lagging this variable by one quarter yields very similar results, which suggest that any simultaneity between the current values of S and D is negligible.

17 A discussion of this appears in [18, pp. 10–13].

18 Thus, Turner notes that '... unlike the redundancy disputes, which become more important in slumps in the car industry's activity, "wage-structure and workload" strikes become more frequent in booms and are thus considerably more disruptive of production' [19, p. 70].

19 For example, see McCarthy [11].

20 It is interesting to note that, while the lag on price changes seems to decay uniformly, there is a tendency for the estimated coefficients on wage changes to be U-shaped. An F test revealed, however, that this difference was not significant at conventional levels of significance: $\dot{F} = 0.82 < F_{0.05}\ (2,48) = 3.2$.

21 See [2, p. 47, n. 29].

22 L takes the value of unity from 1950-I to 1950-IV and from 1964-IV to 1967-II. The appropriate period to assign J the value of unity is more speculative, but the following choice was made: 1950-I to 1950-IV, 1961-III to 1962-II, and 1965-II to 1967-II. This choice corresponds almost identically to those periods during which, according to Smith's multiple regressions [16], an incomes policy had a significantly dampening effect on weekly wage increases.

23 All the previous inferences concerning the included variables and the lag structure on real wages also hold almost identically for specifications which include the J and L variables.

24 Hines [6, p. 225]. In terms of the exposition in the preceding section, the argument is that $y_0 = F(\Delta T, X)$, where X is a vector of other variables. Note that with annual data, ΔP_t, ΔP_{t-1}, D_t and D_{t-1}, together remove only 28 per cent of the variance in ΔT_t in the 1950–67 period.

25 A quarterly series on ΔT was create by calculating a moving average of the annual data, and ΔT was then added to the equation specifications in Table 1. With such measurement errors (which will bias the estimated coefficients towards zero even in the probability limit), it is not surprising that the estimated coefficient on ΔT (lagged or unlagged) was not significant.

26 Note that the industrial composition of the dependent variable appears to display little change over the period: construction constitutes about 19 per cent of the total, transport 15 per cent, textiles 2.5 per cent and the large group consisting of metal industries and goods, engineering, shipbuilding and vehicles hovers around 47 per cent.

27 This is consistent with some of the arguments contained in Clark Kerr and Siegel's commentary [8].

28 A related piece of evidence here is the work of Brechling [3] on regional unemploy-

ment. He regresses regional unemployment rates on total unemployment to derive estimates of (in our terminology) the b_{ij} and significant regional differences are found for the b_{ij}. Since unemployment in a region reflects in part the economic health of the major industries located there, it is likely that differences would also be found in the b_{ij} as estimated from industry unemployment rates.

29 Recall that strikes in coal mining were excluded from the definition of the explicandum in the previous section. Strikes in the construction, transport and metal goods industries formed about 80 per cent of the dependent variable in the regression equations of Section II.

30 On the other hand, the omission of D_t from the estimated relationship at the aggregate level leaves the estimated coefficients on the other independent variables not significantly different from those presented in Table 1. Also, it is well known that the association between the unemployment rate and profits at the industry level is much lower than at the aggregate level.

31 Since there are well-known difficulties concerning the accuracy of the data on U_t^I, the equations were also estimated (where possible) with other indices of business activity for that industry. These production or sales indices yielded results broadly similar to those with U_t^I. Our preference for the U_t^I variable is that it is a labour market, rather than a final product market variable.

32 Not surprisingly, the presence in the estimated equations of industry-specific variables (and, in particular, the industry's unemployment rate) with variables like the aggregate unemployment rate and the time trend, created problems of collinearity. Although in an equation with more than two independent variables collinearity involves the set of moments among *all* regressors, the matrix of zero-order correlations can be instructive in locating those variables with particularly high inter-correlations. Where correlation between two or three variables inflated their estimated standard errors to render the conventional tests based on the t distribution questionable joint tests of significance were performed on the estimated parameters of the collinear variables. For a standard reference for the use of the F distribution in such cases, see Goldberger [5, pp. 173–7].

33 A linear regression containing only the seasonal dummies and the time trend removes 69 per cent of the variance of the dependent variable. Omitting T from equation (3b) reduced the R^2 to 0.54.

34 Broadly similar results obtain for various lags on ΔR_t^I.

35 This type of variable was tried in other industry regressions and the results were as negative as reported here for transport.

36 The negative time trend in coal mining is not the consequence of a declining labour force in the industry. When E_t^I (employment in coal mining) is added as a regressor to the estimated equation, its estimated coefficient is not significantly different from zero (using the standard t test), yet the time trend (T) retains its significance. Alternatively forming the dependent variable (S/E_t^I) yields almost the same results as those in equation (3d).

37 We are thus obliged to use for this test less than half the number of observations available to us in the aggregate strike equation in Section II.

38 The test statistic defines an F distribution as follows:
$F = [(SSR_T - SSR_I) k(v-1)]/k(v-1)] [SSR_I/v(n-k)]$, where SSR_T and SSR_I are the sums of squared residuals from the aggregated model and from the individual industries respectively, k the number of estimated parameters in each regression, v the numbers of industries, and n the number of observations.

39 A comment on the estimating procedures invoked in this section is in order. An alternative technique for estimating the industry regressions here involves incorporating our *a priori* information concerning the absence of certain regressors from a given equation along lines proposed by Zellner [21]. However, the gain in efficiency of this two-stage Aitken estimator is likely to be marginal in this case, for,

although contemporaneous disturbance terms in the different industry equations may well be correlated, the regressors in these equations are likely to be highly collinear. That is, unemployment rates and changes in real wages in different industries tend to move together, so that it becomes questionable whether a slight (if any) gain in efficiency compensates for the greater computational costs of this procedure.

REFERENCES

[1] Almon, S., 'The Distributed Lag between Capital Appropriations and Expenditures', *Econometrica*, Vol. 33 (1965), pp. 178–96.
[2] Ashenfelter, O. and G. E. Johnson, 'Bargaining Theory, Trade Unions and Industrial Strike Activity', *American Economic Review*, Vol. LIX (1969), pp. 35–49.
[3] Brechling, F., 'Trends and Cycles in British Regional Unemployment', *Oxford Economic Papers*, Vol. 19 (1967), pp. 1–21.
[4] Cochrane, D. and G. H. Orcutt, 'Application of Least Squares Regressions to Relationships Containing Autocorrelated Error Terms', *Journal of the American Statistical Association*, Vol. 44 (1949), pp. 32–61.
[5] Goldberger, A. S., *Econometric Theory*, 1964.
[6] Hines, A. G., 'Trade Unions and Wage Inflation in the United Kingdom, 1893–1961', *Review of Economic Studies*, Vol. XXXI (1964), pp. 221–52.
[7] Hobsbawm, E. J., 'Economic Fluctuations and Some Social Movements since 1800', in his *Labouring Men, Studies in the History of Labour*, 1964.
[8] Kerr, C. and A. Siegel, 'The Interindustry Propensity to Strike–An International Comparison', in A. Kornhauser, R. Dubin and A. M. Ross (eds.), *Industrial Conflict*, 1954, pp. 189–212.
[9] Klein, L. R., R. J. Ball, A. Hazlewood, and P. Vandome, *An Econometric Model of the United Kingdom*, Oxford, 1961.
[10] Knowles, K. G. J. C., *Strikes–A Study in Industrial Conflict*, Oxford, 1952.
[11] McCarthy, W. E. J., 'The Reasons Given for Striking', *Bulletin of the Oxford University Institute of Statistics*, Vol. 21 (1959), pp. 17–29.
[12] ——and S. R. Parker, *Shop Stewards and Worshop Relations*, Research Papers 10, Royal Commission on Trade Unions and Employers' Associations, 1968.
[13] Rees, A., 'Industrial Conflict and Business Fluctuations', *Journal of Political Economy*, Vol. LX (1952), pp. 371–82.
[14] Roberts, B. C., *Trade Union Government and Administration in Great Britain*, 1956.
[15] Ross, A. M., *Trade Union Wage Policy*, Berkeley and Los Angeles, 1948.
[16] Smith, D. S., 'Incomes Policy', in R. E. Caves and Associates, *Britain's Economic Prospects*, Washington, 1968, pp. 104–44.
[17] Theil, H., *Linear Aggregation of Economic Relations*, Amsterdam, 1954.
[18] Turner, H. A., *The Trend of Strikes*, Leeds, 1963.
[19] ——, G. Clack and G. Roberts, *Labour Relations in the Motor Industry*, 1967.
[20] United Kingdom, Her Majesty's Stationery Office, *Report of the Royal Commission on Trade Unions and Employers' Associations*, 1968.
[21] Zellner, A., 'An Efficient Method of Estimating Seemingly Unrelated Regressions and Tests for Aggregation Bias', *Journal of the American Statistical Association*, Vol. 57 (1962), pp. 348–68.

9

INTERNATIONAL DIFFERENCES IN THE STRIKE PROPENSITY OF COAL MINERS: EXPERIENCE IN FOUR COUNTRIES

Gaston V. Rimlinger

A comparison of available data on coal miners' strikes in the United States, Great Britain, France, and Germany since the first decade of this century reveals the following patterns.

(1) As indicated by Tables 1 and 2, the United States and Britain had substantially more strikes and larger yearly man-day strike losses relative to employment than the continental countries.

(2) Britain had the greatest number of strikes relative to employment, but the United States was far in front in man-days lost per strike.

(3) Germany had the smallest number of strikes relative to employment, although her man-days lost per strike were not appreciably different from the French and British ratios.

(4) During the nineteen years for which data are available for all four countries, the number of times yearly man-day losses were less than one half for each worker employed was: none for the United States, one for Britain, nine for France, and twelve for Germany.

(5) In five of the eight years reported separately for the Saar territory, man-day losses were less than one tenth for each worker employed.

(6) Continental miners do not lack the ability to organise large strikes. They organised mass strikes of long duration but far more infrequently than their Anglo-American colleagues.

The data on which these observations are based are admittedly incomplete, and, as all strike data, must be taken with a certain reservation. Differences between countries and through time in defining strikes and in reporting and computing employment and man-day losses introduce an unknown margin of error. Moreover, there are unfortunate gaps in the tables because comparable figures for either employment or man-day strike losses were not available on a continuous basis.

However, as far as the data go, they do show substantial differences in strike behavior between Anglo-American and continental miners. Most important, they indicate that mining can be a rather peaceful industry. An investigation of such differences is worthwhile on its own grounds, but the case of the coal industry should be especially interesting in view of the arguments about the role of the coal mining environment advanced by Kerr and Siegel.[1] Their major point is that in spite of international sociocultural differences, certain industries, and foremost among them mining, tend to 'direct workers into isolated masses'[2] which are highly strike prone. The statistical support for this argument consists of a painstaking

TABLE 1

Relative Frequency and Average Magnitude of Strikes

Date	No. of Strikes per 10,000 Workers				Man-Days Lost per Strike			
	U.S.	Great Britain	France	Germany	U.S.	Great Britain	France	Germany
1902			2.25				90,132	
1903			.81				3,376	
1904			.44	.24			1,619	
1905			.41	.48			326	
1906			1.35	1.10			124,674	
1907			1.11	.93			2,315	
1908			.95	.42			773	
1909			.63	.22			885	
1910		2.05	.40	.25		25,954	5,382	
1911		1.63	.60	.15		23,912	1,718	
1912		1.35	1.60	1.97		222,970	2,390	
1913		1.47	1.45	.76		7,962	12,717	
1914		1.50	1.07			23,534	19,633	
1915		.82	.18			21,310	222	
1916		.70	.08			4,636	30	
1917		1.19	.18			9,388	128	
1918		1.52	.18			7,925	978	
1919		1.84	1.24	5.97	35,099	68,221	12,069	
1920		1.73	.81			82,971	176,443	5,985
1921		1.32	.32	1.39	494,510	5,206	9,077	
1922		1.37	.61	1.75	8,039	614	4,155	
1923		1.58	.77		6,360	38,778	16,707	
1924		1.60	.88	.40	8,226	892	87,076	
1925		1.52	.70	.15	21,055	974	7,432	
1926			.58	.03			4,109	268
1927	.71	1.10	.52	.43	447,816	6,255	5,924	10,418
1028	1.04	1.04	.45	.09	91,752	4,660	13,899	46,397
1929	1.38	1.63	.59	.01	4,676	3,765	12,406	12,250
1930	1.09	1.65	.76	.07	14,270	4,420	11,684	144,226
1931	1.20	1.73	.18		30,663	19,374	165	18,126

TABLE 1 (continued)

Relative Frequency and Average Magnitude of Strikes

No. of Strikers per 10,000 Workers   Man-Days Lost per Strike

Date	U.S.	Great Britain	France	U.S.	Great Britain	France
1932	1.15	1.39	.28	99,687	2,586	2,684
1933	2.48	1.45	.33	24,994	3,982	11,299
1934	2.03	1.86	.41	31,648	2,549	2,046
1935	1.31	2.90	.48	48,563	6,304	4,476
1936	1.10	3.60		12,482	3,156	
1937	1.46	5.78		29,321	3,274	
1938	.81	4.65		11,152	1,920	
1939	.93	5.25		147,609	1,399	
1940	1.11	5.03		43,847	1,342	
1941	1.85	6.70		70,317	713	
1942	2.42	7.41		3,861	1,597	
1943	8.78	11.83		21,737	1,060	
1944	18.96	17.65		1,622	1,979	
1945	14.57	18.38		9,626	491	
1946	12.07	18.99		38,823	318	
1947	9.43	14.83		5,302	866	
1948	12.23	15.50		25,411	416	
1949	9.48	12.14		39,780	863	
1950	10.70	12.29		19,958	501	
1951	12.87	15.11		1,672	331	
1952	15.41	16.96		4,765	541	
1953	12.24	14.68		1,264	371	
1954	8.41	20.91		1,851	320	
1955	12.36	25.47		914	624	

Sources: United States: Statistical Abstracts of the United States, 1928, 1949, 1952, 1956. U.S. Bureau of the Census; Historical Statistics of the United States, 1789–1945, pp. 153–154; U.S. Department of Labor, Bulletin No. 651, pp. 151–152.

Great Britain: Statistical Abstract for the United Kingdom, vols. 74, 81; Annual Abstract of Statistics, Nos. 86, 91; Ministry of Labour Gazette, 1910–1956.

France: Direction du Travail, Statistique des Grèves, 1902–1936; Annuaire Statistique, 1902–1935, 1947, 1956; Revue Française du Travail, 1947–1956.

Germany: Statistisches Jahrbuch fuer das deutsche Reich, 1902–1932; Statistisches Jahrbuch fuer die Bundesrepublik Deutschland, 1953–1956.

international comparison of a large number of industries ranked by strike losses over some thirty years.

Logically, the data of Tables 1 and 2 are not inconsistent with the Kerr-Siegel findings, for they tell us nothing about the strike proneness of miners relative to other workers. But they do raise suspicions about the implied insignificance of nonenvironmental factors, especially since Kerr and Siegel themselves note that between 1925 and 1932 the propensity to strike in German mining was 'lower than usual' and frankly admit that they 'have no explanation to offer'[3]. The only other data they have on the German

TABLE 2

Man-Days Lost in Strikes per Worker Employed, 1910–1955

Year	U.S.	Great Britain	France	Germany	Saar
1910	26.37	5.33	.21		
1911	1.35	3.89	.10		
1912	17.34	30.16	.38		
1913	4.08	1.17	1.81		
1914	14.43	3.53	2.11		
1915	3.36	1.75	.004		
1916	4.64	.32	.000		
1917	3.10	1.12	.002		
1918	.67	1.20	.02		
1919	20.30	6.47	8.27	7.19	2.86
1920	7.54	14.45	14.48	1.39	
1921	3.77	65.31	.17	1.26	
1922	87.00	1.10	.04	.73	
1923	4.48	1.00	2.94	2.17	
1924	6.88	1.31	.03	3.46	
1925	21.95	3.15	.07	.11	
1926	8.84	132.36	.24	.001	2.86
1927	31.85	.68	.30	.45	1.38
1928	9.54	.49	.62	.40	.04
1929	.64	.61	.72	.02	.38
1930	1.55	.72	.88	.96	.02
1931	3.73	3.34	.003	.25	.03
1932	11.52	.35	.08		.05
1933	6.16	.57	.38		.002
1934	4.43	.47	.08		
1935	5.56	1.81	.21		
1936	1.37	1.13			
1937	4.29	1.89			
1938	.91	.89			
1939	13.68	.72			
1940	.48	.68			
1941	13.12	.48			
1942	.92	1.18			
1943	19.21	1.26			
1944	3.05	3.49			
1945	14.12	.90			
1946	46.65	.60			
1947	5.04	1.28	7.22		
1948	20.92	.64	21.08		
1949	37.79	1.05	.57	.02	
1950	21.22	.62	.33	.03	
1951	2.16	.50	.70	.02	
1952	7.32	.92	1.06	.000	
1953	1.52	.55	6.33	.005	
1954	1.57	.66	.32		
1955	1.15	1.59	.20	.69	

Sources: U.S., Great Britain, France, and Germany: same as Table 1. The Saar: *Bericht des Statistischen Amtes des Saargebietes,* 1927–1934.

miners, which indicate a high strike propensity, are for 1915–24, but the representativeness of this period may be questioned in view of the political circumstances of the post-war period, the agitation for nationalisation of the mines, and the French occupation of the Ruhr. Moreover, after World War II the German miners have been less strike prone than other German workers, as indicated by Table 3, which compares mining with nine other major industries between 1949 and 1956.[4] In these eight years the miners' strike rank was four times below their employment rank, twice equal to it, and only twice above it.

TABLE 3

Rank Order of Employment and Strike-Losses in German Mining, 1949–56

Mining ranked	1949	1950	1951	1952	1953	1954	1955	1956
By employment	3	3	4	5	4	4	4	4
By man-day strike losses	6	3	6	9	4	9	1	3

Source: Computed from *Statistisches Jahrbuch fuer die Bundesrepublik Deutschland*, 1952–1957.

Can it be validly maintained in the face of these international differences that a mining environment creates a strike-prone 'isolated mass' regardless of a country's cultural milieu? Is the 'isolated mass' a valid concept when applied to coal mining in general? Or are there merely certain factors in a mining environment which work against peaceful relations but which may be either counteracted or reinforced by influences from outside the immediate environment? These are the main questions dealt with in this study. The environmental forces, on which Kerr and Siegel rest their argument, will be examined first. Then an historical comparison will be made of the coal mine work forces in the Saar, Germany, France, Britain, and the United States.

THE COAL MINING ENVIRONMENT

The mining environment influences labor conduct in two ways: first, it constitutes a source of discontent and tension; second, it helps to mold the workers' conduct in response to these emotions. In reality, of course, these two aspects of environmental influence are not as independent as this conceptual separation might imply.

The elements of the industrial environment which may be considered sources of tension and discontent are the nature of the work, the danger surrounding it, the economics of the industry, and its communications problem.[5] Irritation and friction are almost inevitable in a job which not only requires great physical exertion, often under high temperatures and other discomforts, but also depends on close cooperation within and among teams of workers, on the performance of preceding shifts, and on unpredictable natural conditions which may frustrate productive efforts and create problems in the remuneration and allocation of work.[6] Tensions result from anxieties due to danger compounded by darkness and to the witnessing of serious accidents.[7] Economic sources of difficulties arise primarily from the high percentage of wages in the cost of production on the one hand, and a tendency toward unstable coal prices on the other.[8] Moreover, the secular decline in employment in the industry in most countries[9] has promoted widespread feelings of insecurity among the workers. The underground dispersion and isolation of the workers make good labor–management communication, which is an asset to industrial peace, considerably more difficult in mines than in factories.[10]

The major environment-related factors that mold the response to these problems are: (1) the miners' separatism, (2) their habits and intensely felt need of cooperation, and (3) the psychological burden imposed upon them by the danger and arduousness of their job. The natural tendency of these factors is to produce labor solidarity and aggressiveness. However, they may lead also to solidarity but non-aggressive forms of conduct, or to individualistic aggressiveness.

Whether mine workers are isolated geographically or merely segregated in 'miners' colonies' consisting of company houses within or adjacent to larger towns, their location and occupation make them a distinct group of which they themselves, as well as outsiders, are fully conscious. They tend to be strongly aware, one would guess much more so than other workers, that they share a common fate. Their work and recreation habits make them feel different from other workers, even where they have frequent contact with them. They have their own feasts and tragedies, their own institutions and traditions. The organisation of their work relies on a system of 'mutual trust and dependence'[11] and on a 'highly developed sense of collective responsibility'[12]. Close kinship ties among them, their proverbial faithfulness to the trade, and a certain pride of craftsmanship further reinforce their sense of separateness and their cohesion.[13] The combination of all these factors is usually enough to give them a strong feeling of common destiny, which they can translate into united action.

There are a number of reasons why such action often has an aggressive character, namely strong tension, forceful work habits, and sometimes this sense of separateness. Acts of aggression, whether collective or individual, are normal outlets for tension and frustration. The occupation is a source of aggressiveness in the sense that it tends to alienate those who share its hardships from those who do not. Miners, like other workers in similar circumstances, harbor feelings of contempt for people who earn a living in an easy, pleasant way.[14] The work itself justifies a certain amount of recklessness, and the workers easily come to feel that its dangers and hardships are insufficiently recognised and inadequately rewarded. Separatism may promote an aggressive attitude toward management to the extent that it influences the workers' acceptance of authority. Under certain circumstances miners resent every exercise of authority, whether by management or the union, as a form of control imposed upon them by outsiders.

THE CONCEPT OF THE 'ISOLATED MASS'

Not even the combination of all these factors, however, makes it easy to believe that miners have to become an undifferentiated and alienated 'isolated mass' for whom the strike turns into 'a kind of colonial revolt against far-removed authority'[15]. Social life, even in an isolated mining town, is the resultant of a highly complex process. Recent sociological studies of mining communities [16] in England and in the United States show that miners strongly hold to certain common values, but at the same time these studies reveal internal crosscurrents and the possibility for different reactions to the environment, reactions which are influenced by nonenvironmental factors. It is quite possible, as will be shown below, for a socially distinct group like the miners to be well integrated into society and to be rather sensitive to society's opinion of them. And where this is the case, their cohesion and their strong inclination to conform to group values, which is directly related to their separatism,[17] may actually become a major support of disciplined industrial conduct. Under appropriate historical circumstances, it may be possible for management to rely on this inclination as an indirect form of control, for so long as the group as a whole interprets acceptance of managerial authority as proper conduct, deviators will be exposed to strong pressures to comply. In relatively homogeneous and isolated communities such pressures are particularly effective.

In some situations, on the other hand, the mining environment, instead of promoting solidarity, reinforces individualistic tendencies. If, for one reason or another, effective organisation and expression of protest are inhibited, tension and frustration are likely to promote the feeling that fellow workers are guilty for the lack of success, that they are undependable, and that everyone has to look out for himself. This attitude manifests itself in friction between workers, refusals to cooperate, heavy absenteeism, the rise of informal or secret organisations, mutual recriminations, and acts of violence.[18] Miners tend not to remain neutral; their alternative to intense solidarity is very often intense friction.

The extensive literature surveyed for this study leaves no doubt about the miners' sense of separateness but does not support the Kerr-Siegel arguments concerning the formation of the 'isolated mass,' which is an entirely different phenomenon. The main points of the foregoing discussion may be restated as follows: (1) by their occupation the miners are prone to tension and discontent; (2) their response is usually characterised by aggressiveness and solidarity; but (3) aggressiveness may give way to compliance where solidarity lends itself to indirect managerial control; and (4) solidarity may give way to intense individualism where cooperation and collective action are unsuccessful. [19] The miners' proneness or reluctance to strike in a given country clearly depends on the relative strength of these alternative responses. It will be the task of the following sections to examine historically how sociocultural factors may affect these responses to the environment, starting with the most compliant case, the Saar territory, and ending with the most aggressive, the United States.

THE SAAR TERRITORY

Although presently the Saar is again federated with the West German states, it deserves special treatment because its miners have a special history and unique traditions. Unfortunately, official strike records for the region are very incomplete. The longest strike on record occurred in 1923, when the men stayed out for one hundred days.[20] In recent years there have been but few strikes. One-day general strikes took place on October 2, 1950 and on April 8, 1952. Official records also mention scattered partial strikes in various years.[21]

The Saar miners have shown that they can organise massive stoppages but have an impressive record of industrial peace. Even their strikes have been unusually calm and orderly.[22] Their record of work attendance is the steadiest in Western Europe.[23] The decade of the 1920's, which is covered in part by Table 2, was the stormiest period of their history. In addition to the post-war labor upheavals, which shook all Europe, this border land faced the problem of annexation to France. It was a period when the French authorities, acting as a foreign and disliked power, discharged or reassigned thousands of miners as part of their mechanisation program. Yet, work stoppages remained astonishingly few. [24] The right to strike was curtailed only briefly, in 1923–24, by a prohibition of picketing.

In the behavior of the Saar miners historical factors have played a strong and positive role. Their conduct is the product of long-run forces which are embedded in present habits and institutions. Of prime importance among these forces has been the official tutelage of the miners by the state. The old Saar principality 'nationalised' the mines as early as the middle of the 18th century,[25] and they have remained that way ever since. With state ownership went a detailed and vigorous control not only of the miners' work habits but also of their private lives. The state sponsored and controlled guild-type organisations (Knappschaften) which administered various benefits and were designed to cultivate a spirit of loyalty, industry, orderliness, and discipline. An official regulation of 1853 went so far as to declare the elected miners' elders (who represented the workers in the administration of the Knappschaften) responsible for the moral conduct of the 'mine workers, their wives and children'[26]. During the expansion of the second half of the 19th century the authorities continued to make serious efforts to maintain this spirit by supporting such traditions as the old miner's greeting forms, the wearing of the miner's uniform, miners' bands and parades, burial ceremonies, religious observances, and various forms of social insurance.

Trade unions developed very slowly and not until after 1890. Against unionism were the miners' inbred sense of discipline, the fact that many remained part-time peasants, the resistance of the employer (the state) who not only controlled employment in almost all mines but had police power, and a form of Roman Catholic traditionalism that strongly frowned upon resistance to the authority of the master. The workers were always highly conscious of their special, state-protected status, but the character of this cohesion necessarily hindered rather than helped the development of a protest movement.

Although today the vast majority of the Saar miners are considered ardent union members,[27] much of the old attitude and some of the institutions supporting it are still in existence. Their advantages are still legally protected, and they still enjoy a social status unequalled by miners anywhere in the Western world. The esteem of their occupation is such that this is the only area in Europe without a shortage of mine labor, in spite of a rigorous apprenticeship system. The miners are the most important social group of the territory[28] and politicians woo them for support. [29] Unlike in most mining regions, in the Saar valley the miners are not geographically isolated. Most of them live as a minority among other workers and farmers in towns with less than ten thousand inhabitants.[30] Many continue to work their own land with the help of their wives and children. Industralisation in the Saar valley did not sever the laborer from his land nor did it bring in a lot of outsiders. Almost without exception the miners are native to the region. To this must be added the fact that about 75 per cent of them are Roman Catholic, which has helped to continue some corporative religious observances. In most towns the miners participate as a group, with their band, in processions on religious holidays. And in isolated cases they have kept the very old custom of the collective devotion before entering the mine.

The Saar miners are a good example of workers who have a high degree of solidarity but are not strike prone. They are a homogeneous and self-conscious group, and though they are socially distinct, they are not socially isolated. On the contrary, their social position makes them sensitive to social pressures and more or less forces them to live up to the traditional 'honor and esteem' of their occupation. The workers themselves have an obvious interest in protecting this social recognition and in restraining those who would endanger it by undisciplined or unprincipled conduct.

GERMANY

The discussion of Germany will be restricted to the Ruhr basin, which has always been the most important German coal producing area. The Ruhr miners have been more aggressive and more highly unionised than other German miners most of whom today are within the Communist orbit.

There are certain historical similarities between the Ruhr and the Saar, but in the Ruhr, the Prussian state of the mid-eighteenth century did not take over the mines directly. Frederick the Great left the working of the mines to private concession holders, whom he placed under the supervision of mining bureaus. These had the duty to exercise detailed control over managerial, technical, and personnel matters. This system, which remained in force until the 1850's, entailed extensive state tutelage over the workers, although it was not quite as thorough as in the Saar. Still, the miners partook of the honor of civil service [31] and enjoyed various forms of economic protection by the state. [32] The *Knappschaften* system was similar to that of the Saar.

Between 1850 and 1865 the state relinquished its control, and private employers took over the reins. Many of the workers' privileges vanished in the subsequent headlong expansion. Nevertheless they long found it difficult to 'rebel' against their masters, a course of action which was to the early miner as mutiny was to the sailor. Union organisation, which began seriously around 1890, was primarily the work of individuals who stood outside the industry's authority structure and had strong ideological orientations, either Socialist or Christian Social.

The authoritarian tradition has weakened over time but in modified forms continues to the present day. Diverse factors account for its tenacity. The workers who streamed into the area during the expansion of the second half of the nineteenth century were not eager to support a protest movement. Most of them came from the eastern agricultural districts where they had grown accustomed to the coercive discipline of a plantation-type capitalism. The unions' orientation was such that their efforts were never directed toward a day-to-day challenge of managerial authority. The ideal of both Socialists and Christian Socials has never been a social order based on continual tests of strength, but an order based on agreed-upon rules administered in an orderly, disciplined fashion.

Management, of course, has sought to maintain the old ideals. Traditionally, the bearing of the higher managerial personnel has been rather military in character, which is sometimes ascribed to the fact that many of them started their careers in the well-disciplined and honor-conscious civil service. German mine foremen have always been known for their harshness.[33] The recent study of the Mannesmann mines describes their control of the workers as a system of 'iron-handed subordination'[34]' It must be pointed out, however, that except for abuses and occasional insults, the workers by and large accepted 'rigorous but fair' discipline. This acceptance was not merely the result of specific forms of organisation. It was an expression of a work ethic and of a deeply rooted, religiously oriented, concept of the master-workman relationship. Much of this attitude lingers on even though its religious basis has become secularised.[35] Even during the tumultuous days following World War I the Ruhr miners were noted for their conservatism and willingness to compromise.[36] It is especially significant that the 'quickie' strike, which is almost endemic to Anglo-American mines, has never become a problem in German mining. It is handicapped by the disciplinary atmosphere as well as by the workers' responsiveness to a strong public opinion which supports walkouts for 'solid' reasons but denounces 'quickies' as 'reckless insubordination'[37]. The miners are responsive to this attitude because they share the premises on which it rests.

To a certain extent the foregoing characterisation applies to German industry in general and may account for the fact that German workers generally do not have a reputation for strike proneness. Although the objective of this study is limited to a comparison of miners in different countries, it may be worth noting that investigations such as that of the Mannesmann Works,[38] which covered both mines and factories, clearly indicate that authoritarianism has been harsher in the mines. This does not mean that strict discipline per se is a guarantee against strikes. It is effective because the German miners, for historical reasons, have accepted it, and because in their case the strong inclination to conform to group values, attributed to miners generally, has helped to discipline their industrial conduct.

The case of the Ruhr miners is similar to that of the Saar miners, although the Ruhr has had considerably more strikes. This may be explained in part by the fact that the Ruhr miners are a less homogeneous group and do not enjoy the same degree of social recognition as their Saar colleagues. Nevertheless, in neither instance have unionisation and labor solidarity led to an aggressive strike record. In both cases did the industrial environment play a major role in the building of traditions which strengthened rather than weakened the effectiveness of managerial control.

FRANCE

The conduct of the French miners bears similarities to that of both the relatively compliant Germans and the more aggressive Americans. In strike frequency and yearly man-day losses they are not too far removed from their continental colleagues, but the sporadic violence of their outbreaks reminds one of the American experience. During the 1840's, a student notes, the conduct of the miners in northern France was characterised by a 'series of brutal explosions interrupting long periods of calm'[39]. This form of behavior is typical of many workers during the pre-organised stage, but it characterises the French miners throughout most of their history. Their historical literature is sprinkled with references to 'explosions of pain' and 'paroxysms of rage.' These descriptions are not merely an aspect of the literary style of French writers; they have a factual basis in terrible acts of vengeance perpetrated by the workers. Crisis situations, such as mine disasters, were sometimes the sparks that touched off waves of exasperation. The death of hundreds of workers in the Courrière catastrophe of 1906 produced the instinctive reactions of widespread disorder, including rows among workers and battles with the police, and vociferous demands that 'the murderers be punished.' Yet, in spite of their bitterness, the workers often came easily 'back under the yoke, almost without rancor'[40].

More recent examples of explosive situations were the strikes of 1947 and 1948. The 1948 strike was a form of civil war; the miners kidnapped at least one government official and in many places refused to let maintenance crews enter the mines, which were in danger of becoming flooded and unworkable for weeks.[41]

On the whole, nevertheless, the French miners have bowed to a strict managerial discipline. But when they declare industrial war, a deep-seated alienation and bitterness become tragically evident. This is necessarily an over-simplification; yet, it contains the dominant traits of their conduct, traits which reflect their history and social environment. Foremost among the historical factors are a landowning peasantry background, a narrow paternalism and rigid managerial discipline, a repressive governmental attitude, sharply conflicting ideological currents, and the resulting chronic weakness of unionism.

Historically, the legacy of a landowning peasantry has been felt most strongly in the central and southern mines. The workers there were long distrustful of unions; their attitude was that they would be better off if they themselves saved the money needed to support a labor organisation. They were steeped in notions they had formed during their 'self-centered and independent life as small land-owners'[42], a life to which many hoped to return with their earnings to buy more land. They were unwilling to accept the discipline of a voluntary organisation which was both ineffective and suspect. In northern France most workers had severed their connections with the land by the late 19th century, which explains partly why their unions were more highly developed. But even there, support of unionism long remained spotty.

The French government has always had considerable influence on labor–management relations through its regional officials and the *Corps des Mines*. Historically, this influence worked in the direction of supporting a system of quasi-military discipline, which operated not only in the mines but also in the company housing districts, where it was connected with various paternalistic schemes.[43] It was the official attitude that the dangerous nature of the occupation makes rigid discipline an inescapable necessity. In this respect, the French system bears similarities to the German. The important difference lies in the fact that the French miners never achieved the social status of their German colleagues and never enjoyed the same type of governmental protection. Nevertheless, they grew accustomed to look to the government rather than to the unions for basic improvements in their living and working conditions.

Another significant difference between France and Germany has been the conduct of the government during strikes. The French miners have bitter memories of massive uses of gendarmes and troops against them, some of which ended in serious bloodshed and became *causes célèbres* among the working class.[44] In the big strike of 1948 some 30,000 troops and policemen armed with half-tracks, machine guns, and hand grenades were used to drive the strikers from the pits in northern France.[45] The strikers retaliated with hand grenades. During none of the big German strikes did anything similar take place.

With the nationalisation of the mines after World War II, the government became more or less directly responsible for the workers' welfare. Yet, notwithstanding official efforts to improve working conditions through a comprehensive system of benefits and a highly developed grievance machinery, the post-war period has been one of the most strike-ridden in the miners' history. This unexpected result is often described as a 'crise d'autorité'[46], which is attributed to the relaxation of the old disciplinary system under the new laws and to the 'politicisation' of grievances. Because of the interconnections of rival unions with rival political parties, and especially because of the dominant Communist influence, ordinary grievances have become hopelessly enmeshed in political issues. [47] Hence, as a result of internal friction, the French miners are again today, as so often in previous times, prevented from achieving a meaningful participation in the industrial decision-making process.

In the French case neither the unions nor management have been able to take full advantage of the natural solidarity of coal miners. The French miners' unions have a long record of the most bitter internecine warfare,[48] and friction among the workers at the pit level has often been acute.[49] Management has been able to exercise strict discipline but not to gain the workers' acceptance of it. Notwithstanding significant exceptions, the historical record of the French miners lends considerable support to the hypothesis that the mining environment may contribute to the strengthening rather than weakening of the individualistic influences of a country's culture on labor protest.

GREAT BRITAIN

In this section and in the following an attempt will be made to uncover historical reasons for the British and American miners' strike proneness. A cautious reminder may be appropriate at this point. The historical part of this study is not meant to be a full explanation of the miners' behavior. Its major aim is to trace the development of their attitude toward authority, but the effect of this attitude must be combined with the impact of a peculiar environment, for the same historical forces may lead to quite different results in different industrial environments.

Two facts stand out in the history of the British miners: (1) they were able to develop, even before the country's industrialisation, a sense of group solidarity, a certain spirit of independence, and habits of self-defense; (2) during industrialisation sociocultural factors reinforced rather than counteracted these early inclinations.

The British collier of the 18th century led a rough and ignorant life; in Scotland he was a serf,[50] and in the country's major coal-producing area, the northeast coast, he was tied to his job by a yearly bond which strongly reflected his subordinate social position.[51] His master was a wealthy landowner or capitalist lessee drawn from the landed classes.[52] He usually lived in isolation from other workers as well as, of course, from his master. Only rarely did he have access to educational and religious institutions.

Unlike in Germany and in France, in Britain the state did not interfere with labor–management relations in the coal industry. One reason for this was the fact that since the 16th century British coal mines had been legally considered the property of the landowner rather than of the state. Moreover, state interference was unlikely since political power was in the hands of the landowning classes. Consequently, the collier, though nearly a social outcast, possessed a considerable degree of personal independence. His wages and working conditions were largely a matter of local custom and did not reflect short-run market conditions.[53]

For the bulk of the 18th century the British miners remained loyal 'servants' to their masters, following a pattern of conduct established by long-standing customs. However, when customary conditions were upset, the miners rose to their defence. They also acquired a reputation as 'formidable rioters,' especially in years of bad harvests, when rising food prices threatened them with famine.[54] Although these riots were mostly directed against suppliers of food, the workers' 'riotous disposition' was also a warning to employers and constituted a crude but not ineffective defensive weapon. Their ability to act as a group in emergencies, with some semblance of organisation, and their known recklessness could not be ignored, even though they had no direct voice in the determination of living and working conditions.

The rapid expansion of the industry in the late 18th and early 19th centuries undermined the old, traditional relationship between employers and workers. New methods of mining, increasing competition, more unstable markets, and an expanding work force forced local customs to give way in the determination of wages and employment conditions. Moreover, many of the newcomers to the employer rank had little regard for the miners' traditional rights.

Although the miners were not able to organise viable unions until after 1850, long before then their aggressiveness asserted itself.[55]

At first they organised strikes mainly to resist changes in traditional arrangements. However, as their horizons widened under the impact of the political, social, and religious reforms sweeping the country, they began to insist more and more doggedly on improvements in wages and working conditions. The emphasis of these reform movements was on individual freedom and equality and on self-determination. The British miners' record during the first half of the last century is one of increasing insistence that these concepts be introduced into industrial relations.

Viable miners' unions appeared during the third quarter of the 19th century. [56] Most of the leaders of these unions tried to follow a policy of peace and conciliation to gain employer acceptance, but this approach was tenable only so long as market conditions were favorable. With the onset of the depression of 1873 the workers demanded forceful action to resist wage cuts. It was then that the problem of restraining organised miners in Britain became fully evident.[57] The depression weakened the unions but heightened discontent. When unionism revived, in the mid 1880's, it was accompanied by a new spirit of aggressiveness. Under the rising influence of socialism, the mine workers formulated new demands which reflected a more radical view of their situation. The most radical of these demands was for nationalisation of the mines. For this goal they fought for nearly half a century. Yet, its achievement, as is well known, has not led to industrial peace. The miners have almost as many complaints against the new management as they had against the old. [58]

In Britain the impact of the mining environment was counteracted neither by paternalistic discipline, nor by employer interference with the workers' private lives, nor by state participation in the training and disciplining of the work force. Neither the state nor the employers accepted responsibility for the workers' welfare during industrialisation. The liberalism of the 19th century was an insistence that this was each man's own responsibility. But workers who are forced to look after themselves are invited to fight for their interests. The miners had to fight a long, uphill struggle to rise from their lowly position to one of partnership in industrial government. As in all history, this too has been an irreversible process. The miners' struggle established legacies of conflict, and of distrust and independence toward authority which will take some time, if ever, to disappear.

THE UNITED STATES

The American miners differed from their British cousins in two important ways: (1) though their own social status was low, they did not start their industrial struggle in a society where the social subordination of a working class was taken for granted; (2) they felt that their 'rights' did not have to be won, that they were guaranteed by the Constitution, but had to be defended against employers who would usurp them.

Virginia was the birthplace of the American coal industry, but her slave-operated mines were not the birthplace of miner unionism. The birthplace of this unionism was in the North, in Pennsylvania, Ohio, Indiana, and Illinois, where British miners, who often had previous union experience, had come to settle. From these areas stem the historical traits of the American miners' movement. Strikes do not seem to have started until the late 1840's, and, with one exception, unions did not appear until the 1860's.[59] Those which appeared in the early 1860's vanished after the Civil War, and those started in the late 1860's and early 1870's collapsed during the following depression. The advent of viable unions was delayed until the formation of the United Mine Workers in 1890, although promising starts were made in the second half of the 1880's.

The frontier environment of the young coal industry, with its fluid social conditions and its freedom from governmental control, and the dispersion and small scale of the mining operations were important factors in the development of a strongly egalitarian and sometimes fiercely independent attitude on the part of the workers. They felt that they had the same basic rights as the employers and had no reservations about challenging their authority. In one instance, in 1851, they greeted an employer's demand that accrued wages be forfeited in case of strike as 'an insult to American citizenship' and 'threatened the arrest of the mine superintendents for proposing to abridge the rights of American citizenship'[60]. During the 1860's the mine workers' spirit of independence and determination became fully evident.[61] But perhaps its most classic expression is contained in a resolution, passed at the 1874 convention of the Miners' National Association, which urged that the members 'immediately provide themselves with a full supply of the best breechloading rifles which the country affords' to counteract the importation of 'armed banditti and lazzaroni from the slums of the large cities'[62]. J. McBride, one of the early leaders, explained that American miners 'do not cringe or fawn to authority. Many of them left their native land because of the oppression there, and in the hope of obtaining a larger share of liberty here. Hence they resent every intrusion of their rights; and the stubbornness shown by them in many of their strikes . . . shows how dearly they love justice, and how hard they are willing to fight for it'[63]. Andrew Roy, who spent most of his life in and around the mines, described the miners of the 'sixties and 'seventies as 'terrible fighters.' Another observer, John Wilson, the man who later become a prominent English miners' leader, reports that as early as 1864, the year he came to America for a brief stay as a mine worker, guns were used in strikes. 'It was rough while it lasted, and this was the only place where I saw pistols used as arguments to persuade blacklegs not to work'[64]. Unfortunately, that was not the last time guns were used to decide labor issues in American mining.

This heritage of independence and self-assurance is the historical basis of the American miners' aggressiveness. There were, of course, times and places when they seemed subdued. The massive influx of central and southern European peasants after 1880 posed serious problems for worker solidarity and united action, especially in the anthracite regions.[65] But the fact is that the United Mine Workers were able to overcome these problems and, in spite of strong ethnic antagonisms, to assimilate the newcomers.[66] In the southern mines, as is well known, special conditions delayed the rise of unionism, but wherever American miners were able to assert themselves, it seems, they insisted on vigorous action. It is symptomatic that they denounced one of their most famous leaders, John Mitchell, when he became too conciliatory.[67]

Social and historical conditions supporting the environmental tendency toward combativeness are even stronger in evidence in the American than in the British case. The employers were more ruthlessly competitive, and the workers more fiercely independent. Both sides fought with an inner conviction that their 'rights,' however vaguely these may have been understood in a theoretical sense, were inviolable. And it is this typically American characteristic of their combat which helps to explain why their struggles could be so violent and yet not take on a radical orientation.

CONCLUDING REMARKS

The present survey suggests two broad generalisations: (1) the conduct of miners everywhere reflects the impact of a peculiar environment; (2) the inherent environmental tendency toward strike proness may be counteracted or reinforced by sociocultural factors. What miners have in common is the bearing of similar psychological and physical burdens which stem from the nature of their job and the industrial environment. The environment has an influence on how they carry these burdens, but their conduct is also under the influence of sociocultural factors.

Kerr and Siegel have shown statistically that mining is often a strike-prone occupation, but their explanation of this phenomenon cannot be accepted. Their 'isolated mass,' which by definition is socially not integrated, might be replaced by some notion of a 'separatist group' which may or may not be socially integrated, and may or may not be strike prone, depending on the historical situation. Only then does it become understandable why, in spite of certain universal characteristics, miners in a given country may have either very many strikes or practically none at all.

NOTES

1 C. Kerr and A. Siegel, 'The Interindustry Propensity to Strike–An International Comparison,' in A. Kornhauser, R. Dubin, and A. M. Ross, eds., *Industrial Conflict* (New York: McGraw-Hill, 1954), pp. 189–212.

2 *Ibid.*, p. 203.

3 *Op. cit.*, p. 191.

4 The other industries were: Iron and Metal-works, Iron-, Steel- and Metal-fabricating, Machinery and Vehicles, Electrical equipment, Chemicals, Textiles, Building, Printing, and Paper.

5 The sources of labor difficulties have been discussed at length in the rapidly expanding literature on nationalised mines in Great Britain; for the same country see also K. G. J. C. Knowles, *Strikes–A Study in Industrial Conflict* (Oxford: Basil Blackwell, 1952), pp. 164ff; E. L. Trist and K. W. Bamforth, 'Some Social and Psychological Consequences of the Longwall Method of Coal-Getting,' *Human Relations*, IV (February 1951), 3–38; and S. Wellisz, 'Strikes in Coal Mining,' *British Journal of Sociology*, IV (December 1953), 346–366. In the American literature somewhat dated but still highly useful treatments may be found in E. E. Hunt, *et al.*, eds., *What the Coal Commission Found* (Baltimore: Williams and Wilkins, 1925), and in M. van Kleeck, *Miners and Management* (New York: Russell Sage Foundation, 1934); more recent observations and references are contained in G. G. Somers, *Grievance Settlement in Coal Mining*, West Virginia University Business and Economics Studies (Morgantown: West Virginia University, 1956).

6 For an excellent analysis of some of these problems see N. Dennis, F. Henriques, and C. Slaughter, *Coal is Our Life* (London: Eyre and Spottiswoode, 1956).

7 Cf. Trist and Bamforth, *loc. cit.* pp. 7–8. The traditional superstition of the miner is one form of response to these anxieties. For interesting illustrations see P. Sébillot, *Les travaux publics et les mines dans les traditions et les superstitions* (Paris: J. Rothschild, 1894), pp. 443–500.

8 In most countries the industry has had long periods of excess capacity. The short-run industry demand for coal tends to be income elastic but price inelastic. Since the number of firms in the industry is usually fairly large, these characteristics, in conjunction with a low mobility of labor and sunk capital, set the stage for cut-throat competition in slack times. Where wages and prices are maintained by agreement there may still be violent fluctuations in employment.

9 Between 1929 and 1955 employment in U.S. mining declined from 654,944 to 245,600; in Britain from 939,000 to 699,000; in France from 292,242 to 221,000; in Germany the trend has been similar but political shifts of territory make comparisons difficult.

10 Comparative evidence on this point may be found in Institut fuer Sozialforschung, *Betriebsklima. Eine industrie-soziologische Untersuchung im Mannesmann-Bereich* (Frankfurt a.M: Johann-Wolfgang Goethe-Universitaet, 1954), pp. 199ff. For a discussion of the related problem of size of mine and industrial relations, see R. W. Revans, 'Facteurs dimensionnels dans l'exploitation des houillères,' *Annales des Mines*, vol. 144:3 (October–December 1955), pp. 3–15.

11 Dennis, *et. al., op. cit.*, p. 45.

12 J. Chardonnet, *Le charbon, sa production, son rôle économique et social* (Grenoble: Arthaud, c. 1948), p. 171.

13 See P. Vigne, 'Quelques types de psychologie ouvrière–le mineur,' *Droit Social*, XIII (July–August 1950), 279–284.

14 Dennis, *et. al., op. cit.*, p. 33.

15 Kerr and Siegel, *loc. cit.*, p. 193.

16 For a study of a Yorkshire mining town, see Dennis, *et al., op. cit.;* for an American example, see H. R. Lantz, *People of Coal Town* (New York: Columbia University Press, 1958).

17 'One wonders how a people possessing such facets of open rebellion and violence can also be conformists. Yet at certain basic levels these people do possess very pronounced tendencies toward conformity. Our Coal Town people, with intense feelings of separateness, have very real needs to belong, and these needs to belong are expressed through conformity and a fear of non-conformity. Such conformity is a blind, indiscriminate conformity to the values of the majority.' Lantz, *op. cit.*, p. 259.

18 Trist and Bamforth found some of these forms of conduct where patterns of work cooperation had been destroyed. Similar results may occur at the level of union organisation.

19 This last solution may be considered unstable, but that does not prevent its existence even for very long periods of time.

20 R. Obé, *Arbeitsverhaeltnisse im franzoesisch-fiskalischen Saarbergbau* (Published doctoral dissertation, University of Frankfurt, a.M., 1930), pp. 44ff.

21 See Statistisches Amt des Saarlandes, *Saarlaendische Bevoelkerungs und Wirtschaftszahlen* (issued quarterly since 1948).

22 F. Roy, Le mineur sarrois (Paris: Berger-Levrault, 1954), p. 149.

23 OEEC, *Coal Production. Short Term Programmes of Western Europe.* Report of the Ministerial Coal Production Group (Paris: Organisation for European Economic Cooperation, 1952), p. 55.

24 For a more detailed discussion see P. Waelbroeck, 'Industrial Relations in the French State Mines in the Saar Basin: I' *International Labour Review*, XXI (June 1930), pp. 798–836.

25 A. von Brandt, *Zur sozialen Entwicklung im Saargebiet* (Leipzig: Dunker und Humblot, 1904), pp. 3–4.

26 P. Kiefer, *Die Organisationsbestrebungen der Saarbergleute* (Published doctoral dissertation, University of Strasbourg, 1912), p. 121.

27 No official membership figures are published, but it is estimated that of some 60,000 miners in 1952, 55,000 were unionised. F. Roy, *op. cit.*, p. 174.

28 Of the slightly less than one million Saar inhabitants about one fourth depend on the coal industry for their livelihood.

29 At least ten of the fifty members of the Saar legislature in 1954 were miners or former miners. F. Roy, *op. cit.*, p. 176.

30 *Ibid.*, pp. 21–22.

31 E. Gothein, 'Bergbau,' *Grundriss der Sozialoekonomik* (Tuebingen: J. C. B. Mohr (Paul Siebeck), 1914), VI, 332.

32 For a general survey see O. Hué, *Die Bergarbeiter* (Stuttgart: Verlag von J. H. W. Dietz Nachf., 1910–13), 2 Vols. Other major studies are H. Imbusch, *Arbeitsver-*

haeltnis und Arbeiter-Organisationen im deutschen Bergbau (Essen: Gewerkverein christlicher Bergarbeiter, 1908); M. Koch, *Die Bergarbeiterbewegung im Ruhrgebiet zur Zeit Wilhelm II* (Dusseldorf: Droste Verlag, 1954); and M. Baumont, *La grosse industrie allemande et le charbon* (Paris: Gaston Doin, 1928).

33 According to one student, the employers of the 1880's preferred to hire former Prussian army sergeants as foremen. See K. Oldenberg, 'Studien ueber die Rheinisch-Westfaelische Berbarbeiterbewegung,' *Jahrbuch fuer Gesetzgebung, Verwaltung, und Volkswirtschaft*, XXIV (1890), 665.

34 Institut fuer Sozialforschung, *op. cit.*, p. 93.

35 See the recnet study of W. Brepohl, *Industrievolk im Wandel von der agraren zur industriellen Dasienform dargestellt am Ruhrgebiet* (Tuebingen: J. C. B. Mohr (Paul Siebeck), 1957).

36 W. Neumann, *Die Gewerkschaften im Ruhrgebiet* (Koeln: Bund Verlag, 1951), pp. 183, 224.

37 See M. L. Lehmkuehler, 'Streik als soziale Krise des Grossbetriebes eine historischsoziologische Studie ueber den Ruhrbergbau,' *Soziale Welt*, III, 151–152.

38 Institut fuer Sozialforschung, *op. cit.*

39 M. Gillet, 'Aspects de la crise de 1846–51 dans le bassin houiller du Nord,' *Revue du Nord*, Vol. 37 (January–March 1956), p. 21.

40 P. du Maroussem, 'Piqueur sociétaire de la "mine aux mineurs" de Monthieux (Loire-France).' *Ouvriers des deux mondes*, 2nd series, V (1898), 376.

41 *Le Figaro*, October 23, 1948, p. 1. This refusal was allegedly instigated by the Communists, and labor spokesmen declared it alien to the history and tradition of French miners. See the editorial in *Révolution Prolétarienne*, November 1948. However, a similar refusal had occurred in a big strike in 1919; see L. J. Gras, *Histoire économique générale des mines de la Loire* (St. Etienne, 1922), II, p. 888.

42 H. Pin, *Les Mines de houille dans le Gard* (Published doctoral dissertation, University of Lyon, 1914), p. 177.

43 See C. Benoist, 'Le travail dans la grande industries–Les mines de houille,' *Revue des deux mondes*, X (July, 1902), 5–26 and XI (August, 1902), 845–871; A. Amieux, *Des conditions du travail dans les mines* (Published doctoral dissertation, University of Lyon, 1908), and J. Valdour, *Les mineurs: observations vécues* (Paris: Rousseau, 1919).

44 See Gras, *op. cit.*, II, pp. 752–55, I, pp. 345 ff.

45 *Le Figaro*, October 26, November 3, 1948.

46 R. Gendarme, *L'expérience française de la nationalisation industrielle* (Paris: Librairie de Medicis, 1950), pp. 120–122.

47 See R. Quilliot, 'Dix ans de nationalisation des houillères,' *Revue Socialiste*, No. 103 (January 1957), pp. 18–28, and the editorial 'La politisation des houillères nationales,' in *Révolution Prolétarienne*, November 1947, pp. 244–250.

48 See for instance G. Dumoulin, *Carnets de Route* (Lille: L'Avenir, 1938), pp. 48, 113 ff. Inability to deal with management may also lead to the use of terroristic measures by secret organisations. For evidence on this among French miners, see C. Bartuel and M. Ruillère, *La mine et les mineurs* (Paris: Gaston Doin, 1923), pp. 355–383.

49 See Valdour, *op. cit.*, *passim*.

50 If a miner left his master he could be reclaimed and punished as a thief. See T. S. Ashton and J. Sykes, *The Coal Industry in the Eighteenth Century* (Manchester: University Press, 1929), p. 27.

51 S. Webb, *The Story of the Durham Miners* (London: The Labour Publishing Co., 1921), p. 9. The bond was voluntary but only the workers, not the employers, could be legally held to it. Violation often meant jail for the worker.

52 Ashton and Sykes, *op. cit.*, p. 3.

53 '. . . over the greater part of the eighteenth century money wages exhibited remark-

able rigidity,' *ibid.*, p. 115.

54 *Ibid.*, chapter viii, and A. H. Dodd, *The Industrial Revolution in North Wales* (Cardiff: University of Wales Press, 1933), p. 399, and A. H. John, *Industrial Development of South Wales* (Cardiff: University of Wales Press, 1950), pp. 19–20.

55 See E. Welbourne, *The Miners' Unions of Northumberland and Durham* (Cambridge: University Press, 1923), pp. 23 ff., R. F. Wearmouth, *Some Working-Class Movements of the Nineteenth Century* (London: The Epworth Press, 1948), pp. 239–244, and J. L. and B. Hammond, *The Skilled Labourer* (London: Longmans, Green, and Co., 1919), pp. 26 ff.

56 See R. P. Arnot, *The Miners* (London: George Allen & Unwin, 1929), p. 47, and G. D. H. Cole, *A Short History of the British Working Class Movement* (revised edition; London: George Allen & Unwin, 1948), pp. 181–185.

57 See an account by one of their leaders, J. Wilson, *A History of the Durham Miners* (Durham: J. H. Veitch and Sons, 1907), pp. 55, 92, 145–146, 161–162. The workers were in open rebellion against the leaders.

58 See Acton Society Trust, *The Workers' Point of View* (London: Acton Society Trust, 1952).

59 There was one union in the anthracite field in 1848–49; P. Roberts, *The Anthracite Coal Industry* (New York: Macmillan, 1901), pp. 172–173. In the late 1850's the miners in western Pennsylvania organised an 'Equal Justice Society'; H. N. Eavenson, *The First Century and a Quarter of American Coal Industry* (Pittsburgh, Pa.: Privately printed, Koppers Building, 1942), p. 198.

60 A. Roy, *A History of the Coal Miners of the United States*, 3rd ed. (Columbus, Ohio: J. L. Trauger Printing Co., 1907), pp. 51–52.

61 See the collection of documentary evidence in the appendix of E. A. Wieck, *The American Miners' Association* (New York: Russell Sage Foundation, 1940).

62 C. Evans, *History of the United Mine Workers of America* (Indianapolis: United Mine Workers of America, n.d.), I, 61.

63 J. McBride assisted by T. T. O'Malley, 'The Coal Miners,' in G. E. McNeill, ed., *The Labor Movement* (New York: M. W. Hazen, 1887), p. 257.

64 J. Wilson, *Memories of a Labour Leader* (London: T. Fisher Unwin, 1910), p.181.

65 See W. J. Walsh, *The United Mine Workers of America as an Economic and Social Force in the Anthracite Territory* (Published doctoral dissertation, Catholic University of America, Washington, D.C., 1931), p. 92.

66 Cf. W. M. Leiserson, *Adjusting Immigrant and Industry* (New York: Harper and Brothers, 1924), pp. 186 ff.

67 See the acid attacks on him in United Mine Workers of America, *Proceedings of the Twenty-Second Annual Convention* (Indianapolis: Cheltonham Press, 1911), I, 519–568.

International Comparisons

10

SOME INTERNATIONAL ASPECTS OF THE STRIKE MOVEMENT

K. Forchheimer

The first impression given by a comparison between statistics of labour disputes in different countries is that apart from the world-wide strike wave after the first world war, there is little international agreement; strike figures seem to differ completely in this respect from statistics of the economic development, business activity, employment, prices and so on. Yet a closer study reveals some common features.

This paper sets out to show the most important similarities and some of the differences in the general structure and development of national strike movements. It does not discuss the technical diffi-culties of international comparisons in this field.[1] Only such figures are used as seem fairly comparable.

In order to find out the national features of the strike movements, and their similarities and differences, one has to compare the relevant figures over a considerable series of years: one should compare them over a *common* period at least from the beginning of this century. But the available figures do not relate to the same periods. In two countries only (U.S.A. and Italy) statistics start as early as 1880; France followed in 1890, Great Britain in 1893, Germany in 1899, Canada in 1901, Sweden in 1903, and so on. On the other hand, in some countries statistics have been discontinued in the 'twenties or in the early 'thirties (Germany, Italy, partly in France). Furthermore they were interrupted in U.S.A. from 1905 to 1916,[2] and partly in Italy from 1904 to 1907. U.S.A. and German statistics are incomplete in an important respect (data on working days lost by disputes) until 1927 and 1920 respectively. There were, in addition, important changes made in the methods of compilation (statistics of 'results' in U.S.A., several changes in Italy) which impair considerably the reliability of the time series. Discussion in this paper is accordingly limited to a few countries.

THE STRENGTH OF THE MOVEMENT AND ITS COMPONENTS

National statistics on labour disputes present yearly figures showing in a fairly similar way during decent decades:

(1) the numbers of disputes; (2) the numbers of workers involved in disputes; and in addition in some countries (3) the numbers of working days lost by disputes. The number of days lost is likely to be the most comprehensive indication of the strength of labour disputes in a particular country during a particular year. If we analyse the number of days lost in a given period we find that it consists of three elements. If we call

the number of Disputes F (Frequency);
the number of workers involved W;
the number of days lost L,

then $\frac{W}{F}$ stands for the average *Magnitude* of Disputes which we may call M, $\frac{L}{W}$ for the average *Duration* (or perseverance) of Disputes which we may call P. L can be thought of as three-dimensional: $L = F.M.P.$

If, therefore, L gives an indication of the strength of the movement in a country during a given period, then F, M and P indicate the components of the strength, viz. Frequency, Magnitude and Duration of disputes.

Their study turns out to be more useful than the original figures enumerated above; the latter are not independent variables since the number of workers involved is a function of the number of disputes, and the number of days lost a function both of the numbers of disputes and of the numbers of workers involved: we shall find, however, that these figures retain some significance.

To make the figures presented by national statistics internationally comparable, we have to adjust them for the differences in the size of the countries concerned. One could do this by relating the figures to total population, or to the active population (gainfully employed). Since disputes in agriculture are, however, very rare and the ratio between industrial population and agricultural population varies widely from country to country, it is preferable to take only *industrial* wage earners into account.[3]

In the following Tables the numbers of disputes (frequency), the numbers of workers involved and of days lost are presented deflated by the *active non-agricultural population* in each country and in each year. It is true that in some non-agricultural groups labour disputes are also rare, or even non-existent, but it would be difficult to draw the borderline and, furthermore, it would not be easy to get homogeneous figures for the workers employed in these groups in all countries concerned through the whole period in question. On the other hand, the Censuses in all countries concerned provide fairly homogeneous figures giving the active non-agricultural population in the Census years; we get approximate figures for the years in between or after the last Census, by a rough linear inter-polation or extra-polation. There is no need to deflate 'magnitude' and 'duration' which present the ratios between figures relating to the same country in the same year.

1. General Comparison

The most outstanding feature of Table 1 is that the numbers of workers involved in disputes (deflated in the way indicated above) are very similar in all the countries concerned on the annual average during the periods in question. This contrasts, particularly if we take the common period and exclude the years of general strikes of exceptional dimensions, strongly with the very large differences in the other columns; in frequency, magnitude, days lost, the highest figures are four times as high as the lowest, in duration three times as high.

TABLE 1

The Strength of the Strike Movements

Annual Averages		Frequency (Numbers of Disputes per Million of active industrial population)	Magnitude (Workers involved per Dispute)	Workers involved per Million of active industrial population 000's	Duration (Days lost per Worker involved)	Days lost per Million of active industrial population 000's
		1. Whole period covered by statistics				
United Kingdom	1893–1943	40	662	24.6	26.9	662
(without 1926)		(40)	(557)	(22.3)	(22.7)	(506)
France	1891–1935	64	291	18.6	16.4	305
Germany	1899–1931	97	272	26.4	—	—
Sweden	1903–1943	142	195	27.7	42.5	1179
(without 1909)		(142)	(155)	(22.2)	(43.6)	(963)
U.S.A.	1880–1941	84	317	26.6	—	—
Canada	1901–1943	72	263	18.9	18.1	342
		2. Common Period (about 1901–1935)				
United Kingdom	—	34	854	29.1	27.1	791
(without 1926)		(35)	(746)	(25.8)	(21.9)	(565)
France	—	69	306	21.1	16.9[1]	356*
Germany.. ..	1901–1930	100	283	28.3	—	—
Sweden	1903–1935	162	206	33.3	42.6	1420
(without 1909)		(162)	(164)	(26.5)	(42.3)	(1122)
U.S.A.	—	88	327	28.7	—	—
Canada	—	71	241	17.0	22.6	384

*The figures showing 'Days lost' and 'Duration' in France apply only up to 1930.

Nearly the same proportions of the Labour force went on strike in all the countries included in our investigation, on the yearly average of the last four or five decades; it appears therefore that strike proneness is not too different in industrial countries over long periods.[4] But there are nevertheless differences to be observed. The figures of workers involved (per active non-agricultural population) are larger in the United Kingdom, U.S.A. and Germany than in France and Canada; this seems to indicate that differences in the degree of industrialisation are not without importance. Sweden is, however, also included in the former group (even if the huge figures of the General Strike in 1909 are left out of account); differences in the organisation and tactics of workers and employers also play a part.

Since the numbers of workers involved (being the product of frequency and magnitude) are very similar, we can expect that the differences in magnitude are the opposite of those in frequency. The sequence of the countries with regard to the magnitude of their disputes is, indeed, the inverse of that in frequency (United Kingdom, U.S.A., Germany, Sweden); only the countries with smaller numbers of workers involved, France and Canada, fall somewhat outside the pattern. The United Kingdom represents the type with large but relatively infrequent, Sweden the type with frequent but small, disputes; in France and Canada disputes are both relatively small and relatively infrequent, in U.S.A. they are relatively large and frequent. This applies to our whole period and to most of the sub-periods (deviations from the pattern can often be explained by special developments). How can the different patterns of national strike activities be explained?

At first sight, one is tempted to believe that the national statistics define the term 'one dispute' differently; if the numbers of workers involved in disputes are nearly the same in two countries, and if several disputes in the same trade at the same time and for the same purpose were separately counted in one country, and only as one large dispute in the other, the international differences in frequency and in magnitude described above could perhaps be largely explained by differences in definition. If it were so, a better international understanding on the definition involved would be badly needed. But there is no indication that the differences in interpreting the term are so considerable from country to country that such differences in the figures could ensue.

It is sometimes assumed that the differences in the average magnitude of disputes are due to differences in the size of the industrial units in various countries. The sequence of the countries compared according to 'magnitude' is not quite out of tune with this hypothesis: disputes are larger in Great Britain than in France and Canada, and larger in France than in Sweden on the average, but the figures for U.S.A. and Germany do not fit this explanation.[5] Moreover we shall find later on that the magnitude of disputes does not develop over time in accordance with the growth of the industrial units either in general, or in particular countries, though the 'magnitude' tends to grow in highly industrialised countries over the whole period.

It is very probable that the relations between frequency and magnitude of disputes (frequent but small, or large but relatively infrequent disputes) have, above all, something to do with differences in Labour organisation and tactics.

From the small international differences in the numbers of workers involved in disputes per million of the active non-agricultural population it follows, furthermore, that the numbers of days lost (weighted in the same way) come mainly from differences in the duration of disputes. The relevant statistical material is available for four countries only; but the strike movement in Sweden shows by far the highest number of days lost and by far the longest average duration; the loss of working days is smallest and the average duration shortest in France (and similarly in Canada), while Britain is in a middle position.

2. The Trend

Anyone who expects that the strike movement gains momentum–more or less–through the whole period for which we have figures, is certainly mistaken; nor do we find a continuously falling trend, or a rise, say, up to 1920 and then a fall. As far as there is any international trend observable, it changes several times through our period and, moreover, the trend is not the same for all components. It is of little use to compare linear trends through the whole period.

The development of national strike movements shows a very conspicuous agreement in two respects: the common violent rise round 1920, and the subsequent fall to a very low level in the 'thirties. The former is expressed in the frequency, magnitude and duration of disputes, the latter chiefly in frequency. In this period, the strike activity in all countries is strongly influenced by *international*–partly economic, partly political–factors:

In the first transition stage after World War I: economic expansion during the post-war boom, instability of prices lasting longer in some countries than in the others, the general belief that a new era had dawned for Labour (Russian Revolution, the creation of the

International Labour Organisation), expressed in an unprecedented growth of Trade Union membership.

In the early 'thirties: bad economic conditions, above all mass unemployment on a scale hitherto unknown, and a changed Trade Union attitude as to the means of achieving better working conditions shown by the growth of the tendency to strike prevention. It has to be noted that a fall in the numbers of disputes had already started shortly before 1914.

Since economic fluctuations have in general an international scope and do not produce such a similarity of strike movements in other sub-periods, it seems very probable that the common political factors (post-war unrest and the subsequent strike prevention) are mainly responsible for the striking phenomenon of the big international strike wave.

One could break up the whole period into four sub-periods, in each of which there is a kind of international agreement in trend, at least in some of the components: (1) up to 1914 some increase in strike movements, but different behaviour of the component series; (2) a very distinct sharp rise up to the early 'twenties and a corresponding fall in the late 'twenties common to all countries and more or less to all components; (3) a low level in general–a very low level in some of the components–at the end of the 'twenties and the beginning of the 'thirties; (4) finally a certain partial tendency to rise again in the course of the 'thirties and 'forties. But it is not possible to define these sub-periods more exactly; their beginnings and ends do not coincide in different countries. Average figures for identical sub-periods are not significant enough to show the differences in development. The trends in different countries are, therefore, compared by presenting seven years moving averages, to eliminate–as far as possible–cyclical movements which will be dealt with in the next Section. This method is applied in the Table contained in the Appendix.

The violent strike wave after World War I is the most outstanding international feature in *all* the series. But it ebbed away and we have to take account of it when describing the trend only in so far as the subsequent level changed by comparison with the pre-1914 level.

Frequency. Up to about 1908 the (*deflated*) numbers of disputes rose in the countries with a growing labour movement (U.S.A., France, Germany, Italy, but not in the U.K.). There was a temporary setback at one time or another in this pre-war period in most of the countries compared, due to measures or developments unfavourable to Labour.[6] Shortly before the outbreak of war in 1914 there is, however, already a common falling trend to be observed.[7]

In about 1920 the peak of the big strike wave was reached, the fall in frequency was, however, somewhat deferred in countries with drawn out currency difficulties (in Germany till 1922, in France till 1927). The very low level round 1930 is an international feature. There was not only an ebbing of the post-war strike wave, but the level was in all countries lower than before the war.

In the late 'thirties and early 'forties frequency started rising in many countries; it seems that unofficial strikes played a considerable part. It is still an open question whether the return of peace will turn the trend downward again.

Apart from this last phase, the frequency of strikes tended to fall in all countries over the whole period, perhaps with the exception of the United Kingdom where the trend is neither falling nor rising.

The *magnitude* of strikes taken over the whole period seems to be rising, especially in the highly industrialised countries.

Up to 1914 we find no trend movement in any of the countries; it is striking that at this time the average size of disputes is nearly the same in all of them (about 200–300 workers per dispute). But after the big strike wave magnitude remained at a higher level, particularly in the United Kingdom, U.S.A. and Germany (in the United Kingdom the level was exceptionally high between 1912 and 1932, but fell considerably afterwards.)

The *duration* of strikes shows very large international differences in various sub-periods but is–apart from the rise during the big strike wave–distinctly diminishing in all countries with two exceptions: before 1914, duration is increasing in France, Italy and Canada, that is in countries with a growing labour movement (whereas it is decreasing in the United Kingdom also in this sub-period); secondly, in the late 'twenties and in the 'thirties, the development is quite exceptional in Sweden[8] where duration continued to increase enormously after the big strike wave and remained on a very high level at least till 1939.

The shortening of the average *duration* of disputes may be due to the recognition that protracted disputes are as a rule not very efficient weapons for the workers though there may be conditions under which this rule does not apply (Sweden in the 'twenties and 'thirties). The increasing *magnitude* of disputes may–as is frequently assumed–have something to do with the growing size of industrial units; there is, however, no trace of a strict correlation. More important is the organisation of disputes on a national scale. There are no great differences between the countries in the average magnitude of disputes, and the common level is comparatively low, before 1914. At this time, the possibilities and implications of General Strikes for improving the position of Labour were the subject of much theoretical discussion. Sweden was the only country in which it really happened, the General Strike in 1909 being 'proportionally the greatest labour conflict that had till then occurred in any country';[9] it was defeated. In the inter-war period General Strikes became more frequent but their influence on average magnitude was not decisive (with the exception of the 1926 General Strike in Great Britain whose influence is shown in Table 1). But very large strikes on a national scale played a larger part, and this makes for the higher average compared with pre-1914. The fall in the *frequency* of disputes can partly be explained by the increasing average magnitude (one big strike instead of several small ones) but to a much greater extent by strike prevention; the deep depression in the 'thirties may also play a part.

3. *Short Run Fluctuations*

If we want to compare the short run movements of strike figures with the general cyclical movement, the appropriate method which presents itself, and has been used for this purpose, seems to be to look for correlations, *e.g.* with indexes of business activity, over the periods for which we have figures. But this method did not prove useful for investigations on a national scale. Dale Yoder, for instance, by comparing the numbers of disputes and of workers involved in U.S.A. with indexes of business activity came to the conclusion that 'no simple co-variation such as may be measured by linear correlation is observable'[10]. It seems even more hopeless to use this method for international comparisons.

By examining strike figures as deviations from 7 years moving averages (to eliminate the trend) and relating them to the trade cycle, above all to the peaks and trends in strike figures we gain the advantage that we are able to examine each cycle separately, instead of looking for over-all correlations through long periods which are not significant enough.

Among the five series, only *frequency* follows fairly distinctly the cyclical pattern. This reaction is strongest in Great Britain, Germany and Canada, but there is a trace of it in all the countries. This makes for a kind of international agreement in the short run changes of the frequency of disputes.

It is worth noting that as far as separate figures for strikes—in contradistinction to lock-outs—exist, the former follow the cyclical pattern more distinctly than the total numbers of disputes. Some countries did, however, not accept this classification, others abandoned it later for the reason that it is often not as clear as is generally assumed to which group a dispute belongs. But it is not this formal classification (whether it is employers or employees who start the dispute) but the material distinction whether the dispute aims at improving working conditions or at warding off their worsening, which matters most in this respect. Such figures as we have suggest – as could be expected – that disputes concerning wage decreases are at their peak during the downswing of the cycle when disputes concerning wage increases are going down. (The latter are generally more frequent than the former but in some years – for instance in U.S.A. after the boom of 1920 and 1929 – the numbers of wage disputes consisted predominantly of defensive strikes.)

The changes in *magnitude* and in *duration* do not show the same agreement with the cyclical movement as those in frequency. There are mostly two high points, sometimes only one, within each cycle and they coincide only in a few cases with trade booms; they occur rather during the cyclical downward and/or upward movement. The years in which disputes are very large on the average are those in which national strikes break out in one of the big industries. In the United Kingdom and in U.S.A. these are often also years with a long average duration of disputes; in other countries the largest averages in magnitude and in duration fall rather into different years. In any case, the high points in frequency very seldom coincide with those in magnitude and in duration; the most outstanding exceptions fall into the big strike wave round 1920, during which the whole strength of the movement was gathered into an extraordinary effort.

Since frequency, magnitude and duration do – with rare exceptions – react differently to the course of the Trade Cycle, it is not surprising that its influence on their composites is small. There are still some traces of the cyclical pattern in the numbers of *workers involved*, in which frequency plays a large part. But even this last trace of any regular reaction on cyclical movements has gone in the numbers of *days lost;* there is no international agreement and (apart from the big strike wave) the peaks look entirely erratic.

The problem connected with the correlation between strike movements and economic (cyclical) changes has been so far to find out how the latter affect 'industrial unrest' manifested by strikes. It has been taken for granted that, among the strike figures, the numbers of strikes and of workers involved are most likely to reflect them. Our observations suggest that frequency is, indeed, sensitive to the cyclical movements more or less in all countries but that its movements correspond more exactly as far as only aggressive strikes are concerned; the different behaviour of the frequency of defensive strikes is one of the reasons why a strict correlation is not to be expected with the numbers of *all* strikes. But the numbers of workers involved in strikes (aggressive and defensive) are less likely to correspond to the Trade Cycle since they contain an element following a different pattern *viz.* the magnitude of strikes.

Industrial unrest has not been strictly defined. But it seems that only the direct psychological reaction of the workers—in contradistinction to Labour tactics—on changing economic conditions is meant. In the following lines I attempt to show in a few outlines which of these factors determines the changes in each of the three components of the strike movement.

That the short run changes in the *frequency* of disputes follow to a certain extent the pattern of the Trade Cycle, could be explained in two different ways, by tactical considerations and by psychological reactions of Labour. One could mainly emphasise that times of prosperity present better opportunities for improving working conditions than times of depression. No doubt this is true; but it can be objected that very large disputes (mainly controlled by national organisations) do not follow the same pattern and it is not in or near the boom years that workers achieve in fact the best results by disputes. If there is a tactical element in the frequency of disputes it is the tactics of the rank and file, rather than of the leaders. Or, what comes perhaps to the same, frequent disputes are mainly caused by dissatisfaction among the workers; strikes for improvements are frequent when rising prices are not adequately met by rising wages, strikes against a worsening of conditions when the workers are menaced by cuts and especially by wage cuts not justified by a proportional fall in prices. It is true that strikes are also infrequent when the labour movement is suppressed, or loses strength for political reasons, or when the tendency to prevent strikes is accepted by the Labour leaders. But, on the other hand, the most recent increase of frequency is probably due to the psychological reaction of the rank and file against the shortcomings of the official conciliation machinery. On the whole, the frequency of disputes depends less on deliberate Labour tactics than on the natural reactions of the workers to economic or political developments.

Changes in the *magnitude* of disputes, however, do not conform to the cyclical pattern. The best opportunities for large disputes in the main strike prone industries do apparently not arise out of general economic or political conditions but out of situations specific to these industries. Large strikes are in need of financial help from the united Labour movement; they are prompted by or supported for tactical considerations at the top. In contradistinction to frequency, the magnitude of disputes depends mainly on the tactics of the Labour leaders.

In protracted disputes, however, a psychological factor, the embittered mood of the workers or leaders, may also play a large part. Very large disputes of an extraordinary length occur when the attitude of Labour towards employers or towards the Government is particularly embittered, and when Labour feels bound to show its strength even if the opportunity is not good. We may conclude that normally the duration of disputes depends on tactics but largely also on a psychological factor which – as a rule – is *not* rooted in general economic conditions but in the political or personal background of the particular disputes.

NOTES

1 It may also be that strike statistics are particularly unreliable and less significant than those in other fields (see K. C. G. Knowles: 'Strikes and their Economic Context', *Bulletin* Vol. 9, No. 9). It would, however, be even more complicated to assess the importance of these shortcomings for international comparisons than for investigations on a national scale.

2 Figures for 1914 and 1915 were subsequently computed by the Bureau of Labor Statistics. The remaining gap was bridged by J. I. Griffin in his book *Strikes* (1939), pp. 118–132. He used the statistics continued during the interval by seven states (Connecticut, Kansas, Maryland, Massachusetts, New Jersey, New York and Rhode Island) to estimate nation-wide figures, assuming that the share of the seven states in them remained unchanged (47 per cent of the numbers of strikes, 38 per cent of the numbers of strikers); this method is very primitive but is sufficient to indicate the order of magnitude. The estimated figures serve, therefore, to complete the material for the following Table.

3 Comp. Dale Yoder: 'Economic Changes and Industrial Unrest in U.S.A.', *Journal of Political Economy*, Vol. 48, 1940, pp. 227–229.

4 The degree of international similarity is, of course, not the same in all sub-periods. For instance, participation in strikes in the United Kingdom is relatively very small in the years following the Taff Vale judgement (first decade of the 20th century), but relatively large in the post 1918 transition stage; in U.S.A., on the other hand, it is smaller than in Great Britain in this transition stage, but larger before 1914 and in the late 'thirties. But even these extreme differences are less considerable than in frequency, magnitude and duration.

5 International differences in the magnitude of strikes are apparently also due to the different rôle which various industries play within each national strike movement. The extraordinary large overall average magnitude of British strikes in the 'twenties, for instance, is due to a great extent to coal strikes, the average magnitude of strikes in the other industries – though also large compared with other countries – being very considerably smaller. The large size of coal strikes is partly the consequence of large industrial units, but in Great Britain, also due to the national organisation of strikes in this industry during the period in question.

6 In Britain: the Taff Vale judgement (1901) greatly hampered the activity of Trade Unions by making them responsible for damages alleged to have been caused by the actions of their officers, and the numbers of disputes fell; this obstacle was removed by the Trade Disputes Act, 1906, and the Unions caught up with the temporary setback so that frequency rose up to the beginning of the war.

   In U.S.A., a temporary setback in strike activity was caused by the fall in Trade Union membership which had reached a peak in 1887 (about 1 million); 'afterwards the losses suffered by Labor were so great that membership in the early nineties was probably little more than a few hundred thousand' (National Bureau of Economic Research: *The Growth of American Trade Unions, 1880–1923*). The rise in frequency was correspondingly interrupted.

   In Sweden: a severe setback was caused by the failure of the General Strike in 1909; Union membership fell from 1908 to 1910 by almost half. There was a steep fall in frequency at the same time.

7 This tendency is not only visible in 7 years moving averages (the low frequency at the beginning of the war distorting 7 years averages) but also in the original figures.

8 A classification of strikes by duration and workers involved in them, given in official Swedish sources, show differences in detail but would seem to confirm, on the whole, our figures.

9 H. A. Marquand and others: *Organised Labour in Four Continents*, p. 292.

10 Dale Yoder, loc. cit., p. 234.

APPENDIX

In the following Table seven-year moving averages of the main figures showing the Strength of Strike Movements in six countries for which statistics are available are used. The figures showing Magnitude, Workers Involved and Days Lost are deflated by the non-agricultural active population (per million) in each year, to make them comparable. The distorting influence of General Strikes on moving averages is eliminated by inserting–instead of the actual figures of Magnitude, Workers Involved and Days Lost for Sweden in 1909, and for the United Kingdom in 1926, 1927 and 1928 (in the two years following the British General Strike those figures were exceptionally low)–arithmetical averages of the six adjacent years (3 years before and 3 years after the year, or years, in question). It should be kept in mind that the data on which these figures are based are not always homogeneous over time or strictly comparable as between countries. The moving averages, however, sufficiently indicate differences in the strength of the strike movement in various countries.

CHANGES IN FREQUENCY AND SEVERITY OF STRIKES

Year	I. Frequency						II. Magnitude						III. Workers Involved (000)						IV. Duration				V. Days Lost (000)				Year
	U.K.	France	Germany	Sweden	U.S.A.*	Canada	U.K.	France	Germany	Sweden	U.S.A.†	Canada	U.K.	France	Germany	Sweden	U.S.A.§	Canada	U.K.	France	Sweden	Canada	U.K.	France	Sweden	Canada	
1893		39			92			229			269						23							138			1893
1894		39			83			203			285			9			23							128			1894
1895		40			75			176			283			8			22							118			1895
1896	52	46			76		342	183			301			7			22						751	150			1896
1897	51	48			78		229	181			315			9			23		43	16			475	152			1897
1898	48	49			88		214	191			272			9			23		39	16			418	160			1898
1899	45	50			101		215	234			256			10			23		39	16			393	210			1899
1900	40	50			117		228	250			254		17	12			24		39	16			379	231			1900
1901	35	58			124		221	260			234		12	13			28		34	15			294	269			1901
1902	31	63	96		130		209	259	90		219		10	15			28		28	16			172	286			1902
1903	29	70	113		138		229	272	93		201		9	16			27		28	17			175	354			1903
1904	28	73	119		147	109	224	259	95		176	163	8	19	10		26	18	29	18		19	164	349		376	1904
1905	25	80	121		136	102	280	242	98		165	177	6	19	11		23	17	28	18		19	216	346		337	1905
1906	25	85	124	210	127	93	295	206	100		161	191	6	18	12	24	21	17	28	18		24	208	331	963	390	1906
1907	26	96	136	198	121	82	368	202	105	114	165	191	7	20	13	24	20	15	26	19	37	25	267	358	1009	353	1907
1908	30	101	141	179	119	78	480	186	113	105	152	217	10	19	15	24	18	16	25	18	35	32	336	358	1022	483	1908
1909	33	104	140	167	121	82	664	190	109	127	178	232	16	20	17	21	21	18	25	18	34	33	640	352	743	551	1909
1910	41	101	129	143	117	79	665	171	113	115	202	248	25	17	16	20	24	19	27	18	28	34	692	247	714	595	1910
1911	43	93	118	115	108	65	689	183	109	117	216	245	27	17	14	18	24	16	21	16	29	39	751	227	716	581	1911
1912	46	82	107	84	115	62	693	183	112	124	236	221	29	16	13	14	28	15	20	15	32	36	685	188	485	521	1912
1913	46	73	97	90	110	63	699	179	175	114	270	225	30	14	13	13	33	15	17	14	28	31	682	148	396	460	1913
1914	48	64	76	130	120	66	704	213	324	109	274	238	31	14	15	14	35	17	17	10	28	29	645	110	372	479	1914
1915	49	52	59	186	123	74	682	241	408	90	306	260	32	14	15	14	39	20	14	8	27	21	608	260	440	372	1915
1916	53	62	66	215	125	83	724	289	459	104	425	290	33	24	26	17	53	27	13	8	27	21	547	496	627	520	1916
1917	54	70	78	248	123	94	834	361	492	133	446	278	41	36	34	24	55	28	16	10	32	19	669	549	1445	495	1917
1918	52	68	101	266	107	101	1117	446	526	136	479	279	61	39	44	36	56	29	17	10	33	17	1237	520	1615	527	1918
1919	51	74	135	293	106	103	1159	495	567	155	651	315	62	42	57	45	59	31	21	11	35	21	1368	624	1845	593	1919
1920	52	82	146	288	94	100	1174	521	611	213	660	339	63	45	68	52	55	32	24	12	42	23	1432	636	2414	650	1920

(continued on page 232)

*For years 1883 to 1892 figures are respectively, 83, 70, 73, 78, 90, 101, 105, 100, 94, 94. †For years 1883 to 1892 figures are respectively. 334, 333, 319, 305, 285, 263, 235, 209, 238, 269.

§For years 1883 to 1892 figures are respectively. 21, 23, 23, 25, 26, 25, 21, 22, 24.

CHANGES IN FREQUENCY AND SEVERITY OF STRIKES (continued)

Year	I. Frequency						II. Magnitude						III. Workers Involved (000)						IV. Duration				V. Days Lost (000)				Year
	U.K.	France	Germany	Sweden	U.S.A.*	Canada	U.K.	France	Germany	Sweden	U.S.A.†	Canada	U.K.	France	Germany	Sweden	U.S.A.§	Canada	U.K.	France	Sweden	Canada	U.K.	France	Sweden	Canada	
1921	51	86	156	262	77	92	1174	498	561	212	695	364	63	45	74	49	51	30	24	14	45	25	1453	661	2402	646	1921
1922	47	90	163	215	66	81	1156	486	521	287	690	348	59	45	76	56	47	26	26	14	45	30	1468	673	2480	674	1922
1923	40	85	138	190	53	61	1019	435	483	298	571	329	44	36	62	52	29	17	27	14	45	28	1273	540	2405	447	1923
1924	30	69	114	159	40	43	978	372	513	264	577	345	33	22	54	40	23	15	27	13	43	27	1142	289	1585	399	1924
1925	26	72	86	144	32	37	765	287	602	294	585	347	23	20	49	41	19	13	23	15	45	24	565	277	1731	339	1925
1926	25	77	54	123	31	35	801	252	621	277	423	308	23	19	37	36	13	11	20	14	47	20	470	263	1545	244	1926
1927	23	77	42	124	26	33	820	284	587	217	394	281	21	21	27	28	10	9	17	14	45	18	420	291	1005	205	1927
1928	21	68	32	117	24	33	852	268	522	234	380	229	21	19	17	29	9	8	17		47	16	405		1102	136	1928
1929	19	61		110	22	34	881	253		186	388	210	20	17		20	8	7	18		53	11	380		1119	75	1929
1930	19	46		104	24	36	809	259		182	446	196	18	14		18	11	8	16		64	12	331		1234	75	1930
1931	20	45		96	27	41	724	244		194	487	188	16	13		19	14	9	15		65	12	269		1256	75	1931
1932	22	41		87	32	42	666	239		168	492	201	14	12		14	18	10	13		62	11	215		929	97	1932
1933	24			77	36	45	545			166	499	213	12			13	19	13	12		72	12	167		907	103	1933
1934	29			62	50	45	496			221	514	220	13			14	25	13	11		69	10	160		892	142	1934
1935	32			54	56	55	387			239	489	221	11			13	26	15	10		67	8	120		782	138	1935
1936	36			43	62	57	301			207	498	241	11			9	29	15	8		68	7	83		560	136	1936
1937	40			35	64	59	288			189	432	262	12			7	27	17	7		55	7	82		307	133	1937
1938	45			30	72	60	289			178	398	281	13			6	29	21	7		55	6	83		259	124	1938
1939	49			32		71	271			154	359	288	13			5			7		54		79		206	131	1939
1940	55			38		82	270			152	383	334	15			5		30	5		38		77		181	167	1940

11

THE INTERINDUSTRY PROPENSITY TO STRIKE–AN INTERNATIONAL COMPARISON

Clark Kerr and Abraham Siegel

Are certain industries in democratic industrialised nations consistently strike prone, while others are consistently strike free?[1] If the facts give an affirmative answer to this question, then how can this social phenomenon be explained? How do several of the standard theories of industrial peace and industrial conflict fare in the light of these facts? Finally, if it were desired either to encourage or to discourage the propensity to strike in an industry, how best should it be attempted? These are the four questions to which this chapter is addressed.

THE SIMILARITY OF BEHAVIOR

Table 1 gives a generalised grouping of industries, taken from the more detailed Table 2 (see Technical Supplement, p. 285). This generalised grouping is possible because of the uniformity of behavior of certain industries in the eleven countries studied[2] (Australia, Czechoslovakia, Germany, Italy, the Netherlands, New Zealand, Norway, Sweden, Switzerland, the United Kingdom, and the United States).

The assignment of industries from Table 2 to a box in Table 1 is admittedly determined on a somewhat impressionistic basis. Only those industries which show a generally discernible uniformity of behavior in Table 2 are located in Table 1. Many industries in Table 2 do not appear in Table 1 because there are too few observations of them (as rubber) or because, while they are referred to several times (as paper), they are often in a paired grouping with some dissimilar industry (paper and printing) and there are too few separate rankings. The combination of distinct industries into the same statistical grouping is particularly vexatious (clothing and textile and land and water transportation,[3] for example) when each of them separately is an interesting case. The evidence for the placement of one industry (railroad) is partly from general knowledge, since it is not often clearly shown by itself. On the basis of general knowledge alone, several other groups might confidently be placed in this table–domestic servants, government employees, and white-collar workers in the 'Low Propensity to Strike' box–and some reference will be made to them in the discussion.

Manufacturing (general) is, of course, an omnibus description, and the grouping may turn up in the 'Medium' box only because quite divergent patterns cancel each other out. However, it seems more likely that general manufacturing (which includes, perhaps most importantly, metal working) is the significant standard case, and the question then becomes: Why are some industries more strike prone and others less than general manufacturing?

The industries in the 'Medium' box may be divided into two types: those which are quite consistently medium strike prone (general manufacturing, leather, and construction) and those which vary considerably from 'High' or 'Medium high' to 'Medium low' or 'Low' (printing, chemical, and food and kindred products). Industries in the 'Medium' category are likely to be either under balanced environmental pressures toward both conflict and peace or under such little pressure in either direction that force arising from other sources than the industrial environment are predominant.

TABLE 1

General Pattern of Strike Propensities

Propensity to strike	Industry
High	Mining Maritime and longshore
Medium high	Lumber Textile
Medium	Chemical Printing Leather Manufacturing (general) Construction Food and kindred products
Medium low	Clothing Gas, water and electricity Services (hotels, restaurants, etc.)
Low	Railroad Agriculture Trade

While the concern here is exclusively with industries, it is to be expected that individual firms in industries in the 'medium' category should vary more widely one from another than firms in industries in the high-propensity or low-propensity categories. A medium-propensity industry is likely to give wide latitude for individual firm variations, while a high- or a low-propensity one is more likely to demand individual conformity;[4] and general observation attests that there is more uniformity in behavior among coal mines or government bureaus than among general-manufacturing plants.

Before turning to the question of whether there are any reasonable hypotheses to explain the apparently great impact of certain industrial environments on the propensity to strike, five exceptions (see Table 2, p 285) to the uniformity of behavior should be noted:

Trade in Sweden (higher than usual).
Mining in Germany in the second period and in the Netherlands during the second period (lower than usual).
Machinery in Germany (higher than usual).
Automobiles in the United States in the second period (higher than usual).
Agriculture in Italy, in Australia during the second period, and in New Zealand in the first (higher than usual).

For the first two exceptions we have no explanation to offer; but comments on the last three will be made later on.

THE EXPLANATIONS

Hypothesis 1. *The Location of the Worker in Society*. Is there any single theory which will largely explain the facts which we have found? Can we, at one and the same time, explain the high propensity to strike of miners, longshoremen, sailors, and loggers and the low propensity of government employees, grocery clerks, railroad employees, and garment workers? The first hypothesis is that the location of the worker in society determines his propensity to strike and that this location is heavily influenced by the industrial environment.

1. THE ISOLATED MASS. The miners, the sailors, the longshoremen, the loggers, and, to a much lesser extent, the textile workers form isolated masses, almost a 'race apart.' They live in their own separate communities: the coal patch, the ship, the waterfront district, the logging camp, the textile town.[5] These communities have their own codes, myths, heroes, and social standards.[6] There are few neutrals in them to mediate the conflicts and dilute the mass. All people have grievances, but what is important is that all the members of each of these groups have the same grievances: industrial hazards or severe

depression unemployment or bad living conditions (which seem additionally evil because they are supplied by the employer), or low wages or intermittent work. And here is a case where the totality of common grievances, [6a] after they have been verbally shared, may be greater than the sum of the individual parts. The employees form a largely homogeneous, undifferentiated mass–they all do about the same work and have about the same experiences. Here you do not have the occupational stratification of the metal or building crafts, of the hotel or restaurant, or of the government bureau.[7]

It is hard to get out of this mass. The jobs are specialised, and the workers come to be also. Skills are not transferable as they are for stenographers or electricians. Protest is less likely to take the form of moving to another industry and more the character of the mass walkout. Just as it is hard for these workers to move out, so also is it difficult for them to move up. To what higher occupational strata can the longshoreman or the coal miner or the logger rise in the natural course of events? Nor is he likely to be pulled from the mass in other ways. In these communities there are not the myriad of voluntary associations with mixed memberships which characterise the multi-industry town. The force of public opinion must seem rather weak to the logger in the camp or to the miner in the coal patch who never sees 'the public'; and it is no more possible to cut trees than to mine coal with bayonets. The employer throws out few lines to these workers. He is usually an absentee owner who 'cuts out and gets out' in the logging business or exhausts a mine and moves on or hires longshoremen on a casual basis or gets his views of personnel relations from the law on mutiny.[8] The worker is as detached from the employer as from the community at large.

The union becomes a kind of working-class party or even government for these employees, rather than just another association among many. Union meetings are more adequately attended and union affairs more vigorously discussed; and, as one consequence, personal and ideological factionalism and rival unionism are more likely. Strife within and between unions is a sign that the union is important.

The strike for this isolated mass is a kind of colonial revolt against far-removed authority, an outlet for accumulated tensions, and a substitute for occupational and social mobility. The industrial environment places these workers in the role of members of separate classes distinct from the community at large, classes with their share of grievances. These individuals are not members of the ubiquitous middle class but of their own class of miners or longshoremen; and they do not aim to be more considerate of the general community than they think the general community is of them. Thus the isolated mass in a classless society may become something like the isolated class in a class society, more or less permanently at odds with the community at large.[9]

2. THE INTEGRATED INDIVIDUAL AND THE INTEGRATED GROUP. The opposite of the isolated mass is the integrated individual or the integrated group. 'Integrated' is used here not in the psychological but in the sociological sense: absorbed in and unified with society at large. The workers in the industries at the other end of our scale —those in the industries where the propensity to strike is low or medium low (railroad; trade; agriculture; clothing; gas, water, and electricity; the services; and, we might add, government, domestic services, and clerical)–are given an industrial role to play which integrates them better into the general community. They are more likely (with the exception of farm hands) to live in multi-industry communities, to associate with people with quite different working experiences than their own, and to belong to associations with heterogeneous memberships. In these communities their individual grievances are less likely to coalesce into a mass grievance which is expressed at the job level. There are many neutrals in any dispute, and this helps to assure the impartiality of public officials.

In most of these cases the worker either can change his industry fairly readily without losing the value of his skill or has access to higher skilled jobs or managerial or even employer status. Generally, also, the employer is either not so remote or not so callous if remote. The industry has small-scale employing units, or the employer-worker relationship is normally a continuing one. And the community can bring pressure to bear to encourage peaceful conduct. The workers see and feel the general community; in at least three cases (railroads, public utilities, and government) the government asserts the supremacy of the public interest in continuity of service;[10] and in at least one other (clothing) the market for the products makes steady production the *sine qua non* for both investment and jobs. The union, except in the garment trades, where it runs the industry, and the railroads, where it administers seniority, is not so wound into the lives of the workers, and in no instance is it so much the chosen instrument for protest, if it exists at all.

The workers in these industries are generally more dispersed in the general community, more stratified in the hierarchy of jobs in each industry, more attached to their individual employers, more restrained by social pressures, and more able to escape job dissatisfactions without striking than are the workers in the high-propensity industries. The strike is against a known employer and affects a community of which the workers are a part. These workers are contained in society rather than maintained on its periphery.[11]

Several further notes are needed on the hypothesis that the location of the worker in society is the basic determinant of the inter-industry propensity to strike. Agriculture in New Zealand, Australia, and Italy is, during certain periods, an exception to the rule of rural tranquillity. Agriculture has also been an exception to this rule in California and Hawaii. These areas have in common large-scale agriculture. When agriculture moves from employing the single hired hand to large groups of socially isolated workers, it also moves from peace toward conflict. It is also instructive that the automobile and rubber industries, which rank so high in the second period in the United States, are predominantly localised in the special communities of Detroit and Akron, which were also the two homes of the sit-down strike. The experience of two additional industries, while the data on them is by no means conclusive, seems to support this hypothesis. Man-days lost due to strikes have been much above the average in the toy-manufacturing industry in Germany and in quarrying (stone, clay, and sand) and the fabricating activities associated with it wherever they are separately identifiable, and both these industries isolate groups of workers from the larger society.[12]

The location of industries in the 'Medium' box is not so readily elucidated by this hypothesis, although the occasional adventures into the conflict category of the printing and chemical industries might be laid to the well-developed sense of a common community which characterises some printing trades and the frequent geographical isolation of chemical plants; and the consistently 'Medium' behaviour of the general manufacturing, construction, and leather industries, to the balance of pulls toward both group and societal identification. The employees of these industries often form cohesive groups, but these groups are neither isolated from society, on the one hand, nor under strong social pressure to avoid strikes, on the other; and these employees, while they belong to unions, frequently have strong attachments in other directions as well.

In summary, this hypothesis may be stated as follows: (a) industries will be highly strike prone when the workers (i) form a relatively homogeneous group which (ii) is unusually isolated from the general community and which (iii) is capable of cohesion; and (b) industries will be comparatively strike free when their workers (i) are individually integrated into the larger society, (ii) are members of trade groups which are coerced by government or the market to avoid strikes, or (iii) are so individually isolated that strike action is impossible.

Hypothesis 2. *The Character of the Job and the Worker.* The second hypothesis is that the inherent nature of the job determines, by selection and conditioning, the kinds of workers employed and their attitudes, and these workers, in turn, cause conflict or peace. If the job is physically difficult and unpleasant, unskilled or semi-skilled, and casual or seasonal, and fosters an independent spirit (as in the logger in the woods), it will draw tough, inconstant, combative, and virile workers, and they will be inclined to strike. If the job is physically easy and performed in pleasant surroundings, skilled and responsible, steady, and subject to set rules and close supervision, it will attract women or the more submissive type of man who will abhor strikes. Certainly the bull of the woods and the mousy bank clerk are different types of people and can be expected to act differently. Certainly, also, the community is more sympathetic with striking miners coming out of the ground than with school teachers abandoning their desks.

This hypothesis explains a good many of the facts but not quite so neatly as the first. Sailors, longshoremen, miners, and lumberjacks are popularly accepted as being more vigorous and combative types than garment workers, grocery clerks, railway conductors, hotel maids, or cannery employees; they seem to strike more often, and their strikes are also more violent. But textile workers and printing craftsmen, who also strike with some frequency, are not classed as so forceful. Teamsters, farm hands, steelworkers, and construction tradesmen, who are not usually delicate individuals, do not strike with unusual frequency.

Several other elements of the industrial environment were examined, but they did not seem to lead to a general theory of the inter-industry propensity to strike. They may, however, be important factors behind the behaviour of individual industries, or they may explain the different records of the several plants within an industry. These factors are the following:

1. The sensitivity of the industry to the business cycle.
2. The structure of the product market.
3. The elasticity of demand for the product.
4. Labor as a percentage of total cost.
5. The profitability of the industry.
6. The average size of plant.
7. The state of technological change.
8. The rate of expansion or contraction of the industry.

Reference to any or all of these elements, as a careful examination of the characteristics of the industries ranked in Table 1 will make evident, is insufficient to explain the bulk of the facts.

We are left, then, with the two general hypotheses set forth above, of which the former seems the more consistent with the known facts.

The two theories, however, have a uniting thread. Both of them are consistent with the thesis that strikes occur where they can occur, that is, where the working-class community is closely knit and the workers forceful and not where the workers are dispersed and subdued. This is not the same thing, however, as saying that strikes take place where strikes pay, for grocery clerks are probably in a better position to benefit from strikes, if they could develop them, than are textile workers; and railroad workers, than sailors.

The two hypotheses can be combined to state that strikes occur most severely in industries which (1) segregate large numbers of persons who (2) have relatively unpleasant jobs. Mass segregation by itself is not enough, for members of the 'lower gentility' (telephone operators, bank clerks, and the like) would probably not strike frequently, in deference to their lower-middle-class psychology, even if they were put off by themselves in large groups; nor is unpleasant work enough by itself, for scavengers, sand blasters, divers, and chimney sweeps have disagreeable jobs but are so scattered that joint action is almost impossible. The polar cases then may be described as follows: (1) an isolated mass of persons doing unpleasant work and (2) dispersed individuals doing pleasant work.

CERTAIN THEORIES EXAMINED

Two explanations of the ranking of industries by the propensity of the workers to strike have been offered: the location of the workers in society and the character of the jobs and the workers, both of which explanations relate to what may be called the industrial environment; but there are many other theories which can be applied to these data, although not specifically devised to explain them. How adequate are these theories in explaining these particular data?[13]

1. *The economic environment*, which for these purposes we shall define as the market aspects of the larger industrial environment which was discussed above, makes a contribution to an understanding of these data but by itself is an inadequate explanation. The industries located at each extreme have quite various product- and labour-market structures. An elastic demand in the product market may encourage peace,[14] particularly where business may be lost to non-union employers, and an inelastic labour-supply situation may lead workers to strike, since it reflects the fact that it is difficult for them to move out; but an elastic demand for the product may also cause trouble where a union is competing in a wage war with a rival union or is under pressure to match a pattern wage

settlement and where the employer is handicapped in translating higher wage costs into higher prices for fear of losing volume, and an inelastic labour supply may encourage peace if it helps give rise to higher wage rates. Product-market and labour-market forces are, perhaps, more suited to explain variations among firms or between period in the life of an industry than they are between industries over a span of time.

2. *The political environment*, particularly of the unions, has been persuasively adduced as the cause of industrial warfare or peace: the more secure the union and its leaders, the fewer the strikes; the less secure, the more numerous. The unions of grocery clerks, government employees, and agriculture workers, however, have generally less institutional security than those of coal miners, printers, and longshoremen, yet they strike less. More jurisdictional and organisational rivalries usually face the construction and railroad unions than the unions of miners, yet they are more peaceful. In the United States the leader of the mine workers is popularly conceived to have a more secure position than the chief of the airline pilots' association, yet his union strikes more; and peace descended on the West Coast waterfront when the established union leaders became less secure. Certainly the political environment of the union and its leaders is useful, even indispensable, in explaining certain situations at certain times,[15] but it does not provide a generally valid explanation of the interindustry propensity to strike.

Among the industries with a high propensity to strike, while unionism is usually most secure, union leaders and specific institutions may on the average be somewhat less secure than usual. This is consistent with the hypothesis that the 'isolated mass' builds a strong union movement and that active memberships give rise to factionalism. Among the industries with a low propensity to strike, unionism finds its greatest uncertainty and factionalism its least assured market.

Employer associations are particularly strong where the industrial environment is coercive toward conflict (coal mining, logging, longshore, and maritime). While, by increasing the ability to pay of the individual employers, by increasing interemployer uniformity of terms and conditions of employment, and by lowering the level of the union's ultimate demands by raising the cost of strikes, multiemployer bargaining may encourage peace, it finds its origins, in part, in war.

Strikes may better be explained by looking not so much at the organisation as at the membership. They occur most frequently not only in places where the membership is restless because of its

industrial environment, as we have seen above, but also at times of
membership unrest.[16] It is to the reactions of the workers and not
to the tactics of the leaders that we must turn for the more basic
explanations.

3. *Human relations* at the face-to-face level are said by some to
explain not only industrial but even international relations. Mis-
understandings are not inherent in a situation but result from faulty
communications.[17] It may be true that face-to-face relations are
worse between longshoremen and coal miners and their employers
than between grocery clerks and theirs and that, if face-to-face
relations were better between coal miners and their employers,
there would be less conflict. But why are face-to-face relations often
so unsatisfactory between coal miners and their employers? Is it
because they always know less about semantics than construction
workers and their employers, and is it only faulty communication
systems which stand between them and ultimate harmony? And
how are face-to-face relations to be improved? Can it be done by
giving courses in group dynamics and introducing social engineers
into the mines?

It seems more likely that some situations are structured against
good face-to-face relations and that this structure is the more basic
cause and the source of the more basic changes. The climate of
face-to-face relations may be one way of testing and of describing
the degree of conflict or co-operation in an industry, and there may
be occasions when manipulation of these relations alone will bring
great changes,[18] but it seems unlikely that the peace in government
agencies and the warfare on the waterfront are due primarily to the
universal superiority in human-relations techniques of government
bureaucrats over stevedoring contractors. Even if this were the
case, it would still need to be explained why government draws to it
a more skilful elite than the longshore industry. Labour relations
may be a mirror in which the employer sees his own reflection – the
decent employer may see decent relationships reflected back at
him[19] – but why then are employers more decent in one industry
than another? At this point some reference needs to be made to the
industrial environment. *Causa causae est causa causati.*

4. *The trend of historical developments* varies considerably from
one collective-bargaining system to another. In industries with a
high propensity to strike, the origins have frequently been more
violent and time has had less of a subduing effect. The printing
trades tend to be among the earliest organised, as are the coal
mines, but they both continue to be disposed toward conflict long
after other industries have learned to tread a more peaceful Path.
The garment trades in the United States were organised in bitter

struggles but, given an environment which was persuasive toward peace, soon established the standard for tranquil conduct. Both the nature of the birth and the trend of development must be explained by some common causes, for both have been quite uniform for the same industry from one country to another. More than historical accident is at work. The nature of the birth appears to be not purely accidental; so it is necessary to say more than that a bad start leads to poorer continuing relations than does a good one. Since time works fewer wonders with some industries than others, it is necessary to state more than that time smooths the wrinkles in the relationship.[20]

5. *Dominant personalities* certainly leave an imprint on relations in an industry;[21] but why do the coal and longshore industries bring a John L. Lewis[22] and a Harry Bridges to the fore, and clothing, a Sidney Hillman, and why do coal and longshore and clothing industries perform about the same way in other countries without Lewis, Bridges, and Hillman?

6. *Adherence to ideological views* or merely to certain specific attitudes toward the other party profoundly affects bargaining relationships and the propensity to strike. [23] Communist-led unions probably cause more trouble and tough-minded employers invite more than do non-Communist-led unions and softhearted employers. Belligerent unions and reactionary employers seem, however, to be more effect than cause, for the citadels of union radicalism and the hotbeds of employer reaction are found in about the same industries from country to country.[24]

7. It is suggested, particularly by certain economists, that the *selection of good bargaining techniques* can prevent conflict, since strikes never pay and peace does; [25] but all the parties, regardless of industry, have access to the same storehouse and can draw from it the sword or the green table as they wish. Better bargaining techniques can improve some situations, but it is not for lack of bargaining skill that so many strikes have occurred in the coal mines and on the waterfronts of the world.

8. '*Key' bargains* are thought to lead to more conflict than 'satellite' bargains.[26] This thesis cannot be examined very adequately at the interindustry level, since, particularly in the United States, key bargains are made at the company level. However, the key nature of the bargains may explain the comparatively high ranking of the automobile industry in the United States during the second period and of the machinery industry in Germany, where the metalworkers' union is the largest and most powerful union and the normal pattern setter. Again, however, this theory is better at explaining individual situations than at explaining the propensity to

strike industry by industry. The steel industry sets patterns in the United States but is not particularly strike prone, and the longshore industry sets no pattern but is strike inclined.

THEORIES OF THE TRADE-UNION MOVEMENT

The trade-union movement is variously analysed as moving toward 'monopoly,' 'job control,' 'status' in its own trade-union society, 'bureaucracy,' 'power accumulation,' and 'class consciousness.' These are either the ascribed goals or contemplated ends, and it might be thought that, as individual unions reach the culmination of their development, some effect on their proneness to strike would be noticed—more peace in the first five cases and more conflict in the last one. What do the facts on the interindustry propensity to strike show? Generally the industries at the conflict end of the ranking have unions with a greater monopoly in the labour market than have those at the other end of the range. Once job control is obtained by the teamsters peace overwhelms the industry, but longshoremen continue their conflict after job control is seized. The garment workers have achieved a degree of status in a partially self-contained society of their own creation and seldom strike; typographical workers have also and are much less quiescent. The 'iron law of oligarchy' has been confirmed by the coal miners' union in the United States without the dove of peace alighting on the coal tipple. Power has been accumulated by the unions of mine workers sufficient to make governments shake in the face of it, but the unions have not been satiated; but then the process of striving for power never comes to an end. The class-consciousness theory says that (1) workers are becoming more class minded and that (2), when they do, they are more inclined to violence against the surrounding society. While the first part of this theory is of doubtful truth, at least for the United States, the data seem to bear out the second part: workers strike most often and most violently when they are in an isolated mass with a strong sense of group, if not class, consciousness.

This suggests that some strikes have elements of a small-scale revolt against society rather than of bargaining tactics alone. There is a sense of a mass grievance against society and little sense of a community responsibility. The cost of striking is lowered, for there is more group support for the strike and less felt public pressure against it; and the gain in prospect is not alone a better contract but the release of accumulated tensions. The single equation of prospective economic cost against prospective economic gain (which will seldom show a positive surplus) is particularly inappropriate here, for cost and gain are calculated in more than the economic dimension. The revolt element is certainly not present in all strikes or even in many, but the industries where it may be present account for a substantial proportion of the man-days lost. In New Zealand, during the first period, over 80 per cent of all man-days lost were in mining and water transport alone; in Germany, during the second period, mining alone accounted for over 40 per cent of the total man-days lost; and in the United Kingdom, mining and quarrying accounted for almost 50 per cent of the total man-days lost in industrial disputes during the three decades covered (exclusive of the 1926 losses). It was out of the isolated masses of coal miners in Great Britain and of longshoremen in San Francisco that two of the greatest general strikes developed.[27]

SUMMARY

The most general explanation of the interindustry propensity to strike is the nature of the industrial environment and, particularly, its tendency to direct workers into isolated masses or to integrate them into the general community. This hypothesis elucidates the behavior of most of the industries surveyed for most of the time periods covered and does so better than alternative theories. However, it does not explain the ranking of all industries for all the time and is less effective in analysing why industries are medium strike prone than why they are high or low; and thus other explanations are necessary too. We are dealing with complex phenomena and must resort to multiple causation; and, as we have seen, other theories are helpful or essential in explaining certain situations.

The hypothesis of the location of the worker in society is useful for the one task of explaining the interindustry propensity to strike. It has little to say about the behavior of individual firms, except that firms in industries located at the two extremes of the range are more likely to conform to the pattern of their industry than are firms in industries located in the middle of the range. At the level of the firm, many more factors than the industrial environment must be examined, particularly if the industrial environment is 'neutral,' as it appears to be for the bulk of manufacturing. The only explanation this hypothesis offers for the variation of the propensity to strike from one period of time to another is that the propensity will rise or fall in an industry or society as the workers become more isolated in masses or more integrated into society; and the only clues to the causes of international differences in the inclination to strike are that the industry mix of each nation is important, as is also the general integration of workers and their institutions into society.

THE GREATER STRATEGY

'Good' and 'evil' in the industrial-relations field are not subject to discovery by any purely technical explorations but must be defined by the exercise of value judgments. It is generally, although by no means universally, accepted that the apparently endemic warfare in the coal industry is as undesirable as the coerced peace in the railroad industry; yet the first may be as environmentally inescapable as the second is socially inevitable. If we wish, nevertheless, to reduce the intensity of conflict in the industries characterised by a high or medium-high propensity to strike, without resorting to a social strategy of divide *or* conquer in an effort to create environments such as those surrounding the workers in some of the 'Low' or 'Medium-low' industries, what is the most general principle to be followed? It is not making the demand for all products elastic to encourage union-management cooperation, or giving the union a closed shop and an administration safe from the whims of the rank and file for the sake of institutional and leadership security, or training the managerial elite to manipulate the workers the right way, or waiting for time, which solves all problems, to solve this one also, or psychoanalysing the leaders and turning them into more benevolent despots, or suppressing or encouraging certain ideologies or attitudes, or nailing a list of approved bargaining techniques on every conference table, or designating one industry (preferably one with no useful product) to mark the course for the lambs to follow (although all these devices contain some merit), but it is integrating the worker and his associations, and the employer, as fully as possible into the general society without coercion.[28]

The effort should be to increase vertical and horizontal mobility, to encourage a wide variety of mixed associations, to break down barriers between groups and between individuals, to create the mixed community instead of the 'Gold Coast' or the 'back of the yards,' which alike inspire ideological thinking. The opposite road is toward the all-absorbing party of the Communists, the all-absorbing corporation of Mayo,[29] and the all-absorbing union of Tannenbaum.[30] Of the isolated group and the isolated groupless individual, it is the former which is the greater threat to democracy. Rather than either of these, however, we should encourage the limited-function party, the limited-function corporation, the limited-function union,[31] and the unlimited individual. The extreme left and the extreme right alike seek the answer in the monolithic organisation. The democratic approach is for the individual to be many things, but most of all a citizen, and to find his protection from domination from any source in the multiplicity of organisations.

NOTES

1 Man-days lost due to strikes and lockouts are used as the measure of the propensity to strike. Thus an industry may have frequent small strikes of short duration and yet be shown with a lower propensity to strike than one with a few big strikes of substantial length. We are more concerned here with the significance of strikes than with their numerical occurrence.

2 While the data disclose a substantial consistency of behavior, it should be kept in mind that they reflect the experience of only eleven countries over a limited period of time and that the industrial breakdowns are not so numerous nor so comparable from one country to another, or even from one time period to another in the same country, as would be ideally desirable for the purposes of this analysis.

3 A particularly disturbing combination is transportation and navigation in Norway. Do railroads pull down the rank, or do both railroads and shipping rank low? If shipping ranks low, why is the Norwegian experience different from that in the other countries?

4 This is not to suggest that a single firm cannot make a record for peace in a warlike industry or a record for conflict in a quiescent industry but only that it is unlikely to do so.

5 Some of these communities, such as the coal towns, are geographically isolated, while others, such as waterfront districts, are socially isolated within metropolitan communities.

6 Hobsbawm notes that 'the habit of solidarity suggests itself naturally' more in some industries, such as coal mining, than in others. See E. J. Hobsbawm, 'The Machine Breakers,' *Past and Present*, Vol. 1, No. 1 (February, 1952). See also comments by Seymour M. Lipset and Reinhard Bendix, 'Social Status and Social Structure,' *British Journal of Sociology*, Vol. 2, No. 3 (September, 1951).

6a The members of these groups not only have the same grievances, but they have them at the same time, at the same place, and against the same people. In the more peaceful industries their inevitable grievances are dispersed – by stratification of the workers (as in steel), by scattering of the employees (as in agriculture), by absorption of the workers into a mixed community (as in trade), by scattering of the targets (the employer, the landlord, the grocer, and the policemen being quite different people). The 'mass grievance,' not the individual grievance, is the source of the greater social difficulty. It may arise in the environment we are describing here, or may have a cross-industry content – for example, it may result from widespread unemployment, rapid inflation, general wage cuts. It is the mass grievance which leads to 'class' action. The individual grievance can be more readily absorbed and managed by society. Industrial tranquility depends on keeping grievances dispersed so that they may be handled one at a time. Proponents of social unrest are most successful in those places where, and at those times when, grievances are highly concentrated.

7 Occupational stratification may be an unusually important aspect of the industrial environment, affecting the location of the worker in society and his propensity to strike. The iron and steel industry is often located in geographically isolated one-industry towns, and much of the work in it is arduous (see hypothesis 2), yet it is not particularly famous as a centre of strike activity. Only three separate observations of this industry appear in our data (see Table 2), and they are too few for a confident generalisation. The industry, however, seems to rank somewhat above the average ('High' in Germany in the second period and 'Medium' in the United States in the first period and 'Medium high' in the second). It might rank somewhat higher, nevertheless, were it not for the high degree of job differentiation which marks the industry and which both separates one worker from another and creates a ladder for each worker to climb.

8 The industrial environment creates 'bad' employers (just as it does strike-prone workers) who disregard the welfare of their employees because of the casual nature of their connection with them or who undertake to dominate their employees unduly, as landlord and policeman as well as employer, because they are the preponderant power in a one-industry community, or who do both.

9 A third condition is necessary, in addition to the existence of a relatively homogeneous group of workers which is isolated from the general community, for an industry to be especially strike prone; but this condition is almost universally present when the other two are. This condition is the capacity of the group for cohesion. The existence of an identifiable group (such as the clothing workers) is not sufficient by itself nor is the fact of isolation (note the general lack of strikes by fishermen and oil-field workers) nor the two together, if cohesion is difficult for the isolated mass. The great hordes of agricultural harvest hands in the San Joaquin Valley of California have struck, but only with great difficulty, for they are such an inconstant, fluctuating, amorphous group. The capacity for cohesion is dependent on the fairly steady contact of the members of the group, which in turn creates the basis for permanent organisation. Thus the itinerant but occupationally specialised sheepshearers in the western United States have long been organised, since they form a group of constant composition whose members have repetitive contacts with each other, while less specialised agricultural workers have not. An isolated mass can be kept from internal solidarity not only by the turnover of its membership but also by racial, religious, and nationality barriers–a social law on which certain American employers, particularly in earlier times, have founded their recruiting practices. Hawaiian sugar-plantation workers did not become effectively organised until they were 'Americanised.' See Mark Perlman, 'Organised Labor in Hawaii,' *Labor Law Journal*, Vol. 3 (April, 1952). Even agricultural workers strike when they move from a state of individual isolation in an isolated mass to the state of a cohesive isolated mass.

10 Few man-days lost because of strikes do not necessarily indicate an absence of worker unrest, as the experience of the railroad industry in the United States attests.

11 The industries ranked 'Low' or 'Medium low' may be divided into two distinct groups: (*a*) those in which the workers are relatively well integrated individually into the community (agriculture, trade, services), and (*b*) those in which the workers constitute collectively a recognisable group but where the group is under intense social pressure to settle its grievances peacefully (clothing, railroad, public utilities). In the two categories, the industries in the latter have demonstrated the greater inclination toward strikes. In either case, community integration, in contrast to mass segregation, is the key to the explanation of peaceful behavior. The farm hand living in his employer's family, however, is integrated into the community in quite a different fashion from the railroad workers whose union finds strikes socially unacceptable. The farm hands have no group cohesion while the railroad workers have a great deal, but the pressure of society is against their making effective use of it through the strike. A third situation exists where strikes are rare or nonexistent, but it does not show in our data. This is where the workers are not integrated into the community as individuals or through their groups but are so dispersed (lighthouse keepers, hunters, forest-fire lookouts and the like) that no group action is likely. These are the isolated individuals in society.

12 A further illustration, not drawn, however, from the statistical data, is also instructive. Sailors working on oil tankers in the coastal trade of the United States, who are employed steadily by the same employer and have a more regularised family and community life than other seamen, are also less strike prone.

13 There are other tests of the validity of these theories for the explanation of industrial conflict and peace than those of how well they elucidate these data. If

the theories fail this test, this does not mean they will not pass other tests or explain other phenomena.

14 An elastic demand for the products of a firm or a group of firms and an elastic demand for labour have been advanced on occasion as a basic cause of labor–management cooperation. The employer faces stiff competition, and the union does not wish to injure his competitive position. The union, however, may not be so considerate if (a) any job reduction for this firm is matched by an increase in jobs somewhere else for members of the same union organisation and perhaps even for the same workers (as may often happen in local trade and service industries) or if (b) the union or its leaders, for the sake of survival, must make certain wage gains regardless of the potential effects (which may be much delayed) on job opportunities. Union–management cooperation is most likely to result when disturbing actions by the union would cause a loss of jobs to areas outside its job territory *and* where its leaders are in a position to consider this effect as the dominant influence. An inelastic demand for the products is probably more generally conducive to peace since it gives the employer greater leeway in accommodating himself to the union. Then a gap is more likely to exist between the maximum which the employer can readily afford to pay and the minimum which the union can reasonably accept. Richard A. Lester, however, states: 'Practically without exception . . . labor-capital cooperation has been adopted by individual firms with a fairly elastic demand for labor either because of competition within the industry or because of the practice of contracting out for work . . .' (*Economics of Labor*, New York, Macmillan, 1946, p. 697); and 'union-employer cooperation to regulate competition has occurred, for instance in [several industries are enumerated) . . . In such industries price-cutting and wage-cutting are likely to occur to an extreme degree because there is a large number of small employers in the industry, it is so easy to enter the business, and wages are such an important item in total costs.' See *ibid.*, p. 145. Hence the need for the 'stabilising' effect of the union. Shister, in his analysis of union–management cooperation, also emphasises the influence of the economic environment in working for cooperation: 'union–management cooperation has appeared mainly, although not exclusively, when the bargaining unit was in an adverse economic situation.' See Joseph Shister, 'Union–Management Cooperation: An Analysis,' in Richard A. Lester and Joseph Shister (eds.), *Insights into Labor Issues*, New York, Macmillan, 1948, p. 90. Shister states that, if the cost reductions resulting from union-management cooperation involve hourly wage reductions, 'then it is necessary that the employer's demand for labor be elastic over the relevant range. A union would not be likely to agree to reduce wages rates, under union–management cooperation, if it did not see a possibility of gaining more than proportionately in employment and/or income from the wage reduction.' See *ibid.*, pp. 90–91. Further illustration of arguments stressing the economic environment's influence in affecting industrial peace or conflict may be found in Frederick H. Harbison, Robert K. Burns and Robert Dubin, 'Toward a Theory of Labor–Management Relations,' in *Lester and Shister* (eds.), *op. cit.*, pp. 8–14; and in John Dunlop's contribution to 'Framework for the Analysis of Industrial Relations: Two Views,' *Industrial and Labor Relations Review*, Vol. 3, No. 3 (April, 1950), where he states: 'the conditions in the labor market in which the labor services are purchased by the management, and the conditions in the product market in which the output or service is sold' constitute an important aspect of the total environment impinging on the prospects for peace of conflict'.

15 Ross and Irwin conclude that 'differences in the frequency of strikes between one country and another can best be explained by differences in the position of the union and the union leader' and that 'internal factionalism, like external com petition, encourages the development and prosecution of grievances.' See Arthur

  M. Ross and Donald Irwin, 'Strike Experience in Five Countries, 1927–1947: An Interpretation,' *Industrial and Labor Relations Review*, Vol. 4, No. 3 (April, 1951).

16 'Frequent disputes are mainly caused by dissatisfaction among the workers; strikes for improvements are frequent when rising prices are not adequately met by rising wages, strikes against a worsening of conditions when the workers are menaced by cuts and especially by wage cuts not justified by a proportional fall in prices.' K. Forchheimer, *Some International Aspects of the Strike Movement*, Oxford Institute of Statistics Bulletin 10, January, 1948.

17 'According to this approach [*i.e.*, the human-relations' approach], actions and sentiments are the items to be explained: Why do workers increase (or decrease) their productivity? Why do they stay on the job–or go out on strike? Why do they express hostile (or favourable) sentiments toward management? And the analysis of patterns of interaction [where 'interaction' refers to all personal contacts between two individuals or among three or more individuals] seems to me the most effective means of explaining actions and sentiments.' See William Foote Whyte's contribution to 'Framework for the Analysis of Industrial Relations: Two Views.' The economic, social, and political environments are determinants in this schema only in so far as their influences are manifested in specific items of behavior of the people observed within the 'social system' which the plant constitutes. The determining influence in shaping 'sentiments' is the nature of the human relations which prevail: 'The trouble is that people's sentiments cannot be changed by simply telling them that it is a good idea to change their sentiments. In this case [the Chicago plant of the Inland Steel Container Co.], union and management people began with hatred and distrust, while now mutual good will prevails. But the good will was a late arrival on the scene. It only developed *following* far-reaching changes in human relations. This is the sequence of change we see, as a rule: first a change in human relations, then a change in sentiments.' See William Foote Whyte, *Pattern for Industrial Peace*, New York, Harper, 1951, p. 228.

18 For example, by changing the structure of the work group. See E. L. Trist and K. W. Bamforth, 'Some Social and Psychological Consequences of the Longwall Method of Coal-getting,' *Human Relations*, Vol. 4, No. 1 (1951).

19 Clinton S. Golden and Harold J. Ruttenberg, *The Dynamics of Industrial Democracy*, New York, Harper, 1942. 'Management as a general principle, gets the kind of union leadership it deserves. A tough management begets tough union leaders, while a patient, friendly, cooperative management begets a like type of union leadership . . .' (p. 58).

20 See Robert R. R. Brooks, *As Steel Goes*, New Haven, Conn., Yale University Press, 1940. 'There are three stages in the development of successful collective bargaining. The first is the signing of a contract by a company giving a union the right to bargain for its members only. Such a contract often amounts to no more than a letter of introduction. It may be followed by a period of intense conflict between union and management representatives during which the union fights for a permanent status, and the management fights for the *status quo ante*. In the second stage, individual companies concede a stable position to the union and cooperate with it in the adjustment of personal grievances, but the use of the word "grievance" clearly suggests that union–management relationships remain essentially negative. In the third stage, collective bargaining becomes a cooperative relationship directed toward increasing the productive efficiency of the industry. Positive action toward this objective must ultimately lead to industry-wide union–management cooperation by organised workers and associated employers . . .' (p. 190).

21 Several of the case studies in the National Planning Association series 'Causes of Industrial Peace' emphasise the importance of dominant personalities in the

shaping of peaceful relations. For example, 'Perhaps the most important factor [determining the course of the relationship] is the president of the company. His philosophy and his personality have had a great deal to do with the ultimate development of health. . . .' (Douglas McGregor and Joseph N. Scanlon, *The Dewey and Almy Chemical Company and the International Chemical Workers Union*, Washington, National Planning Association, 1948, pp. 63–64); or 'A long and successful evolution has brought about these conditions, but what was the genesis of this evolution? Why did collective bargaining get off to a good start in this industry? The personality of Sidney Hillman played a dominant role. His constructive and honest approach was often an effective substitute for the picket line . . .' (Donald B. Straus, *Hickey-Freeman Company and Amalgamated Clothing Workers*, Washington, National Planning Association, 1949, pp. 70–71).

22 John L. Lewis may very well have made a greater contribution to industrial tranquillity than Sidney Hillman, for he has channeled the ineluctable unrest of the miners into mass strikes called (usually) at a time of year (in the spring) when they cost the nation the very least. Hillman headed a union which has made a record for industrial peace in an industry which is almost always peaceful.

23 See Benjamin M. Selekman, 'Varieties of Labor Relations,' *Harvard Business Review*, Vol. 27, No. 2 (March, 1949). 'Beyond any short-term changes in the bargaining program, accordingly, the ideological structure does constitute the most undeviating and ineradicable conflict pattern in present-day industrial relations. For the party-line leaders accept neither the system of free collective bargaining nor the American democracy of which it is a part. Manifestly, such an undivided focus on external goals means that the ideological structure of relationship possesses no innate potentialities for evolution toward a more accommodative structure of joint dealings. Consequently, the reliance on time and experience, which may prove helpful in other structures, in this one can become a source of actual danger. Only by ousting party-line leaders from positions of union leadership, whether by legislation or by employer resistance or by intra-union action, may this source of conflict be minimised.'

24 Not to be neglected is Communist selection of certain strategic industries for infiltration, including coal mining and water transportation. These industries, however, were the locale of many strikes before the Communists became active, but their efforts certainly have served to intensify the conflict in these already favorable environments.

25 See J. R. Hicks, *The Theory of Wages*, New York, Peter Smith, 1948. 'Under a system of collective bargaining . . . the majority of actual strikes are doubtless the result of faulty negotiation . . . The danger lies in ignorance by one side of the other's dispositions, and in hasty breaking-off of negotiations . . .' (pp. 146–147). For discussions of the importance of bargaining skill and techniques, see also Sumner H. Slichter, *The Challenge of Industrial Relations*, Ithaca, N.Y., Cornell University Press, 1947, pp. 138–145; and *Massachusetts Proposals for Better Industrial Relations*, Boston, New England Council, 1947, pp. 11–15.

26 Harbison and Dubin, Dunlop, and others emphasise the key-bargain hypothesis. Harbison and Dubin point to the difficulties in achieving good union–management relations where labor patterns are set rather than followed, and Dunlop points to the overall difficulties in establishing workable relations for the economy where a few key bargains set the pace for the followers. See Frederick H. Harbison and Robert Dubin, *Patterns of Union–Management Relations*, Chicago, Science Research Associates, 1947. 'The question of corporation survival and maintenance of employment is not so likely to be a determining factor in negotiations between organisations such as General Motors and the GM Department of the UAW. Negotiations between such giants do not conform solely to our economic environ-

ment; indeed they actually tend to create much of the economic environment for the mass production industries. As we have indicated, the forces influencing collective bargaining in the power centres make the development of constructive union–management relations difficult. Here lies the most crucial problem in present-day labor relations . . .' (p. 221). See also John T. Dunlop, 'American Wage Determination: The Trend and Its Significance,' in *Wage Determination and the Economics of Liberalism*, Washington, U.S. Chamber of Commerce, 1947, pp. 41–43.

27 A perusal of Wilfred Harris Crook, *The General Strike*, Chapel Hill, The University of North Carolina Press, 1931, indicates that many of the general strikes evolved from disputes in coal, lumber, textiles, and the waterfront: for example, the 1842 general strike in Britain developed out of a dispute in the collieries as did the 1902 strike in France; the 1904 strike in France began with a lockout of the harbor workmen in Marseilles, and the 1903 strike in Holland also grew out of a dispute which involved the dockers' union; the 1904 strike in Italy developed when troops were sent in to maintain order in a strike of miners; and the 1909 strike in Sweden involved a lockout of sawmill and textile workers (pp. 18–20, 38–39, 115 ff., 185, 283).

28 This is, of course, a prescription which is difficult, but not impossible, to apply to the coal mining or lumber or maritime industries. Actually integration is growing with the introduction of the automobile, the radio, and television, the decasualisation of work on the waterfront and in the logging camp, the increasing acceptance of trade-unions by employers, by government, and by the community at large, and the spread of popular education. The 'homeless, voteless, womanless' worker is now the rare exception, and workers and their institutions share more in the operation of society. With these fundamental changes the industries of high propensity to strike are presumably becoming less conflict inclined, although they may always rank high comparatively. If, instead of reducing conflict through a policy of individual and group assimilation, it were wished to intensify it, then the appropriate social program would be to isolate the workers and immerse them in a segregated organisation.

29 'Mayo gives us instances where industrial administrators have succeeded in making factory groups so stable in their attitudes of group cooperation that men in the groups explicitly recognised that the factory had become for them the stabilising force around which they developed satisfying lives . . . Thus Mayo shows us for the first time in the form of specific instances that it is within the power of industrial administrators to create within industry itself a partially effective substitute for the old stabilising effect of the neighborhood. Given stable employment, it might make of industry (as of the small town during most of our national life) a socially satisfying way of life as well as a way of making a living.' See Wallace B. Donham, 'Foreword,' in Elton Mayo, *The Social Problems of an Industrial Civilisation*, Cambridge, Mass., Harvard University Press, 1945, pp. viii–ix.

30 Frank Tannenbaum, *A Philosophy of Labor*, New York, Knopf, 1951. 'In terms of the individual, the union returns to the worker his "society." It gives him a fellowship, a part in a drama that he can understand, and life takes on meaning once again because he shares a value system common to others. Institutionally the trade-union movement is an unconscious effort to harness the drift of our time and reorganise it around the cohesive identity that men working together always achieve . . .' (p. 10). 'The trade-union is the real alternative to the authoritarian state. The trade-union is our modern "society," the only true society that industrialism has fostered. As a true society it is concerned with the whole man, and embodies the possibilities of both the freedom and the security essential to human dignity. The corporation and the union will ultimately merge in common owner-

ship and cease to be a house divided. It is only thus that a common identity may once again come to rule the lives of men and endow each one with rights and duties recognised by all . . .' (pp. 198–199).

31 See Will Herberg, 'For "Limited" as against "Total" Unionism,' *Labor and Nation*, Vol. 1, No. 5 (April–May, 1946). 'Each kind of organisation has its own proper function in the pluralistic scheme of a democratic society and for its own good as well as for the good of society as a whole, each should confine itself primarily to the sphere determined by that function. There are undoubtedly other purposes and interests of deep concern to workers, who, it must be remembered, are not merely workers, but men and citizens as well. For the furtherance of these purposes and interests there exist a wide variety of organisations – and where none exist new ones may be formed – in which trade unionists may naturally take part, though not as trade unionists but in one or another of the many capacities in which citizens functions in a free pluralistic society.'

For Table 2, see Technical Supplement, p. 285.

12

INFLUENCES ON RELATIVE STRIKE ACTIVITY

A. M. Ross and P. T. Hartman

We have undertaken elsewhere* to explain the decline in strike activity which has occurred in numerous countries. But this decline has not proceeded evenly, nor has it been experienced everywhere. As we have seen, there are four distinctive patterns of industrial conflict among the countries we have studied systematically, and three of the countries are best described as special cases. Presumably there are reasons why strikes in Denmark are so unlike those in Finland, why industrial conflict in the United States is a different matter from that in France. The purpose of the present chapter is to identify these reasons by describing the main influences on relative strike activity with varying incidence in the different nations.

A similar attempt was made in 'Strike Experience in Five Countries.' There several factors were stressed as tending to aggravate industrial warfare: employer resistance, 'voluntary choice between membership and non-membership,' organisational and jurisdictional conflict, internal leadership rivalries, Communist unionism, single-firm bargaining, and the absence of a labor party. In general, the strike was seen as 'a response to difficulties that are encountered by unions in acquiring organisational stability and by union leaders in attaining personal . . . security.' And it was held that 'these difficulties are the result of competition and freedom of choice in various forms: power conflicts with employers, ambiguous loyalties on the part of workers,' etc.[1]

This interpretation worked well enough for Australia, Canada, Great Britain, Sweden, and the United States. All of these countries have similar institutions, including a long-established and well-financed labor movement. All of them put primary reliance on collective bargaining as the main instrument for defining terms of employment. A broader interpretation is necessary, however, for

*This chapter contains several references to other parts of the book from which it comes.

countries in which the whole environment of labor-management relations is different, such as Japan, India, France, and Finland.

For example, 'Strike Experience in Five Countries' held that 'continuous voluntary choice between membership and non-membership is conducive to agitation and strikes' because 'issues are sharpened, grievances promoted, and commotions created in order to keep members in good standing'; but 'when, in contrast, union membership is guaranteed, either by contractual arrangement with employers or social pressure and habit among wage earners, apathy and quiescence can be permitted to set in. . . .'[2] This interpretation is valid where the act of joining the union represents a significant decision, membership is a formal status, and the dues are relatively high. But we find many countries in which union membership is a different kind of phenomenon. The work force of an enterprise joins up more or less as a group, the dues are nominal and are not systematically collected, the line between membership and non-membership is a hazy one, and the worker is not called upon to make a considered, individual decision. The environment is so different that the question of individual choice cannot be analysed in the same way.

The leading influences in relative strike activity which are amenable to comparison between one country and another appear to be the following:

(1) *Organisational stability*
    (*a*) Age of the labor movement.
    (*b*) Stability of membership in recent years.
(2) *Leadership conflicts in the labor movement*
    (*a*) Factionalism, rival unionism and rival federations.
    (*b*) Strength of Communism in labor unions.
(3) *Status of union-management relations*
    (*a*) Degree of acceptance by employers.
    (*b*) Consolidation of bargaining structure.
(4) *Labor political activity*
    (*a*) Existence of labor party as a leading political party.
    (*b*) Labor-party governments.
(5) *Role of the state*
    (*a*) Extent of government activity in defining terms of employment.
    (*b*) Dispute-settlement policies and procedures.

What is the relationship between these influences on relative strike activity, on the one hand, and the reasons for the decline of industrial conflict in several countries (which were discussed in the preceding chapter), on the other? The answer is that the two classifications overlap to a considerable extent but are not entirely congruent. They differ because in one case we dealt principally with Northern Europe and North America, whereas this chapter also covers the Mediterranean-Asian group, Australia, Finland, and South Africa. We must, therefore, have a classification that will explain a broader range of phenomena than we discussed when dealing with Northern Europe and North America. Have we included all the factors that affect the volume and duration of strikes in these 15 countries? We have not, but only those that are amenable to a comparative analysis. Every country – like every individual – is essentially unique, but we must concentrate on features that are subject to comparison rather than those that are singular. We have made a few exceptions, but only a few; if each country had been analysed in its own terms, no generalisations could have been attempted. Furthermore, we could not investigate two or three possible influences because the data were not available. It is possible, for instance, that differences in the industrial structure or 'industry mix' have a bearing on relative strike activity.[3] Actually the distribution of non-agricultural employment among the major economic divisions (mining, manufacturing, etc.) is quite similar in most of the countries. To deal with a more detailed industrial classification would have introduced so many complications that it could not feasibly be done within the confines of this study.

Although these influences on strike activity are described separately, they should not be thought of as independent variables. Actually, much depends on how they fit into the total system of industrial relations in each country. When we state, therefore, that a certain factor is conducive to industrial peace or industrial conflict, we mean that it has such an effect in the context where it is typically encountered. The importance of context will be discussed further in the final chapter.

ORGANISATIONAL STABILITY

In discussing the paucity of strikes in some of the newer countries where nationalism, anticolonialism, and economic planning are prominent factors, we warned against the concept of a universal cycle of union development. Nevertheless, there has been a common cycle of growth in most of the older countries which are studied in this monograph. The early years of the labor movements have been marked by friction, hostility, and confusion. With the passage of time, organisations have become more solid and secure, control over the rank and file has been cemented, and accommodative relations with the employers have been established.

Thus the chronological age of a labor movement may have an important influence on the incidence of industrial conflict. Older movements are more likely to have completed their struggles for existence, recognition, and security, and to be integrated into their national economies. Once this point has been reached, bargaining machinery can be developed to handle economic issues without frequent work stoppages.

Age alone does not tell the full story. Rapid changes in membership can initiate new struggles for worker allegiance and for recognition and acceptance. 'Organising periods' are not always limited to the early years of a labor movement. Membership fluctuations may take place at any time. Pronounced fluctuations are generally conducive to industrial conflict as the unions strive to organise and absorb new members and to settle the most pressing grievances, or struggle to limit their losses and recapture their territory.

LEADERSHIP CONFLICTS

Factionalism encourages the prosecution of issues because the vested officials must protect their position against upstarts lower down in the ranks, while the upstarts must demonstrate that the members are being sold down the river by a tired, indifferent or corrupt Old Guard. In contrast, the only threat to the established officials in a one-party union lies in shop steward revolts at the bottom of the pyramid. Such revolts, which take the form of outlaw strikes, can be choked off quickly if internal discipline is sufficiently effective and relations with employers are good.

Rival unionism is a potent cause of strikes where rivalry is pursued on the basis of comparative militancy in pressing grievances and comparative gains in collective bargaining. A labor organisation must attempt to match the achievements of its rival or rivals and must secure even greater benefits, if possible, regardless of the amount of resistance to be overcome. In the absence of competition for members, the pressure to use bargaining gains as economic weapons is not so great.

In many countries the concepts of bargaining unit and exclusive bargaining agent do not apply. Several organisations may be operating inside what we in the United States would consider a single bargaining unit. Moreover, these organisations may be affiliated with rival federations or trade union centres. Rivalry among unions under these circumstances is even more intense. The striving to outdo a competitor exists not only from one contract negotiation to the next, but from day to day in the plant as well.

That stable union-management relations are difficult to construct under these circumstances would seem obvious.

The union structure most conducive to the elimination of industrial conflict is a unified national movement with strongly centralised control. Under these conditions the central leadership can consciously substitute other tactics for the strike and can restrain the exercise of power by strong subordinate unions.

Finally, where the Communist faction has substantial strength in the labor movement, strike activity is usually stimulated – particularly the use of massive demonstration strikes. In the Communist view, the worker's grievances are not to be settled conclusively within the framework of capitalism. Strikes have an agitational purpose; for although the eventual seizure of power is to be accomplished by military or political means, the 'inherent revolutionary potential of the workers' must be developed and their awareness of class differences sharpened in the meantime. Economic gains resulting from strikes are useful to prove the effectiveness of leadership but cannot be allowed to underwrite any lasting reconciliation. When Communists operate as a minority group within unions, and have failed to achieve top leadership, settlements by the established officials must be denounced as sellouts. It follows that strikes are unlikely to wither away in any democratic country so long as Communists have majority control or strong minority influence within important unions.

We are not stating, however, that Communist leadership will inevitably employ the strike for agitational purposes. Much depends on the party strategy at the time; much depends also on the membership base. The bargaining policies of Communist-led unions in the United States have generally been indistinguishable from those of other unions. Disinterested in ideological unionism, the members have expected a bread-and-butter approach and their expectations have been rewarded. Those left-wing leaders who have survived for any substantial period have practised the same business unionism that is condemned so heartily in Marxist literature. The same can be said of left-wing union leaders in the United Kingdom.

STATUS OF UNION-MANAGEMENT RELATIONS

There are two main types of industrial conflict. The first is basically organisational even though wages and other economic issues may ostensibly be involved. It has dominated the early states of labor-management relations in many countries, where the unions have struggled to win their place in economic society and employers have striven to retain their traditional authority. This phase has come to an end where employers and unions have attained an acceptable balance of power and prerogatives. The usual description is that employers have 'accepted unionism and collective bargaining,' although the process is actually more complicated than that.

Concededly 'acceptance' is not capable of measurement and is difficult to discuss except in stilted terms. It is sufficiently obvious that as long as unions are permitted to strive for power but are thwarted in their every bid, only conflict can result.

The second type of industrial conflict is essentially economic and persists after collective bargaining has become 'institutionalised' and the parties have found ways and means of living together. But as we have seen, even this kind of conflict has virtually disappeared in some countries where the collective bargaining system has become tightly organised and controlled.

There also are two degrees of centralisation in the structure of collective bargaining. Industry-wide bargaining between industrial unions and employer associations constitutes the first degree. It is not necessary that master negotiations cover the entire industry; the resulting agreement can be extended by force of law or by voluntary action. Nor is it necessary that there be a formal industry association with power of attorney. Unless the number of firms is large, informal employer committees can accomplish the same result.

We have already indicated in the previous chapter the reasons why multi-employer bargaining is conducive to industrial peace. Professional leadership eliminates reckless and emotional behavior; the costliness of large strikes serves as a deterrent to both sides; employers are less inclined to resist because they are not in danger of being whipsawed and will not suffer a competitive disadvantage within the industry; unions are less aggressive because intraunion competition is eliminated. The United Kingdom is a good example of a country with this type of bargaining system. Unauthorised or unofficial strikes (the counterpart of local-union strikes in a decentralised bargaining structure) are always a possibility, but in the nature of the case they are generally brief gestures of protest.

The second degree of centralisation is economy-wide rather than merely industry-wide. The labor market is regulated and disciplined as a whole. It is in this state of affairs that the strike is most likely to wither away. In some of the newer countries, governments are moving to organise and discipline the labor market through an alliance with the unions and under the banner of nationalism and anticolonialism. In some of the older countries of Northern Europe a thoroughly consolidated bargaining structure has been created under private auspices. 'Peak associations' or federations of management and labor have been the means of integration. The

officers of such federations represent the broadest possible constituencies and are the farthest removed from parochial pressures.
Of course, this fully centralised system will not work without the
highest degree of subordination and discipline within the federations.

LABOR POLITICAL ACTIVITY

In the preceding chapter we observed that labor parties and labor
governments have contributed toward relinquishment of the strike
by providing a political alternative. We noted that the powers of the
state over income distribution and other aspects of economic welfare
are clearly stronger than the possibilities of collective bargaining,
and that political action is more convenient, dignified, and respect-
able than industrial conflict.

It remains to point out that the existence of a labor party with
close trade union affiliations is perhaps the greatest deterrent to the
use of the strike. We are not speaking of just any labor party,
however, but rather of one which is capable of imbuing the unions
with a feeling of political responsibility. The party must have tasted
political power, or at least must be sufficiently potent to be seen as a
serious contender for power. And there must be a reasonable
prospect of achieving labor objectives through government action.

We emphasise the last point because the existence of strong labor
parties has not eliminated industrial conflict in postwar Finland and
in Australia. In the first case the economic environment has been
too hostile for successful reliance on the political mechanism, and
in the second case the constitutional powers of the federal government are too weak. The federal form of government in the United
States and Canada, with much power located in the states and
provinces, has inhibited successful political action and helps to
explain why unions have relied so heavily on industrial action.

Why is labor political action a deterrent to strikes? First, strikes
are injurious to the political fortunes of the labor party. Middle-
class votes must be attracted if the party is to be successful, but the
middle-class voter is antagonised by strikes and tends to blame them
on the unions. Second, worker unrest is channeled off into the
political sphere. Demands that would otherwise be made upon the
employer are directed against the government instead. If the labor
party comes into power, the deterrent effect is even stronger. The
trade union officials, having invested heavily in the party, are
disinclined to do anything that would have the effect of sabotaging
its program. Moreover, large-scale strikes are always embarrassing
to the administration in power; and if industrial paralysis seems to be

threatened, unpleasant repressive measures may become inevitable. All of this means that the trade union leader who wishes to cooperate with party officials, or is himself such an official, will show maximum restraint in the use of the strike.

ROLE OF THE STATE

We showed in the last chapter that greater participation by government as entrepreneur, economic planner, guardian of labor, and supervisor of union-management relations has been partly responsible for the declining frequency of strikes. We indicated also that labor protest against public employment policies or compulsory arbitration awards is more likely to take the form of brief demonstrations than actual trials of economic strength.

All governments have not assumed these new functions to an equal extent, however. The amount of socialised industry in the United Kingdom, for example, is greater than in Canada. The Scandinavian countries have implemented programs of central economic planning to an unusual extent during recent years, generally under the leadership of labor party governments. France, Italy, and Japan rely on legislation for defining many conditions of employment that are determined by collective bargaining elsewhere. Australia has an elaborate system of compulsory arbitration, whereas the government of the United States remains aloof from most industrial disputes except for offering mediation services.

INFLUENCES ON STRIKE ACTIVITY AND THE FOUR 'PATTERNS'

In Chapter 3 we classified most of the countries we have studied under four patterns of industrial conflict, and in the present chapter we have attempted to describe the principal influences on relative strike activity. It is now time to bring these two classifications together.

We think that a significant association can be shown between national patterns of strike activity, on the one hand, and the condition of the labor movement, union-management relations, and political institutions on the other. In the nature of the case only a broad and general association can be expected, however. There are so many unique and special causes at work in particular countries that a perfect correlation is out of the question. In fact, if a simple and mechanical relationship could be established, there would be reason to suspect that we were dealing with shallow and verbal categories rather than with real distinctions.

Having sounded this caveat, we may turn to the four patterns of industrial conflict. What is said below will be discussed in much greater detail in the remaining chapters of this volume.

THE NORTH EUROPEAN PATTERN – FIRST VARIANT

This pattern, found in Denmark, the Netherlands, the United Kingdom, and Germany, is characterised by a nominal propensity to strike and a low or moderate duration of strikes. These countries have mature labor movements with firm and stable memberships. (The postwar German labor movement, as Kerr has noted, is a revival of the pre-Hitler movement with remarkably little change.) Leadership conflicts are subdued: there is one dominant central federation in Denmark, the United Kingdom, and Germany. (It is true that three federations have coexisted in the Netherlands for upwards of four decades, but their competition has not been so vigorous as to provoke industrial conflict.) The Communist faction has been notably weak in all four countries.

By virtue of industry-wide negotiations and the influence of central federations, collective bargaining structures have become highly centralised, although the degree of consolidation varies from one country to another. Industrial unions and industry associations do the negotiating in the United Kingdom, for example, whereas much power is concentrated in the Danish and Dutch central federations. There are strong labor or social democratic parties, which have organised or at least participated in the government, except in postwar Germany.

There is a fair amount of public enterprise in the United Kingdom, but not a great deal in the other nations. Neither is there much reliance on the state for defining important conditions of employment. On the other hand, all four governments have had active programs of intervention in bargaining disputes. Compulsory arbitration was practised in the United Kingdom until 1951, and the machinery was retained on a voluntary basis in a number of key industries. In Denmark the legislature has frequently intervened, generally by enacting mediation proposals into law. An official Board of Mediation in the Netherlands has authority to approve, modify, or disapprove collective agreements, extend their provisions to employers and workers not directly covered, and set wages directly in some cases. The 'extension' system is also used in Germany.

THE NORTH EUROPEAN PATTERN – SECOND VARIANT

This pattern is defined by very infrequent but long stoppages. The labor movement, the bargaining system, and political context in

Norway and Sweden are similar in most pertinent respects to those in Denmark, the Netherlands, the United Kingdom, and Germany. The only significant difference we have identified is that Norway and Sweden generally maintain a hands-off policy in labor-management controversies, whereas more active intervention has been practised in the other countries. This is not a very convincing explanation of the remarkable disparity in average duration of strikes. Differences in the 'industry mix' may be significant, and doubtless additional causes are at work.

THE MEDITERRANEAN-ASIAN PATTERN

This pattern includes France, Italy, Japan, and India. Participation in strikes is very great but duration is short. Labor movements entered the phase of mass organisation, or reorganised from scratch, subsequent to World War II. Union membership does not involve an important personal or financial commitment and has often been an ephemeral phenomenon. Rival unionism and internal leadership conflicts have been endemic; there has been a powerful Communist faction in each of these countries, which has made chronic use of the massive demonstration stoppage as an agitational tool.

Labor-management relations, like the labor movements themselves, are weak and unstable. The unions have not really been accepted by employers and are not in a position to negotiate on an equal basis. Although the forms of multi-employer bargaining are used in some of these countries, the subject matter of bargaining is rather insubstantial. The significant conditions of work, for the most part, are either set by the government or remain within the employer's control. The unions are normally too poor to undertake long strikes.

All these countries have two or more left-wing parties affiliated with different branches of the labor movement. They are bitterly divided, however, a far cry from the unified labor or social democratic parties of Northern Europe. As a consequence, conservative governments have occupied the stage during the past decade. No single labor party has come sufficiently close to political power that the strike policy of its affiliated unions has been affected. (In recent years, however, collaboration between the Congress Party and the largest group of Indian unions has had a definite influence on strike activity.)

There is a surprising amount of public enterprise in France, Italy, Japan, and India. Moreover, as noted above, many important terms of employment are defined by the state rather than collective bargaining; unionism is so weak in the industrial sphere that unrest is focused on the political process. Thus labor protest is frequently directed against the government, a further reason for the popularity of brief demonstration strikes.

THE NORTH AMERICAN PATTERN

The North American pattern, found in the United States and Canada, is characterised by a moderately high propensity to strike as well as a relatively long duration. Insofar as large-scale organisation is concerned, the labor movements are younger than those in Northern Europe but older than those in the Mediterranean-Asian group. There were wide swings in union membership until the 1940's, but the intensity of organisation has become more stable in recent years.

The status of union leadership is likewise in transition. Historically, rival unionism, jurisdictional conflict, and internal leadership struggles have all been prevalent in the United States and Canada. Communist influence was significant in numerous unions between 1935 and 1950. But with the expulsion and atrophy of the Communist unions, the development of no-raid agreements, and the merger between AFL and CIO, there has been a notable tendency for jurisdictional lines to stabilise. Furthermore, political rivalry inside unions has diminished as the organisations have become more stable and the leaders have grown older. It is possible, however, that technological changes will revive the conflict between craft and industrial unionism and encourage competition over the growing army of white-collar workers.

The major employers in the United States and Canada generally resisted unionism until the latter part of the 1930's. In subsequent years labor organisations have increasingly been accepted and incorporated into the industrial system. Here again the situation is midway between the Northern European countries, where collective bargaining became 'institutionalised' early in the present century, and the Mediterranean-Asian group, where collective bargaining is still weak and undeveloped. Bargaining structure in the United States and Canada is more decentralised than in any other country we have studied. About five-sixths of all labor contracts in the United States are negotiated in single-employer units, and most of the multi-employer contracts cover local areas only. Canada's collective bargaining system is very similar.

Political processes in the United States and Canada, like bargaining structure, are consistent with relatively frequent and rather long industrial disputes. The important conditions of employment are determined privately rather than by government: the minimum wage laws are not very significant from a practical standpoint; paid vacations, holidays, etc., are not covered by legislation; and even a private system of social security has developed. A successful labor party has not emerged in either country, and the central orientation of the labor movement is industrial rather than political. Finally, although compulsory mediation is practised in Canada, the United States maintains a laissez-faire policy towards most types of industrial disputes.

NOTES

1 A. M. Ross and D. Irwin, 'Strike Experience in Five Countries,' *Industrial and Labor Relations Review*, 4 (April 1951), p. 336.
2 *Ibid.*, p. 337.
3 See Clark Kerr and Abraham Siegel, 'The Inter-Industry Propensity to Strike – An International Comparison,' in A. Kornhauser, R. Dubin, and A. M. Ross (eds.), *Industrial Conflict* (New York: McGraw-Hill Book Co., 1954), pp. 189–212.

THE NATURE OF BRITAIN'S STRIKE PROBLEM

A REASSESSMENT OF ARGUMENTS IN THE DONOVAN REPORT

W. E. J. McCarthy

While the Report of the Royal Commission on Trade Unions and Employers' Associations was being prepared it became increasingly obvious to those who were involved that most people outside were only interested in what the report was going to say about strikes. It seemed likely that if the Commissioners came out in favour of the *status quo*, or advocated the introduction of simple but draconic legal penalties to be imposed on all unofficial strikers, they would be denounced by some and applauded by others, but at least they would be understood. If, on the other hand, they listed a number of detailed proposals for long-run reform, prefaced by a statistical analysis of the nature and significance of Britain's strike problem—most people would not get the point.

In the end the Commissioners opted for a limited statistical analysis and concentrated on long-run reforms.[1] But the results were not as bad as had been feared. For the most part the long-run proposals, when suitably simplified and coarsened by passage through the mass media, seemed to find general acceptance. Indeed, many public men (who had argued quite differently before the Commission, or in those innumerable articles headed '*Waiting for Donovan*') paid the Commission the most sincere of compliments: they claimed to have been advocating similar things for years.

Yet curiously enough the analysis of Britain's strike problem, which seemed to be an essential part of the case for bargaining reform, attracted far less attention, and to judge from most editorials, articles and speeches on strikes since Donovan it has not been understood yet. Obviously a much sharper and more provocative assault on conventional wisdom than that provided by Chapter Seven of the Donovan Report was required.

IS BRITAIN REALLY STRIKE PRONE?

It was for this reason that Professor Turner's recent Occasional Paper published under the eye-catching title of *Is Britain Really Strike Prone?*[2] was welcome. The occasion of its publication was also superbly timed: the height of the public debate over the so-called 'penal clauses' in the Government's White Paper, *In Place of Strife*.[3] Partly as a result of this, Turner's serious analysis of some of the underlying trends in recent strike statistics has been widely quoted. Perhaps in this way it has helped to direct the public mind away from an unhealthy and sensational interest in particular disputes—especially those that happen to take place in the so-called 'strike prone' industries like car manufacture and the docks. There is even hope that some of Professor Turner's more significant general points may make a more lasting impression on leader-writers than Chapter Seven of the Donovan Report.

But Turner also claimed to have uncovered a number of errors and exaggerations in the Donovan Report, said to be repeated in the Government's White Paper. The central aim of this article is to assess his arguments in this respect with two objectives in mind: first, to see how far his criticisms of the Donovan analysis are justified; second, to work towards a re-statement of what seems to be the nub of Britain's strike problem.

Turner's basic position is that three important and influential publications in recent years have exaggerated the seriousness of Britain's strike problem. These publications are the Donovan Report, the Labour Government's White Paper, and the Conservative Party's policy document *Fair Deal at Work*.[4] Throughout most of his paper he insists on lumping all these three together, because whatever their differences of emphasis they all contain 'one proposition on which they appear virtually unanimous. This is the allegedly high liability of British society to industrial conflict, and the supposedly damaging effect of labour unrest on the British economy'[5].

Turner further argues that in substance 'the three documents are at one in their assertions as to the facts, and their conclusions as to the effects which follow from them'[6]. The elements of this common view can be summarised as follows:

1. The British economy has experienced much more frequent small stoppages than others.
2. Britain is unusual in that most strikes are unofficial and unconstitutional.
3. Unofficial and unconstitutional strikes, which are usually small, short but unpredictable, are 'more economically

damaging' than (say) a big official stoppage which involves 'the same total of lost working days'.

4.   In Britain the frequency of such strikes 'is tending to increase– while the frequency of official strikes is not'.

Turner assumes throughout that the proposals for dealing with strikes in the Donovan Report, The White Paper and *Fair Deal at Work* depend on all four of these assumptions being true. He therefore sets out to show that they 'are (to say the least) highly dubious'[7].

INTERNATIONAL COMPARISONS

The first assumption is said to derive from the table of international strike statistics given in the Donovan Report.[8] (This is repeated in Appendix Two of the White Paper.) This table was used in the Report to show that on the evidence available Britain had a comparatively high incidence of strikes per worker employed. In fact the table listed fifteen countries and indicated that Britain was 'worse' than nine and 'better' than five. The White Paper drew on this evidence to assert: 'Compared with other countries we have a large number of strikes in relation to our workforce'[9].

Turner's point is that the figures in Donovan do not stand up to examination, because different countries have such different definitions of what is to count as a strike. He also claims that most countries for which there is any reliable information 'appear to define strikes in a way that is more restricted than the British definition'. It follows from this that if these other countries adopted *British* definitions they would record a higher incidence of strikes per worker than they do now. Conversely, if Britain adopted *their* definitions it would not appear to be so strike prone.

In fact the question of definitions is a rather complex one. It is true that almost all countries have slightly different definitions of what is to count as a strike for the purpose of their official statistics. But some are more restrictive than others in some respects while being more all-embracing in other ways. The Secretariat of the Donovan Commission, which was responsible for the table, was well aware of these problems. A considerable time was spent in correspondence with the I.L.O. trying to obtain reasonably comparable figures. In the end it was decided that the figures obtained from the I.L.O. could be said to represent 'a broadly accurate picture' although it was pointed out that 'the difficulty which always exists in making strict international comparisons is greater than usual in this case because different countries adopt different criteria in deciding whether a strike is too small to be included in the statistics'.

A further look at the information that was available to the Donovan Commission does not convince one that the criticisms made by Turner can be sustained. He argues that of the countries listed in the Commission's table there are only nine where 'minimum definitional information' is available.[10] Since 'six have definitions which would exclude from their strike statistics many incidents which are included in British figures' it follows that 'the frequency of disputes in the U.K. should appear comparatively high'[11]. The implication, to me at least, seems to be that Britain is not *really* strike prone, or at least not as relatively strike prone as Donovan's rough-and-ready table would seem to imply. This is because, by and large, in countries for which there is reliable evidence, more strikes drop through the definitional net. It follows that if Turner's arguments could be followed to their logical conclusion (i.e. if those countries he wants to exclude could be excluded, and known differences in definition allowed for) they would lead to another table which would show Great Britain in a much more favourable position. An attempt will be made to show that what evidence there is does not point in this direction. It seems on the contrary, that Britain's comparative strike position looks worse after following Turner's suggestions, insofar as this is possible. The evidence for this assertion is contained in Table 1.

TABLE 1

Minimum Definitions

	Stoppages per 100,000	Working days lost		Duration		Number of Workers
1. Australia	63.8	10		—		—
2. United Kingdom	16.8	100	or	1 day	and	10 workers
3. Canada	15.8	10		—		—
4. United States	13.2	—		1 day/shift	and	6 workers
5. Finland	10.8	100	or	4 hours		—
6. Japan	7.6	—		4 hours		—
7. Denmark	5.5	100		—		—
8. Norway	0.6	—		1 day		—
9. Germany	NA	100	or	1 day		—

This table presents the strike ratios in the Donovan Report for the nine countries which Turner considers provide 'minimum definitional information'. Countries are ranked in order of their ratios and it can be seen that of the nine Britain has a 'worse' record than any seven and a 'better' record than one i.e. Australia. Definitional information provided by the I.L.O. to Donovan is classified under three heads: (1) the *minimum number of working days lost* which countries may require before a given strike is to count; (2) *minimum duration periods*; (3) *minimum number of workers on strike*. Where there is no entry for a given country in respect of one of these categories there is no prescribed minimum below which a strike will not be counted.

The United Kingdom occupies the second position in this table, but it should be obvious that it has a definition of what is to count as a strike that is far *more* restrictive than that of countries to either side of it. Thus both Australia, which heads the list, and Canada, which lies third, only require that a strike should result in a loss of ten working days. They impose no minimum duration in respect of the length of a strike and no minimum number of workers involved. By contrast the United Kingdom's definition is much more restrictive. Turner appreciates this when he writes, of Australia, that it is its relatively permissive definition which results in the fact that 'the frequency of strikes in Australia should appear to be four times as high as that in the U.K.'[12].

But Australia and Canada are not the only countries where it is plausible to suggest that the Donovan table, on Turner's arguments, actually understated Britain's comparative strike ratio. Finland and Japan count all strikes that last more than four hours, and Finland also includes those that last less than four hours if they result in a loss of one hundred days. On this evidence it seems that Finland has a less restrictive definition than Britain; therefore it is impossible to agree with Turner who says, at one point, that it is 'an open question' whether its definition would yield higher or lower figures than Britain's.[13] It is also difficult to agree with his judgement on Japan. Of course, it is true that strikes in Japan which result in a loss of a hundred days, but which last less than four hours, will not be counted. The question is: Are there likely to be more of these in Japan than there are strikes in Britain that last between four hours and a day but result in a loss of less than a hundred days? In other words: Is Japan more plagued by large numbers of workers who strike for very short periods (e.g. large-scale demonstration strikes, which often have political overtones) than Britain is affected by small groups who stop work for slightly longer periods (e.g. small-scale demonstration strikes, usually related to shop floor grievances)? Bearing in mind what is known about both countries this seems extremely implausible. Yet it is clear that Turner must have included both Japan and Finland among the six foreign countries whose definitions contribute to a situation in which 'it seems quite natural that the frequency of disputes in the U.K. should *appear* comparatively high'.

Most other countries in the above table are more easily dealt with. Germany's definitions are much the same as Britain's, though Turner once again includes them in his six. More importantly, however, since the Commission was uable to find a comparable figure in respect of strikes per worker, and Turner does not seek to remedy this deficiency, Germany's position is hardly relevant to the argument. Denmark's definitions are slightly more exclusive than the British one, since it only counts strikes that result in the loss of a hundred working days. Strikes that have a smaller loss than this, but which last a day or more and involve at least ten workers, are counted in Britain. Norway's definition is also more restrictive than Britain's, since it excludes strikes that last less than a day altogether – i.e. it does not go on, as Britain does, to make an exception for strikes lasting less than a day if they result in the loss of a hundred working days.

Finally, the United States position is the most complex of all, and it seems that the only possible conclusion is that it is 'an open question' whether Britain counts a greater proportion of strikes than it does. The U.S.A. excludes strikes lasting less than a day or shift even if they do result in the loss of a hundred working days. On the other hand, as Turner points out, it also allows in some strikes Britain would exclude – e.g. those involving between six and nine workers which result in less than a hundred working days lost. Once again the question is: Are there more strikes of the first sort in the U.S.A. than there are strikes of the second sort in Britain? Once again there is no way of knowing for certain.

What is clear is that Turner's method of calculating the effect of applying American definitions to Britain is open to challenge. He suggests that this would mean that Britain's ratio of 16.8 strikes per hundred thousand would be reduced to 'about 11.0'. Since it would then compare with Donovan's score of 16.8 for the United States he concludes that 'the frequency of strikes in the United States was not less than in Britain, but significantly greater'[14]. But this calculation is based on a misreading of a table in the annual article on strikes in the *D.E.P. Gazette*, for Turner assumes that 'about 40 per cent' of the strikes recorded in the United Kingdom would be excluded from the U.S. data because they last less than a day. Yet, as he admitted,[15] this statement is subject to challenge on two counts:

1.   The British statistics in question refer to the percentage of strikes lasting 'Not more than one day', rather than those lasting '*less* than a day'.

2. In any case the comparisons used (which actually produce a figure of 35.6 rather than 40.4) refer not to 'the most recent year' but to the period 1964–66. Yet in recent years the percentage of British strikes lasting a day and less have actually been falling–i.e. from 38.6 in 1964 to 34.3 in 1965, 33.3 in 1966, 29.1 in 1967, and 28.6 in 1968.[16]

Of course, there is no way of knowing how many strikes in Britain last *just* a day. Turner claims that his 'inspection of strike reports shows that there are very few' but he does not claim to have inspected a representative sample, and gives no details. [17] In the circumstances can the verdict of *Is Britain Really Strike Prone?* really be accepted? This clearly assumes that the U.S. *must* be regarded as one of the six countries with a more restrictive definition than Britain. It certainly cannot be maintained that there are figures which *prove* that in America strikes are more frequent than they are in Britain.

To summarise–if the I.L.O. information is correct it is difficult to accept Turner's argument that the table in the Donovan Report was 'unfair' to Britain. At least three of the countries in his list of eight (i.e. Australia, Canada and Finland) include more strikes than Britain does. Two more (i.e. Japan and the United States) have definitions that are more restrictive in some respects and less restrictive in others. Only two (i.e. Norway and Denmark) have definitions that are clearly and significantly more restrictive than those of Britain. Far from the Report of the Royal Commission being 'unfair' to Britain it was, if anything, unfair to Australia, Canada and Finland. Far from definitional adjustments demonstrating that Britain was not strike prone, they are more likely to push her nearer to the top of the international league table set out above.[18]

But of course it may well be argued that attempts to refine still further Donovan's rough-and-ready analysis are in any case misconceived. It could be said that there are so many imponderables in the collection and comparison of international strike statistics that any attempt to produce improvements by refining definitions, or taking into account differences in definitions, are largely valueless. Indeed, if Turner had contented himself with pouring scorn on the value of international comparisons in general, there would have been little to grouse about in this part of his paper. As it is, while he does not succeed in his attempts to show that Donovan's tables were perversely inverted, he does raise grave doubts about the basis of international comparisons, especially those relating to strikes per worker employed. Looking back it seems that the Commission might have done better to spell out, in some detail, why strike comparisons across different countries and cultures, with varying institutional and industrial structures, are such doubtful tools of analysis. The main difficulty was, of course, that so many people *feel* that Britain *is* more strike prone than other countries. If the Commission had simply said that it was impossible to say one way or another from the figures, little would have been done to meet this feeling.

BRITAIN'S STRIKE FIGURES

Even if it was admitted that those responsible for the Donovan Report oversimplified the complexities of this particular problem, in an effort to provide some easily understood figures, it does not follow, as Turner seems to assume, that the whole of the Report's analysis of Britain's strike problem falls to the ground. It is here that he seems to have been less than fair.

To demonstrate that, it is necessary to look again at the actual use made by Donovan of international comparisons. It is obvious, from reading the whole of Chapter Seven, that essentially the argument rested on an evaluation of *British* strike trends. The table on which Turner is so hard was referred to briefly in the text, where it was mainly used to suggest that in respect of workers involved and working days lost (contrary to popular opinion) Britain's record was relatively good. The fact that the table did provide evidence for the belief that Britain might have a comparatively large number of strikes for the size of the workforce was immediately followed by a qualification to the effect that the evidence was based on admittedly imperfect 'international comparisons'. The whole pattern that emerged from these comparisons was subsequently described as an 'impression' and it was pointed out that in any case this 'impression' was 'confirmed by a closer examination of our own figures'[19]. There then followed a much longer and more detailed analysis of British strike trends, which took up most of the rest of the Chapter. In this analysis official British statistics were used to show:

1. A general increase in strikes over the last ten years in virtually every industry outside mining.
2. That on the evidence available the probability is that the overwhelming majority of these strikes were both unofficial and unconstitutional.
3. That most of them were also small and short.
4. That there has been no similar general increase in the numbers of official/constitutional strikes.

Turner nowhere really contests this evidence. But it is crucial to the policy advanced by Donovan. It is, moreover, much more reliable than any evidence which could possibly be based on international comparisons. For what matters in strike statistics, as Turner admits, is constant definition, stability in collection methods and a continued and marked trend. If these all exist and the results support and reinforce other evidence collected in other ways certain conclusions can justifiably be drawn. This is the case here.

To begin with, the figures do show a marked and more or less steady increase in the number of strikes in industries outside mining. This can be seen from the table below which includes 1968 figures that show no sign of reversing the trend.

It can be seen from this table that in all the industries named, apart from mining, the total number of strikes is up on ten years ago; sometimes by magnitudes of 3 or 400 per cent. Most notable of all, perhaps, in the large residual group 'All other industries' recorded strikes have risen since 1958 by over 500 per cent: moreover, this increase is not confined to broad industrial groups. This can be seen from the more detailed breakdown into some 49 industrial groups that is published in the *D.E.P.*'s annual article on strikes in the Gazette. This shows that in 1968 there were recorded strikes in 47 groups and that in every case but one the number of strikes was higher than in 1958. Once again the only industry to record a reduction in strikes was mining. Of course it is true that if one looks at British strike statistics *as a whole* they are not rising; Donovan nowhere suggests that they are. On the other hand it seems to be slightly misleading to suggest, as Turner does, that the 'general trend of unofficial strikes' is moving 'pretty clearly downwards'. His argument is that while 'there was an increase in the frequency of strikes in the Second World War' and 'this trend resumed again in the post-war period up to the late 1950s . . . this increase was very largely concentrated in a narrow range of industries and was not, apparently, maintained in the 1960s'[20].

But the figures in the table above do not support this view. It is true that the *total* of recorded strikes rose more or less steadily till the period 1957–61, since when it has remained more or less stable at figures slightly below those for that peak period. But this 'apparent' stability and slight improvement is grossly misleading (as Turner pointed out several years ago in a well-known inaugural lecture at Leeds.)[21] For it is entirely the result of an extremely rapid shrinkage in the number of mining strikes–i.e. from almost two thousand in 1958 to just over two hundred in 1968. As a result, instead of accounting for about four-fifths of all strikes, mining now accounts for less than one strike in ten. It is only because there are a tenth of the

TABLE 2

Number of Stoppages by Broad Industrial Groups – 1958–68

	Mining and quarrying	Metals and engineering	Ship-building and marine engineering	Vehicles	Textiles and clothing	Construction	Transport and communication	All other industries	Total all Industries other than mining	Total all industries
1958	1,964	121	97	84	29	178	83	73	665	2,629
1959	1,311	117	85	135	25	171	88	101	782	2,093
1960	1,669	305	74	174	41	215	179	180	1,163	2,832
1961	1,466	300	91	157	41	286	138	209	1,220	2,686
1962	1,207	344	78	166	46	316	134	174	1,242	2,449
1963	993	329	66	173	46	168	133	161	1,075	2,068
1964	1,063	458	91	217	57	222	180	242	1,461	2,524
1965	743	506	129	221	44	261	179	274	1,611	2,354
1966	556	405	84	214	30	265	178	208	1,381	1,937
1967	399	540	96	272	61	256	208	293	1,717	2,116
1968	225	547	134	315	68	272	326	463	2,225	2,350

Note: In some instances stoppages affected several industrial groups, but they are shown only once in the last two columns above.

mining strikes that there used to be that there has not been a record increase in the total number of strikes, for the number of strikes outside mining is now almost four times what it used to be!

In the face of these figures, it really is surprising that Turner should imply that the increase in strikes in Britain in the sixties has more or less burnt itself out, and that those increases that remain are 'very largely concentrated in a narrow range of industries'. Surely the reverse is the case. The increase is 'general' and affects most industries. It also shows no sign of abating.[22] The improvement, on the other hand, appears to be more or less confined to mining. If present trends continue outside mining even the total disappearance of all mining strikes will not be sufficient to prevent an increase in the strike level of about three hundred strikes a year. This will very soon result in an all time high in recorded strikes!

Of course the main reason for the great decrease in mining strikes is well known and quite unique; it results from the unprecedented shrinkage in the number of workers employed. This has been said to account for over half the improvement, after making allowance for the kind of pits that have been closed. The other major factor is probably the disappearance of piece-work, for many years the main cause of most mining strikes, together with the major restructuring of the industrial relations system in mining which has developed over the last ten years.

This leads on to the use Donovan makes of these strike trends, and its supporting evidence. It is an essential part of the argument that a general and more or less steady increase in the number of small-scale unofficial/unconstitutional strikes over most of British industry is symptomatic of the growth of workplace bargaining within an increasingly ineffective and disordered system of industry-wide formal agreements. In this way, it is said, the figures complement and reinforce what is known about the central malaise of British industrial relations from so many other sources – numerous N.B.P.I. Reports, the Reports of Courts of Inquiry, and the researches arising out of Donovan's own workshop relations surveys. Taken together all this evidence indicates that things are not right, and are unlikely to become better, left to themselves. This is the central core of Chapters Three to Seven of the Donovan Report. It is this argument which is used to support its specific proposals for dealing with strikes.

FURTHER CRITICISMS

Turner's other criticisms of Donovan's analysis of strikes are more easily answered. Donovan did not suggest that Britain was 'unique' in its problem of unofficial and unconstitutional strikes. It is *Fair Deal at Work* that might be said to have made this claim, and it is from this publication that he quotes.[23] He may or may not be right to suggest that America has as high a proportion of unconstitutional strikes as Britain does but it does not seem that his evidence proves this beyond reasonable doubt.

He relies on the fact that U.S. statistics distinguish strikes which take place 'during the duration of labour contracts' and suggests that in recent years over a third of all U.S. strikes have been 'irregular' in this respect. But can it be assumed that strikes in America during the course of contracts are necessarily irregular? Certainly they need not be 'in breach of agreement'. It is normal practice in the U.S. to specify those matters which are subject to the procedural strike ban for the duration of the contract, and to arrange for these matters to be dealt with by arbitration. But is it rare for *all* matters to be subject to a strike ban during the period of the contract? As Stieber showed in his paper for the Donovan Commission,[24] excluded issues were found in about a quarter of the agreements examined in a recent American study. These included wage adjustments, job classification problems, production standards, discipline questions, overtime issues and management rights disputes. Outside this area most other agreements were in fact operated in ways that permitted certain 'constitutional' strikes during the course of the contract. For, as Stieber demonstrated, it was not usual for the parties to the bargaining process in the United States to agree to forego *all* use of the strike or the lockout during the period of their main collective contract. As he put it 'only a small proportion of agreements provided for arbitration of all unsettled grievances without exception'[25]. It follows from this that strikes arising during the duration of labour contracts cannot be assumed to be necessarily 'in breach of agreement' in the British sense. In any case even if, as Turner claims, 'the majority of them may well have been'[26] this would not result in a proportion of unconstitutional strikes which approaches that commonly supposed in Britain.

What can be proved, and what was actually assumed in both the Donovan Report and the White Paper, is that insofar as Britain has a strike problem it takes certain limited forms. What was being argued was that as Turner himself says Britain is not often troubled by the massive confrontations of the late 1920s or the kind of general strike that still occurs in countries like Italy, France and Finland. This is why the British record, in terms of workers involved in strikes, and in numbers of working days lost, looks comparatively good.

BRITAIN'S REAL STRIKE PROBLEM

The British problem is a different one, and it takes two forms: (1) A steady upward creep of small-scale unconstitutionalism which sometimes results in the creation of a strike-prone group in particular firms or plants. (2) The fact that sometimes unconstitutionalism results in the odd strike which causes a disproportionate amount of damage to the national economy and results in large numbers of workers who are not involved being laid off. Curiously enough, after criticising both the Donovan and the White Paper's analysis, Turner comes round to suggesting that Britain may have a strike problem of this second sort. This is why he ends by proposing something like the White Paper's Conciliation Pause. He advocates legislation along the lines of the 'Presidential Seizure' procedures in the United States. As described by him these are clearly designed to deal with the occasional disproportionately damaging strike, and they work in not dissimilar ways.

Turner's assertion that both Donovan and the White Paper assumed that small and unconstitutional strikes were *intrinsically* more damaging than large constitutional ones is also without textual justification, which is not surprising since it is self-evidently absurd. Once again the relevant quotations are those from *Fair Deal at Work*.[27]

More importantly, Turner misrepresents the arguments in the Donovan Report about the psychological effects of strikes on management. The nub of its case was that in an increasing number of establishments, where occasional strikes or other workshop sanctions were used, there was a danger of escalation into a strike-prone situation. As the Report put it, 'managements tend to be worried lest the situation deteriorate'. This fear, it was argued, could affect managerial readiness to innovate and could lead to inflationary settlements. It was because the Commission was concerned with the effect of such fears that it concluded that the evidence of its own researches, and British strike statistics, justified it in maintaining that Britain's strike pattern had 'serious economic implications'[28].

It must be admitted that a statement of this sort is in the last analysis beyond statistical challenge. The figures do not contradict it, but they cannot be said to prove it one way or the other. It is, at base, a matter of impression or judgment. Personally I have always thought that the Donovan Report grossly oversold the psychological deterrent effect of strikes; it has always seemed to me a managerial excuse, the first refuge of the lazy and the last ditch of the cowardly. Good managers make much more use of the more sophisticated point that all change has to be paid for in one way or another, and sometimes it is just not worth the price. However, even in its crude Donovan form this view certainly cannot be disposed of, as Turner argues, simply by pointing to the fact that in many short strikes management can make up lost time afterwards by using more overtime.

CONCLUSIONS

It should be clear by now that Turner's last point, concerning the overall trend in British strikes, has already been answered and that his paper represents no serious challenge to the analysis of the nature of Britain's strike problem in the Donovan Report. On the other hand, *Is Britain Really Strike Prone?* does contain some useful correctives to the more extreme statements of those who pronounce in public about the nature of Britain's strike problem.

Turner is basically right to warn that too much cannot be made to turn on international comparisons. He is almost certainly correct to suggest that *most* countries have a high proportion of unofficial/ unconstitutional strikes. (After all, most strikes in most places are extremely short, very small and arise out of decisions taken on the spur of the moment. It is doubtful if the workers concerned thought about their procedural position, or if most of their executives ever got to hear about their actions.) Turner is on more disputable ground, but many would agree with him, when he argues that most short strikes have little or no real cost.

He is mistaken when he seeks to force into a common framework, as a preparation for a common attack, *Fair Deal at Work*, the Donovan Report and *In Place of Strife*. This results in doubtful arguments and is apt to impair the more worth-while parts of his analysis. It also prevents him from discussing the more complex and circumscribed view of the nature of Britain's strike problem which is actually contained in Donovan and the White Paper–a view which parts of his paper indicate he does not really oppose. Above all, perhaps, Turner's determination to prove that all three documents are equally wrong sometimes leads him to write as if he actually believed that Britain had no strike problem at all. A conclusion which some of his readers, and many of those who have picked up parts of his argument, would very much like to believe.

NOTES

1 *Royal Commission on Trade Unions and Employers' Associations 1965–68: Report*, Cmnd 3623, H.M.S.O., London, 1968.
2 H. A. Turner, *Is Britain Really Strike Prone?: A Review of the Incidence, Character and Costs of Industrial Conflict*, Occasional Paper 20, Cambridge University Press, May 1969.
3 *In Place of Strife: A Policy for Industrial Relations*, Cmnd 3888, H.M.S.O., London, January 1969.
4 *Fair Deal at Work*, Conservative Political Centre, London, 1968.
5 H. A. Turner, *op. cit.*, p. 3.
6 H. A. Turner, *op. cit.*, p. 4.
7 H. A. Turner, *op. cit.*, p. 44.
8 *Report, op. cit.*, p. 95.
9 *In Place of Strife, op. cit.*, p. 8.
10 H. A. Turner, *op. cit.*, p. 6.
11 *Ibid.* p. 9.
12 *Ibid.*, p. 9.
13 *Ibid.*, p. 15
14 *Ibid.*, p. 14.
15 See a letter by H. A. Turner to *The Times Business News*, 20 May, 1969.
16 See *D.E.P. Gazette*, H.M.S.O., London, May, 1968.
17 In his letter to *The Times Business News*.
18 Certainly they would be likely greatly to narrow the gap between Britain and Australia, and would presumably result in Britain appearing as much more strike-prone than Canada. On the other hand, since the strike ratios of Norway and Denmark are extremely low on Donovan's figures, one would have to assume a very great deal to believe that they could be inflated to a point where they were likely to overtake Britain.
19 *Report op., cit.*, p. 96.
20 H. A. Turner, *op. cit.*, p. 18
21 H. A. Turner, *The Trend of Strikes*, Leeds University Press, 1963, p. 8.
22 Indeed at the time this article was written (i.e. December, 1969) the as yet incomplete figures for strikes outside mining appeared to be running at levels considerably above those for 1968. See *D.E.P. Gazette* for October 1969 (p. 951) which records a figure for the first nine months of 1969 over 400 above the comparable figure for 1968. An industry wide breakdown of these figures reveals a continued shrinking in mining strikes and a similarly 'general' rise elsewhere.
23 H. A. Turner, *op. cit.*, p. 4.
24 J. Stieber, 'Grievance Arbitration in the U.S.: An Analysis of its Functions and Effects', in *Three Studies in Collective Bargaining*, Research Paper No. 8, Royal Commission on Trade Unions and Employers' Associations, H.M.S.O., London, 1968.
25 J. Stieber, *op. cit.*, p. 10.
26 H. A. Turner, *op. cit.*, p. 21.
27 H. A. Turner, *op. cit.*, p. 4.
28 *Report, op. cit.*, p. 112.

TECHNICAL SUPPLEMENT TO CHAPTER 11
(pages 233–253)

Usable data were found for eleven countries, and the rankings prepared from these data are set forth in Table 2. Data were examined for six additional countries but in each case were inadequate:

Belgium   Man-days lost in industrial disputes, by industry, were not published until very recently.

Canada   No employment figures are available to match against man-days lost.

Denmark   Man-days lost are shown by occupation instead of by industry.

Finland   Data on man-days lost are given by occupation and by industry, but no comparable employment data are available.

France   Man-days lost are published in aggregate but are not broken down by industry.

Union of South Africa   No employment data are available to match against the data on man-days lost given by industry and occupation.

The essential facts on the data for the eleven countries follow:

Australia   Man-days lost and trade-union membership data are available for fourteen industry groups for approximately three decades, which have been divided into three periods in Table 2.

Czechoslovakia   Data on man-days lost are available for the same twenty industry groupings for the period 1921–1936 (except for 1926–1928 and 1931). Employment data for the same industry groupings are from the 1921 and 1930 censuses.

Germany   Data on man-days lost are available for twenty-one industry groupings for the period 1915–1924 and for twenty-four industry groupings for 1925–1932; and employment data, for the same groupings for 1907 and 1925. It has been assumed that employment ranking in those 2 years was representative for the two periods respectively.

Italy   Data on man-days lost are available for seventeen industry groupings only for the 8 years 1916–1923. Trade-union membership data for the same groupings are available for 1921.

Netherlands   Data on man-days lost are available for twenty-one industry groupings for the period 1918–1940 (except for 1919 and 1927). Comparable employment data are taken from the 1920 and 1930 censuses of industry. The data are divided into two periods in Table 2.

New Zealand   Data on man-days lost are available for approximately three decades (except for 1944 and 1945) for fifteen industry groupings; and trade-union membership statistics, for the same groupings for 1924–1948. The periods set forth in Table 2 were selected for the consistency of behavior in each period.

Norway   Statistics on man-days lost and workers covered by collective agreement are available for nineteen industry groupings for 1925–1949, but Table 2 is based only on the period to 1939 since strikes were banned during the war.

Sweden   Man-days lost and workers covered by collective agreement are available for the same fourteen industry groups for 1920–1937.

Switzerland   Data on man-days lost are available for the period 1927–1949 for ten industry groupings and are divided in Table 2 into two periods, 1927–1939 and 1940–1949, with employment data for 1930 and 1941 taken as representative for the two periods respectively.

United Kingdom   Data on man-days lost are available for only six industry groupings. The ranking in Table 2 is based on the calculations of K. C. G. Knowles of man-days lost per worker in employment for the period 1911–1945.

United States   Man-days lost and employment estimates are available for twenty-one industry groupings for the period 1927–1941 and for twenty-eight groupings for 1942–1948.

The industries for each period in each country (except the United Kingdom) were ranked, first, by number of man-days lost and, second, by volume of employment (or by union members or by workers covered by contract, as the case might be). In the first instance (employment), the propensity to organize and then to strike is shown; and in the second and third (union members and workers covered), to strike after being organized. The difference is not so great, however, as might at first appear, since in four countries where employment data were not used (Australia, New Zeland, Norway, and Sweden), unionization is very widespread. We should have preferred to use employment data throughout since we are concerned with the propensity of the workers in an industry to strike or, since organization is normally a prerequisite to striking, to organize and then to strike. Generally, workers who are not easily organized are also the ones who do not readily strike once they have been organized. And then the relation of the one rank to the other was noted. Table 2 shows the industries in their resultant ranking. They have been arbitrarily divided into five categories as follows:

High	Man-days lost rank substantially above employment rank
Medium high	Man-days lost rank significantly above employment rank
Medium high	Man-days lost rank significantly above employment rank
Medium	About the same ranking for both
Medium low	Man-days lost rank significantly below employment rank
Low	Man-days lost rank significantly below employment rank

Man-days lost, in each case, are the total of man-days idle because of both strikes and lockouts. 'Masked strikes' and 'slowdowns' are not included.

TABLE 2
Interindustry Propensity to Strike

	High	Medium high	Medium	Medium low	Low
Australia 1919–1929	Mining Shipping, wharf labor, etc.	Wood, furniture, sawmills, etc. Books, printing, etc.	Other manufacturing industries Other land transport Engineering, metal works, etc. Building	Domestic, hotel, etc. Miscellaneous Food, drink, etc. Railway and tramway services	Pastoral and agriculture Clothing, textiles, boots, etc.
1930–1939	Mining Shipping, wharf labor, etc.	Pastoral and agriculture Other land transport	Engineering, metal works, etc. Food, drink, etc. Other manufacturing industries Wood, furniture, sawmills, etc. Books, printing, etc.	Domestic, hotel, etc. Clothing, textiles, boots, etc. Building Miscellaneous	Railway and tramway services
1940–1946	Mining Shipping, wharf labor, etc.	Books, printing, etc. Food, drink, etc. Other manufacturing industries	Building Other land transport Wood, furniture, sawmills, etc. Engineering, metal works, etc.	Domestic, hotel, etc. Pastoral and agriculture Clothing, textiles, boots, etc.	Railway and tramway services Miscellaneous
Czechoslovakia 1921–1936	Mining and metallurgy Quarrying and stoneware	Pottery and glassware Skins, leather, etc. Textile industry Chemical industry Paper industry	Building Wood Gas, water, and electricity Rubber Machines Printing Metals Clothing	Banks, etc. Food and drink	Hotels and restaurants Agriculture Commerce and auxiliary branches
Germany 1915–1924	Machinery Mining (coal, salt, etc.) Chemicals	Wood and wood products Printing and publishing Quarrying	Metals Forestry and allied products Fishing and animal husbandry Textiles Transportation and communication Leather Paper Gardening Arts and crafts	Construction Hotels, inns, etc. Health and sanitation Food, drink, tobacco, etc.	Clothing Trade
1925–1932	Musical instruments and toys Iron-, steel-, and metal- works Quarrying Iron and metal extraction	Machinery (including vehicles) Electrical machinery, precision instruments and optical industries Rubber and asbestos Fishing Textile Wood and wood products Paper and printing	Chemicals Construction Mining Theater, music, sports, etc.	Clothing Gardening and animal husbandry Leather and linoleum Transportation and communication Water, gas, and electricity Food, drink, tobacco, etc.	Hotels, restaurants, etc. Health and sanitation Trade

Interindustry Propensity to Strike (continued)

	High	Medium High	Medium	Medium low	Low
Italy 1916–1923	Mining (extraction industries)	Food and drink Stone, clay, and sand Textiles	Skins and leather Buttons, etc. Paper and printing Metallurgy and machines Precision instruments and precious metals Clothing Transportation and communication Wood, straw, and allied industries Construction	Agriculture	Chemical industries Production and distribution of power, light, heat, and water Commerce and public services
Netherlands 1918–1929	Manufacture of goods of wood, cork, and straw Mining and peat cutting Manufacture of earthenware, glass, lime, and stoneware	Building and related industries Applied art Chemical industries Paper industry	Metal industry Diamonds and other precious stones Printing industry Fishing and hunting Transport Food, drink, and tobacco Textile industry Insurance	Leather, oilcloth, and rubber industries Gas, water, and electricity Clothing and cleaning	Agriculture Credit and banking Commerce
1930–1940	Fishing and hunting Paper industry	Textiles Manufacture of earthenware, glass, lime, and stoneware Manufacture of goods of wood, cork, and straw Building and related industries Clothing and cleaning	Metal industry Mining, peat cutting Diamonds and other precious stones Applied art Food, drink, and tobacco Printing Chemicals Gas, water, and electricity Insurance Transport	Credit and banking Leather, oilcloth, and rubber industries	Agriculture Commerce
New Zealand 1920–1934	Mines and quarries Transport by water	Wood, etc.	The land (farming) Food, drink, etc. Power, heat, and light Metal Accommodations, meals, and personal services Skins, leather, etc.	Stone, clay, glass, and chemicals Miscellaneous Paper, printing, etc.	Clothing, footwear, and textiles Transport by land Building and construction
1935–1939	Mines and quarries Stone, clay, glass, and chemicals Transport by water Wood, etc.	Power, heat, and light	Paper, printing, etc. Food, drink, etc. Metal Skins, leather, etc. Building and construction		Miscellaneous Transport by land Clothing, footwear, and textiles Accommodations, meals, and personal services The land

Interindustry Propensity to Strike (continued)

	High	Medium high	Medium	Medium low	Low
1940–1948	Mines and quarries Transport by water	Wood, etc. Stone, clay, glass, and chemicals Power, heat, and light Accommodations, meals, and personal services	Skins, leather, etc. Food, drink, etc. Paper, printing, etc. Building and construction Metal	Clothing, footwear, and textiles Transport by land	The land Miscellaneous
Norway 1925–1939	Textiles Mining and quarrying Extraction of metals	Paper Leather and rubber Publishing and printing Metal industries	Food and tobacco Clothing Forestry Wood Gas and electricity Construction Hotels and restaurants Oils and lubricants	Chemical industries	Trade Transportation and navigation Miscellaneous
Sweden 1920–1937	Mining and quarrying	Leather, skins, and rubber	Forestry and wood Construction Paper and printing Chemicals Textiles and clothing Agriculture and fishing Food Other industries Commerce and trade	Metallurgy and construction of machines Land and water transport Public institutions and enterprises	
Switzerland 1927–1939		Leather and rubber Mining Wood and pottery Textile industry	Construction Clocks and jewelry Chemicals Metals and machines		Clothing Transport
1940–1949	Mining Wood and pottery		Chemicals Leather and rubber Construction Textiles Metals and machines Clocks and jewelry		Clothing Transport
United Kingdom 1911–1945	Mining and quarrying	Textiles	Metal and engineering industries Transport and communication Building and construction industries	Clothing	

Interindustry Propensity to Strike (continued)

	High	Medium high	Medium	Medium low	Low
United States 1927–1941	Anthracite-coal mining Bituminous-coal mining	Lumber, timber, basic products, furniture, and finished lumber products Textiles and apparel Leather and leather products Transportation equipment (including autos and auto equipment) Miscellaneous manufacturing industries	Construction Transportation, communication, etc. Stone, clay, and glass products Nonferrous metals and their products Tobacco manufacturing Iron and steel and their products Machinery (including electrical)	Services, personal, business, and others Food and kindred products Paper and allied products, printing, publishing, and allied industries Chemicals and allied products, products of petroleum and coal	Trade Other nonmanu-facturing industries Agriculture, forestry, and fishing
1942–1948	Bituminous-coal mining Anthracite-coal mining Stone, clay, and glass products Automobiles and automobile equipment Rubber and rubber products	Leather and leather products Textile-mill products Lumber and timber basic products Nonferrous metals and their products Iron and steel and their products	Food and kindred products Products of petroleum and coal Transportation equipment (except autos) Machinery (except electrical) Paper and allied products Tobacco manufacturing Transportation, communication, etc. Construction Furniture and finished lumber products Electrical machinery	Printing, publishing, and allied trades Chemicals and allied products Miscellaneous manufactur-ing industries	Trade Apparel and other finished products Other nonmanu-facturing industries Services, personal, business, etc. Agriculture, forestry, and fishing Finance, insurance, and real estate

Sources: Australia–*Official Yearbook of the Commonwealth of Australia;* Czechoslovakia–*Manuel statistique de la république tchécoslovaque* and *Annuaire statistique de la république tchécoslovaque;* Germany–*Statistiches Jahrbuch für das deutsche Reich* and *Statistik der deutschen Reichs;* Italy–*Annuario statistico italiano;* Netherlands –*Jaarcijfers voor Nederland;* New Zealand–*New Zealand Official Yearbook;* Norway–*Statistisk Arbok for Norge;* Sweden–*Arbetsinstallelser och Kollektivavtal samt Forlikningsmannens Verksamhet;* Switzerland–*Statistiches Jahrbuch der Schweiz;* United Kingdom–K. C. G. Knowles, 'Strikes and Their Changing Economic Context,' *Bulletin of the Oxford University Institute of Statistics,* September, 1947; United States–*Handbook of Labor Statistics,* 1947 ed., *Statistical Abstract of the United States,* and *Strikes in the United States 1880–1936,* U.S. Bureau of Labor Statistics (Bulletin 651); and *Yearbook of Labor Statistics,* General-international Labor Office.

BIBLIOGRAPHY

Short Bibliography with special reference to the U.K. and International Comparisons. Place of publication is London unless otherwise stated. Where a particular chapter is especially relevant this is noted.

ALLEN V. L. Power in Trade Unions. Longmans. (1954).

ALLEN V. L. Trade Union Leadership. Longmans. (1957).

ALLEN V. L. Militant Trade Unionism. Merlin Press. (1966).

ASHENFELTER O. and JOHNSON G. E. 'Bargaining Theory, Trade Unions and Industrial Strike Activity'. American Economic Review. (1969), pp. 35–59.

BESCOBY J. and TURNER H. A. 'An Analysis of Post-War Labour Disputes in British Car Manufacturing Firms'. Manchester School, Vol. 29. (1961), pp. 133–160.

BLACKBURN R. and COCKBURN A. (eds.) The Incompatibles: Trade Union Militancy and the Consensus. Harmondsworth: Penguin. (1967).

BLUMLER J. G. and EWBANK A. J. 'Trade Unionists, the Man Media and Unofficial Strikes'. British Journal of Industrial Relations, Vol. 8. (1970), pp. 32–54.

CLACK G. Industrial Relations in a British Car Factory. Cambridge. Cambridge University Press. (1967).

CLACK G. 'How Unofficial Strikes help Industry'. Business. (July 1967), pp. 42–47.

CLEGG H. A. 'Strikes'. Political Quarterly, Vol. 27. (1956), pp. 31–43.

CLEGG H. A. The System of Industrial Relations in Great Britain. Oxford: Blackwell. (1970).

CLEGG H. A. How to run an Incomes Policy and why we made such a mess of the last one. Heinemann. (1971). Chapter 8.

CLEGG H. A. and ADAMS R. The Employers' Challenge. Oxford: Blackwell. (1957).

CLIFF T. The Employers' Offensive. Pluto Press. (1970).

COATES K. and TOPHAM A. Industrial Democracy. Panther. (1970).

CYRIAX G. and OAKESHOTT R. The Bargainers. Faber and Faber. (1960). Chapter 6.

DENNIS N., HENRIQUES F. and SLAUGHTER C. Coal is our Life. Eyre and Spottiswoode. (1957).

DEVLIN, Lord. Chairman of Committee of Inquiry, Port Transport Industry. Final Report. H.M.S.O. Cmnd. 2734. (1965).

DONOVAN, Lord. Chairman of Royal Commission on Trade Unions and Employers' Associations. Report. H.M.S.O. Cmnd. 3623. (1968). Chapter 7.

DUNLOP J. T. Industrial Relations Systems. New York: Holt. (1958).

DRUCKER P. 'Why Men Strike'. Fortnightly Review. (February 1947).

ELDRIDGE J. E. T. (ed.) Industrial Disputes. Routledge and Kegan Paul. (1968).

EVANS E. W. and GALAMBOS P. 'Work stoppages in the U.K., 1951–64; A Quantitative Study'. Bulletin of the Oxford Institute of Economics and Statistics, Vol. 28. (1966), pp. 33–57.

EVANS E. W. and GALAMBOS P. 'Work stoppages in the United Kingdom 1951–64 A Reply.' Bulletin of Oxford Institute of Economics and Statistics, Vol. 28 (1966), pp. 283–284.

EVANS E. W. and GALAMBOS P. 'Work stoppages in the United Kingdom 1965–70'. Bulletin of Economic Research, Vol. 25. (1973), pp. 22–43.

FLANDERS A. The Fawley Productivity Agreements. Faber and Faber. (1964).

FLANDERS A. Industrial Relations: What is wrong with the System? Faber and Faber. (1965).

FLANDERS A. Trade Unions. Hutchinson. (7th Edition 1968).

FLANDERS A. Management and Unions. Faber and Faber. (1970).

FLANDERS A. and CLEGG H. A. The System of Industrial Relations in Great Britain. Oxford: Blackwell. (1964).

FOOT P. The Postal Workers and the Tory Offensive. Socialist Worker. (1971).

FORCHHEIMER K. 'Some International Aspects of the Strike Movement'. Bulletin of the Oxford Institute of Statistics, Vol. 10. (1948), pp. 1–24.

FOX A. Industrial Sociology and Industrial Relations. Royal Commission Research Paper No. 3. H.M.S.O. (1966).

FOX A. 'Managerial Ideology and Labour Relations'. British Journal of Industrial Relations, Vol. 4. (1966), pp. 366–378.

FOX A. and FLANDERS A. 'The Reform of Collective Bargaining from Donovan to Durkheim'. British Journal of Industrial Relations. Vol. 7. (1969), pp. 151–180.

GOLDTHORPE J. H., LOCKWOOD D., BECHHOFER F. and PLATT J. The Affluent Worker: Industrial Attitudes and Behaviour. Cambridge: Cambridge University Press. (1968).

GOMBERG E. L. 'Strikes and Lockouts in Great Britain'. Quarterly Journal of Economics, Vol. 59. (1944), pp. 92–106.

GOODMAN J. F. B. 'Strikes in the United Kingdom: Recent Statistics and Trends'. International Labour Review, Vol. 95. (1967), pp. 465–481.

GOODMAN J. F. B. and WHITTINGHAM T. G. Shop Stewards in British Industry. McGraw-Hill. (1969).

GOULDNER A. W. Wildcat Strike. Routledge and Kegan Paul. (1955).

GOVERNMENT SOCIAL SURVEY. Workplace Industrial Relations. H.M.S.O. (1968).

HANSON C. G. 'Trade Union Law Reform and Unofficial Strikes'. National Westminster Bank Review (August 1968), pp. 47–61.

HAWKINS K. Conflict and Change: Aspects of Industrial Relations. Holt. (1972).

HOPKINS S. V. 'Industrial Stoppages and their Economic Significance'. Oxford Economic Papers, Vol. 5. (1953), pp. 209–220.

HUGHES J. and MOORE R. A. Special case? Social Justice and the Miners. Harmondsworth: Penguin. (1972).

HYMAN R. Strikes. Fontana. (1972).

JACKSON D., TURNER H. A. and WILKINSON F. Do Trade Unions Cause Inflation? Cambridge: Cambridge University Press. (1972). Chapter 3.

KERR C. Labour and Management in Industrial Society. New York: Harper. (1964), pp. 148–166.

KNIGHT K. G. 'Strikes and Wage Inflation in British Manufacturing Industry, 1950–68'. Bulletin of the Oxford Institute of Economics and Statistics, Vol. 34. (1972), pp. 281–294.

KNOWLES K. G. J. C. Strikes: A Study in Industrial Conflict. Oxford: Blackwell. (1952).

KNOWLES K. G. J. C. 'Strikes and their Changing Economic Context'. Bulletin of the Oxford Institute of Statistics, Vol. 9. (1947), pp. 287–306.

KNOWLES K. G. J. C. 'The Post-War Dock Strikes'. Political Quarterly, Vol. 22. (1951), pp. 266–290.

KNOWLES K. G. J. C. 'Strike-proneness and its determinants'. American Journal of Sociology, Vol. 60. (1954), pp. 213–229.

KNOWLES K. G. J. C. 'A Comment'. Bulletin of the Oxford Institute of Economics and Statistics, Vol. 28. (1966), pp. 59–62.

KORNHAUSER A., DUBIN R. and ROSS A. M. (ed.) Industrial Conflict. New York: McGraw-Hill. (1954).

KUHN J. W. Bargaining in Grievance Settlement. New York: Columbia. (1961).

LANCASTER T. 'A Stochastic Model for the Duration of A Strike'. Journal of the Royal Statistical Society A., 135. (1972). pp. 257–271.

LANE T. and ROBERTS K. Strike at Pilkingtons, Fontana. (1971).

LEESON R. A. (ed.) Strike. Allen and Unwin. (1973).

LIVERPOOL UNIVERSITY, Department of Social Science. The Dock Worker. Liverpool: Liverpool University Press. (1955).

LOCKWOOD P. 'Arbitration and Industrial Conflict'. British Journal of Sociology, Vol. 6. (1955), pp. 335–347.

MARSH A. Industrial Relations in Engineering. Pergamon. (1965).

MARSH A. I., EVANS E. O. and GARCIA P. Workplace Industrial Relations in Engineering. Kogan Page. (1971).

MATHEWS J. The Ford Strike. Panther. (1972).

MCCARTHY W. E. J. 'The Reasons Given for Striking'. Bulletin of the Oxford University Institute of Statistics, Vol. 21. (1959), pp. 17–29.

MCCARTHY W. E. J. The Role of Shop Stewards in British Industrial Relations. Royal Commission Research Paper. No. 1. H.M.S.O. (1966).

MCCARTHY W. E. J. 'The Nature of Britain's Strike Problem'. British Journal of Industrial Relations, (Sydney) Vol. 7. (1965), pp. 144–163.

MCCARTHY W. E. J. and PARKER S. R. Shop Stewards and Workshop Relations. Royal Commission Research Paper No. 10. H.M.S.O. (1968).

MCKELVEY J. Dock Labour Disputes in Great Britain. New York State School of Industrial and Labour Relations. Bulletin, No. 23. (1953).

MEREDITH J. 'Psychological Aspects of Strikes'. Penguin Parade. Second Series II. Monpurgo. (ed.) (1948).

MINISTRY OF LABOUR. Written Evidence to the Royal Commission. H.M.S.O. (1965).

MULVEY C. 'Unemployment and the Incidence of Strikes in the Republic of Ireland 1942–66'. Journal of Economic Studies, Vol. 3. (1968), pp. 73–88.

OXNAM D. W. 'International Comparisons of Industrial Conflict'. Journal of Industrials Relations, (Sydney) Vol. 7. (1965), pp. 144–163.

PARKER H. M. D. Manpower A Study in War-time Policy and Administration. H.M.S.O. and Longmans. (1957). Chapter XXV.

PATERSON T. T. Glasgow Limited, Cambridge: Cambridge University Press. (1960).

PATERSON T. T. 'Why men go on strike.' Listener. Vol. XLIX. (29/1/53), p. 167.

PATERSON T. T. and WILLETT F. J. 'Unofficial Strike'. Sociological Review, Vol. 43. (1957), pp. 67–94.

PENCAVEL J. H. 'An Investigation into Industrial Strike Activity in Britain'. Economica. Vol. 37. (1970), pp. 239–255.

REVANS R. W. 'Industrial Morale and the Size of Unit'. Political Quarterly, Vol. 27. (1956), pp. 303–311.

RIMLINGER G. V. 'International Differences in the Strike Propensity of Coal Miners: experience in four countries'. Industrial and Labor Relations Review, Vol. 13. (1959). pp. 389–405.

ROBERTS B. C. (ed.) Industrial Relations: Contemporary Problems and Perspectives. Methuen. (1962).

ROBERTS B. C. Trade Union Government and Administration. Bell. (1956).

ROSS A. M. and HARTMAN P. T. Changing Patterns of Industrial Conflict. New York: Wiley. (1960).

SAMS K. I. 'The Devlin Committee and Unrest in British Ports'. Journal of Industrial Relations, (Sydney) Vol. 9. (1967), pp. 65–71.

SCOTT W. H., BANKS J. A., HALSEY A. H. and LUPTON T. Technical Change and Industrial Relations, Liverpool: Liverpool University Press. (1956).

SCOTT W. H., MUMFORD E., McGIVERING I. C. and KIRKBY J. M. Coal and Conflict. Liverpool: Liverpool University Press. (1963).

SILVER M. 'Recent British Strike Trends: A Factual Analysis, British Journal of Industrial Relations, Vol. 11. (1973), pp. 66–104.

STIEBER J. 'Unauthorised Strikes Under the American and British Industrial Relations Systems'. British Journal of Industrial Relations, Vol. 6. (1968), pp. 232–38.

TURNER H. A. 'The Crossley Strike' Manchester School, Vol. 18. (1950), pp. 179–216.

TURNER H. A. The Trend of Strikes. Leeds University Press. (1963).

TURNER H. A. Trade Union Growth, Structure and Policy. Allen and Unwin. (1962).

TURNER H. A. Is Britain Really Strike-Prone? Cambridge: Cambridge University Press. Occasional Paper No. 20. (1969).

TURNER H. A. and BESCOBY J. 'Strikes, Redundancy and the Demand Cycle in the Motor Car Industry'. Bulletin of the Oxford Institute of Statistics, Vol. 23. (1961), pp. 179–185.

TURNER H. A., CLACK G. and ROBERTS B. Labour Relations in the Motor Industry. Allen and Unwin. (1967).

WEDDERBURN K. W. The Worker and the Law. Harmondsworth: Penguin. (1971).

WELLISZ S. 'Strikes in Coal-Mining'. British Journal of Sociology, Vol. 3. (1953), pp. 346–366.

WHITTINGHAM T. G. and TOWERS B. 'Strikes and the Economy'. National Westminster Bank Quarterly Review. (1971), pp. 33–42.

WHITTINGHAM T. G. and TOWERS B. 'The Strike Record of the United Kingdom; An Analysis'. Industrial Relations Journal, Vol. 2. (1971), pp. 2–8.

WIGHAM E. L. What's Wrong with the Unions? Harmondsworth: Penguin. (1961).

WILSON D. F. Dockers. The Impact of Industrial Change. Fontana. (1972).